Legal Control of
Racial Discrimination

Laurence Lustgarten
School of Law, University of Warwick

First published 1980 by
THE MACMILLAN PRESS LTD
London and Basingstoke
Associated companies in Delhi Dublin
Hong Kong Johannesburg Lagos Melbourne
New York Singapore and Tokyo

Filmset in Great Britain by
VANTAGE PHOTOTYPESETTING CO. LTD
Southampton and London

Printed in Great Britain
by J. W. Arrowsmith Ltd, Bristol

ISBN 0 333 24387 0 (hard cover)
0 333 24388 9 (paper cover)

Legal Control of
Racial Discrimination

To my Parents

Contents

Part I
The Meaning of Discrimination

Part II
Discrimination in Employment

Part III
Enforcement

Preface

I

This book is neither simply a study of law in the form of a textual exegesis, nor of race relations in a general sense. It is rather a look at a social problem – the ill treatment and inferior material conditions of a portion of the nation's population marked off from the majority by colour and ethnic origin – through the eyes of a lawyer. Consequently much that a sociologist, social psychologist or economist would include in a work on this general subject is not to be found: nothing is said about theories of racial stratification, of prejudice or of microeconomic models of discrimination. Conversely, much of the work is devoted to matters that the black letter lawyer has defined out of his realm, as with the chapters on the condition of racial minorities in employment and the theoretical examination of concepts of discrimination. Thus the social reality of racial discrimination and disadvantage defines the setting of the study, a substantial proportion of which is devoted to a highly detailed examination of the Race Relations Act 1976 ('the Act' or 'the 1976 Act') and related employment law.

Moreover, if law, while constrained by the wider social structure, simultaneously helps to alter it, one must examine the extent to which the legal structure – a shorthand for a complex of institutions, inherited habits of thought and modes of procedure, and the roles and ideology of the profession – may itself channel or block the effort to achieve a particular social reform by legislative enactment. Just as one does not fully comprehend 'society' if one treats law as a discrete factor, or ignores its specific provisions, so one does not understand 'law' if it is regarded simply as a system of rules, concepts and formal procedures. This sense of an interlocking and dynamic – perhaps the best adjective is 'kaleidoscopic' – relationship has shaped the definition of the issues considered here, the relative importance accorded specific topics and the overall organisation of the study.

Analysis is made all the more difficult by the fact that the central concept under scrutiny is philosophically problematic and highly contentious. Early in this study I became fascinated by the way in which the evolution of the legal concept of discrimination mirrored policymakers' altered perceptions of a social problem. I also found the effort to come to grips with the moral and philosophical dilemmas raised by some of the proposed remedies almost physically painful, and became convinced that non-whites in nations like Britain and the United States would remain locked permanently in inferior conditions with little assistance from anti-discrimination law unless the concept was broadened to take adequate account of the element of collective deprivation. I have attempted to formulate at least the rudiments of a suitably expanded concept in the last section of Chapter 1. Readers may judge whether the effort has succeeded, but I am certain that philosophical and jurisprudential analysis is essential to adequate treatment of the subject.

This study is confined to discrimination in employment, although there are occasional mentions of other spheres. This arises partly from length limitations imposed by the economics of publishing, but the primary importance of employment in dictating the economic position of minorities seems clear enough. Moreover, the analyses in Parts I and III are for the most part capable of direct application to other areas, like housing, by anyone with knowledge of them. The restriction also facilitates examination of the way in which employment discrimination and the governing law fit into the broader framework of industrial relations and labour law. Consequently, the criminal prohibition of incitement to racial hatred now found in s. 70 of the Act, and the wider problems of public order and protection of minority communities from racist attacks, are entirely omitted. For the same reason, little is said about the immigration laws, despite the fact that they are the most explicitly discriminatory legislation presently in force in Britain.

Given a perspective which sees law in relation to the social phenomenon to which it is addressed, discussion of sex discrimination had to be omitted. Although various forms of discrimination may share certain behavioural sources, sex discrimination ultimately derives from the different social roles occupied by women, in turn an outgrowth of the family, one of the most fundamental institutions of society. Nor do women live, or function economically, separately from men in daily life in the way that blacks may move in realms utterly apart from most whites. Moreover, different institutions and practices serve as barriers to the economic advancement of minorities than to women. Given these contextual variations, it would be impossible in a work of this length to do either subject justice. However, since many of the provisions of the Sex Discrimination Act 1975 and the RRA are identical, a large part of the discussion of case law concerns litigation under the SDA, and anyone more concerned with that problem should find this book relevant.

The study aims to reach a wide and diffuse audience. I should hope that it would be of interest to scholars and students of law and social science generally, to persons who may wish to learn of their rights or obligations under the Act, and equally to that amiable figure whom I hope is not a pleasant fiction – the general reader/concerned citizen. This has meant attempting to strike a balance between stating what is elementary or obvious to the legally-trained specialist and leaving the layman in ignorance. I have found this extraordinarily difficult and must ask the indulgence of those who may intermittently be bored or mystified, since I am quite sure that in places I have not got the balance right.

II

Theorising on a breathtakingly vague, and often vacuous, level has become the vogue in academic social science in this country over the past few years. It now seems impossible to pick up a book which does not seek to locate its particular subject-matter in the context of late/corporate/crisis-ridden/virulent capitalism. None the less, whilst individual efforts are only too easy to parody, the intellectual movement has had the valuable result of making scholars aware that any topic they have defined as a social problem has both a temporal – i.e. historical – dimension, and a structural one – that it is part of the deeper-lying social organisation and power relationships of the society that produced it. This theoretical orientation has the further virtue of reminding an author that he cannot escape having an implicit sociology and moral standpoint that shapes his work, whether or not he expresses them. I should thus explain why I have chosen not to articulate certain assumptions which implicitly underpin my analysis and approach.

The first concerns the general theoretical relationship between law and economic and/or social change. The first of these is well beyond my present needs except where discussed at one point in the opening chapter. Though I have found broad accounts relating the development of law to the evolution of capitalism, whether Marxist or Weberian in orientation, historically quite illuminating, they seem less useful in analysing the role of law within a short and contemporary period. Within this tight frame, I posit that legal factors exercise an independent and often strong influence; in the present jargon, that law is relatively autonomous.

The question of the relationship of law to social change is really a way of asking the same theoretical question within the narrower time frame and under the influence of a sociological tradition, largely American, which does not posit even the underlying paramountcy of economic factors. This tradition has produced a vast amount of writing, much of it concerned to examine the effect of various constitutional decisions of the Supreme Court.[1] I fear, however, that most of the studies I have read have not proven very helpful, since they either theorise at a level so general that I at any rate cannot apply them to a concrete problem, or because the theories produced are a form of premature generalisation, seeking to extrapolate conclusions from a narrow case study into a shaky structure which cannot support the intellectual weight loaded upon it. Therefore, in addition to certain postulates about legal remedies set out at the beginning of Chapter 12, I have adopted certain assumptions. These are that enactment of a law genuinely intended to achieve a certain end may be more or less successful, depending upon whether it is well designed in terms of four factors:

(1) *Clarity*, both in the policy it is supposed to implement and in the precise statutory language;
(2) *Internal inconsistency* – being without important debilitating exemptions or loopholes;
(3) Whether it contains *effective enforcement procedures*;
(4) Whether *adequate resources* are allocated to bringing about the proclaimed end.

Within this framework I also emphasise the importance of the ideas and perceptions of those formulating policy; I am confident that good faith failures of understanding are both common and critical in explaining outcomes.

For different reasons two other important questions are omitted. The first is any general analysis of the causes of racial discrimination. Again, I have found general typologies either unconvincing or incapable of illuminating the specific situation that concerns me – the condition of black workers in Britain in the late 1970s. I would agree that there is a significant element of truth in the analysis offered by Professor Rex[2] which stresses that the problems considered here cannot ultimately be seen apart from the broader social process of black immigration from poor former colonies in the Third World to (largely) undesirable jobs in advanced industrialised countries. None the less this clearly is an oversimplified picture, since – to mention only two obvious points – Greece and Turkey were not colonies of Germany or Switzerland, and the condition of white migrant workers in these countries (and of Iberians in France) is at least as unequal and unpleasant as that of blacks in Britain. At least in the present state of theorising there are severe limits in what general theories can usefully add to policy-oriented analysis of a specific problem. Marxist analysis has in my opinion been of even less value; only recently have more sophisticated writers of this orientation begun to acknowledge that race is not simply class in some peculiar guise or disguise.[3] Thus I have dealt with the question of causation at the level of empirical observations about the forms and incidence of employment discrimination. I have assumed that an effectively designed law – judged by the criteria enunciated in the preceding paragraph – would cause people to change their behaviour, given that it is addressed primarily to businessmen whose goals are profit and avoiding distractions, not becoming political figures or folk martyrs.

The second omission is consideration of why the legislation was enacted.

One often hears what may be termed the 'pacification' or 'conspiracy' theory
– that its real purpose was to defuse black protest or the emergence of a
strong black political movement, to give the appearance of responding to
grievances but in reality to do little.[4] Doubtless policymakers sought to avoid
long-term troubles, but as an explanation of the mainsprings of policy I find
this quite unconvincing: my own view, shortly and dogmatically stated, is
that the legislation, especially that of the 1970s, proceeded from the moral
concern of a relatively small number of individuals, within and outside the
government. In a sense which requires no apology, it was an elitist measure,
carried through, as was the sex discrimination legislation, with surprisingly
little organised support or opposition from both beneficiaries and affected
interests. My criticisms of the statute thus proceed by taking entirely
seriously the proclaimed objective of reducing discrimination and pointing
out where it seems likely to fail. I emphasise the extent to which the flaws
result from errors of perception and analysis, timidity, and from the influence of constraints imposed by the normal workings of the legal system.
Adherents of the 'pacification' theory may of course see in my criticisms –
which are numerous and at times severe – confirmation of their views, but
this divergence is the essence of scholarly controversy.

III

The book is divided into four parts. The first examines the concept of
discrimination, both as a philosophical problem and a matter of statutory
interpretation. Analysis of the precise grounds of discrimination governed
by the Act, and of discrimination by means of victimisation, round out this
conceptual section. Part II commences with a review of findings about racial
discrimination and disadvantage in employment and then explains the
application of specific provisions of the Act. Part III looks at the machinery
created for the enforcement of the Act. The Coda, after a brief recapitula-
tion of the main criticisms voiced earlier, offers some speculations about the
prospect of achieving significant advances in racial equality in the 1980s.

A few points relating to the use of legal material should be mentioned.
The first is that repeated reference is made to case law under the American
federal Civil Rights Act of 1964. Not only, as will be seen, was this
legislation in many respects the progenitor of the British statute, but
increasingly American sex discrimination and equal pay cases are cited with
respect by English courts,[5] which may be expected to make at least as great
use of them in construing the 1976 Act. It is argued in Chapter 2 that, if
the Act is to work, courts and tribunals must adopt the kind of policy-
orientated interpretation long employed by American judges and, if Lord
Denning is correct, by the European Court of Justice;[6] in Chapter 11 it is
suggested that some aspects of the approach of the American courts to

evidentiary questions be adopted. I do not wish to be understood to argue that the American approach to statutory interpretation, or other aspects of that legal system, are generally superior. However, for reasons I hope are found convincing, it seems extremely unlikely that Parliament's declared objective of reducing racial discrimination and disadvantage by legal means can be achieved without substantial alteration of several traditional doctrines, habits of thought and modes of proceeding characteristic of the English legal system. The American practice is therefore more than usually relevant.

Second, there is very little reported case law on the Act. Most litigation does not go beyond industrial tribunals, whose decisions are usually unreported and difficult to obtain, and are in any case of limited importance as precedents. Although I have cited such material where it seemed appropriate and was accessible, I have given unusually great emphasis to Parliamentary discussion, particularly in Standing Committee. This material is of course supposed to be a sealed book to judges, but there is no reason why a scholar should impose such blinkers on himself, particularly as many important issues of policy, and questions of interpretation, considered here were directly addressed in that forum.

I have spoken throughout entirely in terms of English law, although the Act applies equally to Scotland. However, the minuscule non-white population north of the Border, and the minor importance of matters not subject to uniform statute law, permitted me, without obvious embarrassment, to preserve my invincible ignorance of Scottish law.

It is not possible to have the notes placed at the bottom of each page. I regret the inconvenience of reference and have tried to mitigate it by asterisking those notes which supplement the argument in the text, rather than simply cite a legal or academic source. It also seemed desirable not to clutter the text with the unnecessary mention of case names where a note would suffice. However, for legal specialists to whom the detail is important, the Table of Cases is organised to facilitate more precise reference, in the manner explained at the head of the table. The notes appear at the end of relevant chapters.

Certain sections of the Act are of particular importance, and at certain points in the text arguments are made based on the precise wording of certain provisions. A Statutory Appendix consisting of critical sections and those whose language readers might wish to examine themselves, has therefore been compiled.

In contrast to the Preface, I have tried to avoid the use of the first person singular throughout the text. This is not to give the impression of a spurious objectivity – it should be obvious that I want to see racial discrimination ended and racial inequality diminished – but because an author's persona has always seemed to me an awkward interloper in scholarly work.

I have followed the illogical but prevailing English practice of using the term 'black' to describe both the various Asian ethnic groups as well as West Indians. Like virtually all studies and public discussion, I have omitted consideration of African and Chinese minorities in Britain.

I was able to take account of material available to me as of 31 December 1979.

IV   A BRIEF HISTORICAL CONSPECTUS

Apart from requiring innkeepers and common carriers to offer their facilities without regard to colour or race, the common law imposed no restrictions on the power of private persons – employers, landlords, shop-owners and the like – to refuse to have dealings with any person on these grounds, or indeed any others. Legislation was therefore required to impose rules of public law on hitherto private decisions. Private Members' Bills were first offered in the 1950s, but the initial legislation did not come until the Race Relations Act 1965. Apart from its criminal prohibition of incitement to racial hatred it was a very limited enactment. It prohibited only the 'practice' of discrimination in 'places of public resort' (s. 1) and, with exceptions, discriminatory restrictions on the disposal of tenancies (s. 5). Its inadequacies became increasingly apparent, and under the aegis of a new Home Secretary, Roy Jenkins, the ground was prepared for further legislation. A report by an independent research organisation, Political and Economic Planning (PEP), published in April 1967, documented the vast extent of racial discrimination in Britain.[7] Later in the same year, a committee of lawyers led by Professor Harry Street produced an analysis (the 'Street Report') of the possible forms and mechanisms of enforcement and amendment anti-discrimination law might contain.[8] Its analysis drew heavily upon the experience of American states and Canadian provinces. In the following year the Race Relations Act 1968 ('the 1968 Act') made employment discrimination, with certain exceptions, unlawful for the first time in British history. It also extended the sweep of the legislation in relation to discrimination in housing and the provision of goods, facilities and services. Administratively, it reconstituted and strengthened the Race Relations Board ('the Board'), which was supposed to receive and investigate complaints of violations and achieve satisfactory redress of the victim's grievance. Some, but by no means all, of the proposals in the Street Report found their way into this legislation.

Flaws and weaknesses in the 1968 Act soon emerged, particularly in relation to the mechanism of enforcement and the narrow definition of discrimination. In 1973 PEP undertook another national survey, and in a series of Reports that soon followed, documented the persistence of massive discrimination, particularly in employment.[9] Meanwhile awareness of the diverse dimensions of discrimination began to broaden, and in 1970 the

Equal Pay Act was passed, although it did not take effect until 1975. When
the Labour Party took office in 1974, Roy Jenkins was once again Home
Secretary. The Sex Discrimination Act 1975 (SDA) soon emerged, with
many provisions drawing upon the Board's experience and criticisms of the
1968 Act. The Race Relations Act 1976 followed. All legislation concerning
racial discrimination is now found in this statute; its predecessors are wholly
repealed. The Board has been abolished and replaced by the Commission
for Racial Equality ('the CRE' or 'the Commission').

University of Warwick   L. L.
15 January 1980

NOTES

1. A large sample may be found in L. Friedman and S. Macaulay, *Law and the
Behavioural Sciences* (Bobbs-Merrill, 2nd edn, 1979) chap. 3, esp. pp. 488–98,
which lists numerous studies. See also Evan, 'Law as an Instrument of Social
Change', in A. Gouldner and S. Miller (eds) *Applied Sociology* (Free Press, 1965)
pp. 285–93.

2. In *Race, Colonialism and the City* (Routledge, 1973), pp. 203–23. See now also
J. Rex and S. Tomlinson, *Colonial Immigrants in a British City* (Routledge, 1979)
chap. 1.

3. Gabriel and Ben-Tovim, 'Marxism and Race', 7 *Econ. & Soc.* 118 (1978).

4. This theory has been most fully articulated by Sivanandan, 'Race, Class and the
State', 17 *Race & Class* 350 (1976). See also Freeman and Spencer, 'The State, the
Law and Race Relations in Britain Today', (1979) 31 *Curr. Leg. Probs* 117.

5. E.g. *Clay Cross (Quarry Service) Ltd* v. *Fletcher*, [1979] 1 All E.R. 474, 478
(Lord Denning M.R.), 481 (Lawton L.J.); *Shields* v. *E. Coomes (Holdings) Ltd*,
[1979] 1 All E.R. 456, 464 (Lord Denning M.R.), 470 (Bridge L.J.); *Ministry of
Defence* v. *Jeremiah*, [1979] 3 All E.R. 833, 836, per Lord Denning M.R.

6. See his comments on the European Court's 'teleological' method of interpretation in *James Buchanan & Co. Ltd* v. *Babco Forwarding & Shipping (U.K.) Ltd*,
[1976] 2 W.L.R. 107, 112. It should be noted, however, that on appeal, [1978] A.C.
141, the House of Lords was distinctly hostile to Lord Denning's eulogisation and
application of 'Continental' methods of interpretation, at any rate in the circumstances of that case.

7. It was published in popular form as W. Daniel, *Racial Discrimination in
England* (Penguin Books, 1968).

8. H. Street *et al.*, *Report on Anti-discrimination Legislation* (PEP, 1967).

9. The popular version (see Table of Abbreviations) is cited repeatedly in this
book. The relevant original Reports, both published by PEP, are *Racial Disadvantage in Employment* (Report No. 544, June 1974) and *The Extent of Racial
Discrimination* (Report No. 547, September 1974).

Acknowledgements

We in Britain are enduring a period dominated by politicians and media sages who would have us believe selfishness is a social virtue and anything of value must be measured in cash. I therefore take a particular pleasure in stating that in addition to the normal reliance of scholars on the published work of others, I could not have written this book without the generous contribution of time, effort and ideas of literally dozens of people. Lack of space precludes naming all of them here – many are acknowledged in various note references – particularly as a full list would include a substantial proportion of my colleagues at Warwick and Queen's University, Kingston, Ontario. Several were kind enough to read, criticise and discuss drafts of various chapters. Numerous persons in diverse Faculties of universities throughout the country, and in several departments of government, courteously and promptly supplied me with unpublished information. I wrote to all of them as a stranger; virtually no one refused assistance.

Every scholar writes on a more than half-covered slate; even Newton averred, 'I could not have seen so far, had I not stood on ye shoulders of giants'. I should like to pay tribute to three books on this general subject, cited so often as to be mentioned in the Table of Abbreviations: Bob Hepple's *Race, Jobs and the Law* (2nd edn); Antony Lester and Geoffrey Bindman's *Race and Law*, and Ian Macdonald's *The Race Relations Act 1976*. In scope, ambition and intended audience they are very different from each other, and from the present study – which in many respects attempts to pick up the trail where the first two left off – but I should be well pleased if many people regarded my work as highly as I do theirs.

The Nuffield Foundation's generous award under its Small Grants Scheme enabled me to obtain the services of Vicky Giles, Rob Ross and Paul Statham as research assistants at various stages. Their efforts facilitated and accelerated completion of many aspects of the book. Thanks are also due to the British Institute of International and Comparative Law, and Messrs Sweet & Maxwell/Stevens, for their kind permission to reprint portions of articles first appearing in journals published by them, and to Her Majesty's

Stationery Office for permission to reproduce portions of the Race Relations Act 1976 in the Statutory Appendix.

I am deeply indebted to my secretary, Sally Venables, and her colleagues, for typing repeated drafts of the manuscript despite the pressures of a great volume of other work, and difficulties engendered by my pre-literate handwriting and several requested deadlines which, in retrospect, seem blatantly unreasonable.

My wife, Donna Dickenson Lustgarten, bore more than her fair share of the emotional strain involved in the writing. She has also made a significant contribution to the arguments in Chapter 1, and to the language and clarity of a goodly portion of the whole book.

Despite these great debts, all brickbats relating to errors, omissions and confusions must be aimed at my head alone.

Table of Cases

NOTE: Cases appearing in italics are those which are referred to by name in the text. The page in the text and the corresponding footnote are given together in the Table below, along with all other places in which the case is cited.

Thus, '*Cassell & Co. Ltd* v. *Broome* 187, 231/238' indicates that the case appears in a footnote on p. 187, and by name in the text on p. 231 with the corresponding footnote on p. 238.

Table of Statutes

Please note that the table of Statutory Instruments appears overleaf.

Statutory Instruments

Table of Abbreviations – Law Reports

A.C.	Appeal Cases (House of Lords)
All E.R.	All England Reports
Ch.	Chancery
C.M.L.R.	Common Market Law Reports
E.C.R.	European Court Reports
I.C.R.	Industrial Case Reports
I.R.L.R.	Industrial Relations Law Reports
K.B.	King's Bench
Q.B.	Queen's Bench
W.L.R.	Weekly Law Reports

American Cases

F. 2d	Federal Reports, Second Series
F. Supp.	Federal Supplement
L. Ed. 2d	Lawyer's Edition, Second Series (Supreme Court)
P. 2d	Pacific Reports, Second Series
U.S.	United States (Supreme Court)

Works frequently cited

1. *de Smith* – S. A. de Smith, *Constitutional and Administrative Law* (Penguin Books, 2nd edn, 1973). I have preferred this edition to the subsequent one, written by others following the author's death.
2. *Hepple* – B. A. Hepple, *Race, Jobs and the Law* (Penguin Books, 2nd edn, 1970).
3. *Lester and Bindman* – A. Lester and G. Bindman, *Race and Law* (Penguin Books, 1972).
4. *Macdonald* – I. Macdonald, *The Race Relations Act 1976* (Butterworth, 1977).
5. PEP Report or *Racial Disadvantage* – D. Smith, *Racial Disadvantage in Britain* (Penguin Books, 1977).
6. *Runnymede Seminar* – *A Review of the Race Relations Act 1976* (Runnymede Trust, 1979).
7. *W. & P./B.* – E. Wade and G. Phillips, *Constitutional and Administrative Law*, 9th edn by A. Bradley (Longman, 1977).

Part I
The Meaning of Discrimination

1
Concepts of Discrimination –
History and Theory

This chapter will examine the meaning of discrimination in convergent but analytically distinct ways. We look first at its evolution in British legislation, considering simultaneously how these statutory changes embodied an altered view of the problem of racial inequality, and then analyse diverse concepts of discrimination at a more abstract level. Ultimately our concern is with the way in which discrimination may be applied as a legal concept. Any such definition, however, is at bottom the expression in a peculiar specialised vocabulary of what may, rather loosely, be termed a social-philosophical concept; and it is only when work at this level is complete that the translation into law may begin. Hence both levels of analysis are undertaken.

Ideas arise in particular historical circumstances, which in the present instance means out of specific political and social conflicts. However, once created, they exercise an independent influence and the failure of a given social policy may be due as much to intellectual weakness as political opposition. Hence this chapter moves repeatedly between the levels of abstract ideas and particular social phenomena, as well as including analysis of statutes and judical decisions that have arisen in response to both.

Much of the material discussed here derives from the United States, both the direct source of British legislation and the centre of the most thoughtful philosophical and legal analysis of various approaches. This theoretical sophistication is perhaps less a tribute to innate acuity than to the greater pressure of political conflict over a longer period, but it is a resource Britain would be foolish to ignore on nationalistic grounds. Moreover, legal and intellectual developments have had nearly fifteen years to make some impact on American life, and one can speak with at least some empirical grounding about the effect of certain policies by reference to the United States in a way that would simply not be possible if one's vision were restricted to Britain. And precisely because ideas bear the imprint of their historical origins, the decision whether to import policies and legislation from another country must take account of the extent to which its strength depends upon less portable factors in its homeland. Thus certain ideas are initially explored and criticised within an American context. That assessment is then qualified by considering whether they would be equally appropriate to Britain.

I EVOLUTION OF THE STATUTORY DEFINITION

The 1968 Act defined discrimination as treating a person 'less favourably than he treats or would treat other persons', which by a separate subsection explicitly included segregation. This precise language has been carried over into s. 1 (1)(a) of the present Act (see Statutory Appendix). Both elements reflect a common understanding of the behaviour they wish to suppress: it is seen as a deliberate wrong perpetrated by one individual against a specific victim. The discriminator, however, need not act with malice or dislike; the legal definition of discrimination has always subsumed but gone beyond actions based upon prejudice. Put another way, behaviour rather than attitudes has always been the focus of the law; the discriminator cannot escape responsibility by showing that his heart was pure but that he acted to propitiate others. This is a point of major importance, for one of the main conclusions of the PEP study examined in detail in Chapter 5 is that employment discrimination largely results from inaction rather than deliberate policy, which in turn stems in substantial measure from acquiescence in and fear of disturbing the strong racial hostilities of a very small minority.[1]

This concept of discrimination gives no assistance to those not in fact equal, among whom number a substantial majority of non-whites in Britain and the United States. For reasons of history, relatively few would have the educational and professional qualifications or experience necessary to meet standard criteria for employment. In the United States, it became clear soon after the 1964 Civil Rights Act outlawed employment discrimination that unless the original understanding of the problem was broadened, the Act would have minimal effect on the inferior position of blacks as a group. The courts responded, and in 1971, in *Griggs* v *Duke Power Co.*,[2] a rare unanimous Supreme Court expounded a concept of discrimination whose key element was disproportionate adverse effect, not mere intentional inferior treatment.

This idea slowly crossed the Atlantic. A lecture by a distinguished American civil rights lawyer expressed it forcefully and seems to have influenced important figures connected with the Board.[3] However, when in September 1974 the Labour Government issued a White Paper containing proposals for legislation against sex discrimination, there was no indication that the traditional notion of intentional, or direct, discrimination was to be broadened. Soon thereafter the Home Secretary, Roy Jenkins, visited the

United States. On his return a new provision outlawing 'indirect discrimination', drawn directly from *Griggs*, was added to the Bill. In Standing Committee discussion a Minister explained the new clause by quoting passages from the judgment in *Griggs*,[4] one of the very few occasions in Parliamentary history when the meaning of a proposed statute has been explained by reference to the case law of another nation. The Race Relations Bill contained an identically worded provision which was approved after full consideration by a different Standing Committee. The precise statutory language, found in s. 1 (1)(b) and reproduced in the Appendix, will be analysed in detail in Chapter 2. It may be summarised by saying that a person alleging indirect discrimination must prove five things:

(1) that the respondent applied a 'requirement or condition' such that the 'proportion of persons'
(2) of the 'same racial group' as the complainant who
(3) 'can comply' with it is
(4) 'considerably smaller' than the proportion of those not of his group who can satisfy it, and
(5) that the result is to his 'detriment'.

Once he carries this burden it falls to the employer to show that the challenged requirement is 'justifiable'.

The borrowing from the United States was deliberately selective. One serious weakness of the new statutes is that they imported only the expanded concept of discrimination and left behind the essential concomitant procedural and remedial elements. (This is explored in detail in Chapter 12.) Further, for what are ultimately moral and philosophical reasons, the practice variously known as reverse or affirmative or positive discrimination – the setting of targets, in reality indistinguishable from quotes, for the percentage of minorities to be hired or promoted within a given period – has also been rejected. It is thus unlawful – except in meticulously specified instances where race is a 'genuine occupational qualification' (below, pp.145–8) – to give preference to a non-white because of his race; the white person adversely treated could lodge a complaint of direct racial discrimination.

This does not mean that no positive steps may be taken; the law does not prevent efforts to help those in fact unequal to achieve equality. Hence employers, trade unions and statutory and approved private training bodies may now offer special training programmes, assistance and encouragement to non-whites to enable them to qualify for positions for which they are wholly or disproportionately absent (see below, pp.25–8).

The significant evolution undergone by the law in less than a decade mirrors a growing and radically transformed understanding of the subordinate position occupied by racial minorities. To see how the aims, techniques and probable limitations of the law have altered, one must examine in depth the various concepts of discrimination that have been articulated, the social and ethical problems they raise, and their consequences for the operation of law.

II CONCEPTS OF DISCRIMINATION

One may begin with a broad distinction between two distinct, and ultimately conflicting, ideas of racial equality. Drawing upon Leon Mayhew, these will be called the 'equal opportunity' and 'fair-share' approaches;[5] a later writer has similarly differentiated between 'process-oriented' and 'result-oriented' approaches.[6] In its purest or most extreme form the first accepts that discrimination has been abolished when all formal and deliberate barriers against blacks have been dismantled. Its concern stops with determining whether the factor of race has caused an individual to suffer adverse treatment. At the furthest point at the other end of the spectrum the unalloyed fair-share approach is concerned only with equality of result, measured in terms of proportionality. Its inherent logic leads to the adoption of quotas as a remedy once a finding of discrimination is made.

The two approaches derive from different, also ultimately conflicting, philosophical foundations. Equality of treatment is inherent in the feeling of a fundamental human connectedness. In the striking phrase of Patrick Fitzgerald, 'Why would it be offensive, at the end of King Lear, for only Lear and Cordelia to take bows, and not the minor characters? It would be like equating the minor characters with tables and chairs. It is not just a question of equality, but of humanity.'[7] Grounded in sentiments so deep, it is consequently a minimalist view, requiring only that each individual be judged by the same standards – whatever these may be in any particular instance – and not favoured or disfavoured by the application of socially ascribed status characteristics. It is the concept of just treatment appropriate to an abstract philosophical system, and to individuals who are recognised in any given society as factually equal; put another way, it is the principle that would surely be chosen by persons in John Rawls' 'original position'.[8]

The fair-share approach, by contrast, is more complex and controversial. It is also of much more recent origin, having arisen in response to a history of ill treatment of socially distinct groups – which history, it is argued, makes the defining group characteristic relevant to the distribution of social goods. Justice is therefore seen as collective, at least in the negative sense that it is considered wrong for the ill-treated group to have proportionately less of whatever is valued. The fair-share idea also embodies what Robert Nozick calls 'a patterned distribution' – a norm based upon abstract philosophical principles by which a given distribution is to be judged.[9] This norm, whilst not necessarily socialist or egalitarian, does entail a judgment about the relative deserts of different groups; as such it is incompatible with the liberal individualism of the nineteenth century, which not only accepted the results of the market but could not conceive of enquiring into the handicaps some competitors brought with them when they entered its competitions. However – as one might have suspected from its American antecedents – the fair-share approach is in no way compatible with great inequalities of income, wealth and social resources: it merely requires that blacks fit into the existing patterns of inequality in the same proportions as whites.

At both the philosophical and legal levels the latent conflict erupts when the fair-share approach requires denial of something desirable to a white person in order to achieve justice defined in terms of collective advancement. The daunting task confronting policymakers and theorists is to minimise the extent of the conflict, to transcend the limited effectiveness of the first approach while avoiding the injustices of the second. No more important question exists in relation to racial discrimination than how to eliminate the inferior conditions of blacks without trampling upon other important social values.

DIRECT DISCRIMINATION

This concept is the legal expression of the equal opportunity approach. It sees acts of discrimination as isolated and intentional specific wrongs. It paints an intensely individualistic picture, at the centre of which stands a model victim: a middle-class person whose education, occupational skills or income entitle him on widely accepted criteria to some opportunity which he is denied solely because of race. This understanding derives from both the liberal notion of formal equality before the law and the dominant Western conception of justice going back to Aristotle, which commands the equal treatment of equals. One could only deny the claim of such a man by arguing that his race made him unequal, a view relatively few people in the post-Nazi and post-Imperial era are willing to state openly.

Historically, direct discrimination has been the dominant conception, remaining virtually unchallenged until the late 1960s, and is the form that in its initial stages of optimism and inexperience anti-discrimination law has taken wherever it has been enacted.[10] The unadorned moral repugnance of deliberate racist behaviour, unredeemed by any social value, perhaps explains its pre-eminence, but it was also linked to the initial method of enforcement. Intent is an essential element in the great majority of criminal offences, and criminal sanctions were often the only means of enforcing the earliest anti-discrimination laws (as remains true in France today). Indeed the criminal law approach moulded the Government's proposals for the first British legislation in 1965; only after an intensive lobbying campaign which disseminated persuasive evidence from various American states of the ineffectiveness of reliance upon criminal penalties was it rejected at the last moment.[11]

From this perception of the problem flow two importance consequences.

First, the law's intention is directed to the alleged discriminator, not to his victim. Because the discrimination must be 'on racial grounds' the precise basis of his action must be determined. Thus a court or tribunal must consider detailed evidence about the events of a specific situation, and must weigh the plausibility of alternative explanations – the complainant was ill-mannered; another applicant appeared in person after he 'phoned, etc. – and the credibility of conflicting stories in order to determine why the defendant treated him in a particular way. The only pertinent question is the legality of the defendant's treatment of the particular complainant; the process is viewed as a private law matter of one individual with a grievance against another. Each complaint of discrimination thus becomes a highly particularised 'case',[12]* and the social structure and power relationships which ultimately determine the situation of racial minorities remain hidden from the sight of the law.

Second, because the evil is defined in individualistic terms it tends to be equated with *different* treatment of any sort on the basis of race, not merely with *inferior* treatment, particularly as segregation is prohibited as well. Thus colour-blindness becomes a central value. This encourages employers, education and housing authorities, and governments to adopt an attitude of *laissez-faire* whilst, inevitably, the position of minorities stagnates or deteriorates; it also deprives anyone concerned with the problem of the information essential to intelligent analysis of policy. In Britain this may be seen most clearly in the debates, as yet unresolved, over voluntary or compulsory racial record-keeping, which have been marked by substantial contradictions on the part of government and notable changes of mind in the late 1970s.[13]*

This view of discrimination had to be dislodged from pre-eminence if a realistic view of the problem was to be taken. However, its continuing importance in anti-discrimination law should not be discounted. The great majority of complaints of discrimination since the 1976 Act became effective have concerned this form of treatment: the persistence of overt racialism in Britain ensures that the law will be repeatedly invoked in relatively straightforward situations, as well as more subtle ones.

INDIRECT DISCRIMINATION

This concept shifts the inquiry of the law from the respondent's purposes to the impact of his practices on members of a disadvantaged group. The change of perspective followed from the realisation in the United States that the social problem of discrimination is not primarily a matter of intentional acts of individuals. It is fundamentally deep-seated and impersonal: characteristic terms in the vocabulary of enforcement are patterns, practices, structures and effects.[14] The impact of this new understanding on the law was most fully manifest in the *Griggs* case. The Court there held that use of employment tests or educational qualifications as prerequisites for hiring and promotion fell within the statutory proscription of 'discrimination' unless those prerequisites had 'a manifest relationship to the employment in question'.[15] Invoking the legislative purpose 'to achieve equality of employment opportunities', Burger C. J. declared:

> Congress has now required that the posture and condition of the job-seeker be taken into account. . . . The Act proscribes not only overt discrimination, but also practices that are fair in form, but discriminatory in operation . . . good intent or absence of discriminatory intent does not redeem employment procedures or testing mechanisms that operate as 'built-in headwinds' for minority groups and are unrelated to measuring job capability.[16]

Thus discrimination is now understood as the substantive inequality of racial groups. The emphasis, however, is still on the fact of *racial* difference: inequalities of class, status and power are as such not touched by the law. Nor is racial inequality *equated* with those other forms of stratification, even though in the experience of most blacks they may be inseparable; in one important case the Supreme Court rejected the argument that differentials on the basis of income or wealth was in effect discrimination against racial minorities.[17] However, within the framework of existing systems of stratification, prohibition of indirect discrimination attempts to eliminate policies and practices which disproportionately disqualify or disadvantage racial minorities. Where these are expressed as criteria of some sort – e.g. seniority, test results, length of residence – the criteria themselves, though containing no mention of race, are called into question. Here the essential difference from direct discrimination emerges clearly: under that conception, so long as a non-racial criterion is applied, the fact that it heavily disadvantages blacks is irrelevant in law. Moreover – a key point not sufficiently appreciated – once such a criterion is condemned, it cannot be applied to anyone, regardless of race. Thus whites who have been excluded from a particular job for lack of a qualification held to be indirectly discriminatory with gain from the working of the broader concept; indeed it is quite probable in Britain, with its small black population, that in many instances numerically more deprived whites than blacks will benefit. A recent and important example of this 'spillover' effect is the experience of the 'open admissions' programme of the City University of New York. In 1970 the University abandoned its previous admissions standards and broadened the criteria for acceptance, intending to facilitate the entrance of black and Hispanic students. In effect – although the programme evolved in response to political protest rather than litigation – the University conceded that its former requirements were indirectly discriminatory. The first comprehensive study of the scheme, completed in 1978, reported that a large proportion of those admitted were in fact students from white ethnic minorities who would also have hitherto been denied admission.[18] This point emphasises as well the substantial overlap between social and racial disadvantage; it may also in future years lead to increasing dissatisfaction with the political decision to refuse to use legal methods to attack social inequality directly.

Although American law was historically the source of the broader understanding, there were other resources, apparently untapped, closer to home. The EEC prohibitions on nationality discrimination discussed in Chapter 3 have produced a substantial case law before the Court of Justice. Quite early in the history of the Community, academic legal writers – who in the civil law tradition are a more influential source of law than in England – recognised that what they variously called 'material', 'covert' or 'indirect' discrimination ought also to be proscribed.[19] Not until 1969 was the problem considered by the Court of Justice, which declared that refusal to employ anyone who had not served in the member state's armed forces, a criterion obviously excluding all but its own nationals, violated the Treaty.[20] In a subsequent case the Court expressly stated that the Treaty rules 'forbid not only overt discrimination by reason of nationality but also all forms of covert discrimination which, by the application of other criteria of differentiation, lead in fact to the same result'.[21] Later cases have decided that a residence requirement for permission to act as a legal representative,[22] and a refusal by the French Bar Council to recognise university qualifications received in another member state, despite their certification as equivalent by a French university,[23] were impermissible infringements on the Treaty right of freedom of establishment. In both cases it is clear from the judgments that the Court was aware that the rules it invalidated were types of indirect discrimination, although did not use that precise description. This jurisprudence has begun to weave its way into British law, notably in the bold decision of the National Insurance Commissioner in *Re Residence Conditions*.[24] In the case Art. 7 of the Treaty, a general prohibition on nationality discrimination, was not only held to be directly applicable, but to invalidate more restrictive eligibility requirements for those born outside the United Kingdom. The Commissioner reasoned that this requirement must almost necessarily result in indirect discrimination on grounds of nationality to the detriment of nationals of other member states.[25]

It is noteworthy that courts confronting radically different social problems within profoundly dissimilar legal and intellectual traditions have arrived at a similar understanding of the problem of unequal treatment. This suggests strongly that a concern for the effectiveness of the law necessitates the broadened understanding of discrimination.

In two fundamental respects, however, the *Griggs* approach and its British statutory equivalent go beyond the concept articulated by the Court of Justice. The latter, perhaps in part because of the nature of the specific cases that have come before it, has been concerned only with formal rules which adversely affect persons because of a legal and political status, that of nationality. Indirect discrimination in Britain, however, is ultimately concerned with the *economic and social* position of *groups*. The statute expresses this by making the social and economic status of the complainant's 'racial group' the touchstone of the legality of the challenged 'requirement'. If as a consequence of the group's unequal 'posture and condition', to recall a phrase from *Griggs*, the requirement has a greater adverse effect upon minorities, it will be unlawful (unless proved 'justifiable').

In essence the law has recognised and protected a group interest. This interest arises from the disabilities imposed by the majority upon those who possess the involuntary and unalterable characteristic of colour. Until these can be reduced to insignificance, all non-whites share a common interest in the enhancement of the group's economic and social position. This is so because each individual will suffer from the ascription of undesirable traits which supposedly mark the group, even if he has no sense of loyalty or participation in it. It is also true because when enough outstandingly able members of the group achieve success and esteem in the eyes of the majority, the perception of other members of the group becomes more favourable, and the common run of them come to be treated on their merits as individuals. Thus the existence of the group interest is not everlasting; it persists only so long as group membership produces disadvantages, and is widely thought to be a mark of superior status. Throughout this time the advance of the group and of individuals is inseparable.

English law is strongly individualistic. It knows only persons, and responds to the reality of collectivity, if at all, by recourse to fiction. Thus vast commercial enterprises become a legal person, the limited company. Where this personification has not been brought about – notably in the case of trade unions – the courts have been manifestly confused.[26]

Why this is so is a large question which has yet to be adequately answered. The depth of analysis and historical investigation required is, regrettably, beyond the scope of the present work, but a few general speculations may perhaps be permitted.

The individualism of contemporary law – whose effect on the way in which social issues are distorted by narrowing when translated into legal questions has already been noted (above, p. 8) – seems clearly to be the result of historical development. It is connected with what Kamenka and Tay describe as the shift from *gemeinschaft* to *gesellschaft* law.[27] In brief, this means that the function of law has altered from the maintenance of ongoing relationships in an organic community in which people repeatedly encounter each other in a variety of roles, to resolving disputes among parties linked only by intermittent discrete relationships in fragmented spheres of life. Law thus alters its form and functions as the agrarian feudal community gives way to the individualism of capitalist industrial society. One consequence is that legal recognitions of collective rights or statutes gained in pre-capitalist times – for example, that of common land use, or the characterisation of Benchers of the various Inns of Court as a 'corps by custom' – lose their original meaning and decay into quaintness. Whether the collective dimension of human life will again be recognised in legal conception in the next 'stage' of development – whatever that may be, and assuming some such evolutionary schemata adequately conceives Western history – remains to be seen. It does seem clear, however, that ethnicity is the primary vehicle through which the reality of collectivity has begun to be recovered on a social level, and that this has begun to have legal impact.[28] Thus whatever the destiny of *gesellschaft* law,[29] the conflicts engendered by the vastly increased diversity of populations within every industrialised nation – a product of the labour mobility, cheap transport and economic confederations of the last quarter-century – and by the revival of long-quiescent minority identifications, will force legal theory to accommodate the claims upon the legal system that will emerge.

The concept of indirect discrimination does recognise the group character of the *wrong* suffered by individuals. This is a significant jurisprudential advance, and one essential to the effectiveness of anti-discrimination legislation. However, the statute does not go so far as to create group rights, in the sense that a racial minority, or entity purporting to represent it, can invoke the remedial power of a judicial body. This may, however, be a logical and necessary next step in the evolution of the law, and later in this chapter consideration will be given to the ways in which a racial minority might *as a group* achieve collective remedies through the legal process.

The prohibition of indirect discrimination may also be seen as an attempt to spread the responsibility for reducing racial disadvantage far more widely than was previously possible. Under earlier legislation an employer whose policy was scrupulously to treat blacks and whites identically could detach his operations from the reality of racial disadvantage: if, for whatever reasons, few non-whites could satisfy his employment qualifications, that was simply unfortunate. Now, however, the law as a practical matter requires him to review his employment practices with an eye to their long-term effects. If blacks are absent from the labour force, or remain concentrated in the worst jobs, he must at least ask why, for he may find his firm the defendant in a legal action or the object of an administrative investigation. Whether self-initiated reform of this kind will significantly improve employment opportunities for non-whites will, however, depend entirely upon how trenchantly indirect discrimination comes to be interpreted.

Two further species are to be found within the genus indirect discrimination. The first may be best illustrated by the hypothetical example of a local authority which has long required five years' residence within its boundaries as a condition of eligibility for council accommodation. Three years after the arrival of a sizeable number of non-white immigrants, and in response to a campaign to 'Keep Council Housing White', it doubles the length of the residence requirement. The ten-year rule is not overtly racialist, and would also exclude some whites, but *ex hypothesi* would exclude all blacks. Clearly this would be indirect discrimination, but unlike the case of a long-established employment practice, or indeed the five-year residence requirement itself, it was employed as a deliberate device of racial exclusion. The Act recognises that this discrimination by subterfuge, or intentional indirect discrimination, is a distinct problem. Generally a complainant who wins an indirect discrimination case is not entitled to damages; however, unless the respondent cannot disprove the element of intention, this prohibition does not apply (see further below, pp. 233). Of course the discriminatory purpose of a seemingly racially neutral criterion may not be as easy to prove as in the illustrative example.

The other sub-class of indirectly discriminatory acts are those which perpetuate the effects of past formal discrimination. This has been an important issue in American litigation, where past deliberate and in some instances legally sanctioned discrimination meant that blacks were in an inferior position in terms of seniority or job transfer rights. It was also a central element in one of the most important cases under the Sex Discrimination Act, *Steel* v. *Union of Post Office Workers.*[30] For many years the Post Office had refused to classify women as 'permanent full-time', relegating them to the somewhat incongruous category of 'temporary full-time'. When this discriminatory treatment was ended in 1975, women received seniority rights only from that date. This meant that when Mrs Steel, a full-time postwoman since 1961, applied for a more desirable assignment, she had less seniority than a man hired in 1972. The Employment Appeal Tribunal (EAT) had little difficulty in deciding that she had suffered indirect discrimination. Given the history of openly practised sex discrimination, one may expect many cases of this kind.

In relation to racial discrimination the problem may be expected to take a somewhat different form. Even before 1968 few employers or trade unions operated overt or acknowledged colour bars, nor was such discrimination supported, let alone mandated, by law. However, tacit arrangements, many of which remain unadmitted even today, quite effectively denied blacks employment or promotion in particular industries.[31] Consequently any agreement or practice that maintains the effect of this prior intentional discrimination would itself now be unlawful unless otherwise 'justifiable'. The point seems most likely to arise in the context of experience requirements and seniority rights. With regard to the latter it may be noted that the Act gives more protection to victims of discrimination than the American legislation as authoritatively interpreted. The Civil Rights Act of 1964 contains an exemption for differential treatment 'pursuant to a bona fide seniority or merit system'.[32] Although some thirty lower court decisions had held that seniority systems which entrenched the effects of pre-Act discrimination (which at the time was not unlawful), were not within the exemption because they were not 'bona fide', in 1977 the Supreme Court overruled this line of cases.[33] It now appears that only where the seniority arrangements themselves constitute discrimination can the exemption be avoided. Moreover, even where a seniority system entrenches the effects of discrimination occurring *after* the passage of the Act, and hence unequivocally unlawful, the Court held that the exemption overrides the proscription of discrimination.[34] As the *Steel* judgment shows, the absence of any such exception in British legislation ensures that the law will not be made into a device for maintaining the pattern of past discrimination for the succeeding generation. An industrial tribunal subsequently awarded Mrs Steel seniority retrospective to 1969, nearly seven years before sex discrimination became unlawful.[35]

Indirect discrimination, then, is a substantial enlargement of a social and legal concept, one at least potentially sensitive to the realities of racial disadvantage. It also contains important limitations. It is not a single-minded attempt to eliminate all substantive racial inequality, for it is still rooted in the equal opportunity concept. It incorporates a balancing of interests which is worked out in each particular case when the adjudicating body determines whether a practice which disproportionately excludes or hinders blacks is none the less 'justifiable'. Even the sceptical approach to such claims suggested in Chapter 2 would accept the existence of situations where racial disadvantage would be outweighed by other factors, and it is by no means clear that such an approach will be adopted. For those to whom the eradication of racial disadvantage is a goal which does not admit of such dilution, the concept of indirect discrimination cannot be regarded as the final step or reasonable limit of legislation. Others, particularly lawyers and administrators who have been concerned to devise remedies for past discrimination, have argued that fire must be fought with fire. These paths merge in a more controversial concept.

FAIR SHARES AND REVERSE DISCRIMINATION[36]*

Reverse discrimination may take several forms, which Professor William Gould has enumerated as 'quotas, ratios, goals and timetables'.[37] These can range, *inter alia*, from absolute preferences, e.g. the next twenty persons hired shall be drawn from minority groups; to hiring ratios, e.g. a rule that minority groups must comprise x per cent of the next 100 persons engaged; to a use of ratios terminating when minorities reach a certain percentage of the workforce; to selection procedures establishing more lenient standards for non-whites which may, as in the celebrated *Bakke* case,[38] be combined with a policy of reserving a specific number or proportion of places for minorities.

Historically reverse discrimination developed in the United States, not as part of a concept of discrimination, but as a remedy for past intentional discrimination. Thus, the argument ran, if blacks have been deliberately treated in an inferior manner and whites have improperly benefited at their expense, it is reasonable to make recompense by the same criterion – race – that defined the basis of the ill treatment. Additionally, on what may be called the working level, when discrimination has been proven, an appropriate remedy must be formulated. In so doing, how can one avoid taking racial factors into account? Conversely, how does one determine when the effects of past discrimination have been eradicated, so that administrative or judicial orders may cease to operate, or resources be directed elsewhere? One plausible answer to these questions is to assume that but for the effects of past or present injustice, individuals from various social groups would occupy various levels of jobs, qualities of housing and so forth in roughly identical proportions. This in turn assumes that natural ability or intelligence – concepts of manifold uncertainty – are genetically equally distributed in the aggregate among social groups (though obviously not among individuals) or – more modestly but perhaps more cogently – that these concepts are largely meaningless except as socially developed, hindered, recognised and in general determined. It follows that the absence of racial minorities in proportion to their numbers from a particular workforce or from desirable jobs is *prima facie* evidence of the workings of discrimination. It further follows that one can be sure that discrimination has ended only when what may be called 'proportionate representation' has been reached. This state also defines when the remedies cease to be required, although since their use began so recently, it cannot be specified how long they will be necessary. Hence the otherwise powerful point that reverse discrimination measures permanently entrench racial differences, contrary to the fundamental principles of anti-discrimination law, is turned aside. The same form of analysis may be applied to broader manifestations of racial inequality than the employment practices of a single company, such as national or regional differentials in income and unemployment.

This compensatory and practical view coalesces with one grounded in principle. Some believe that proportionate representation is itself a desirable goal, that social justice may be equated with a 'fair share' of social goods for each distinct group, and further that minority groups are not treated with equal respect until their members occupy important positions in proportion to the group's numbers. In the United States this accords with an established tradition of politicians in the urban North-East and Mid West who when selecting a slate of candidates tried to achieve 'a balanced ticket' – one containing representatives of each sizeable ethnic group.[39] For those who believe that the success of minority individuals serves as an example and a spur to the efforts of others among a disadvantaged group, such an arrangement may be regarded, not as a squalid political deal, but as a practical method of according minority groups equal esteem.

It should be emphasised, however, that no anti-discrimination statute yet enacted embodies this idea. Indeed, the American Civil Rights Act, under which reverse discrimination policies have frequently been ordered, contains a provision prohibiting the granting of 'preferential treatment' to any minority individual or group 'on account of an imbalance' – i.e. because measured by its presence in the relevant region or work force, the group is under-represented.[40] This provision has been uniformly interpreted to mean that preferential remedies can only be justified by a demonstrated history of discrimination, and that 'imbalance' as such is not sufficient to call forth such remedies.[41] The element of redress is thus an essential prerequisite, although it is not always clear to what extent the element of intention must be present to make out that history.[42]*

Reverse discrimination programmes, having unfortunately pre-empted the term 'affirmative action', have been operated widely in the United States in the spheres of employment and higher education, but apparently not in housing. They have not even been tentatively suggested for matters like the distribution of wealth, access to health care (extraordinarily expensive there) or – except in the wake of deliberate segregation[43] – quality of primary education. Yet these inequalities, particularly the first, are as important – indeed are inseparable – as those in employment and higher education which are thought to require extraordinary remedies. This limited scope reflects the central flaws in the idea itself, which themselves arise from legal, political and philosophical influences.

The most striking feature of these programmes is their compatibility with the ethos of liberal individualism. For all the rhetoric about recognition of group wrong, the process of compensation remains firmly within the framework of competition among individuals. This while preferences based upon race are justified by reference to unfair treatment committed over centuries by unspecifiable persons now dead, society as a whole does not make recompense. Instead specific employers are the defendants in legal actions, and individuals in competition for a job or place in higher education suffer the actual effects of the granting of preferences, since it is they who actually lose the opportunity which, had the usual criteria been employed, would have been there. This is an extraordinary way to allocate social responsibilities and costs. If 'society' – a shorthand for government, a wide range of major private institutions and predominant opinion – has been responsible for the inferior treatment of blacks, why should a person who has worked hard to acquire qualifications and has developed a sense of self based in part of his abilities, be denied employment because of new-found societal concern about discrimination?

Here it is necessary to insist upon a distinction between those persons who, whether or not by desire, had gained directly from the practice of discrimination and those who had not.[44]* An example of the former is the man who would have obtained his preferred assignment had Mrs Steel not brought her complaint (above, p. 13). In that situation the postman personally would have benefited from the effects of demonstrable past discrimination against an identifiable victim. It would therefore have been fair for Mrs Steel to have taken his place, particularly as the onset of the litigation would have put him on notice that his selection was contingent and thus not allowed him to develop reasonable expectations of entitlement. (In this connection it is vital that complaints be heard quickly, since protracted litigation would encourage the initially successful applicant to 'settle in' psychologically and perhaps make financial or other plans on the assumption of permanence.) But where a white applicant has gained no wrongful advantage, to shunt him aside impersonally, due to the operation of a timetable or quota, is to use him as a means to a social end. The irony is that this end – the rectification of injustice – is in this instance carried out by fundamentally unjust means, since the person who suffers has neither contributed to nor been favoured by the injustice. The only sense in which he could be said to have gained, is that the inferior social conditions of blacks will probably have eliminated some potential competitors. Whether this actually accrued to his personal advantage is wholly speculative, and too remote to require recompense from him. In any event, like all whites, he will be subject to increasing competition from blacks when effective anti-discrimination law enables them to achieve the positions their abilities and qualifications should command. Marginal whites must lose when arbitrary racial barriers are torn down: the essence of fairness is that abler people are preferred to the less suitable. This result, painful enough when founded upon a conception of justice shared by those who lose out, becomes intolerable when achieved by arbitrariness. It may of course be argued that the remedial process must start somewhere, and that the alternatives to racial preferences are either doing nothing, or an approach so far-ranging that the opposition it would excite would in the end make it come to nothing. However, in reality such a more radical view, which may be called society-wide or collective compensation, has not been seriously considered. (Some suggestion of what this might comprehend appears on pp. 19–20 and pp. 31–7 below.)

It is possible that one important reason for this failure is the structure of law itself. At least as presently understood, legal rights are inherently very specific – enforceable against a particular person, or a narrowly defined class of persons, rather than against 'society' or 'the state'. Even where the substance of the right – or its correlate, a duty – is expressed in general terms – e.g. reasonable care in the law of tort – the extent to which it may be asserted, or is owed, is also curtailed. As Lord Atkin stated in perhaps the single most influential judicial speech delivered in this century, 'The injunction, "Love thy neighbour" becomes "Do not injure thy neighbour", and the lawyer's question, "Who is my neighbour?" receives a restrictive answer.'[45] This outlook is particularly dominant in English law, as may be seen, to take an example from Professor Lawson, in the tenacity with which it adheres to the notion of privity of contract.[46]

This creates a radical disjunction between 'law' and economic or social 'policy'. The former is not only marked off by its distinctive set of functionaries, language, organisation and mystique; it is subject to sharp limits on what is thought to come within its domain. Thus once something is regarded as a matter of policy, its substance becomes wholly a matter of the judgment of officials of government, which may be the product of prudence, the search for popularity, prejudice, whim or historic vision. The important point is that it is subject to no control but electoral accountability. By means of various doctrines which form the core of administrative law, largely concerning procedural fairness and standards to which the exercise of discretion must conform, the courts have imposed certain limits on the mechanics of official decision. But only rarely – and then in circumstances of great controversy[47] – does the legal process address itself directly to the policy as such. Thus while the courts may insist that the Criminal Injuries Compensation Board must comport with certain procedural standards,[48] they cannot establish, abolish or amend the scheme itself; and although they may interpret the statutory standards of eligibility for a social security benefit, they cannot set the rate or decide that another form of benefit would be socially more desirable. Hence the things that probably matter most to people in an inferior social or economic position remain beyond the reach of the law. It is inconceivable, for example, that any anti-discrimination statute would contain provisions enabling a judicial body to declare that a deflationary economic policy which resulted in disproportionate unemployment for blacks constituted unlawful indirect discrimination, or to make the same judgment about a decision to switch £X million from renovation of inner-city housing to construction of a Highland motorway. That this idea sounds bizarre is not merely due to the political fact that no government would agree to tie its hands in this way. It arises also from what are thought to be inherent institutional limits on the competence of judicial bodies to address these sorts of questions adequately. Moreover, and doubtless due partly to the influence of these factors, no workable legal concept has yet been developed of a 'right' to employment, adequate housing or various forms of social provision. Although some of these are described as rights, at least in qualified terms, in various international documents,[49] at present this expresses at most an aspiration. Certainly the intellectual tools for their incorporation into a legal system have yet to be forged. Yet in reality opportunities whose existence is in substantial measure determined by the economic and expenditure policies of government – steady employment at adequate wages, decent housing and effective schools – matter far more in the aggregate to the advancement of minorities than the hiring or promotion of individuals and the policies of particular companies or housing authorities. The limits of the legal concepts and procedures thus far developed impose serious restrictions on the effectiveness of the legal process to rectify racial disadvantage, and part of the attraction of remedies involving reverse discrimination is that they fall well within the normal working of the legal system. They require only an order that a relatively small number of individuals be employed, and that appropriate records be kept. Such remedies requires minimal judicial supervision of institutions or immersion in day-to-day administration – far less than courts in the United States, though not in Britain, have often undertaken in fields such as restrictive practices (anti-trust), review of decisions of regulatory bodies, reform of prison conditions and legislative reapportionment.

However, use of racial preferences in selected areas is not simply the result of structural limitations in the legal process, but also of political decisions reflecting the power of certain interests. This may be seen by considering who bears the brunt of reverse discrimination programmes. The most striking thing is that they apply largely to the young. This is inevitably true of selection for higher education but has been equally so in employment. It is at the junior job levels – trainees and the bottom rung of progression ladders – that preferences have been applied. Indeed the American courts, which have often upheld quotas at entry level, have been notably reluctant to order their use of higher ranks.[50] This phenomenon is particularly noteworthy because one would have expected it to be more characteristic of a strict equal opportunity approach. With racial barriers dismantled the fact that blacks had previously been prevented from acquiring the qualifications, connections or experience required for higher level jobs is irrelevant, and anyone lacking such assets may continue to be denied advancement. Reverse discrimination programmes, which purport to recognise the importance of history, could be expected to be sensitive to this problem. However, thus far they have given only minor emphasis to supplementary training or accelerated promotion for persons who have been in the labour force for substantial periods. Thus managers and executives, foremen, professors and the like – those who have actually achieved relative eminence in part as a result of the exclusion of black competitors – continue to enjoy their trained gains, while compensation is exacted from members of the succeeding generation. The process is a peculiar form of oppression of the young by the middle-aged. This invalidates one important rationale offered for reverse discrimination, the theory that race as a criterion for allocating benefits is acceptable only when the majority acts to its own detriment and to benefit the minority.[51] 'The majority' is not a monolith, and what really occurs is that its entrenched members act to forestall perceived threats to social order, or to still moral unease, by foisting the burden of compensation on to less powerful groups within it.

The narrow scope of reverse discrimination remedies – the use of racial preferences in filling a limited number of jobs or places in higher education – manifests a similar political character. If, as a consequence of discrimination, racial minorities have lower average incomes than whites, no law of nature, or of economics, prevents enactment of legislation to provide supplementation of income for those economically injured. For that matter the manifest racial inequalities of wealth could be remedied by capital payments to members of a group who have been deprived of opportunities to acquire it. In other contexts it is recognised that undeserved handicap merits societal recompense. Legislation in force for some years in New Zealand grants social security benefits to the congenitally disabled; the Pearson Commission proposed adoption of a similar scheme in Britain.[52] Many social security systems provide what in Britain is known as the 'special hardship allowance' – an increase paid to an industrially injured worker whose incapacity requires him to take a lower-paid job.[53] Unlike discrimination, neither loss is the result of injury inflicted by those who (through the agency of the state) finance the compensation.

These forms of recompense, cut from the same cloth as the loss, hardly seem administratively impossible. Yet only one scholar has even tentatively explored any variant of these ideas,[54] none of which has come close to finding a place on the agenda of serious political possibilities. Such remedial measures, if financed through progressive taxation, would of course place a heavier proportion of their burden on the better off. They would also logically lead to underprivileged whites asking whether their position is purely due to personal desert: compensation for racial discrimination in this manner carries with it the potential for attacking the legitimacy of economic equality in general. This radical implication has no doubt made such an approach unattractive to public officials, leaders of industry and others called upon to devise remedies for discrimination.

The reverse discrimination approach, on the contrary, is the ideal way to set white and black workers at each other's throats. This may not have been intentional. Reverse discrimination is a child of the affluent 1960s, when it seems to have been assumed that employment and educational institutions would expand indefinitely. Thus even if a white person were shouldered aside in one competition, something almost as good would always remain. Those days are over; and it is unlikely, especially in Britain, that we shall see their like again. The reality now is that one person's preference is another's unemployment, and the concentration of reverse discrimination programmes in blue-collar employment ensures that working-class whites will come to regard the advancement of blacks as a threat to themselves. As theirs is hardly a position of privilege, the justice of this is difficult to defend.

Apart from the way it imposes burdens on the young and the relatively less well off, reverse discrimination is open to objection on other scores. Perhaps the most important is that use of racial preferences inherently creates a small group of élite beneficiaries. For the unskilled and semi-literate they may as well not exist. Only those already within hailing distance of existing selection standards are in any position to benefit: a relative handful of individuals, doubtless the most energetic and probably drawn from among those of relatively favoured social background.[55] The opening of doors to them is part of the process that has been come to be known as 'creaming the poor' – assisting the very top of a submerged group whilst ignoring the rest. It seems increasingly clear that this is precisely what is happening in the United States at the moment, although reverse discrimination is obviously not the only cause. In the words of W. J. Wilson's important study, *The Declining Significance of Race:*[56]

> As the black middle class rides on the wave of political and social changes, benefitting from the growth of employment opportunities in the growing corporate and political sectors of the economy, the black underclass falls behind the larger society in every conceivable respect. The economic and political systems in the United States have demonstrated remarkable flexibility in allowing talented blacks to fill positions of prestige and influence at the same time that these systems have shown persistent rigidity in handling the problems of lower-class blacks.

Other studies confirm this conclusion, emphasising that whilst blacks did achieve relative income gains in the late 1960s, they were received in greatest proportion by the educated, the young, and those of relatively high socio-economic family background.[57] Almost certainly most of those with degrees from prestigious universities gained admission under some sort of preferential policy.[58]* The remainder – the great majority – exist in conditions ranging from sparse adequacy to desperation, and their relative position has substantially worsened: in 1978 blacks made up a higher percentage of those living in poverty than was true ten years earlier and the rate of unemployment among them was more than double that of whites.[59] This confidence of growing prosperity for a relatively small black middle class and deprivation and isolation for the majority points to a striking paradox: reverse discrimination reinforces prevailing inequality. Such programmes have never been directed to changing the economic and social policies which perpetuate the disadvantages of the black poor. There was of course a War on Poverty, proclaimed with loud alarums. However a truce was declared almost immediately as the fiscal appetite of the real war, in Vietnam, became increasingly voracious. Above all, no systematic attempt was ever made to reduce black unemployment to white levels, let alone those then prevailing in Western Europe; and it is the condition of widespread unemployment – a permanent feature of black life in urban America – which, along with slavery, is the main cause of black deprivation. The War on Poverty, reflecting its individualist orientation, concentrated heavily on educational programmes, designed to equip those below working age to compete in the labour market in the indefinite future. It did very little to enable their parents to earn adequate income then and there, or indeed to ensure that jobs would be available for those young people who had received educational assistance.

A different line of criticism of reverse discrimination is that it is misdirected, for the beneficiaries were not themselves victims of ill treatment, merely the heirs of those who were. The position seems initially attractive, but sweeps far too broadly. If the inferior social and economic position of an individual is due to the inherited effects of ill treatment of his forebears, he presently suffers demonstrable injury and may justly be awarded compensation. (This contention would appear less controversial if the deprivation concerned property. The primacy of property rights in political and legal thinking and the concomitant absence of theory according similar status to claims based upon wrongful appropriation of labour or denial of access to job opportunities or public services is a serious handicap to securing public acceptance of the responsibility to redress the wrongs of discrimination.)

The point of abrasion is where the claim is made on behalf of everyone in the group, rather than the deprived section of it. Thus whilst the forebears of a black executive or professional may well have suffered severe ill treatment, it is difficult to specify his own loss. It could be argued that being black is enough of its own to constitute injury,[60] but it is doubtful whether one could explain this to a black friend while looking at him straight in the face. The element of condescension apart, it is important that anti-discrimination efforts do not attempt to be too ambitious, lest they fail utterly. The legal process is generally concerned with compensation for material loss, which is relatively easy to establish and readily quantifiable. There are exceptions – notably the award of damages for emotional injury or pain and suffering in tort actions, and the interest in one's reputation recognised in the law of defamation – but they are few. It is the deprivation of economic interests that creates the strongest case for recompense for racial minorities; it follows that only those who, measured against national norms, are relatively deprived, may justifiably advance claims. Yet once it is accepted that membership of the group is not sufficient *of itself* to command entitlement, then the limitation of such assistance to members of that group becomes difficult to defend. The inclusion of blacks from comfortable circumstances and the exclusion of poor whites are equally illogical and without justification.

Thus both the remedial method of outright racial preferences, and the claim for compensatory treatment for *all* members of an ill-treated minority, must be rejected. It does not follow, however, that a racial minority, as a group, has no valid claim for compensatory treatment. It is quite clear that the disproportionate presence of non-whites in bad housing, poor schools, low-wage employment and the dole queue is in significant measure due to discrimination, for which the state, as the agent of those who have imposed this treatment, must take responsibility. A submerged racial minority in these circumstances has compelling moral claims upon the state for assistance to overcome those particular disabilities. It is neither paradoxical nor inconsistent to reject racial preferences whilst advocating special assistance of this type. The former benefits a limited number of individuals, probably not those most damaged by history, at the expense of other more or less randomly chosen individuals who themselves have done no wrong. The latter is a collective claim against the whole society, which ensures that most deprived members of the group will receive some recompense for the group-inflicted injury, and that the costs of compensation are spread far more broadly among the majority, and hence more fairly. Only when the bounds of the individualism which underpin and tightly restricts the present scope of efforts to compensate for past racial discrimination are transcended will it be possible to develop policies which can attack its legacy of collective deprivation with any realistic hope of success. The precise legal mechanisms by which these claims may be translated into legal rights is discussed later in this chapter.

Thus far we have treated reverse discrimination largely as a philosophical question of political and moral principle. However, as noted in the introduction to this chapter, one cannot ignore the fact that the idea took concrete forms, and much of its moral force, from its specific origins in the America of the 1960s. When the philosophical issues are discussed in relation to the history of the settlement of non-whites in Britain other considerations appear, which undermine many of the assumptions giving the arguments for reverse discrimination much of what limited validity they possess. This is not, however, to advocate the view that no remedial measures are required as a matter of justice.

Perhaps the most important factor is that the permanent presence of racial minorities, except for small colonies in a few seaport districts, is of very recent origin – at most the past thirty years. There are some ominous signs, particularly the unemployment levels of young West Indians, but as will be seen in Chapter 5, it is far too early to conclude that even one section among the immigrants is destined to form a permanent underclass like blacks in American ghettos. This does not justify complacency, either about the extent of overt discrimination or of various forms of disadvantage. It is merely to point out that the key predicate for reverse discrimination – blatantly inferior conditions of a racial minority – is not yet firmly established. Certainly the inferior circumstances of blacks in Britain is hardly surprising, from either an historical or comparative perspective. The Irish who emigrated here in the nineteenth century, and the Jews who arrived in the late Victorian and Edwardian years, were at first desperately poor and often ill treated.[61] The first generation of Southern and Eastern European immigrants to the United States were similarly among the despised and rejected, and it has taken at least two generations for them to come near to catching up with the established ethnic groups in level of income and other measures of success.[62] Similarly, the so-called *gastarbeiter* who came by the millions to the prosperous countries of Western Europe over roughly the same period of New Commonwealth immigration to Britain, are if anything more thoroughly submerged in the worst jobs and wretched housing,[63] despite the fact that the great preponderance of them are white. It was predictable that rural immigrants, often with few technical skills and speaking either a substantially different form of English or none at all, should not at once prosper in a highly industrialised urban society. Their disadvantage has been badly exacerbated by deliberate discrimination, but disadvantage in any event there would have been.

A second difference arises from the fact of voluntariness. American blacks are of course overwhelmingly descendants of slaves, who have had no alternative but to make their way in the country which has oppressed them. Political refugees from East Africa apart, black immigrants came willingly to Britain to better their economic lot, and for many even the most menial job here represented a marked improvement.[64] Most retain the option of returning to their countries of origin. None of these points applies to their British-born children, and none justifies discrimination against the immigrant generation. They do, however, make inapplicable what may be termed the 'captive victim' argument that has carried such persuasive force in the United States.

Finally, the law, the authoritative expression of society's attitude, has never required or encouraged the inferior treatment of racial minorities, as was for decades true in the United States. The common law was formally neutral, and from 1965 hesitant statutory steps were taken to outlaw discrimination. In conjunction with the other points enumerated, this may explain the absence thus far of any widespread sense of an obligation to redress an historical injustice which has been such an important mainspring behind the movement of government policy and legal development in the United States. In Britain appeal to the wrongs of the past is more likely to meet with puzzlement or angry denial.

The 1976 Act firmly repudiated reverse discrimination. This decision flowed from the avowal in the White Paper of the 'principle of non-discrimination' as the fundamental value of the legislation.[65] It thus rejected the view, often advanced in support of reverse discrimination policies, that only 'invidious' discrimination – that of the majority against a politically impotent minority – is objectionable.[66] As we have seen, the precise statutory language, outlawing 'less favourable treatment on racial grounds' permits no such distinction.

Rejection of reverse discrimination does not mean that the equal opportunity approach, even at its broadest, marks the outer limit of acceptable legal and social measures to combat racial disadvantage. The prevalence of deliberate discrimination in Britain and its impact on the lives of non-whites firmly puts the responsibility of redress upon the shoulders of the majority. Moreover, historical injustice is not the only justification for remedial policies. It is hardly sensible to wait until what the White Paper called a 'vicious downward spiral of deprivation' has been firmly established before taking action: an ounce of prevention is not merely worth a pound of cure, it is much less expensive. The paramount question is how this situation can be avoided without infringing other important values, particularly the non-discrimination principle. The Act attempts a partial solution; some other possibilities are considered below.

III SPECIAL ASSISTANCE WITHIN THE EQUAL OPPORTUNITY FRAMEWORK

Reverse discrimination programmes are a response to the previous wrongful use of race as a criterion of selection. A further important reason for the use of racial preferences is that under present conditions the evenhanded use of truly job-related standards would often do little to assist the advancement of minorities, who have not been equipped to satisfy them. A primary response to this fundamental fact has been to establish minimum qualifications, lack of which would exclude anyone, and then to give preference to minority applicants who satisfy them over whites with higher qualifications. It is as yet too early to tell whether those so favoured do the jobs with reasonable skill; if not, the objections of principle will be reinforced by powerful practical considerations. However, their force may be substantially minimised by an alternative approach. This is to proceed from the opposite pole, to leave non-discriminatory standards unchallenged and provide assistance to minority persons to enable them to compete on truly equal terms.

The 1976 Act takes a long stride in this direction. It authorises a derogation from the principle of non-discrimination by permitting the granting of special assistance to minority group members alone in certain circumstances. The provisions are complex, and there is as yet scant information on whether and how they are being used. Hence they can only be discussed in the abstract, and analysis of the issues of principle they raise is combined with a detailed look at the various forms of assistance which may be given by particular bodies.

EMPLOYERS AND TRAINING BODIES

The most important provisions are found in s. 38. Under these, an employer who wishes to 'encourage' only persons of a particular racial group[67]* to 'take advantage of opportunities' of doing particular work in his employ, does not discriminate if he fails to extend the same encouragement to white persons.[68] Similarly, and more controversially, he is permitted to afford minority *employees* alone 'access to facilities for training' – which would include providing such training himself – to qualify them for particular work.[69] The former is largely concerned with recruitment and may include measures like advertisements in the minority language press and special recruitment efforts in areas or schools with large numbers of blacks; it may also comprise informal actions like suggesting to particular minority employees that they apply for higher level jobs.

None of these options would supplement the occupational skills of minority workers. This is not true of the second provision. Under it existing minority employees may be given training which white employees are denied. Some kinds of training do not in any real sense exclude whites, to whom they would be irrelevant. The most important example is language or literacy classes for those whose unfamiliarity with English prevents them from doing any but the most menial work. Other training, however, whether in formal programmes like apprenticeships or secondment to courses, or informal on-the-job arrangements, could as readily be used by whites, and the employer's ability to exclude them is indeed a form of discrimination. But it is discrimination within tightly drawn boundaries. It does not permit racial preferences in hiring, nor result in the employment of unqualified persons. It merely permits those who have actually been unable to acquire the necessary skills to do so. Thus equipped to compete on equal terms, they are then left to take their chances along with everyone else. Since the persons benefiting from the special training were *ex hypothesi* actually disadvantaged, such preferential training assists those for whom minority status can fairly be equated with economic deprivation.[70]* The exclusion of disadvantaged whites from such training opportunities is a far less severe loss than their exclusion from an employment for which they had acquired qualifications, particularly as there are other state-run training schemes for which they would be eligible. Their injury may be regarded as *de minimus*, and the derogation from the principle of non-discrimination justified by the closeness of the connection between the disadvantage and the remedy.

It is important to emphasise that under s. 38 the wall between preferences in training and those in employment remains unbreachable. The confusion between the two was manifest in the controversy that flared over the employment policy announced by Camden Council in January 1978.[71] Many of the components of the policy, such as improved training schemes, advertisements describing the Council as an 'equal-opportunity employer', and training of interviewers to the fullest capabilities of non-white applicants, seem clearly to come within the envisaged use of the section, and indeed do not significantly adversely affect whites. But the statement by the Council spokesman who announced the policy that 'If two people of equal ability but of different colour apply for a job, we will pick the coloured person because coloured people are so under represented at the moment' is plainly outside s. 38, and would – unless race were a genuine occupational qualification for a particular job, a question discussed below (pp. 145–8) – constitute unlawful discrimination. The dangers of misunderstanding are two-sided: while the spokesman overstated the breadth of the statutory exceptions to the non-discrimination principle, opponents of the policy did not seem to realise that s. 38 provides substantial scope for thoughtful efforts by employers to minimise the effects of psychological barriers to the advancement of blacks, as well as more obvious credential barriers. It would also authorise in-service training and career development schemes where members of any ethnic minority have been concentrated in low-level positions. Individuals thought suitable, but who lacked necessary formal qualifications, could be promoted on a tentative basis, to give them the opportunity to prove themselves able to perform the work with the help either of on-the-job training or secondment to a training course. So long as they were not simply given the job on grounds of race, and genuine efforts were made to assist them to measure up to generally accepted standards of performance, this is precisely the sort of innovation s. 38 was designed to encourage.[72]

An employer cannot, however, simply decide that efforts to overcome racial disadvantage are morally and socially desirable and institute a special assistance programme. Certain statutory conditions must be satisfied. These require that, within the previous year, either no minority persons are doing the particular work for which training or encouragement is being offered,[73] or that the proportion of them doing that work is 'small' compared either with their proportion of his total workforce, or with the minority percentage in the surrounding area from which he normally recruits.[74]

These conditions are far from stringent. That the assistance must concern 'particular work' allows that employer to define what may be called the 'target job' narrowly, specifying a particular skill or grade. Thus it is permissible for a large contracting firm which may have numerous black carpenters, but few black plumbers, to offer training in the latter craft alone; it is irrelevant that overall it may employ a sizeable number of black skilled workers.

Similarly, the condition that no blacks are doing the particular work will be met by a surprisingly large number of firms. The PEP Survey in 1973 found that approximately one-third of the plants studied, all in areas with a population at least 1 per cent non-white, had *no* minority employees at all. Even in areas of at least 4 per cent immigrant population, 30 per cent of the plants had less than 2 per cent non-white workers.[75] Perhaps even more common is the situation where there are few if any non-whites in higher level jobs, and a large number in undesirable work, such as cleaning or unskilled foundry or textile mill jobs, in which there may be no whites at all. So long as the proportion in an upper-level job is 'small' compared to the proportion working in that 'establishment' – e.g. there are 3 non-whites out of 300 skilled workers, but they comprise 40 per cent of the labourers and all the cleaners in the plant – preferential training may still be undertaken. The same is true if the figure is 3 out of 300 is 'small' compared to the percentage of non-whites in the employer's normal recruitment area, even though it is commensurate with the percentage of his total minority employees. What constitute 'small' is an important unanswered question. It appears that the variations do not have to be substantial for the section to apply. This may be inferred from comparison of this provision with s. 1 (1)(b), which requires that a 'considerably smaller' proportion of minority persons must be able to satisfy a requirement before it can be held indirectly discriminatory. The absence of the qualifying adverb in s. 38 supports the view that lesser and relative slight disparities are sufficient.

Training bodies are permitted to offer identical forms of special assistance to minority persons, subject to the same preconditions.[76] The only difference is that the realm of comparison of minority participation is not a particular workforce, but all of Great Britain.[77] Moreover, to emphasise the permissive character of the special assistance provisions, where the training body believes that minority under-representation in particular work, while not true of the entire country, is true of an 'area', it may offer encouragement and training to minority persons 'who appear likely to take up work in that area'.[78] The training body is left to define the 'area'. Thus if it appears that there are substantial numbers of black skilled workers in inner city areas but very few in a New Town – a comparison for example between London and Milton Keynes – a training body may either encourage them to seek employment in the latter locations, or offer training to other blacks who lack the skills but who state willingness to work there. In view of the concentration of blacks in economically stagnant areas, and conversely their relatively rare presence in growing areas such as New Towns, this provision could prove important. 'Training body' is defined to include all official bodies such as the Manpower Services Commission.[79] Before a private training body, such as one the established by an employers' association in a particular industry, may offer special assistance under this section, it must be designated by an Order made by the Home Office.[80]

TRADE UNIONS

The question of special assistance here is less controversial, because the element of competition between black and white workers is virtually absent. Trade unions and analogous associations[81] are also permitted under s. 38 to train minority persons alone to 'fit them for holding a post of any kind in the organisation', or encourage them to attempt to do so.[82] The preconditions correspond to those applying to employers. In view of the surprisingly high level of trade union membership among minority workers (below, p. 164), and their notable absence from positions of trade union leadership, there will be little difficulty in satisfying them.

In addition, where only a 'small' proportion of eligible minority persons are members of a particular trade union, the organisation can undertake membership drives directed at minority workers alone.[83] The marked tendency among blacks to join trade unions suggests that this provision will be of value primarily in situations where in the past they have been excluded from membership. Thus a union which has genuinely undergone a change of heart (or, perhaps more realistically, a change of officers) may make use of this section. However, where trade unions exercise job-control functions (below, pp. 174–5) they are unlikely to wish to recruit *any* additional members, let alone non-whites.

OTHER SPECIAL ASSISTANCE

The foregoing provisions may be used only by the specific bodies designated in them. A separate provision, s. 35, authorises 'any act' which affords minorities access to facilities or services to meet their special needs – in regard to education, training, welfare and related benefits. Any public or private body or person whose activities touch on these areas may make use of this somewhat vague provision, which in terms would encompass anything from the establishment by a Health Authority of classes on birth control taught in Punjabi to special circularisation of black areas by a private housing association, announcing vacancies in its flats. The Government seem to have thought this clause would be used largely to authorise special language classes,[84] but since neither the 'special needs' of minority groups nor the statutory language are thus limited, its potential scope is substantially broader. It would, for example, be lawful for a local authority to hire social workers (of any race) to work specifically with West Indians, or for the Home Office to grant funds to a community action project among a particular minority group. Private organisations or philanthropists would be similarly unrestricted, subject, however, to s. 34 of the Act, which ordains that restrictions on grounds of colour in any charitable instrument are to be ignored and the benefits conferred by the instrument be made available to all persons otherwise eligible.

EVALUATION OF THE
SPECIAL ASSISTANCE PROVISIONS

As the White Paper stated, 'if the principle of non-discrimination is interpreted too literally and inflexibly it may actually impede the elimination of invidious discrimination and the encouragement of equal opportunity'.[85] The inclusion of these provisions is in effect the statute's alternative to reverse discrimination. It is also a recognition that effective legislation must do more than clear away obstacles, even in the more socially aware sense embodied in the concept of indirect discrimination. The three sections cover a very wide area, do not contain unduly rigid restrictions and offer broad scope for imaginative efforts to enable blacks to compete effectively by enabling them to acquire the necessary information and skills. None the less, at certain points they are incomplete or of limited value.

First, the employment provisions apply only to efforts to recruit or promote black workers. The implicit assumption is that demand for labour would ensure the availability of opportunities. With present and projected levels of unemployment, this is probably unduly optimistic. As such this is not a criticism of the legislation, but it does indicate its limits: there are no special assistance provisions relating to unemployment, lay-offs or work-sharing. In such situations the factor of direct competition between workers critically alters the balance of considerations, and the argument about *de minimus* injury offered in support of minority training programmes cannot be made. If employers, particularly in the industrial sector, are more concerned with shedding labour than training it, s. 38 may prove a well-intentioned irrelevance. On the other hand, if an employer were substituting white-collar employees for manual workers, s. 38 could prove important, for he could invoke it to retrain black employees in jobs soon to be abolished to fit them for the positions.

Two other criticisms may be offered, based on the contrary assumption that economic factors will not vitiate the provisions at the outset. The first is that whilst employers may encourage any minority persons to apply for work, they may only offer 'access to facilities for training' to existing employees. The purpose of this limitation is unclear. It would prevent an employer concerned about equal opportunity from establishing a training programme for unemployed non-whites to qualify for jobs he expected to fall vacant. If he did not need them until they had learned the necessary skills under the present statute he would have to waste money employing them before training or abandon the idea.

The second point is critical. All the special assistance provisions are purely voluntary. Employers and others hostile to racial equality, or simply indifferent, need not do anything. Moreover, outside one or two industries, workers in plants of any size are likely to be represented by one or more trade unions. It is improbable that an employer who wished to establish a special assistance programme could do so without their assent. Refusal to co-operate by either the shop stewards representing his workforce, or by their trade union at a higher level, would not be illegal. It would be rash to predict responses, but objections for reasons good and bad can readily be imagined. Initiatives in this area can readily be stifled by either of the main parties to industrial relations.

This raises the question whether the assistance provisions ought to be mandatory. The objections to such an extension are easy to imagine: it would force employers to incur additional expense, and create resentment among excluded whites. Little can be added to the previous discussion on the latter point, save to note that the reasons offered in support of compensatory assistance did not depend on whether its provision was voluntary or mandatory.

The objection based upon expense would certainly be loudly proclaimed.

It may, however, be short-sighted. At present society as a whole incurs substantial expense in lost productivity and social security payments arising from the under-employment and unemployment of racial minorities. If imposing responsibility on employers for equipping them with necessary skills is more efficient than reliance upon state schemes alone, the allocation of costs in this manner would be sensible. Moreover, if it were thought necessary, a partial subsidy could be provided, as is now done with statutory redundancy payments and the Temporary Employment Subsidy scheme. The duty to operate an assistance programme plainly could not be universal: exclusions would be provided for firms far away from present or projected areas of non-white settlement, or which genuinely anticipated contraction of the number of their employees in jobs for which training would be necessary. There would clearly be problems of definition surrounding such exclusions, but these would be of a kind normally encountered in drafting social legislation. The important point is that it is reasonable to suppose that in many industries there are desirable jobs for which many non-whites lack qualifications which they will need training and encouragement to acquire. This may be provided most effectively by the employer with whom the vacancies will arise, whose expenditure on training will then be a strong incentive not to discriminate in hiring. Creation of a legal duty, enforced by civil sanctions, would also enable employers and trade unions concerned about racial disadvantage to override internal opposition; obedience to the law is a far firmer ground from which to combat indifference or bigotry than appeal to moral sentiment. Finally, in comparison with what may be expected under ss. 37 and 38, imposition of a legal duty would greatly broaden the access of non-whites to assistance efforts, and thus go some way to redress the group disadvantage they have suffered in Britain on account of race.

TOWARD A COLLECTIVE REMEDIAL CONCEPT OF DISCRIMINATION

All the concepts of discrimination discussed thus far have conceived it in a negative sense, as some form of adverse treatment. The special assistance provisions are seen as desirable remedial action, justifying derogation from the principle of non-discrimination, not as part of the concept of discrimintion itself. This seems unduly restrictive. Separating the remedy from the injury makes the former discretionary, rather than a right in the sense that compensation for tortious injury or deprivation of property has come to be regarded as a right. Consequently the existence of measures designed to counter the effects of discrimination are dependent on economic and political factors whilst other remedial measures are not: public expenditure cuts tear housing construction and further education, but do not impose limits on compensation for compulsory purchase or for torts committed by Crown servants. This fusion of injury and remedy is one vital advantage of securing recognition of an interest or value as a legal 'right'. Another is that once an interest achieves the status of a right, it is accorded greater respect and acceptance by those to whom it does not extend than would be true of a mere assertion of need or social utility.[86]* Achieving this recognition is partly a matter of political struggle, but a coherent theoretical structure that enables the new right to be assimilated to the established legal process is also essential.

No legal concept of discrimination incorporating as an inseparable element *collective* entitlement to remedial assistance has yet been formulated. What follows is a tentative effort to sketch such a theory. It will doubtless prove inadequate, but is presented in the hope that others may find within it some fragments useful for development of more sophisticated and coherent ideas. Two points should be made plain at the outset. First, what is proposed is an extension of the statutory definition of discrimination to be undertaken by Parliament, not that the present Act should be reinterpreted by the courts. Second, the concept is meant to supplement, not to displace, those presently found in the statute. No attempt is made to formulate the precise language that would most clearly express it in statutory form.

The starting-point may be found in *Lau* v. *Nichols*,[87] an American Supreme Court case little known in Britain, in which a class action was brought on behalf of 1800 children of Chinese ancestry attending schools in San Francisco. None spoke English, and the schools did not provide them with supplemental instruction, nor teach the standard curriculum in a language they did understand. Their action was based upon a provision of the Civil Rights Act which forbids racial discrimination in any undertaking carried out by a recipient of federal government financial assistance. Students in California schools are required to attain proficiency in English before receiving a diploma. In the absence of any effort by the education authority to ensure that these students had a chance to acquire that proficiency, the Court concluded, 'It seems obvious that the Chinese-speaking minority *receives fewer benefits* than the English-speaking majority from the respondent's school system which *denies them a meaningful opportunity to participate* in the educational program'[88] (emphasis supplied). The court held unanimously that this constituted 'discrimination'.[89]

It must be emphasised that the education authority was in no way responsible for the plaintiff children's inability to benefit from its standard mode of instruction. None the less its failure to make any compensatory efforts to enable them to achieve equivalent benefit to that received by the majority was ruled unlawful. In other words, an attitude of *laissez-faire* in the face of manifest racial inequality is itself a form of discrimination.

This is a powerful idea, one which may be the foundation-stone for constructing a concept of discrimination fully responsive to the reality of racial disadvantage. As a *matter of law*, it places the fact of substantive inequality at centre stage; only when the respondent authorities take some active steps to combat this inequality do they fulfil their legal responsibility. Thus the fair-shares concept of non-discrimination is given forceful application, but without the use of racial preferences that violate other ethical precepts. Moreover, this view of discrimination gives full weight to the element of collective deprivation, whose existence must be demonstrated before the law may be invoked. Thus, if a sprinkling of minority persons were the only ones unable to achieve equivalent benefit from the instruction offered the responsibility would fall upon them to obtain supplementary assistance; as one concurring Justice put it, 'numbers are at the heart of this case'.[90] This reflects an important characteristic of anti-discrimination legislation: it is not addressed to the problems of persons, numerous in any society, whose individual circumstances or misfortunes hinder their advancement. The question of discrimination arises only when members of a minority group – particular one which has suffered a substantial measure of deliberate inferior treatment – are found disproportionately among the ill favoured. And since collective injury is the evil, it should follow that collective redemption is required, i.e. efforts to reach all within the group who have suffered loss.

Application of the collective fair share (or 'meaningful participation') concept of discrimination would be far from painless. It demands a shifting of resources which may be substantial where a minority group has hitherto received little benefit. It remains open to those with effective power – who almost certainly will be drawn from the majority, whether or not in some ideal sense they represent it – to choose whether to accept that the resources available to majority group recipients of the particular service or benefit will be diminished, or to increase the overall allocation to prevent this result. In the present condition of virtually all Western societies – that of faltering economic growth and an ascendant harsh conservative political ideology – the result would be sharp political conflict. But the battle would be open and the choices clear; it would be carried on among the majority, and could not be resolved by foisting the inevitable sacrifices upon luckless individuals, as happens with use of racial preferences. Rather the costs – for once a literal, not merely metaphorical description – would be borne by all who contributed to the public purse according to the existing procedures which purportedly reflect some notion of ability to pay. They would thus not only be far more widely spread but, being financial, qualitatively different and far less onerous than denial of an opportunity which may never again be open to the excluded person. The sense of *totality* which suffuses the loss suffered by the victim of racial preferences has no counterpart in a small extra tax burden.

The concept of discrimination suggested here bears a strong resemblance to the idea of 'positive discrimination' advocated in the Plowden Report and the suggestions of other government advisory bodies in Britain in the 1960s. The crux of that idea was that areas or groups of persons with particularly severe problems of deprivation should receive disproportionately large shares of resources to counter it.[91] It has been applied in varying degrees to education and housing programmes, and the 1977 White Paper, *Policy for the Inner Cities* and the simultaneous announcement of the quadrupling of appropriations for the Urban Programme are in this vein as well.[92] The critical difference is that these proposals are not concerned with legal rights, but with policies thought to be socially desirable, whose implementation remains purely a matter of political expediency. The collective fair-share notion incorporates the idea of substantive equality into the law, by making deviation from it a test of legality, not merely the wisdom, of the activity in question. It would be a long stride toward closing the unfortunate gap that now exists between legality and policy.

It should be noted that, but for the intervention of a General Election the crux of the concept of discrimination proposed here would have made its appearance in legislation in Britain. The Local Government Grants (Ethnic Groups) Bill, the subject of a five-hour Second Reading Debate in March 1979,[93] would have permitted local authorities to receive funds from the Home Office to defray expenditure for the purposes of 'removing disadvantages from which an ethnic group suffers' or 'securing that the services provided by the local authority are as effective in relation to ethnic groups as they are in relation to the rest of the community.'[94] The Bill fell short of embodying a legal concept of discrimination in that it established an entirely permissive administrative regime, and did not conceive of the process as establishing positive rights of individuals or groups. Thus no local authority was required to incur expenditure for these purposes, and the Government consciously chose not to impose a statutory duty to do so.[95] Hence no member of a disadvantaged minority could have compelled an authority to equalise its services. None the less the Bill may perhaps be seen as first hesitant step in Britain towards acceptance of a legal standard of substantive material equality among ethnic groups. It was also, in view of the breadth and importance of local authority functions, of far broader scope than judicial developments in the United States: cases like *Lau* have arisen only under a few statutes involving federal government financial assistance to specific programmes.[96]

A critical part of translating the collective fair-share understanding of discrimination into a workable legal concept is enunciating manageable standards. What degree of deviation from a standard of equality is permissible before an opportunity ceases to be 'meaningful'? Put another way, to what extent can a racial minority receive 'fewer' benefits without discrimination being found? Such questions of degree commonly arise in the application of a vast range of legal rules, in both civil and criminal law.[97] In some areas such as tort and crime, and for reasons of history rather than considered judgment about institutional competence, the courts have long experience and consider themselves expert in answering them. However, most English lawyers and judges would regard the sort of questions raised in *Lau* as inappropriate for judicial resolution. In *Lau* this difficulty was mitigated by two factors: the complete – and undisputed – absence of any effort by the education authority to take account of the plaintiffs' language handicaps, and the fact that the court was not compelled, or indeed requested, to formulate a remedy. The plaintiffs merely asked that the authority 'be directed to apply its expertise to the problem and rectify the situation.'[98] Thus the Court simply found a violation of the law, and placed the responsibility to prepare a remedy on the defendant. Its decision was no more an overweening exercise of judicial power or a trespass upon the administrative domain than was consideration by the Court of Appeal whether the Metropolitan Police were devoting sufficient resources to the enforcement of the obscenity laws,[99] or indeed the decision in the well-known *Tameside* case. There the courts, having reviewed evidence concerning the attitude of the education authority, the teachers, the amount of time and manpower available and the state of the building programme, determined that the Secretary of State could not properly have concluded that an authority which had abandoned plans for the introduction of comprehensive schools had acted 'unreasonably'.[100] That decision was, of course, highly controversial, but not one of the eight judges in the Court of Appeal and House of Lords regarded the issues as inappropriate for judicial consideration.

More troublesome would be the situation not presented in *Lau*: where the authorities had made some effort to ensure that racial minorities were able to make effective use of a facility, but with demonstrably little impact. For example, special language tuition one hour per week would seem palpably inadequate, but what of one hour each day? Realistically, substantial deference would need to be paid to the authorities' initial judgment about what specific measures were appropriate to ensure equivalent benefit. Ultimately, however, the proof of the pudding would be in the eating – persistent marked racial disparities would be unlawful and require further responses until reduced to insignificance.

One area in which this concept of discrimination would have especial impact is that of public services, of which local authority housing, personal social services and education are prime examples. It is impossible to survey all the potential applications, but two critical ones may be mentioned. The virtual absence of Asians from council housing is well documented,[101] but may possibly be explained by their preference for owning their own homes. Also firmly established is that West Indians live in council housing in roughly the same proportion as whites, but in accommodation of inferior quality on less desirable estates.[102] This is obviously not the result of choice, and over and above eliminating direct discrimination, this substantive inequality would become unlawful.

A second example is the disproportionate spending on personal social services for old people.[103] In light of the much younger age structure among non-whites (below, p. 111 n.20) it is evident that they receive less than their proportionate share of such expenditure. Thus programmes appropriate to their different needs and the skills of social services departments would be required; one plausible candidate is enlarged crêche facilities.

It is impossible to predict what forms remedies under the collective fair-share concept might take, for its object is to make the responsible officials formulate policies to achieve greater minority 'participation'. This may necessitate injection of extra resources, or only that certain allocation procedures or selection criteria be altered or abandoned. The important point is not the prescription of any particular course of action, but the refusal of the law to tolerate inaction in the face of racial inequality.

This approach would reinforce existing provisions of the Act, which place local authorities under a general statutory duty to carry out their functions with a view to eliminating discrimination and promoting equality of opportunity (s. 71), and impose a similar duty upon local education authorities (s. 19). In essence it commands substantive equality of effectiveness in the use of public resources as among racial groups. In no sense does it require any given level of expenditure, nor the deployment of such resources in any particular way: decisions about what constitute public needs are not translated into legal questions. However, once the choice is made to provide some benefit the proposed concept would require that minority groups receive value for money. In some cases a higher proportionate expenditure on behalf of minorities may possibly prove necessary. That, however, would stem from the reality of racial disadvantage, not from *a priori* legal determination that a particular need exists. The law would not require that the state provide decent housing, only that, if it does so, minorities must receive proportionate benefit.

In the sphere of employment the concept would have to be used somewhat differently, since employers do not provide benefits freely available to all. Nor do their operations embody attempts to achieve social integration or express society's partial commitment to the values of caring and community. Thus, unlike the case of public services, it seems appropriate to invoke the proposed concept only where discrimination as now understood as the Act has led to a disproportionate absence of blacks from desirable jobs – i.e. to overcome the effects of unlawful acts.

One remedy might be to insist that employers undertake recruitment efforts by means of channels known to be heavily used by non-whites, such as the ethnic minority press, schools' career services and the Department of Employment. Of even greater long-term importance would be to require discriminatory employers to establish programmes to train blacks in the skills required for desirable jobs that are part of his operations. With training opportunities available across the wide range of industry and commerce, those previously relegated to a narrow sphere of largely unskilled work would begin to enjoy a reasonable range of occupational choice.

Such training schemes would have to be maintained for some extended period, but the employer would not be compelled to hire any of the participants, who would be drawn from the minority general public, not just employees. This limitation expresses an important principle. The purpose of the remedy is to ensure that blacks generally are as well equipped as whites to take their chances in fair competition for employment, not to mandate the hiring of anyone on a racial basis. That such schemes would be generally accessible means that the remedy may reasonably be expected to reach substantial numbers of people, and because it consists of training it is tailored to the nature of the wrong – the deprivation of the opportunity to acquire and use occupational skills. In essence, in the field of employment the proposed concept of discrimination would result in something very like a requirement that discriminatory employers operate schemes now permissible under s. 38 (above, pp. 25–8). As the discussion of that section sought to demonstrate the exclusion of whites from such programmes is morally acceptable, particularly as under the idea put forward here establishment of training schemes would be required only when the employer has discriminated.

V

The analysis offered in this chapter yields few general conclusions. On an historical level the initial individualistic conception of discrimination has been augmented by one which is responsive to the historical and collective reality of racial disadvantage. The reflection of this intellectual advance in a statutory evolution of less than a decade bespeaks an unusual awareness in some key policymakers. None the less the law in its present state accords these elements substantially less than full recognition. The analysis in the previous section may perhaps be of assistance in mapping the contours of a concept that incorporates them more adequately, and is capable of being applied by lawyers and administrators. The inordinate difficulties surrounding this effort have two distinct roots. The first, and much the most discussed, are the ethical and social dilemmas raised by some of the proposed concepts and their concomitant remedies. The second is the poverty of jurisprudential thought concerning group rights and social welfare rights. The present individualism of legal thinking is a serious constraint on the use of the legal process to achieve racial equality.

NOTES

1. PEP Report, pp. 312–13.
2. 401 U.S. 424 (1971).
3. L. Pollak, *Employment Discrimination – The American Response*, published in

pamphlet form by the Runnymede Trust in 1974. Its intellectual impact may be noted both in the Preface by the then Chairman of the Race Relations Board, Sir Geoffrey Wilson, and in the reference by Geoffrey Bindman, the Board's legal adviser, in 'The Law and Discrimination – Third Thoughts', 3 *B.J. Law & Soc.* 195 (1976).

4. Official Report, Standing Comm. B. 22 April 1975, col. 48.

5. L. Mayhew, *Law and Equal Opportunity* (Harvard U.P., 1968) pp. 59–74.

6. Fiss, 'The Fate of an Idea Whose Time Has Come', 41 *U. Chi. L. Rev.* 742, 764 (1974).

7. This occurred in private conversation with Professor Fitzgerald, formerly of the Law Faculty of the University of Kent, now of Carleton University in Ontario. I am most grateful for his comments on this chapter.

8. J. Rawls, *A Theory of Justice* (Harvard U.P., 1971) pp. 17–22.

9. R. Nozick, *Anarchy, State and Utopia* (Harvard U.P., 1974) pp. 155–64.

10. This is true of the definitions contained in all the anti-discrimination laws enacted by numerous American states, Canadian provinces, New Zealand and the Australian Commonwealth and states.

11. The story is detailed in *Lester and Bindman*, pp. 110–16.

*12. This point must be qualified somewhat. If it is alleged that an employer operates a colour bar, or some other blanket exclusionary *policy*, the inquiry may be directed, at least in part, to whether the allegation is true. If the class action device described in Chap. 12 is available, once this fact was established, it would be unnecessary for each class member to prove that the policy was applied in his case.

*13. Two examples: even though an amendment to require racial record-keeping in some instances was rejected by the Government (below, p. 214), several Ministers subsequently urged employers and housing authorities to do so. Similarly, members of the National Union of Teachers flatly refused in 1972 to collect racial data about their pupils. By 1977 it had become clear that this attitude was hampering development of policies designed to improve performance of black pupils, and the Union's President publicly reversed his position.

14. There were the terms used in an influential Congressional Committee Report, quoted by Dean Pollak, above, n. 3.

15. 401 U.S. at 432.

16. Idem at 431.

17. *James* v. *Valtierra*, 402 U.S. 137 (1971).

18. I am drawing here on an account in the *New York Times*, 24 December 1978, of a study by Professor D. Lavin and two colleagues. I am unaware whether it has been published.

19. See B. Sundberg-Weitman, *Discrimination on Grounds of Nationality* (North-Holland, 1977) chap. 8.

20. *Ugliola* v. *Württembergische Milchver A.G.*, (1970) C.M.L.R. 194.

21. *Sotgiu* v. *Deutsche Bundespost*, [1974] E.C.R. 153. The reasoning of the Court also contains a notion analogous to what the Act calls 'justification'.

22. *Van Binsbergen* v. *Bedrijfsvereniging Metaalnijverheid*, [1974] E.C.R. 1299.

23. *Thieffrey* v. *Conseil des Avocats*, [1978] 3 W.L.R. 453.

24. [1978] 2 C.M.L.R. 287.

25. Idem at 291.

26. A confusion manifest most obviously the *Bonsor* v. *Musicians' Union*, [1956] A.C. 104.

27. These terms derive from the German sociologist F. Tonnies. See Kamenka and Tay's illuminating essay, 'Beyond the French Revolution: Communist Socialism and the Rule of Law', 21 *U. Tor. L.J. 109* (1971).

28. See N. Glazer and D. Moynihan (eds), *Ethnicity* (Harvard U.P. 1975), *passim*.

For a wide-ranging account of constitutional arrangements designed to protect ethnic minorities, see C. Palley, *Constitutional Law and Minorities* (Minority Rights Group, 1978).

29. E. Pashukanis, a Soviet legal theorist of the 1920s, argued that a Socialist state would produce a new form of law, which he labelled bureaucratic-administrative. His theory is discussed by Kamenka and Tay, op. cit. His major work, *Law and Marxism: A General Theory*, was republished in this country by Ink Links in 1978.

30. [1977] I.R.L.R. 288, EAT. See the illuminating note by McCrudden, (1977) 6 *I.L.J.* 241.

31. See, e.g. *Hepple*, p. 92.

32. S. 703 (h).

33. *International Brotherhood of Teamsters* v. *United States*, 431 U.S. 324 (1977).

34. *United Air Lines, Inc.* v. *Evans*, 431 U.S. 553 (1977).

35. *Steel* v. *The Post Office*, [1978] I.R.L.R. 198.

*36. This subject has generated a scholarly literature seemingly rivalled in size only by that devoted to the existence of God. I list here the main sources I have consulted. They represent a wide range of views; none has had an especially strong influence of which I am conscious on my own thinking.

Perhaps the most useful sources are two periodicals, *Analysis* and *Philosophy and Public Affairs*, which have printed numerous papers on the subject over the past eight years. M. Cohen *et al.* (eds) *Equality and Preferential Treatment* (Princeton U.P., 1977) collects several of those printed in the latter. Others are A. Goldman, *Justice and Reverse Discrimination* (Princeton U.P., 1979); W. Gould, *Black Workers in White Unions* (Cornell U.P., 1977) chap. 5; R. Dworkin, *Taking Rights Seriously* (Oxford U.P., 1977) chap. 9; Symposium, 75 *Col. L. Rev.* no. 2 (1975); B. Bittker, *The Case for Black Reparations* (Yale U.P., 1973).

Of the philosophical works I am perhaps most sympathetic to the position taken by Goldman, whose book, however, was not available to me until I finished the second draft of this chapter. Moreover his definition limits reverse discrimination to the spheres of education and employment – a restriction I think unnecessary – and his idea of group compensation is much narrower than the one offered in the concluding section of this chapter.

37. W. Gould, *Black Workers in White Unions* (Cornell U.P., 1977) chap. 5.

38. *University of California Regents* v. *Bakke*, 438 U.S. 265 (1978).

39. For some sympathetic descriptions see the chapters on the political behaviour of the various ethnic groups in N. Glazer and D. Moynihan, *Beyond the Melting Pot* (M.I.T. Press, 1963).

40. S. 703 (j).

41. E.g. *Contractors Assn of Eastern Pa.* v. *Sec. of Labour*, 442 F. 2d 159 (3rd Circ. 1971); *S. Ill. Builders Assn* v. *Ogilvie*, 471 F. 2d 680 (7th Circ. 1972).

*42. What is unclear is whether purely indirect discrimination would call forth reverse discrimination remedies. All the cases with which I am familiar have contained elements of direct discrimination, or at least practices institutionalising the effects of past direct discrimination.

43. *Milliken* v. *Bradley*, 433 U.S. 267 (1977).

*44. Because those who have gained will by definition have been in previous competition for employment, this distinction will often coincide with the *age* of the persons involved, as well as the related factor of relatively high job level. The first point is discussed further on p. 19.

45. *Donoghue* v. *Stevenson*, [1932] A.C. 562, 580.

46. F. Lawson, *Remedies of English Law* (Penguin Books, 1972) pp. 253 ff. He contrasts this with American law, which has extended the scope of obligations of contracting parties by use of concepts such as the third party beneficiary.

47. Notably in cases where ratepayers challenge expenditure by local authorities as *ultra vires.* See especially *Roberts* v. *Hopwood,* [1925] A.C. 578, in which the wages paid by George Lansbury's Poplar Borough Council were denounced by Lord Atkinson as based upon 'eccentric principle of Socialist philanthropy', and *Prescott* v. *Birmingham Corpn,* [1955] Ch. 210.

48. *R.* v. *CICB, ex p. Lain,* [1967] 2 Q.B. 864 (C.A.).

49. Especially in the U.N. Universal Declaration of Human Rights (1948), and the Covenant of Economic, Social and Cultural Rights approved by the General Assembly in 1966, and in the European Social Charter.

50. See the discussion in B. Schlei and P. Grossman, *Employment Discrimination Law* (BNA, 1976) p. 1211. A good example is the judgment in *Bridgeport Guardians* v. *Bridgeport Civil Service Commn,* 482 F. 2d 1333 (2nd Circ. 1973), in which quotas ordered for employment of police constables were upheld, whilst those for sergeants were overturned.

51. As argued by Ely, 'The Constitutionality of Reverse Discrimination', 41 *U. Chi. L. Rev* 723 (1974).

52. Report of the Royal Commission on Civil Liability, Cmnd 7075 (1978) chap. 27.

53. Social Security Act 1975, s. 60 (1). The Workmen's Compensation Acts in Canadian provinces and American states almost uniformly contain similar provisions.

54. B. Bittker, *The Case for Black Reparations* (Yale U.P., 1973).

55. I must admit that this statement is based on my impressions, gained while attending élite American universities, but others more recently at similar institutions with whom I have spoken, black and white, have the same impression. As far as I know, no study of the social characteristics of the beneficiaries of the various affirmative action programmes has been published.

56. W. J. Wilson, *The Declining Significance of Race* (University of Chicago Press, 1978) p. 22.

57. See especially Freeman, 'Black Economic Progress since 1964', *Pub. Int.* no. 52 (Summer 1978) *passim*; also S. Levitan *et al., Still a Dream* (Harvard U.P., 1975) chap. 1, who point out (p. 21) that some of the apparent gain was a statistical artifact due to migration from the South to the North, a higher-wage area; Hogan and Featherman, 'Racial Stratification and Socio-Economic Change in the American North and South', 83 *A.J.S.* 100 (1977).

*58. They would constitute the age cohort of those aged 25–9 who show such gains in Freeman's data for 1975 (op. cit. n. 57). Preferential admissions programmes had been operating since the early 1960s in some élite universities; see R. O'Neil, *Discriminating Against Discrimination* (Indiana U.P., 1975) chap. 1.

59. I draw here on a report by Lawrence Marks in the *Observer,* 5 March 1978.

60. This might be one psychological dimension of the idea of 'status harm' advanced by Fiss, 'Groups and the Equal Protection Clause', 5 *Phil. & Pub. Aff.* 107 (1976).

61. An interesting study of the response of the social services to the influx of Irish and Jews, which then compares their response to New Commonwealth immigration, is that of C. Jones, *Immigration and Social Policy in Britain* (Tavistock, 1977).

62. See the discussion and data in Greeley, 'The Ethnic Miracle', *Pub. Int.* no. 45 (Fall 1976) pp. 20–37.

63. For a general comparison, now unfortunately somewhat dated, see S. Castles and G. Kosack, *Migrant Workers and Class Structure* (Oxford U.P., 1973).

64. One example: The 1967 PEP Report found that 59% of all Pakistani immigrants had been unemployed before coming to the United Kingdom. This figure dropped to 5% here, which was, however, double the national unemployment rate at that time.

65. Cmnd 6234, para. 57.
66. Notably in *DeFunis* v. *Odegaard*, 507 P. 2d 1169 (S. Ct Wash. 1973), *dismissed as moot*, 416 U.S. 312 (1974), and by Ely, op. cit. (above n. 51).
*67. Which s. 3 (1) defines broadly to include any group defined by nationality, ethnic or national origins as well as race or colour. See further below, pp. 00–00.
68. S. 38 (1)(b).
69. S. 38 (1)(a).
*70. It still would not reach the truly submerged, the semi-illiterate and wholly unskilled. For them something more is needed, such as perhaps the idea suggested on pp. 31–4.
71. I draw here on reports appearing in *The Times*, 28 January–3 February 1978.
72. The Social Services Department of Islington Borough Council were planning to introduce such a programme, which has been shelved as a result of expenditure cuts. I am grateful to Mr John Rea Price, Director, for this information.
73. S. 38 (2)(a).
74. S. 38 (2)(b).
75. PEP Report, pp. 94–5. The Report uses 'immigrant' as a shorthand for 'non-white', which in the early 1970s was accurate enough with respect to adults.
76. S. 37.
77. S. 37 (1).
78. S. 37 (2)(a).
79. S. 37 (2)(a), incorporating by reference s. 13 (2)(a) and (b).
80. S. 37 (3)(b), to be read in conjunction with s. 74 (1). At the time of writing, no application has been made.
81. Professional and employers' associations may equally make use of the provisions described.
82. S. 38 (3)(a).
83. S. 38(5).
84. Official Report, Stdg Comm. A. 27 May 1976, cols 460–3.
85. Para. 57.
*86. A point made long ago by Bentham, who castigated claims based upon 'natural rights' as attempts by the claimant to gain allies in the achievement of whatever end recognition of the right was supposed to produce. See, e.g., his comment quoted in D. Lloyd, *Introduction to Jurisprudence* (Stevens, 4th edn, 1979) p. 172 n. 9. Of course accepting the truth of Bentham's political analysis does not entail rejecting the desirability of rights, when socially established.
87. 414 U.S. 563 (1974).
88. 414 U.S. at 568.
89. A concurring opinion of three Justices relied on administrative regulations interpreting this provision to reach the same result. Other courts have applied the statutory interpretation in *Lau* where Spanish-speaking children were similarly denied the benefit of education (*Serna* v. *Portales Municipal Schools*, 499 F.2d 1149 [10th Cir. 1974]); where a Spanish-speaker claimed the help without charge of an interpreter to obtain unemployment compensation (*Pabon* v. *Levine* 70 F.R.D. 676 [S.D.N.Y. 1976]); and where a similarly worded statute required that handicapped persons not be denied the benefits of federal programmes (*Lloyd* v. *Regional Transport Authority*, 548 F. 2d 1277 [7th Cir. 1977]).
90. 414 U.S. at 572, per Blackmun J.
91. *Children and Their Primary Schools* (H.M.S.O., 1967) (the Plowden Report) and *Report of the Committee on Housing in Greater London*, Cmnd 2605 (1965) (the Milner Holland Report), are the key documents.
92. Cmnd 6845. See further D. McKay and A. Cox, *The Politics of Urban Change* (Croom Helm, 1979) chap. 7. This is not the place to assess the validity of the theory

that deprivation is spatially concentrated in particular urban areas, which has received substantial empirical criticism.

93. H. C. Hansard, vol. 964, cols 55–174, 12 March 1979.

94. S. 1 (2)(a) and (b), respectively, of the Bill.

95. This emerged in response to the probing of various backbenchers; the Minister's reasons (vol. 964, col. 168) were by no means lucid.

96. See the cases cited in n. 89.

97. See the extraordinary catalogue of more than 50 examples produced by Lord Simon of Glaisdale in *Knuller Ltd* v. *D.P.P.*, [1973] A.C. 435, 487–8.

98. 414 U.S. at 565.

99. *R.* v. *Metropolitan Police Commr, ex p. Blackburn* (No. 3), [1973] Q.B. 241.

100. *Secretary of State for Education* v. *Tameside M.B.*, [1976] 3 All E.R. 665. Under s. 68 of the Education Act 1944 the Minister must be satisfied that a local education authority is acting 'unreasonably' before he may issue directions.

101. E.g. *Racial Disadvantage*, pp. 210–15.

102. E.g. in ibid. pp. 236–7, and the Report by the Runnymede Trust, *Race and Council Housing in London* (1975).

103. K. Jones and A. Smith, *The Economic Impact of Commonwealth Immigration* (Cambridge U.P., 1970) p. 96.

2
Indirect Discrimination –
The Legal Issues

In Chapter 1 we examined the philosophical premises underlying the concept of indirect discrimination, as well as the history of its incorporation into British legislation, but postponed consideration of its precise legal expression and likely practical effects. That is the task of the present chapter, which examines seriatim each legal element in the statutory definition (s. 1 (1)(b); see Statutory Appendix for full text).

The following are the issues which have to be determined in cases of alleged indirect discrimination:

(1)   Has the respondent applied a 'requirement or condition'?

This phrase is of central importance, for its interpretation determines the range of activities and decisions that the Act may regulate. It clearly is meant to apply to criteria of selection and prerequisites for employment; the White Paper instanced prohibitions on the wearing of turbans or saris and minimum height requirements. Whilst some of these rules, such as the clothing requirements, affect only certain groups of non-whites, and others like the height requirement would also bar a sizeable percentage of whites, even though they presumably exclude a disproportionate number of minority persons, they are equally examples of a 'requirement or condition'. More important is that so long as they are used to restrict employment, their particular *form* – written or unwritten, a purely managerial decision or a 'shop-floor understanding'[1] reached between workers and managers – is irrelevant to their legality. This is a key point, for the characteristic preference in British industrial relations for shared understandings, custom and informal methods of settling disputes rather than formal agreements and precise interpretations, would make anti-discrimination laws a nullity if they could be applied only to formally proclaimed rules. Similarly, a rule of guidance, generally but not invariably applied – such as a 'preferred profile' of characteristics of the desired candidate for a post – should also come under this head.[2]

Thus broadly understood, 'requirement or condition' is readily applicable to employment situations where some sort of credential or test is required. Formal tests may be considered in two categories: those specifically concerned with proficiency in English ('language testing') and those which seek to gauge candidates' aptitude and intelligence ('employment testing').

Language testing has proven a serious roadblock to employment opportunities for Asian immigrants. It has been used in controversial circumstances both in relation to highly skilled jobs, as with the Temporary Registration and Assessment Board (TRAB) test for doctors,[3] and as a condition of employment for unskilled manual work. The latter has already produced a major legal battle.[4] Seven men from Bangladesh, who had worked at British Steel's Scunthorpe plant for periods of from six to twenty years and then left their employment at various times, were rejected when they reapplied for their old jobs after failing the Corporation's language test (which apparently was introduced some time after the most junior applicant had first been hired). Although the main issue in the case concerned the justifiability of the tests (below, p. 57) the complainants were in an unusual – and strong – position, because unlike most applicants they all previously held the jobs in question and had received satisfactory evaluations. Their demonstrated competence immediately cast doubt upon BSC's assertion that those unable to pass the test could not perform satisfactorily.

Although it might seem that a reasonable command of English would always be an essential prerequisite for adequate job performance, this is not necessarily so, particularly where the immediate supervisor speaks the worker's language, or where the establishment of a sizeable ethnic work group (below, p. 103) has in effect made a foreign language the prevalent tongue. Although this action was settled on terms favourable to the complainants – who received substantial *ex gratia* compensation and were re-engaged and provided with in-plant English-language training – and thus has no value as legal precedent, it vividly illustrates how the validity of apparent truisms may crumble when exposed to serious scrutiny. It suggests too that complainants challenging an English competence requirement in other contexts should press respondents to demonstrate the justification of the requirement itself, not merely the means chosen to test it.

The incidence of general employment testing is an empirical question of great importance, but one not discussed when the Act was considered in Parliament, and which has received insufficient investigation. Only two surveys, which fall well short of providing a comprehensive picture, have been conducted.[5] Their conclusions may be briefly summarised:

1. The use of testing increased in the 1960s, but never became standard practice. By the mid-1970s its growth had stopped, and a substantial proportion of firms have never used tests of any sort.

2. Tests are most frequently used for clerical staff, or for initial entrants such as apprentices or graduate trainees. Only rarely are they used for managers or 'operatives'.

3. General ability/intelligence tests are much the most common type used.

4. Very large firms (over 2000 employees) are much the most likely to use this selection device. No particular industry differs markedly from the general pattern.

5. Very few attempts to validate the tests have been undertaken, and those rare efforts 'have tended to demonstrate the inadequacy of procedures'.[6]

This research does not support firm conclusions, but it appears that use of tests is far from the norm in British industry, and particularly rare for shop-floor workers. Other formal requirements, notably scholastic credentials, are also used to an unknown extent, probably mostly for white-collar and higher-level trainee positions. Thus it seems likely that few unskilled or semi-skilled jobs are subject to any articulated 'requirement or condition'. The PEP research indicated that all groups of non-whites are substantially more likely than whites to be found in jobs at this level; in the extreme case, that of Pakistanis/Bangladeshis, the proportions are 58 per cent versus 18 per cent.[7] Thus if the phrase were confined to instances where objective qualifications are used, the expanded meaning of discrimination would, at least in the near future, be irrelevant to a large proportion of non-whites seeking employment, and severe limits placed on the applicability of the statute.

However, this unduly restrictive interpretation of the term is not inescapable. The absence of formal, objective criteria does not mean that no standards at all govern employment decisions. Even when a company hires on a 'walk-in' basis, applicants are generally asked about a host of matters, such as prior experience, work record, reasons for leaving previous employment and record of arrests and convictions. Since the employer must be satisfied on these points before the applicant will be hired, these 'personal' criteria function as requirements or conditions of employment. This wider interpretation accords with the policy of the Act to prohibit the use of standards that unintentionally but effectively disadvantage racial minorities, and the discriminatory potential of these and similar personal criteria is substantial, as in the case of an experience requirement in a type of job or industry from which blacks have previously been deliberately excluded.[8]

Of other employment practices that may be expected to be challenged as indirectly discriminatory, perhaps the most important is the use of subjective criteria. This is discussed below (pp. 121–2) in the context of promotion. Another cluster of prerequisites relates to the grounds of nationality or national origins rather than race: possession of a U.K. university degree; membership of a U.K. professional association; place of birth; residence period; or work experience in this country.[9] Indeed the first decision upholding a complaint of indirect discrimination under the Act concerned one such issue. In *Bohon–Mitchell* v. *Common Professional Examination Board*[10] the complainant was an American, married to an English doctor and resident here, who had received a degree in English from an American university. She wished to read for the Bar, and was told by the accrediting authorities[11] that as an overseas graduate with a non-law degree, she must take a two-year course. Non-law graduates from British or Irish universities were permitted to do a one-year course. Since the requirement bore much more heavily upon persons not of British or Irish nationality or national origin – the tribunal did not distinguish between these grounds – and the purported justification of ensuring that barristers had sufficient knowledge of 'the English way of life' was rejected, it was struck down.

Another issue that may arise in future is that of employment bars to persons with arrest records. Unlike a conviction an arrest is simply the result of an unreviewed and very possibly arbitrary decision by one particular policeman. The widespread use in London of 'sus' charges against young West Indians presents the most obvious instance,[12] particularly as – unlike a bank's refusal to hire someone arrested for theft – the charge is both incredibly vague and unconnected to any traits of behaviour that may make a person unfit for a particular job. In at least one American case such a blanket policy was held to be unlawful discrimination.[13]

A second problem of interpretation is the extent to which 'requirement or condition' includes methods of regulation – explicit or implicit – of activities that are *ancillary* to hiring, promotion, training and dismissal. Thus vacancies in a plant may not be publicly advertised because the practice is for employees to be told of them in expectation that they will pass on the information to friends or relations. Although a person unaware of a vacancy obviously cannot apply for it, the method of soliciting applicants is not a 'requirement or condition' of the job itself.

Here the new concept of discrimination interlocks with another innovation in the recent anti-discrimination statutes. An employer is now forbidden by s. 4 (1)(a) to discriminate 'in the arrangements he makes for the purpose of determining who would be offered that employment'. The Government included 'arrangements' among the prohibited activities in order to reach recruitment practices that were probably outside the previous legislation,[14] and it seems clear that an announcement to employees of the existence of vacancies would come within the new clause. It would also appear that even where the employer takes no specific step such as an announcement, but relies on personal referrals through the existing workforce to fill vacancies, he world still be within the reach of the statute, for his reliance on this 'arrangement' is a positive course of conduct. Thus it would be within the jurisdiction of an industrial tribunal to recommend that a company no longer rely on personal or word-of-mouth referrals as its primary method of recruitment. This example is of particular practical importance, for relations and friends are the single most important source of information about vacancies used by those seeking work.[15]

A similar instance of a now-questionable recruitment practice is that of soliciting applications from persons drawn from sources from which non-whites are largely absent. This point received considerable attention when the Sex Discrimination Act was considered, for several MPs were concerned that the 'old boy network' was indeed a literal truth.[16] The same issue would arise under the Act where recruitment had been limited to public schools or schools with an insignificant number of blacks whilst nearby schools with a higher minority population had been ignored. Similarly an employer who recruits through channels unlikely to reach many blacks, whilst refusing to use others, such as Jobcentres, which would, may also be skating on thin ice.

A somewhat unusual employment practice was held unlawful in the first successful case of indirect discrimination on grounds of race, *Hussein* v. *Saints Complete House Furnishers*.[17] The employer, whose premises were in the centre of Liverpool, sought applicants from the City Careers Service, but stipulated that he did not want youths 'from the city centre'. His reason was that unemployed friends of the new recruit who lived nearby would amble over to the shop, make nuisances of themselves and drive customers away. However, by 'city centre' he meant the Liverpool 8 district, in which the majority of the city's black population live. Although the tribunal accepted that he had no intention to exclude black applicants, it concluded that to exclude persons from an area which is 50 per cent black and limit recruitment to areas, none of which is more than 2 per cent black, is unlawful. This decision also illustrates that a negative requirement – you shall not live in a particular area – which applies to a disproportionately large number of blacks, is as unlawful as the more common positive requirements – you must have a particular educational qualification or test result – which disproportionately fewer of them may satisfy.

The 'requirement or condition' language seems an unnecessarily cumbersome way of expressing the intention to prohibit policies, practices and procedures that have a disproportionate adverse effect upon minorities. The term does, however, support an interpretation that encompasses virtually all important decisions in the sphere of employment without going so far as to make unlawful the mere absence or under-representation of minorities discrimination *per se* – a policy the legislation plainly rejects. Consequently employers are now responsible for ensuring that no aspect of their operations creates a situation where non-whites unjustifiably suffer significant disadvantage. This expresses the Act's focus on results, not merely on clearing away deliberate barriers; it may also spur employers to take steps on their own initiative to counter indirect discrimination. If the result is to make elimination of disadvantage less dependent on litigation and administrative enforcement, the gain in speed and savings in cost will be substantial.

(2) Are the disadvantaged persons of the 'same racial group' as the complainant?

In most discussions of race relations it is customary to speak of the non-white or black minority. Although all non-whites do share certain disabilities it is quite inaccurate to imagine that the economic and social circumstances of Punjabi Sikhs, Pakistani Muslims, West Indians, and Asian refugees from East Africa are identical or even similar. Consequently an employment criterion may disadvantage some but not all sub-groups among the non-white population. A minimum-height requirement would affect all groups of Asians but not West Indians, whilst a requirement of several 'A'-levels for a Building Society clerk would eliminate most West Indians educated here but probably – the data are inconclusive[18] – not disqualify British-educated Asians. Thus whether the relevant group for purposes of establishing or negating indirect discrimination is the specific group to which the complainant belongs, or all non-whites, may affect the outcome of litigation.

The only part of the statute that touches on this issue is s. 3 (2):

> The fact that a racial group comprises two or more racial groups does not prevent it from constituting a particular racial group for purposes of this Act.

It appears from the exceedingly brief discussion in the Standing Committee that this subsection was intended to assist those who wished to give training appropriate to the needs of particular minority groups.[19] The Government seem to have overlooked the converse and more contentious problem of group definition for purposes of litigation. The precise wording of s. 3 (2) would permit all non-whites to be classified as one 'racial group', and also – though this is somewhat more difficult – to allow all Asians to be regarded as one group.[20]*

Equally on a fair reading it should not preclude finer differentiation. For example Pakistanis, or persons born here of West Indian percentage, may each be regarded as a 'racial group', for they share a distinct 'ethnic or national origins', and the statute's definition of the term explicitly recognises that a person may belong to more than one racial group.[21]* Permitting the narrowest as well as the widest possible definition also accords with the design of the statute to eradicate disabilities visited upon an individual because of his membership in a group. Thus a prerequisite for employment that disadvantages *any* identifiable racial minority ought to be regarded as prima facie unlawful.

(3) 'Can' the complainant 'comply' with the requirement?

In *Price* v. *The Civil Service Commission*,[22] one of the first indirect discrimination cases to reach the Employment Appeal Tribunal (EAT), interpretation of this phrase was the primary question presented. On a straightforward reading it poses no difficulties: 'can' simply means 'are able to', and once a disparity is established (whatever the appropriate standards and procedure) discrimination is proved. However, an industrial tribunal, construing it with a strictness bordering on severity, had rejected a claim that the maximum age limit of 28 for applicants for Executive Officer posts in the

Civil Service constituted indirect sex discrimination. The fact that large numbers of women withdraw from the labour market in their twenties because of family responsibilities was, in the tribunal's view, a matter of choice and therefore irrelevant. The EAT emphatically rejected this interpretation, and held that

> It should not be said that a person 'can' do something merely because it is theoretically possible for him to do so: it is necessary to see whether *he can do so in practice*.[23] (Italic added).

The important point to emerge from the judgment in *Price* is that the interpretation of 'can comply' involves solely a finding of fact, and excludes questions of causation, or what by analogy may be termed 'contributory fault'. In the context of racial discrimination this means, for example, that in a case involving clothing requirements, the tribunal will not be required – or indeed permitted – to inquire whether fashion, custom or religion has led the complainant to adopt a particular dress, or – if an educational test is in issue – whether poor schools or lack of ability have prevented his racial group from reaching the same level of academic achievement as whites.

Moreover, in the sentence immediately following that quoted above, the EAT instructed tribunals to take account of 'current usual behaviour' in deciding the question of ability to comply. Consequently what may be called 'general social facts' may become important evidence, as where the tendency of whites and non-whites to associate more closely with members of their own racial group is the basis of a challenge to recruitment through personal referrals. The EAT's common-sense interpretation of this phrase will ensure that unwarranted obstacles are not placed in the path of complainants, and that few will fall at this hurdle.[24]

(4)   Is the proportion who can comply 'considerably smaller'?

In determining how great a disparity the application of a requirement must produce before it will be judged indirect discrimination a tribunal must make a decision that is ultimately arbitrary: whether the line is drawn at a difference of 5, 16 or 28½ per cent is a decision not wholly within the boundaries of rationality. By demanding the variation be 'considerable' the statute tells the tribunal to disregard small differences, with no indication of what that might mean. However, as the Minister of State said in committee, absent a 'mathematical formula' written into the Act, 'any word which modifies is bound to be an elastic concept'. He suggested that 'significantly', which was offered as a more stringent alternative, would in reality come down to the same thing.[25]

In the United States a rough rule of thumb was recently evolved after years of experience of litigation: a minority selection rate less than 80 per cent that for whites is taken as evidence of discriminatory impact.[26] However, this is a guideline, not a rigid rule, and lesser differentials may be taken as evidence of discrimination where the defendant's actions have disproportionately discouraged black applicants. Conversely, disparities exceeding 20 per cent may fail to establish impact if not statistically significant. No such guidelines have been evolved here, and thus far the cases under both statutes have involved disparities so marked that analysis of this issue has not been required. It is impossible, without the experience of a much larger number of cases and formal investigations, to determine whether a different figure would be more appropriate to Britain. One ought also to be aware of arithmetical intricacies: if the acceptance rate for whites is 70 per cent, the relevant figure for blacks is 56 per cent (4/5 of 70), *not* 50 per cent.

This provision, and indeed all numerical aspects of proof, may be more troublesome in race than in sex cases. In the latter, one can normally assume that 50 per cent is the proper figure in making demographic comparisons and that requirements which affect women because of their role in family life will either disadvantage a sizeable proportion of them, or none at all. By contrast all non-whites together comprise roughly 3 per cent of the population, and whenever one makes percentage comparisons based upon small numbers the figures are apt to be unreliable. For example, if a requirement is applied to 100 whites and 10 non-whites, the particular talents of each non-white affects the comparative results ten times as much as the particular talents of each white. This means that the figures for non-whites are far more likely to be a statistical artefact, the product of chance. It also means that the figures produced by either side in litigation cannot be expected to satisfy the statisticians' test of 'significance'. With a far smaller population and lower proportion of minorities than the United States, we must be content with less sophisticated data. This is not a serious loss, since the acquisition of such material is expensive and time-consuming, and not at all appropriate to the relatively cheap and speedy adjudication expected of British tribunals.

(5)   Is the inability to comply to the complainant's 'detriment'?

There remains a final hurdle: s. 1 (b)(iii) requires the complainant to prove that the discrimination is to his 'detriment'. This term is also used in the general employment provision of the Act to reach any discriminatory act not otherwise specified (see further below, pp. 130–1) and essentially means anything unpleasant. Thus in the *Bohon–Mitchell* case (above, pp. 45–6) the complainant would have been compelled to spend an additional year as a student, during which she would have had to support herself and been unable to earn her living. This financial hardship was held to be detriment. Nor does the ill effect have to be material. Although employment-related examples do not come as readily to mind, the greatly disproportionate classification of West Indian pupils without mental deficiencies as Educationally Sub-Normal (ESN) results in lowered self-respect, self-confidence and aspiration: detriment may be psychological in its impact.[27]

Although the burden of proving detriment rests upon the complainant, this should not be understood as a 'but-for' test; it does not require him to demonstrate that he would otherwise have been employed. In the *British Steel* case (above, p. 44) the Corporation were prepared to argue that even if the particular test was not justifiable the complainants had suffered no detriment because their poor English would have prevented them from passing *any* test. Since this contention would have effectively required the complainants to demonstrate what an appropriate test would be, which goes well beyond the burden of proof imposed upon them by the Act, it seems clearly mistaken.[28] To take a less extreme example, it would also be a misapplication of the 'detriment' requirement to compel the complainant to demonstrate that indirect discrimination alone prevented his selection. In effect he would have to prove himself clearly superior to all his competitors – a practical impossibility.

It is also quite irrelevant under the Act. The fact that 'arrangements' are now covered indicates clearly that discrimination is unlawful where the result is to prevent the victim receiving full consideration and is thus never properly compared with rival applicants. Such an interpretation of 'detriment' would also be based upon a fundamental misconception of the purpose of anti-discrimination legislation. It is not intended to ensure that a non-white (or woman) gets the job or promotion he or she wants; it insists only that the applicant be fairly considered. The new understanding of discrimination broadens the category of what will be regarded as 'unfair' criteria and practices, but – here the rejection of a pure 'fair-share' approach is explicit – its focus still centres on the process of decision, not the ultimate result. Thus the minority person suffers injury, and the statute is transgressed, whenever the process of decision is tainted by discrimination, not only when he would obviously have succeeded had he been white. Practicality and principle conjoin to urge that 'detriment' be interpreted to mean simply that the process of selection has in any degree been affected by the existence of the challenged requirement or condition.

The apparent purpose of the 'detriment' provision was as a sort of *locus standi* test, to ensure that the litigant has personally been affected by the practice he challenges. At first blush this seems unremarkable, but coupled with the absence in Britain of the class action procedure described in Chapter 12, it in fact creates a serious impediment to the invocation of the Act. Its consequence is that whether even an unmistakably discriminatory practice can be declared illegal will depend on the more or less fortuitous occurrence that a given individual has the interest, tenacity and courage to assert his rights. He may also require an unusual degree of asceticism. An employer worried about the cost or other problems that may attend changing an entrenched practice might find it politic to make a particularly good settlement offer to the occasional complainant. What would seem good fortune to the latter would for the employer be far cheaper than compliance with the law. This 'resist and withdraw' tactic was quite common in early American employment litigation until the courts made clear that such arrangements would not block their scrutiny of the employer's operations. But under the present statute, once the complainant withdrew his case, the tribunal would lose jurisdiction to correct the illegality of the employment practice, regardless of how severely it affected others. It seems wrong, as well as strikingly inefficient, that the law's effectiveness should turn so much on the character of the individual who happens to have been affected by a policy of general application. This difficulty is only fractionally overcome by the power of formal investigation granted the Commission for Racial Equality (CRE), which may proceed against a 'discriminatory practice' even where no specific victim can be identified (s. 28; below, p. 243). With numerous other responsibilities competing for its limited resources the Commission can at best play a supportive but secondary role to enforcement by individuals. Hopefully this central artery will not be blocked by the detriment clause, which in this respect highlights the failure of the Act to align its narrowly individualistic procedural and remedial provisions with its awareness of the collective dimension of discrimination, reflected above all in s. 1 (1)(b). This wider point is examined in detail in Chapter 12.

(6) The Justification Defence

A 'requirement or condition' that indirectly discriminates against non-whites is not necessarily unlawful. Once the complainant established discrimination it is open to the employer – who carries the burden of proof – to demonstrate that the practice is 'justifiable'. In a purely negative sense this is perhaps the most important single term in s. 1 (1)(b), for an interpretation that gave extensive deference to customary employment practices would reduce it to insignificance. A critical defect of the statute is that it fails to articulate any standards to direct tribunals called upon to make this judgment.

A PURPOSIVE APPROACH TO INTERPRETATION

The critical question is why this provision is in the statute. Put another way, why is not any practice proven to be disadvantageous to minorities simply outlawed? The explanation is grounded in policy: the value of preventing the exclusion of non-whites cannot always be paramount. But in the scheme of what, for Britain, is an innovative and comprehensive enactment, this can be true for only the most compelling reasons, which may be roughly defined as the safe and efficient operation of a business. Thus no anti-discrimination law requires an employer to hire unqualified persons, but effective legislation does insist that the criteria governing qualifications truly measure competence, and do not simply express prejudice, preconception or unthinking custom

If this analysis is correct, much of the extended Standing Committee debate over whether 'justifiable' should have been replaced by 'necessary' was misconceived, a point nicely illustrated by the confusion of the Under-Secretary for Employment, who managed to define the former by reference to the latter.[29] He offered two main arguments against the proposed amendment. He defined necessary to mean something like 'inescapable' – a somewhat strained interpretation – and thus contended that it was too restrictive. Conversely those who favoured the substitution gave an unduly latitudinarian meaning to 'justifiable', taking it to denote any explanation not patently specious. The Minister's second point was more cogent: he thought 'justifiable' connoted a more objective test than 'necessary'.[30] Both sides in the debate seemed to share the same ends, whilst having conflicting understandings of each other's formulations.

Another look at the extract from *Griggs* quoted in Chapter 1 may cast further light on the issue:

> The touchstone is business necessity. If an employment practice which operates to exclude Negroes cannot be shown to be related to job performance, the practice is prohibited.

It must be emphasised that the idea of job-relatedness first articulated in *Griggs* is not to be found in the statute; it is understood as *inherent* in the concept of discrimination itself. Bearing in mind that Britain has received the *Griggs* concept of discrimination whilst setting out in a clearer and more systematic manner the sequence in which the reviewing body must make particular legal judgments, it seems appropriate that the justifiability test should require the employer to prove that the practice in question is job-related. This interpretation gives effect to the explanation of the new concept of discrimination offered in the White Paper, which used the phrase 'substantially related to job performance' without acknowledging its origin in *Griggs*. Indeed its omission may simply have resulted from the fact that the Act also governs a range of non-employment matters, each of which would have required analogous formulations. It also accords quite strongly with the sense, if not the precise language, of what both sides in the Standing Committee discussions were attempting in their disparate fashions to convey.

Job-relatedness – 'a manifest relationship to the employment in question'[31] – means above all that the requirements of the job itself, not the expressed or assumed preferences of customers or other employees, must provide the guidelines. Thus it is no justification of a discriminatory practice to argue that it was agreed with trade union representatives,[32] or that its elimination and the employment of non-whites might cause withdrawal of business, strikes or other labour trouble, or would necessitate expenditure on developing new employment criteria.[33] Of course it is more convenient and cheaper to continue existing practices, or to pander to the prejudice of employees or customers, but acquiescence in the discriminatory *status quo* is precisely what laws against discrimination are designed to disturb. Though these consequences may well ensue, they are precisely the sort of considerations the statute subordinates to achieving equality of opportunity. Profitability, it must be emphasised, should not decide the matter.

Only requirements inherent in the job may be regarded as justifiable. This seemingly abstract concept is in fact quite realistic, for it forces employers at first instance and then tribunals to make a practical appraisal of job content, cocking a sceptical eye at traditional restrictions and the more recent, albeit limited, vogue for credentials and testing. The result will surely be to eliminate many practices that have excluded able people and have been carried on primarily through habit and neglect; in numerical terms more whites than non-whites will be the gainers. An effective anti-discrimination law is a powerful source for what is truly 'rationalisation' of industry – the clearing away of mythologies surrounding employment practices, and their replacement by prerequisites that demonstrably help select the most competent people.

The key legal issue is developing a workable test of job-relatedness. The one standard that must be ruled out at the start is that of good-faith belief in the validity of a qualification. The test must be objective, for the issue is not the intention of the employer but the effect of the practice. Concretely this means that the challenged requirement must demonstrably and significantly contribute to industrial efficiency or safety, a test that cannot be satisfied by belief, good faith or otherwise, but only be empirical evidence. This may be hard to come by, but that argues for abandonment of the discriminatory practice, not acceptance of prevailing dogma.

The justification provision is an integral part of the compromise of principle embodied in the Act. Had an unalloyed 'fair-share' approach been taken, the mere under-representation of minorities would have been prescribed: the reason for their disadvantage would have been irrelevant. However, the statute also accepts that industrial efficiency (and fair treatment of qualified whites) are values which should not be trampled in the pursuit of racial equality. There is an inevitable tension between these considerations, but it can be satisfactorily resolved by a rigorous and sceptical approach toward efforts at justification which requires firm evidence that the challenged practice actually achieved the purported objective.

It may be thought that the approach taken here to the interpretation of 'justifiable' represents an alien, indeed specifically American, approach to the construction of a statute. Certainly no British court or tribunal could look at the Committee deliberations discussed throughout this chapter, nor would it be instinctively receptive to the arguments derived from legislative purpose and practical necessity. However, given the capacious and protean character of the term 'justifiable', it is difficult to see how inquiry into the principles underlying the statutes can be avoided, even under the traditional 'mischief' rule. Clearly nothing can be justified in the abstract; references must be made to criteria which establish an order of social values. Since these are notably absent from s. 1 itself, the interpreting body must look to the general principles and structure underpinning the statute as a whole.

If this approach is rejected as being too vague there would seem to be but two alternatives, each even less attractive. The first is unbridled judicial lawmaking: giving meaning to the phrase by infusing the policy preferences of the interpreters themselves. The second, and more likely, is adoption of the attitude of extreme deference the courts continue to take when administrative decisions are challenged by persons asserting personal or political rights.[34] Perhaps the most pertinent example is the judgment of Lord Denning M.R. in *Cumings* v. *Birkenhead Corpn.*[35] Rejecting a claim that the defendant education authority acted *ultra vires* in adopting a policy of allocating students to Roman Catholic and non-Roman Catholic schools that effectively prevented pupils crossing over from one system to the other, he reiterated the familiar test of reasonableness: only if the policy were adopted on 'unreasonable, capricious or irrelevant' grounds would it be regarded as *ultra vires*. 'If the policy is one which could reasonably be upheld for good educational reasons, it is valid. But if it is so unreasonable that no reasonable authority could entertain it, it is invalid'.[36] Here he harked back to one of the *loci classici* of the reasonableness test, the judgment of Warrington L.J. in *Short* v. *Poole Corpn.*[37] It is worth recalling that after stating the principle, Warrington L.J. added: 'It is difficult to suggest any act which would be held *ultra vires* under this head, though performed bona fide'.[38] There is a wide gulf between caprice or unreasonableness and affirmatively demonstrating that something is justified, and if the tribunals and courts are to be faithful to the Act, ensuring that the responsibility it imposes on the employer is a real one, they can only draw upon the policies and perspectives of the Act itself.

It should be recognised that the task placed upon tribunals and courts hearing such cases is an unusual one, and not the least novel feature of recent discrimination legislation.[39]* These bodies must make substantive judgments about the appropriateness of private decisions, drawing upon evidence and supported by a mode of interpretation, both of which are outside the ordinary compass of English jurisprudence. The degree of innovation can be seen particularly clearly by comparing the law of unfair dismissal, perhaps the only other area which provides scope for such regulatory decisions. The vast majority of unfair dismissal cases concern narrow questions of the employee's capability, qualifications and conduct,[40] and the evidence offered is of the concrete and personal kind that is the stuff of ordinary civil litigation. There *is* a relatively small number of cases which call for policy judgments – those concerning unfair selection for redundancy and the fairness of dismissal procedures[41]* – but there remains a significant difference: in these situations the tribunal draws upon notions of fairness and appropriateness widely held within industry to reach its decision, and its ability to do so is much enhanced by the contribution of the 'wingmen' drawn from workers and employers. Discrimination cases do not build upon such a consensus. The legislation seeks to impose an external set of considerations whose application will often disrupt established practices which have been agreed by precisely the groups represented by the lay tribunal members. Furthermore, the relevant evidence will often concern patterns and effects that are national in scope, or at any rate stretch far beyond the actions and relations of the complainant and respondent (see below, Chapter 11). Where tribunals in unfair dismissal cases are essentially concerned to remove arbitrariness as measured by existing norms, in indirect discrimination cases the norms themselves are often in issue, to be judged by the alien standards of the statute. Whether the new legislation will be effective in reducing racial disadvantage will depend significantly on whether all elements of the legal system show sensitivity to the underlying moral force and particular policy judgments expressed in it. One cannot be terribly optimistic.

The major practical question is what sort of evidence should be acceptable to prove job-relatedness. Clearly it must be factual – that is, more than received wisdom – but equally it must have an objective basis. Thus it is not enough that banks *think* their trainees need four 'O'-levels, including English and Maths; and it is not enough that those with such qualifications seem to perform well in the job. The critical question is whether those without the specified qualifications would perform equally well. The credential or employment test must be validated in a manner that convincingly demonstrates that the relationship between the qualification and job performance is not a matter of chance, that evaluations of job performance are themselves reasonably objective, and that groups whose performance on tests and at work are being. compared are properly defined. This is a very complex matter, which requires at least elementary knowledge of professional validation standards and certain statistical techniques. In the United States, with a long tradition of use of economic and sociological data in the courts, judicial scrutiny of validation studies has assimilated such materials, and the Supreme Court decision in *Albemarle Paper Co.* v. *Moody*,[42] with its discussion of testing techniques and references to 'phi coefficients' and other arcana deserves to be better known here. The Court drew heavily upon very detailed Guidelines prepared by the Equal Employment Opportunities Commission;[43] the CRE's draft Code of Practice (below, pp. 248–9) stresses that selection tests should be validated and refers employers to a forthcoming Report of the Joint Working Party of the British Psychological Association and the Runnymede Trust, which presumably will set out professionally accepted methods and standards.[44]* One aspect of this problem was presented in the British Steel litigation. Included in the settlement was an admission by BSC that the tests which the complainants failed had not been professionally devised, and the company retained an expert in selection testing who, along with a similar person chosen by the CRE, will review the language testing at the Scunthorpe plant and may presumably recommend use of a better-designed examination.

This feature of the BSC case is, as noted above (p. 45), characteristic of all testing in this country: virtually none has been subject to proper validation, and the same is presumably true of academic qualifications. All must therefore be regarded as suspect under the law, particularly the general ability/intelligence tests, which are the most commonly used and which have repeatedly failed to survive critical examination in American litigation, including *Griggs* itself.

The validation issue is by no means limited to testing, which is in any case relatively uncommon in this country. To be justifiable, all prerequisites for employment must be shown empirically to select employees who will perform more efficiently. Word-of-mouth hiring, for example, is not designed to ensure the quality of the workforce, but to save outlay on recruitment; this would be insufficient to overcome its discriminatory effect. Height and clothing requirements, unless proven to assist job performace or prevent safety hazards, would also fail. More difficult would be a requirement that applicants have a minimum amount of job experience. This probably would exclude a disproportionate number of non-whites, certainly so if there has been a history of direct discrimination. The inquiry into justification would have to consider whether the job is one for which formal or informal on-the-job training is commonly given. There is a strong tradition in much of British industry that one learns a job 'sitting by Nellie' – watching and imitating an experienced workman. This often applies to skilled as well as semi-skilled jobs, and where the complainant can prove this to be so, or where it is known to exist – here the industrial knowledge of the tribunal wingmen may be valuable – the justifiability of experience as a prerequisite becomes questionable. Similarly, requiring completion of a lengthy apprenticeship may be vulnerable if expert testimony can demonstrate that shorter forms of training produce equally qualified people.

THE CASE LAW

The approach of the EAT to the justification provision has not been altogether consistent. In *Steel* v. *Union of Post Office Workers*,[45] Phillips J., the then President, laid down guidelines for tribunals considering the issue.

He noted that the statute places the onus of proof of justification on the employer, and declared that this was not to be discharged lightly. Here he drew upon similar statements made in Equal Pay Act cases, which in so far as they were intended to suggest that the respondent is under a greater burden of proof than is generally required in civil litigation, were later expressly repudiated by the Court of Appeal.[46] However, the issue is not ultimately one of proof of fact, but of legal conclusion. What the *Steel* judgment – which included an extensive quotation from *Griggs* – seemed in fact to be saying is that the 'requirement or condition' must be objectively, or genuinely, *required* – not merely convenient, traditional, assumedly useful or even apparently reasonable. In deciding this question a tribunal 'must weigh up the needs of the enterprise against the discriminatory effect of the requirement or condition'.[47] Thus a balancing test must be conducted, although with the considerations on each side qualitatively so different, this is clearly a sensitive task. One critical element in the balance is the question of degree; the greater the exclusionary impact on minorities the clearer must be the demonstrated need for the practice.[48]

Potentially the most important of Mr Justice Phillips' instructions was the last:

> Fifthly, it is right to distinguish between a requirement or condition which is necessary and one which is merely convenient, and for this purpose it is relevant to consider whether the employer can find some other and non-discriminatory method of achieving his object.[49]

In its use of the term 'necessary' and rejection of a convenience standard, and in its willingness to look for a less discriminatory alternative before accepting a claim of necessity, this approach seems to be a rigorous application of the 'job-relatedness' test suggested in this chapter. It is also consistent with decisions of the European Court of Justice, which has applied a strict test in determining whether restrictions on various Treaty rights are 'justified' by the need to safeguard *ordre publique* or public health, safety or morals.[50] It is therefore difficult to explain the observations of the same judge in the *Price* case, decided four days later. Speaking there of the possibility of a challenge to the attainment of two 'A'-levels as a prerequisite for employment as an Executive Officer in the Civil Service, he opined that 'the Civil Service Commission would have had little difficulty, if the attack had been limited in that way, in establishing that the condition was justifiable'.[51]

With respect, this remark – admittedly *obiter dicta* inserted somewhat casually at the end of the judgment – cannot be reconciled with the guidelines carefully elaborated in *Steel*. The purpose of a rigorous justification test is precisely to prevent unreflective acceptance and continuation of employment practices which have never received adequate review. How does one *know* that two 'A'-levels are necessary for competent Executive

Officers? The Commission may have made that judgment after a thorough evaluation of the job, but that cannot be conclusive. It is merely evidence, which doubtless will carry considerable weight, but its accuracy must be left open to the complainant to dispute, particularly as testimony by experts on testing and its validation may be essential to the proper adjudication of justifiability. Moreover, where the respondent has made no serious effort to evaluate whether an employment prerequisite is truly job-related, that fact should point emphatically toward the conclusion that it is not justifiable. The *Steel* guidelines are a forceful and realistic application of the job-relatedness standard; one hopes they will not be watered down by uncritical acceptance of 'things as usual'.

At present there appears to be some divergence in approach to the justification question between the English and Scottish EAT. In *Singh* v. *Rowntree Mackintosh Ltd*[52] the latter upheld the refusal of a confectionery factory in Edinburgh to employ production workers with beards, even though this would exclude all Sikhs.[53] The company had apparently consulted a food and drugs officer of the local authority, and defended the requirement as needed to achieve the highest possible standard of hygiene. However, there was also evidence that the company did not impose this rule in six of its eight U.K. plants, which one would have thought seriously undermined its defence. The judgment of Lord McDonald, though not questioning the *Steel* test, speaks in terms of something called 'commercial necessity' – potentially a dangerous dilution, since any practice that aids profitability could readily be so described. At best his analysis is a weak application of *Steel*; whether this represents a fundamental disagreement or merely a response to the facts of the particular case remains to be seen.

One justification that has been successfully pleaded is discrimination by statute. Thus in one case[54] a hospital refused to employ an American citizen with American qualifications because regulations under the National Health Service Reorganisation Act 1973 required the holder of the particular post to have a specified British qualification or some 'equivalent'. When the Whitley Council refused to accept the equivalence of his American qualifications the hospital, against its wishes, rejected him. Its argument that the indirect discrimination on grounds of nationality or national origin was justified by the command of the regulations was accepted. This seems correct, since, unlike the rule overturned in *Bohon–Mitchell*, the hospital had no choice in the matter, indeed presumably would have been acting unlawfully in hiring the complainant. This defence also shades into reliance on the general exception in the Act for discrimination done 'in pursuance of any enactment' (s. 41; above, p. 74). It is unclear how often such justifications may be available; the key unanswered question is whether a justification based on a statutory *discretion*, rather than command, will be upheld.

The most difficult questions concerning justification of discriminatory practices arise when the role and interests of incumbent white workers are added to the picture. The present analysis, tracking the path of the committee debates and the phrasing of the statute itself, has regarded discrimination as wholly a question of employer preferences, policies and interests. In fact, although under the Act the employer has the legal responsibility, many practices or rules, notably those governing apprenticeships, progression opportunities and selection for redundancy or lay off, may reflect even more strongly the interests and collective power of the workforce. To take one example, especially pertinent in the current depression, the 'last-in-first-out' principle (LIFO) governing layoffs and redundancies may very well not be what the employer would have chosen since it tends to lose him the youngest, presumably fittest and most adaptable of his employees. But trade unions commonly support this principle because it protects their members' major asset: the ability to earn a living.[55]* Apart from the serious re-employment difficulties faced by older workers made redundant, a growing number of financially valuable rights, achieved through collective bargaining or conferred by statute, now surround continuous employment. Given the lopsided distribution of wealth in Britain, these rights appurtenant to one's job are in effect the main form of capital possessed by workers below retirement age. Other powerful reasons, such as the avoidance of favouritism and arbitrariness, preventing victimisation of trade-union activitists and others regarded as troublemakers, and simplicity of understanding and administration, further support acceptance of the LIFO principle.[56]*

The impact of LIFO in layoffs and redundancies will unquestionably fall disproportionately heavily on blacks, often the most recently employed, particularly in the more desirable jobs. Yet so compelling are the interests of all workers in continued employment that protection of those interests should, it is submitted, carry the day. Moreover, variation of a LIFO arrangement to prevent discharge of recently hired blacks would appear to leave the employer open to unfair dismissal claims by whites discharged instead, and any system that overtly took race into account would itself be an illegal form of direct discrimination, no matter that its purpose was to benefit non-whites.[57]

Whatever the merits of the foregoing arguments on the substantive point, they share a common defect: they are based on judgments of the author, not upon values readily ascertainable in the statute. Nor are they in any sense related to characteristics of a particular job. This is inevitable: most trade-union-influenced rules are not designed to achieve maximum efficiency or productivity, but to protect the security of their members – usually a conflicting interest, at least in the short run. It is difficult to see how the legal issue may be resolved, other than by appeal to broad considerations of policy. The collision of interests of black and white workers presents the most poignant situations likely to arise in indirect discrimination cases.

Some way must be found to distinguish between legitimate and illegitimate interests: as *Steel* itself demonstrates, white men may achieve preferences and opportunities due to the shabby treatment of minorities within the workforce. By channelling resolution of the issues into the juridical mould of complainant v. employer the statute aggravates the difficulties. Perhaps the only satisfactory solution would be for Parliament, in addition to explicitly writing the job-relatedness test into the Act, to specify any practices not fitting analytically within that test, like LIFO, that it wishes to deem justifiable. It is hoped the list would not be a long one, and that the principle of *expressio unius est exclusio alterius* would be emphasised.

The field of indirect racial discrimination is as yet virtually unmarked by decided case law. There is some indication that tribunals initially found the concept difficult to grasp: in the first year of the Act roughly 20 per cent of complainants raised the issue, but none was upheld.[58] Unfortunately the figures do not reveal whether any of these, like the subsequent British Steel case, were successfully settled, and the general complainant success rate rose substantially after the first year. Interpreted in a manner sensitive to the spirit and policy of the Act, s. 1 (1)(b) could have a wide and beneficial effect upon equal opportunity and more rational selection criteria. This chapter has pointed out only some of the more readily identifiable practices that would require revision or abandonment by employers.

NOTES

1. This term is taken from *Hepple*, p. 85.
2. In *Bains* v. *Avon C.C.* (1978) EAT 143/78, the EAT left open the question whether such a 'preferred profile' would, as argued in the text, come within the phrase.
3. This test, which also includes questions testing professional competence, is discussed in a publication of the former Community Relations Commission, *Doctors From Overseas – A Case For Consultation* (1976).
4. The issues and the terms of settlement were reported in *The Guardian*, 31 Jan 1979.
5. F. Sneath *et al.*, *Testing People at Work* (1976), and K. Miller and J. Hydes, *The Use of Psychological Tests in Personnel Work* (1971), both published by the Institute of Personnel Management.
6. Pearn, 'Exploring the Meaning of Indirect Discrimination in Employment', in *Runnymede Seminar*, p. 45.
7. PEP Report, p. 73.
8. An experience requirement may also be vulnerable under the Act when formal or informal on-the-job training is normally available to employees. See further above, p. 57.
9. See Bindman and Grosz, 'Indirect Discrimination and the Race Relations Act', in *Runnymede Seminar*, p. 40.
10. [1978] I.R.L.R. 525.

11. S. 12 outlaws discrimination by 'qualifying bodies', i.e. those which govern admission and set qualifications for various professions.

12. See, further, C. Demuth, *'Sus' – A Report on the Vagrancy Act 1824* (Runnymede Trust, 1978), for statistics and criticism.

13. *Gregory* v. *Litton Systems, Inc.*, 316 F. Supp. 401 (1970), affd 472 F. 2d 631 (9th Cir. 1972).

14. Official Report, Standing Comm. A, 4 May 1976, col. 135 (Mr J. Grant).

15. See, e.g. *General Household Survey 1973* (H.M.S.O., 1975) table 3.11, indicating how respondents had found their present employment.

16. See especially the comments of the Under-Secretary for Employment, Mr J. Fraser, in Official Report, Standing Comm. B, 22 April 1975, cols 47–9.

17. [1979] I.R.L.R. 337 (Liverpool I.T.).

18. J. Taylor, *The Half-Way Generation* (NFER, 1976) chap. 14. The author notes that his conclusions on this point differ from those of earlier studies.

19. Official Report, Standing Comm. A, 4 May 1976, cols 129–30.

*20. Arguably Asians, despite the great differences among them, are perceived by whites to be of a different 'colour' or 'ethnic origin' from both whites and people of West Indian origin. By s. 3 (1) these are among the defining characteristics of a 'racial group'.

*21. S. 3 (1) states that 'references to a person's racial group refer to *any* racial group into which he falls' (italic added). Since persons may share the same 'race' or 'ethnic origins' yet be of different nationality – also included within the statute's definition of 'racial grounds – it is obvious that the Act contemplates multiple group membership. Similarly, s. 3 (2), quoted in the text, makes no sense except on the understanding that a person may be a member of more than one racial group.

22. [1977] I.R.L.R. 291.

23. Idem at 293.

24. The use of judicial notice in establishing 'current usual behaviour' is considered on p. 213 below.

25. Official Report, Standing Comm. A, 27 April 1976, cols 38–40.

26. I am relying here on the account of American practice presented in *Ind. Rel. Leg. Info. Bull.* no. 187, November 1978, p. 6.

27. Failure to involve disciplinary proceedings against whites who inflict racial abuse on a black employee might be regarded as detriment to the latter if he had complained to the employer.

28. British Steel's position is reported by Bindman and Grosz, op. cit. p. 33.

29. This occurred during consideration of the Sex Discrimination Act 1975, in which the justification provision was extensively discussed. See Official Report, Standing Comm. b, 24 April 1975, cols 63–78.

30. Idem, col. 72 (Mr J. Fraser).

31. 401 U.S. at 432.

32. This attempt at justification was rejected by an industrial tribunal in a case of indirect sex discrimination. See *Meeks* v. *National Union of Agricultural and Allied Workers*, [1976] I.R.L.R. 198, para. 18.

33. These purported justifications have been rejected in what seems to be the leading American appeals court cases, *Robinson* v. *Lorillard Corp.*, 444 F. 2d 791 (2nd Circ. 1971), and *United States* v. *Bethlehem Steel Corp.*, 446 F. 2d 652 (4th Circ. 1971).

34. See further, J. Griffith, *The Politics of the Judiciary* (Fontana, 1977) *passim.*

35. [1972] Chap. 12.

36. [1972] Chap. 12, 37.

37. [1926] Chap. 66.

38. [1926] Chap. 66, 91.

*39. This is also true of cases arising under the 'material difference' provision of the Equal Pay Act 1970, s. 1 (3), amended. This is, however, really another aspect of legislation against discrimination which for a variety of reasons has been isolated from, and preceded, more thoroughgoing statutory prohibition of sex discrimination.

40. EPCA, s. 57 (2). S. 57 (3) requires the employer to show that he acted 'reasonably' in dismissing the employee in the light of these three criteria.

*41. Under the rubric of 'reasonableness' tribunals may determine whether dismissal was too severe a sanction for the employee's misconduct (see especially the EAT's decision in *Mansfield Hosiery Mills* v. *Bromley*, [1977] I.R.L.R. 301), and whether, even though the employer had reasonable grounds for dismissal, he followed an unfair procedure, which could make the dismissal unfair, though compensation could be substantially reduced, as in *W. Devis & Sons Ltd* v. *Atkins*, [1977] A.C. 931.

A reasonableness test is also applied in redundancy cases, where the main policy issue that has confronted tribunals has been evaluation of the employer's economic judgment; specifically, whether alternative employment within the company or group could have been found for the employee instead of making him redundant. See, e.g., *Vokes Ltd* v. *Bear*, [1974] I.C.R. 1 (N.I.R.C.).

42. 422 U.S. 405 (1975).

43. 422 U.S. at 430–5.

*44. It should be emphasised, however, that the CRE's Code of Practice (see further below, pp. 248–9) carries less weight with English courts than do Regulations issued by administrative agencies in the United States courts.

45. [1977] I.R.L.R. 288.

46. *National Vulcan Engineering Insurance Group Ltd* v. *Wade*, [1978] 3 All E.R. 121.

47. [1977] I.R.L.R. at 290.

48. This is the approach taken by the American courts. See B. Schlei and P. Grossman, *Employment Discrimination Law* (Bureau of National Affairs, 1976) pp. 146–8.

49. [1977] I.R.L.R. at 291.

50. Notably in cases under Art. 36 and Art 48, concerning respectively freedom of movement of goods and of labour. The rigorous approach of the European Court is well exemplified by Case 104/75, *Adriaan de Peijper* (1976) E.C.R. 613, decided under Art. 36.

51. [1977] I.R.L.R. 291, 294.

52. [1979] I.C.R. 544.

53. Who were treated as a 'racial group' within the meaning of s. 3; see above, pp. 47–8, and below, p. 77.

54. *Zeigler* v. *Kensington etc. AHA*, (1978) COIT 803/133 (London Central I.T.).

*55. In reality the operation of the LIFO principle is likely to be less straightforward than the text might suggest. Often trade unions are not able to secure management acceptance of it, and some sort of compromise is reached. Moreover, the practical working of a LIFO scheme in determining who is actually selected for redundancy depends critically on how widely the field of those to be considered is defined. The field may be defined as narrowly as one section, or as widely as the entire plant, or indeed the entire workforce of a group of companies.

*56. The Court of Appeal has given its stamp of approval to the LIFO principle. Where trade unions and management have agreed to a LIFO procedure this will be considered fair. Where there is no agreed procedure there is in effect a presumption in favour of LIFO, in that the employer must show good reason for use of other criteria if the selection for redundancy is not to be held unfair. See *Bessenden Properties Ltd* v. *Corness*, [1974] I.R.L.R. 338.

57. Nothing in the prohibition of direct discrimination in s. 1 (1)(a) permits consideration of the reasons purportedly justifying the use of radical criteria. Reverse discrimination is wholly foreclosed.

58. The figure of 20% is taken from an unpublished paper of Mr J. C. McCrudden, Balliol College, Oxford. Not until late October 1978, in the *Bohon–Mitchell* case, was a complaint of indirect discrimination upheld.

3
The Grounds of Discrimination

Those designing anti-discrimination legislation must at the outset make three fundamental choices. One concerns the areas of behaviour to be regulated: employment, housing, personal and public services and so forth. These may be called matters of scope.

A second, related question is that of application: to whom should the legislation speak? Non-discrimination provisions in a Bill of Rights – whether one that overrides conflicting legislation, as in the United States, or is merely of equal authority with other statutes, as in Canada – cover only the actions of the State of public bodies;[1]* the same is true of the European Convention on Human Rights. Though the present Act contains some exclusions of scope (fewer, however, than did its predecessors), it applies to virtually all private persons and institutions as well as to local authorities and the nationalised industries. However, s. 41 exempts discriminatory provisions in statutes, delegated legislation and acts done as arrangements made pursuant to Ministerial approval. These reservations were needed and will be used primarily to immunise discriminatory treatment of aliens, notably but not exclusively in matters of immigration.

The final key decision is specifying what grounds of differential treatment are to be prohibited; put another way, the legislature must declare which personal or group attributes are to be deemed illegitimate grounds of decision in the areas regulated.

The 1965 and 1968 Acts outlawed discrimination only 'on the ground of colour, race or ethnic or national origins'. This narrow 'race formula'[2] may be contrasted with other more ambitious approaches. The European Convention on Human Rights, to which Britain has been a party since it came into force in 1953, forbids 'discrimination on any ground such as sex, race, colour, language, religion, political or other opinion, national or social origin, association with a national minority, property, birth or other status'.[3] The United Nations Universal Declaration on Human Rights contains an almost identical provision. A growing number of writers have proposed that the Convention be enacted as a U.K. Bill of Rights.[4] Should this occur, our discrimination law would be transformed overnight from one outlawing unfavourable treatment on a small number of specified grounds, to one containing a compendium as comprehensive as that incorporated into the municipal law of any nation.[5]* This point seems to have been largely overlooked in the current debate on the need for a Bill of Rights,[6]* a rather startling omission when one considers that the hallmark of the British approach to anti-discrimination legislation is its caution and specificity.

This may be seen through several examples. Perhaps wisely, Britain is unique among common law countries in its creation of a separate statute and enforcement authority for its provisions against sex and marital status discrimination, which were not enacted until a decade after it first began to legislate against racial discrimination. Religion and political opinion have both been carefully excluded from each Race Relations Act, but are the only grounds of discrimination proscribed by the Fair Employment (Northern Ireland) Act 1976. Despite occasional pressure from back-benchers, no government has ever proposed to ban discrimination on the basis of age, although this has been covered by federal legislation in the United States since 1967.[7] Additional grounds prohibited in various Canadian jurisdictions,[8] such as past criminal record (British Columbia), source of income (Manitoba), 'social conditions or civil status' (Quebec) and physical handicap (Nova Scotia) have also been passed over.

Thus the 'race formula' expresses a clear and deliberate policy of proscribing only a few selected grounds of discrimination. Nevertheless substantial difficulties of interpretation have arisen out of its sparse language.

NATIONAL ORIGINS AND NATIONALITY

Stanislaw Zesko was a British ex-serviceman who though resident in this country for over twenty years, had retained his Polish citizenship and was thus of Polish 'nationality'. Twice he was refused a place on the waiting list for a council house in the London Borough of Ealing solely because he did not meet the Council's requirement that he be 'a British subject within the meaning of the British Nationality Act 1948'. The reasons for the adoption of this requirement are obscure; it did not serve to exclude non-white immigrants since under that Act the citizen of any Commonwealth country was, and is, a British subject.[9] Perhaps Ealing, which had a heavy concentration of Polish refugees, was indeed attempting to keep out people like Mr Zesko. In the event, following the statutory procedure then in effect (below, p. 189), a complaint was made on his behalf to the Race Relations Board, which formed the opinion that he had suffered discrimination on grounds of his 'national origins'. In *Ealing London Borough Council* v. *Race Relations Board*[10] this view was upheld, but the decision was reversed on direct appeal to the House of Lords, with only one dissent.[11]

Lord Donovan, in perhaps the clearest judgment, equated national origins with 'nationality received at birth'.[12] This is something an individual cannot alter, even though he may emigrate and change his allegiance. This factor gives national origins its affinity with race; both are ineradicable characteristics, independent of personal choice, which frequently give rise to hostile stereotypes. Nationality, by contrast, is primarily a legal category, commonly – though less so in Britain than elsewhere – equivalent to citizenship, which may, with the approval of the authorities, be changed at a person's election. Indeed Mr Zesko, during the course of the litigation, chose to become a naturalised British subject and was immediately placed on the Council's waiting list, a fact that influenced the Lords' interpretation, since it demonstrated that his former nationality, not his ancestry, had been the basis of his exclusion.[13] In the absence of any clear indication elsewhere in the statute, 'national origins' was held not to include nationality, and the Council's requirement was therefore not lawful.

The *Ealing* decision occasioned substantial criticism from academic lawyers.[14] Yet however undesirable on policy grounds, as a matter of interpretation it seems unexceptionable. The majority gave the statutory language its national meaning, and did not obstruct any clear legislative intent; indeed its position accorded with that taken by Bob Hepple in his thorough analysis of discrimination in the employment of aliens.[15] It is particularly noteworthy that the United States Supreme Court, which with extraordinary liberality has construed the Equal Protection Clause of the Fourteenth Amendment to cover aliens as well as racial minorities, and thus voided numerous state laws barring aliens from public benefits and employment,[16] reached the identical result in a markedly similar case decided nearly two years later. In *Espinoza* v. *Farah Mfg Co.*[17] a Mexican citizen was denied employment by the company, whose labour force was overwhelmingly Mexican–American, i.e. American citizens of Mexican ancestry. She claimed this was discrimination on the basis of 'national origins', a term also used in the federal Civil Rights Act of 1964. All but one of the Justices rejected this argument, as well as the alternative contention that the 'citizens-only' hiring policy constituted indirect discrimination on this ground. In a brief judgment the Court interpreted the phrase to mean ancestry or extraction, not the legal category of citizenship. As in the *Ealing* judgments the question was treated as a straightforward exercise in linguistic analysis.

More important than its technical accuracy, however, was the potential for discrimination by pretext created by the *Ealing* case. An employer could argue that his refusal to hire a black immigrant applicant was due not to his race, but to his foreign allegiance; however implausible, the contention would have to be discredited with sufficient clarity to satisfy a court before the employer could be found to have acted unlawfully. More practically perhaps a local authority which restricted eligibility for council housing to

U.K. citizens or 'patrials' (see below) could have excluded most non-white families without breaking the law. Consequently when, with a slight change of style, the 1976 Act outlawed discrimination 'on racial grounds', the meaning of 'racial' was extended to include nationality as well as national origins,[18] and tucked away among the interpretation provisions is the elucidation that nationality includes citizenship.[19]

SOME QUESTIONS OF POLICY

Race, colour and ethnic and national origins are all ascribed characteristics; they are also quite clearly irrelevant bases of decision in the areas governed by the legislation. Nationality, by contrast, is much more a matter of personal choice; its irrelevance is also far less obvious. As a legal concept it is rooted in feudal allegiance;[20] sacrifices of comfort, property and even life are routinely demanded in its name. Prima facie it seems reasonable that such advantages as the state may provide be limited to those upon whom it may impose such burdens. The legal framework merely institutionalises the fact that national identity remains a uniquely powerful symbol of political allegiance, easily overcoming competitors such as class. This is particularly true of this island nation, whose self-consciousness, not to say insularity, has historically been one of its most striking characteristics. Furthermore, few discretionary powers are more jealously kept unbounded by all governments than those concerning the granting of citizenship and control over entry and expulsion of foreigners. Hence the 1976 extension requires scrutiny and invites a certain scepticism.

As might be expected, the prohibition is far more limited in the public and political spheres than in relation to private persons. Not only are the immigration laws left untouched; so are the restrictions on government employment of aliens (below, p. 153) and on their right to vote. These latter reservations would at first sight seem justified by the need for undivided allegiance among those who participate in public life. Yet British practice has long been unusually liberal in this respect, as a result of the exigencies of Empire and the influence of Commonwealth ties: citizens of the Irish Republic and of the New Commonwealth can vote in British elections, work in the Civil Service and hold the office of police constable, all of which are forbidden to aliens. Moreover, it may be argued that anyone living in a country for a considerable time is affected by community decisions and ought to be permitted to participate in them. This view gains force from the way the electoral system treats students, who are permitted to vote in their university constituencies, in which they may live little more than half the year.[21] Since the mid-1970s immigrant workers have had the vote in local elections in Sweden, with no apparent subversive result, and pressure to permit nationals of EEC countries to vote in member states where they reside may be expected to increase in the near future. In a world of multinational companies, large-scale labour mobility and developing regional economic integration, the justification for barriers against aliens in the public sphere must increasingly be called into question.[22]*

Apart from the exemption of discrimination authorised by statute or delegated legislation, the general applicability of the broadened race formula is subject to but two minor exceptions. The first permits discrimination on the basis of 'nationality, place of birth, or period of residence in a particular locality' in the selection of athletes to represent a country, place or area.[23] Thus a long-resident immigrant, indeed even one who acquires U.K. citizenship, may be excluded from a team representing any of the British nations in international competition. This exception seems unduly wide, since it gives far more leeway for discrimination than most sports authorities have sought to practice. Thus Bruce Rioch, born in Aldershot of Scottish parents settled in England, captained the Scottish side that qualified for the World Cup; the dependence of county cricket teams on West Indian and Asian players hardly needs documentation; and it was choice of employment, not nationality, that cost the South African Tony Greig the captaincy of English cricket. On the other hand, the exemption does preserve the legality of the Yorkshire County Cricket Club policy of refusing to play anyone not born in the county.

The other exemption makes a limited incursion into the broad proscription against discriminatory advertisements. In general the Act does not apply to employment or training for employment outside Great Britain (see below, pp. 141–2); nevertheless it is illegal to publish an advertisement indicating an intent to discriminate in recruitment for such employment.[24] Thus a South African firm could not advertise for white managers, nor the Saudi Arabian Government for non-Jewish technicians, even though a representative of those employers could refuse to interview such persons if he were recruiting in this country. However, it remains lawful to advertise for persons of particular nationality.[25] This exception seems reasonable in so far as it permits a foreign state or company to limit applications to their own nationals who may be resident here. It does, however, leave some scope for covert discrimination: a South African advertisement for 'United Kingdom nationals' would have the effect of making ineligible a large (though decreasing) proportion of non-whites settled in this country. It is as yet unknown whether this exception will be deliberately used in this fashion.

THE IMPACT OF U.K.
ENTRANCE INTO THE EEC

Quite independent of the change effected in 1976, discrimination on grounds of nationality is also forbidden by several provisions of the EEC Treaty, which upon our entrance in the European Communities became part of British municipal law, displacing any inconsistent Act of Parliament.[26]* In addition to a general prohibition against this form of discrimination (Art. 7) the Treaty also contains similar provisions regarding free movement of workers (Art. 48 ff.), freedom of establishment (i.e. self-employment in business – Art. 52 ff.) and freedom to provide services (Art. 59 ff.). This coexistence of the Act and the Treaty has created a situation of great complexity, due to the fact that, whilst they outlaw discrimination on the identical ground, their application, scope and methods of enforcement are all significantly different.

The Act in principle applies to all private individuals and associations, unless specifically exempted. The Treaty is much more limited. Whilst it has long been accepted that the provisions concerning free movement of workers applied to private employers,[27] Art. 59 has been given a narrower reading. Indeed it was first thought that Art. 59 applied only to public authorities, but in *Walrave and Koch*[28] the European Court of Justice held that it invalidated discriminatory rules made by private organisations. However, the Court did not embrace the views of the Advocate-General, who suggested that Art. 59 should reach discriminatory acts of private persons. Moreover, it appears that for Art. 59 to be invoked the discrimination must flow from some sort of collectively agreed formal rules, not merely from custom and practice. Neither of these significant restrictions is present in the Act. Although the point has not been authoritatively settled, it has been argued persuasively that in this respect Art. 52 should be read identically with Art. 59.[29]

The question of scope is even more confused. The Act has been carefully constructed to allow several delicately crafted exceptions; the Treaty merely states a simple prohibition. However, the scope of the Treaty is subject to a fundamental limitation, inherent in the nature of the European Communities: it is limited to 'economic activity'.[30] In principle this of course is far narrower than the Act, but it is unclear to what extent this term will be held to comprehend ancillary matters that may impinge upon employment and commercial matters. For example, discrimination in housing obviously makes it difficult for an immigrant to work in a foreign country. This is recognised by the principal Regulation governing free movement of workers, which provides for equal access to public and private housing.[31] There are doubtless other matters, not specifically covered by Regulations or Directives, in which discrimination would impinge upon the objectives of the Community or other rights created under its laws, thus bringing into play the Treaty prohibitions.

The question of who will interpret the anti-discrimination provisions of the Treaty cannot be answered with confidence. Under Art. 177 national courts and tribunals may refer questions of Community law to the European Court for a preliminary ruling.[32]* Precisely when they should do so remains unsettled. In one important case, *H. P. Bulmer Ltd* v. *J. Bollinger S.A.*,[33] the

Court of Appeal took a narrow view of the circumstances in which reference was required; Lord Denning M.R. enunciated a set of 'guidelines' whose restrictiveness has received substantial criticism.[34] Whilst his lead has been followed in several instances,[35] in others it has not;[36] it is safe to say that the judicial system has not yet reached a *modus vivendi* with Community law in this respect. The practical importance of the question lies in the likely divergence in the manner of interpretation. Although the English bodies and the European Court would both be interpreting the Treaty, the latter would not be guided by an English conception of precedent, but would instead adopt an interpretation directed above all at achieving the goals of the Community. It is possible that the contrasting approaches might affect the result in a particular case.

The different means by which Treaty rights and those created by the Act may be vindicated are considered in the general context of enforcement in Chapter 10.

The prohibitions of the Treaty against nationality discrimination of course only extend to nationals of EEC member states. Anyone else in Britain suffering discrimination on this ground must draw his rights and find his remedy in the Act alone. As the latter is wider in scope and application, this should not cause injustice. However, this may not be true in the other member states. There is, for example, no racial discrimination legislation in West Germany, whilst the French statute, which relies entirely on criminal penalties for its enforcement, has yet to be invoked.[37] Moreover, it uses the word *nation* in its list of prohibited grounds, which seems to be subject to the same ambiguity that emerged in the *Ealing* case: nationality discrimination may not be unlawful. In the absence of effective municipal legislation the Treaty is the only potential source of protection of people from Britain against this form of discrimination. Equally important is that the Treaty not merely prohibits various restrictions on economic activity, but is also a source of positive rights. Thus Regulations under it ensure that social security contributions in one member state entitle the contributor to equivalent benefits in another,[38] and that academic and professional qualifications are 'mutually recognised' throughout the Community.[39]

However, these protections and benefits are available only to those who are nationals of a member state, and in this context 'national' is a term of fine art. On joining the Community each state was permitted to denominate its nationals, and there was no requirement that the term be co-extensive with citizenship or similar status. Britain chose a restrictive definition. This may be found in a Declaration appended to the Treaty of Accession, and in essence limited the status of 'EEC national' to citizens of the United Kingdom and Colonies who have the right of abode in this country and are thus exempt from U.K. immigration control.[40*] (More precisely, they are 'United Kingdom nationals' for EEC purposes only; the term 'EEC national' is used here as a convenient shorthand.) This definition excludes most of the white Commonwealth citizens whose 'patriality' status under the Immigration Act 1971 underlined the deliberately racialist character of that legislation. Thus an Australian who is 'patrial' because one of his parents was a U.K. citizen born here[41] – and thus has an absolute 'right of abode', i.e. an unrestricted right to enter and remain in this country[42] is none the less not an EEC national because he is not a citizen of the United Kingdom and Colonies. On the other hand, the category would comprise the Kenya Asians – citizens of the United Kingdom and Colonies – who entered this country either before or despite the attempt of the Immigration Act 1968 to keep them out, and have been settled here for five years, since they automatically become patrial and hence have right of abode when that period expires.[43] Also included would be Commonwealth citizens or British protected persons who have been naturalised or registered as U.K. citizens and have thereby acquired the right of abode as well.[44] It will be seen that the status of EEC nationality is interwoven not only with the unholy tangle of immigration law, aptly called the most 'complicated body of rules in the whole of our constitutional law'[45] but also with citizenship law, which is almost equally daunting.[46] It is also clear – one of the few matters in this area is – that the definition of EEC national is neither as intentionally nor effectively racialist as the concept of patriality, since it includes categories of black persons and excludes classes of white whom the Immigration Act 1971 treats in precisely the opposite manner.

Nevertheless it was obvious at the time that the majority of non-white immigrants to this country were excluded from the benefits of this status, and since as recently as 1965 more than three-quarters of the non-whites in Britain were born elsewhere,[47] nearly all non-whites of working age were outside the definition. Since the Declaration was made in 1972 the picture has changed somewhat; the Kenya Asians who came to this country in the late 1960s have now been settled here for five years and thus acquired the right of abode. However, several important categories of people remain excluded. The greatest injustice arises with the Uganda Asians, whose moral claims and rights under international law to entrance into Britain were finally recognised, but who despite being otherwise stateless persons, are not *entitled* to U.K. citizenship by registration; they are merely eligible on the same footing as aliens for naturalisation after five years' residence here, and the decision is left entirely to the unreviewable discretion of the Home Office.[48] Second and numerically the largest are Commonwealth citizens settled in this country. Although s. 1 (2) of the Immigration Act 1971 granted them indefinite leave to remain and s. 1 (5) guaranteed that their freedom to come and go would remain unaffected, they none the less do not have the right of abode. This is because their ancestry makes them ineligible for patriality, and other provisions of that statute make plain that these guarantees fall short of freedom from immigration controls.[49] Citizens of Pakistan in a similar position are now technically a distinct category since the departure of that country from the Commonwealth has led to their becoming aliens.[50] Finally, there is a small group of persons affected by the retrospective operation of the removal provision of the 1971 Act.[51] Although an amnesty announced by the Home Office in April 1974 ensures that they cannot be removed from the country, they can probably never become eligible for consideration for U.K. citizenship – for them the key to the right of abode. This disability follows from the requirement that those applying for citizenship be 'ordinarily resident',[52]* a phrase which the Court of Appeal interpreted in 1971 as requiring lawful entry.[53]

Those excluded by the Declaration are not freely entitled to enter other Community member states to seek or take up work, to practise a profession (a matter of particular importance to the 10,000 New Commonwealth doctors practising here) or to establish a business, but are subject to whatever restrictions on aliens a particular country choses to impose. They may not even enter the other nations as readily on a holiday visit, and they are barred from employment within the Community administration, which allocates jobs by quotas based on nationality. More bizarre is the exclusion of children under 16 whose parents are not EEC nationals from the reciprocal arrangements for free or subsidised medical care available to a national who falls ill in another member state, even if the child was born in Britain and is therefore not only a U.K. citizen but patrial.[54]*

It is apparent that both the numbers and percentage of non-whites not qualifying as EEC nations will steadily diminish as a result of the acquisition of patriality by settled immigrants and normal population growth. None the less the proportion of non-whites barred by the terms of the Declaration will continue to exceed the proportion of whites so excluded, probably for decades to come.

The expansion of the race formula in the 1976 Act seems to have proceeded without sufficient awareness of its implications for rights within the EEC. Consider the case of an employer who refuses to hire a Jamaican national because the job, though based in Britain,[55] involves work in France, and his lack of EEC nationality would hamper his ability to work in that country. Although it could pedantically be argued that the denial of employment was due to the difficulties he would encounter at the hands of the French authorities, these are obviously so directly the result of his nationality (or more precisely, lack of the appropriate one) that the decision was taken on 'grounds' of the applicant's nationality. In addition, in this case the employer has made EEC nationality a 'requirement' for employment, one which a 'considerably smaller' proportion of blacks than whites could fulfil. His action would thus raise the issue of indirect discrimination (s. 1 (1)(b), considered in detail in Chapter 2. As will be seen (Chapter 12), an industrial tribunal would have the power to declare that the employer has acted unlawfully, recommend that the applicant be employed, and, in the case of direct discrimination, award damages.

Whether the employer would have a defence to the claim of direct discrimination[56] is a matter of nearly ineffable obscurity and complexity. The fact that he was merely following in his own Government's footsteps would not of itself give him any legal toehold. The only exemption in the Act which might avail him is that applying to acts done 'in pursuance of any enactment' (s. 41 (1)(a); above, p. 65). Whether he has acted 'in pursuance of' the Declaration is problematical. This phrase has only received judicial construction in the context of now-repealed statutes concerning limitation of actions, which imposed shorter periods where the defendant had acted 'in pursuance, or execution, or intended execution' of another Act of Parliament.[57] The leading cases[58] do not address the point explicitly, but seem to equate 'pursuance' with 'execution', which suggests the carrying out of duties imposed directly on the actor by the statute. If this view is correct the subsection would not assist the employer, who is merely paying heed to legal rules when taking a private decision. That his liability under the Act ultimately arises from government action which would almost certainly be unlawful were it not for its immunity from the Act is not an irony he can be expected to savour.

This point can hardly be regarded as settled, but is positively pellucid in comparison with the question whether the Declaration is an 'enactment'. As it is appended to the Accession Treaty one must consult the European Communities Act 1972, which states *inter alia* that the 'restrictions . . . created or arising by or under the Treaties . . . are without further enactment to be given legal effect or used in the United Kingdom.'[59] 'Treaties' are defined with unusual breadth to include not only the Accession Treaty itself, but any 'protocol or annex' thereto.[60] Any legal instrument thus described thereby becomes part of British law – an 'enactment'. It appears that the Declaration, which is unilateral, does not come within these categories. Cmnd 4862-1, the Official document setting out the legal instruments relating to United Kingdom membership in the EEC, contains the Act of Accession, eleven 'Annexes' and thirty 'Protocols' – all of which are specified in something called the 'Final Act', which presumably is not itself an annex. The last paragraph therein states: 'Finally the following declarations [including that defining United Kingdom nationals] have been made and are annexed to this Final Act.'[61] All this suggests – no stronger word is possible – that the Declaration is not itself a 'protocol or annex' to the Accession Treaty and therefore is not part of British municipal law.

There are further wrinkles which cannot be fully explored here. One writer has argued that the Declaration is unlawful as applied to persons like Uganda Asians, who have no other citizenship and legal right to reside elsewhere;[62] another urged that it is illegal under Community law.[63] The first point seems quite persuasive, though the manner in which a person in this situation could challenge the legality of the Declaration is far from clear. The second has been subject to withering criticism.[64] At one time there appeared to be scope for the view that Arts 48–51 – which of all the Treaty discrimination provisions affect the greatest number of persons – should not be tied to nationality, since they speak of 'workers', unlike Arts 52 and 59, which refer to 'nationals'. However, this view now seems unsustainable in light of the decision of the European Court in *Kermaschek*.[65] There the complainant, a Yugoslav national, claimed that her social security contributions in the Netherlands should have entitled her to unemployment benefit in West Germany, where she had gone to live with her German husband. The Court upheld the language of Reg. 1408/71, made under Art. 51, which restricts the transfer of social security rights to workers who are nationals of a member state.

Whatever the adjudication of all these questions may ultimately produce, the present position is wholly unsatisfactory. The basic problem is that the extension of the prohibited grounds of discrimination in the Act has been superimposed on the pre-existing conflict between the British Government's desire to control non-white immigration and its duty to give effect to EEC rules on freedom of movement. Consequently the precise legal rights and duties of employers, prospective workers and officials are dependent on legal questions of a spectacular arcaneness, closely resembling a series of Chinese puzzles. The only straightforward and definite way out of the labyrinth is for Britain to include within the definition of 'United Kingdom national' all persons with indefinite leave to remain here, which would embrace virtually all Commonwealth immigrants. There seems no defensible reason to deny people who are permanently part of British society, and enjoy protection against discrimination on nationality grounds under British law, the wide range of benefits of the nation's membership in the EEC. Indeed Professor K. R. Simmonds, who drew attention to some of these problems at the time of British accession, wrote that 'there is evidence that earlier the Commission would have accepted *all* Commonwealth immigrants not subject to immigration controls as "United Kingdom nationals" for this purpose'.[66] He did not elaborate, but in an analogous situation the Council of Ministers offered in 1968 to extend the free movement provisions to Surinam and the Netherlands Antilles, which for domestic reasons was rejected by those territories.[67]

No justification for the restrictiveness of the definition was offered by the Government; indeed when the matter was discussed in Parliament, the then Home Secretary betrayed no understanding of the questions on this score raised by members of both parties.[68] The only plausible defence is based on the idea of reciprocity: French citizens have no treaty rights in India, so why should the reverse be true?[69] This ignores the unique complexity of British citizenship law, which creates categories of persons, such as the Uganda Asians, who possess U.K. passports and are otherwise stateless, but are denied full civic rights such as freedom from immigration controls. It also passes over the fact that, Holland apart, Britain alone among the Nine has a large number of non-white immigrants who arrived with civic and political rights and have become an unseverable part of the national community. This legacy from the Imperial past cannot responsibly be brushed aside, however convenient some may now find it to do so.

RACE AND COLOUR

Neither of these words has yet required judicial elucidation. Indeed one would have thought their meaning identical, a view taken by the draftsmen of the United Nations Universal Declaration on Human Rights.[70] Yet in two places the Act draws a distinction between them. A charitable instrument may restrict benefits to persons defined by reference to any of the grounds within the race formula except colour,[71] and an exception to the proscription of discrimination in admission to clubs permits an association whose main object is to cater for 'persons of a particular racial group defined otherwise than by reference to colour' to discriminate in its selection of members except on the basis of colour.[72]

The notion that it is permissible to discriminate on grounds of race but not colour sounds peculiar if not indeed coherent. The only way in which the distinction makes any sense is when one recalls the linguistic usage of an earlier era, exemplified by Viscount Dilhorne's description of Mr Zesko as being 'of the Polish race'.[73] The intended meaning is what might more appropriately have been called 'ethnic group' – Scottish, Polish, West Indian and so forth – rather than whites as against blacks, or vice versa. Thus the Indian Workers' Association need not admit English or Pakistani applicants, and a bequest to establish an old people's home for Jews may still be given legal effect. It remains impermissible to establish a scholarship fund for whites only – in this context which is not a 'race' but a 'colour'.

ETHNIC ORIGINS

This term also has yet to receive judicial consideration. Lester and Bindman describe it as an anthropological term devised as an alternative to 'race' to avoid any connotation of innate biological differences among human population groups.[74] If this were its only meaning, its inclusion would scarcely be necessary, since the Act was drafted and will be interpreted by lawyers, not anthropologists, who may be expected to give everyday words their meaning in common speech. Of greater practical importance is another use of the term, more common in North America than in Britain but frequently used by sociological writers here. In this sense it means the ancestry, not of an individual, but of his forebears; by extension, it refers to any socially distinct minority group. Thus the children of Polish post-war refugees are British nationals, and their nationality received at birth – their national origin – is also British, but their ethnic origin is Polish. The use of this term has evolved in a different social context, in which descendants of white immigrants retain some sense of separate identity and are regarded as in some ways distinct from the majority, which thus far has not occurred in Britain. None the less the possibility remains: while British-born people of Polish ancestry seem to consider themselves entirely British, and to be so considered, the same may not be true of, for example, the children of Cypriot immigrants.

Indeed this is particularly likely to occur among the descendants of some Asian immigrants, whose social distinctness from the majority may be as much a function of culture as of colour. Differences in language, diet, communal symbolic loyalties and dress would all be expressions of personal identity, proceeding from an individual's ethnic origins, and adverse treatment owing to dislike of such behaviour would at the least constitute indirect discrimination. This broad interpretation appears also to have been intended by the Government. The White Paper mentioned prohibitions on the wearing of turbans as one example of a policy that might be caught under the indirect discrimination provision.[75] Obviously this would primarily, if not solely, affect Sikhs, whose separate identity originally emerged in the form of religion, a ground which, as will be seen, is deliberately excluded from the Act. None the less it is submitted that Sikhs, like Jews (below, pp. 78–9), are perceived as a distinct cultural group, rather than one whose adherents subscribe to a particular theology, and are therefore properly regarded as a distinct ethnic group. Without discussing the point, the Scottish EAT accepted that it had jurisdiction to consider the claim of discrimination presented by a Sikh who had been denied employment for refusal to shave his beard.[76]

Moreover, the term 'ethnic' alone among the prescribed grounds will plausibly encompass gipsies. Although in some legal contexts 'gipsy' has been interpreted to include any itinerant[77] the severe hostility encountered by the travelling people who are widely believed to be descendants of Romany immigrants from eastern Europe – whatever may be the facts of any specific traveller's genealogy – is akin to the most unpleasant forms of racial prejudice and discrimination. Since most are native-born, and descended from several generations of persons born here, 'national origins', particularly as that term has been understood in the various judgments in the *Ealing* case, would not seem to fit them. Although the particular disadvantages facing gipsies cannot be discussed in this book, it may be pointed out that particularly in regard to local-authority services they suffer serious and well-documented discrimination.[78]

In terms of numbers and immediate relevance, however, the most important application of the ethnic category is in relation to Jews. All three Acts have steadfastly refused to include religion among the prescribed grounds, for reasons less than convincing. In 1968 the Government may have felt that the inclusion of religion would have increased the pressure for application of the Act to Northern Ireland, which is opposed;[79] however this justification, if such it be, was absent in 1976 when Parliament was simultaneously outlawing discrimination in employment on this precise ground – for Northern Ireland alone.[80] The issue was the subject of a long debate in the Standing Committee to which the Bill was remitted after Second Reading.[81] Several Members spoke in favour of including religion among the prescribed grounds, a position rejected by the Minister of State, Brynmor John. Among his objections were that there had been no consultation with affected bodies; that exceptions, e.g. for religious education, would have to be carefully drafted; and that there would be serious problems of definition, particularly in respect of various Christian denominations. These points all seem valid, but could be satisfied by thoughtful draftsmanship. However, his two main arguments were, first, that the new concept of indirect discrimination would cover much religious discrimination, and second, that it was largely unnecessary in view of the progress made through voluntary changes in matters such as the wearing of turbans, and the diminution of historic discrimination against Jews.

The first contention is almost certainly mistaken. It need only be pointed out that the race formula applies identically to both forms of discrimination; even though indirect discrimination has a broader meaning and reaches previously unregulated practices and policies, it still only applies on the 'grounds' specified. Thus, for example, the refusal to hire a Muslim because the existing Hindu workforce would object is a clear case of deliberate religious discrimination. It is certainly a strained reading of the statute to view this as indirect discrimination on grounds of national origins, even if the victim were a Pakistani, since not all his fellow countrymen are Muslims and, in common with all immigrant minorities, an increasing proportion of Muslims are British-born or have acquired U.K. citizenship.

The second point is more problematic. Even as the Minister spoke, the influence of world politics was increasingly impinging upon employment practices in this country. After the rise in oil prices following the Middle-East war in October 1973, Saudi Arabia and other Arab oil-producing nations became dramatically more important customers of Western firms. Saudi Arabia has long barred Jews from its territory, and it and some other states made clear that regardless of any individual's political sympathies, it did not wish to do business with Jewish-owned companies or with companies that employed Jews in prominent positions. No systematic research has been done on the impact of this policy on the employment of Jews by British firms; what follows derives from a discussion with Dr J. Gewirtz of the Board of Deputies of British Jews.[82]

Dr Gewirtz, who handles all complaints of discrimination received by the Board of Deputies, reported that employment discrimination against Jews was virtually unknown before international pressures began to be felt. He added that there is also scant discrimination in matters like admission to membership of private clubs. He noted that, unlike the situation of most non-whites, this form of discrimination involves professional people, often in high-level managerial positions. He had received 'about a dozen' complaints in three years, the small number being due to the fact – not unique to Jews – that 'people don't want to complain', as well as 'a widespread belief that the law does not cover Jews'. Most of the complaints involved hiring, although a few concerned dismissals. In his view substantially greater numbers of people had suffered discrimination of this kind than were personally known to him.

Thus, although the seriousness of the problem cannot be fully gauged, it certainly exists, and the Minister's comments begin to sound somewhat complacent. The exclusion of 'religion' from the statute raises the question whether the present law is competent to control discrimination of this type. The better view is that it is. Parliament was informed by the Home Secretary in 1965, during the debate on the first Act, that Jews would enjoy its protection, and according to Maurice Orbach MP, by 1968 leaders of Jewish organisations had repeatedly been reassured on this point by subsequent Home Secretaries.[83] The Race Relations Board took the same view;[84*] in addition, at least one criminal prosecution for incitement to racial hatred – which uses the same race formula as the anti-discrimination provisions – has included a charge of distributing anti-Semitic stickers.[85] The statutory category into which Jews most readily fit is that of 'ethnic origins' and it would seem well-established that the absence of mention of religion does not place them outside the Act. It does mean, however, that the exclusion of Jews from an institution, such as an Anglican school, with a particular doctrinal character, is not unlawful.[86*]

Thus the present position is that adverse treatment of members of a socially distinct minority whose distinctiveness includes religion constitues unlawful discrimination on grounds of ethnic origin. However, the statute does not apply either where the victim's religion as such is the cause of the discrimination – as in the barring of a Roman Catholic of English ancestry from an élite club, or in the Hindu–Muslim example mentioned earlier – or where the exclusion follows from the sectarian character of the institution.

There is a further dimension to religion discrimination which was not perceived when the Act was debated, but which has subsequently found its way to the courts in a variety of guises. This concerns whether a person whose devotional practices put him in some conflict with established arrangements – which reflect the habits of the majority – may require the authorities to accommodate his particular needs. The most prominent example is the judgment of a divided Court of Appeal in *Ahmad* v. *ILEA*,[87] which rejected a claim by a devout Muslim schoolteacher that he should have been permitted time off at full pay during school hours to attend services at a nearby mosque, as he believed his faith required him to do. He relied both on s. 30 of the Education Act 1944, forbidding disqualification or discrimination against teachers for their religious views, and upon Article 9 of the European Convention of Human Rights, guaranteeing freedom to 'manifest' one's religion or beliefs – subject, as with all the rights in the European Convention, to limitations necessary to safeguard public order, health, morals and the rights of others. Although, as has been seen, (above p. 66 and n. 5) English courts will attempt to construe Parliamentary enactments to avoid conflict with the Convention, only Scarman L.J. (now Lord Scarman) was persuaded that Art. 9 should be used as an aid to construction of s. 30 so as to conclude that Mr Ahmad's dismissal was unfair. A claim by a Chassidic Jew, who informed the authorities after the date for a public inquiry had been set but three weeks before it was to take place, that he religious beliefs prevented her attendance on the day, that Art. 9 required that she be permitted to participate on an alternate day, was similarly rejected.[88] By contrast the statutory concept of 'genuine objection on grounds of religious belief' which makes unfair the otherwise lawful dismissal of an employee who refuses to join a trade union where a closed shop exists[89] has been construed with notable liberality by the EAT.[90] Behaviour based upon religious belief has also brought adherents of minority faiths into conflicts with the criminal law.[91]

These claims raise quite different and far more difficult questions of balancing competing policies than the relatively straightforward issue of prohibiting bars to employment or access to housing services and goods which affect minority groups with distinctive religions. Even if, unlike Lord Denning in *Ahmad*,[92] one regards them as attempts to achieve practical recognition of religious diversity rather than attempts to secure 'preferential treatment', one cannot treat them as absolute entitlements, only as factors to be weighed more heavily than has hitherto been the case. Moreover, ultimately the judgment of the relative weight to be given to the competing considerations must be made by a tribunal or court whose sympathy for pluralism may be blunted. An excellent example is the response of the American Supreme Court to an amendment to the Civil Rights Act requiring employers to make 'responsible accommodation, short of undue hardship, for the religious practices' of their employees. In *T.W.A.* v. *Hardison*,[93] the Court upheld the dismissal of a Saturday Sabbatarian whose relative lack of seniority made straightforward swapping with other employees impossible. The unusually angry dissent of Brennan J.[94] shows graphically that what is perceived to be undue hardship is not simply a matter of bureaucratic rationality, but ultimately of the value the decision-maker places on respect for minority rights. Thus even if, following the universal practice in Canadian and American jurisdictions, religion were added to the present grounds of discrimination, the response to the more difficult claims made in its name would remain problematic.

These then are the main problems surrounding the interpretation of the race formula. Three subsidiary points may be made. First, it is unnecessary to enter into prolonged analysis of whether Jews or gipsies are 'really' an ethnic group, or whether Indians are actually of a different 'race'. The law is concerned with preventing persons who are members of identifiable minority social groups from suffering disabilities because of that membership. It is irrelevant that, even in cases of intentional discrimination, the discriminator may not dislike the group for reasons conforming to traditional stereotypes. For example, the Saudis' attitude towards British Jews is not motivated by religious animosity or a dislike of their supposed attitudes toward money, or for that matter education. It is purely political, being based on the view – hardly wholly irrational – that Jews are likely to be sympathetic to Israel. It is objectionable, however, not merely because a specific Jew may in fact be strongly anti-Israel, or anti-Zionist, but because the effects of their animosity do not extend to anyone who takes that particular political position, only to those identifiable by a distinctive social characteristic – in this case ethnic origins. Potentially at least they may be isolated from the rest of the community and become objects of execration. It is the attempt to divide people along these lines that the law forbids. Ironically, this point is best illustrated by a recent case in which a man who sought employment as a chauffeur was turned away by the employer, a Jew and active Zionist, when he revealed that his father was Arab. The respondent's claim that his motive was political and based on fears for his safety was rejected, since no effort was made to learn anything of the beliefs and affiliations of the applicant, whose mother was English and who was born and raised in this country.[95]

Second, a point already briefly mentioned, the term 'grounds' should be read to include any characteristic or legal status inherent in or a direct product of an individual's race, colour, etc. Thus, to take what one would have supposed to be a fanciful example, refusal to hire someone who spoke with a foreign accent (as distinct from inability to speak English adequately) would constitute discrimination on grounds of national origins.[96]*

Finally, the phrase is not limited to discrimination suffered because of one's own characteristics, but also comprehends unfavourable treatment received by one's spouse, companions, business associates and so forth. Rather surprisingly it took a decade for this point to be squarely presented for adjudication, and in *Wilson* v. *T.B. Steelworks Co. Ltd*,[97] a white woman denied employment because of her marriage to a black man succeeded in her claim of racial discrimination. The Industrial Tribunal, following dicta of Lord Simon of Glaisdale,[98] had no difficulty in concluding that this was discrimination 'on racial grounds'. Not long thereafter the EAT, clearly disturbed that the 'unfortunate and righteous complainant' would otherwise be unprotected, held that a barmaid allegedly dismissed for disobeying instructions that she turn away black customers could seek redress under the Act.[99] The broad prohibition of discrimination 'on racial grounds' expressed in s. 1 was held to override 'all apparent limitations expressed in other sections which had the effect of denying justice to someone who was victimised'.[100] Thus if unfavourable treatment is connected to any element in the race formula it is unlawful; and the range of protected persons is to be generously understood.

NOTES

*1. In the United States, for example, there must be 'state action' before a person may invoke federal constitutional rights; the determination of what this comprises has generated an enormous body of case law. Even more restricted is the Canadian Bill of Rights, which applies only to matters concerning the legislative authority of the Parliament of Canada (s. 5 (3)).

2. This phrase is taken from Dickey, 'The Race Formula of the Race Relations Acts' [1974], *Jurid. Rev.* 282.

3. Art. 14. The current version of the Convention and its subsequent protocols may be found in F. Jacobs, *The European Convention on Human Rights* (Clarendon Press, 1975), which also provides detailed commentary on each Article.

4. The most influential voice has been that of Lord (then Lord Justice) Scarman in *English Law – the New Dimension* (Stevens, 1974).

*5. Although in international law the European Convention is binding on the United Kingdom, it is not part of British municipal, i.e. domestic, law, because it has not been enacted as such by Parliament. However, the courts will often attempt to construe statutes so as to avoid conflict with the Convention, as in *Waddington* v. *Miah*, [1974] 1 W.L.R. 683 (H.L.), and *R.* v. *Home Secretary, ex p. Bhajan Singh*, [1976] Q.B. 198, although Lord Denning subsequently disparaged it as containing 'wide general statements of principle . . . [which] are not the sort of thing we can easily digest'. *R.* v. *Chief Immigration Officer, Heathrow, ex p. Salamat Bibi*, [1976] 3 All E.R. 843, 847.

A number of European nations, including West Germany, Holland and Italy, have incorporated the Convention into their municipal law.

*6. The advocates of British adoption of the Convention such as Lord Scarman and Professor Michael Zander (*A Bill of Rights* (Barry Rose, 1976)) omit it entirely, and the Home Office discussion document, *Legislation on Human Rights* (1976) gives it a passing mention in one sentence in para. 3.23.

7. Age Discrimination in Employment Act of 1967.

8. These examples are taken from Hunter, 'Civil Actions for Discrimination', (1977) 40 *Can. B. Rev.* 106, 106 n. 2.

9. British Nationality Act 1948, s. 1 as amended.

10. [1971] 1 Q.B. 309 (Swanwick J.).

11. [1972] A.C. 342, [1972] 1 All E.R. 105. The dissenter was Lord Kilbrandon.

12. [1972] 1 All E.R. at 108.

13. [1972] 1 All E.R. at 108 (Lord Donovan), at 112 (Viscount Dilhorne), and at 118 (Lord Cross of Chelsea). Despite the change in Mr Zesko's status, the legal question remained important to him, since the Lords' judgment meant that his place in the housing queue would be determined by the date he was naturalised, not when he applied for accommodation.

14. Notably by Hucker, 'The House of Lords and the Race Relations Act' (1975) 24 *I.C.L.Q.* 284. See also J. Griffith, *The Politics of the Judiciary* (Fontana, 1977) pp. 87–8.

15. *Hepple*, pp. 48–59.

16. See especially *Graham* v. *Richardson*, 403 U.S. 365 (1971) (state welfare benefits); *In re Griffiths*, 413 U.S. 717 (1973) (admission to state Bar); *Sugarman* v. *Dougall*, 413 U.S. 634 (1973) (employment in competitive class of state civil service). A sharply divided court has, however, refused to upset alienage bars to the employment of state police, *Foley* v. *Connellie*, 435 U.S. 291 (1978), and teachers, *Ambach* v. *Nowick*, 60 L. Ed. 2d 49 (1979).

17. 414 U.S. 86 (1973).

18. S. 3 (1).

19. S. 78 (1).

20. *de Smith*, p. 419.

21. *Fox* v. *Stirk*, [1970] 2 Q.B. 463.

*22. The limitation of the present study to employment prevents discussion of nationality discrimination in provision of public benefits, of which the most controversial present examples are the admission quotas and higher fees for overseas students in further and higher education. These are lawful under s. 41 (2) (above, p. 65) and D.E.S. Circular 8/77.

23. S. 39.

24. S. 29 (1).

25. S. 29 (3).

*26. The supremacy of Community law, forcefully enunciated in the early 1960s in cases such as *Costa* v. *ENEL*, (1964) C.M.L.R. 425, has if anything been asserted more boldly in the recent European Court judgment in *Amministrazione delle Finanze dello Stato* v. *Simmenthal (No. 2)*, (1978) 3 C.M.L.R. 263. The impact of British accession to the EEC upon the doctrine of parliamentary sovereignty has been one of the most popular bones for scholarly gnawing. See *de Smith*, pp. 45–6, 79–82; *W. & P/B.*, pp. 112–14, 126–30, and articles cited in both works.

27. This seems clear from the main implementing provision, Reg. 1612/68, which in many particulars affects private employers.

28. [1974] E.C.R. 1405.

29. Leleux, 'Recent Decisions of the Court of Justice . . .', in F. Jacobs (ed.) *European Law and the Individual* (North-Holland, 1976) pp. 82–3. (This book is hereafter cited as *Jacobs*.)

30. The phrase in Art. 2 of the EEC Treaty. The judgment in *Walrave and Koch*, above, states clearly that activities which cannot be so classified are not affected by Community law.

31. Reg. 1612/68, Art. 9.

*32. A court or tribunal 'against whose decisions there is no judicial remedy under national law' *must* make such a reference. It is as yet unclear whether any British court or tribunal besides the House of Lords falls under this description.

33. [1974] Ch. 401.

34. [1974] Ch. at 422–5. See the comments of Jacobs, 'When to Refer to the European Court', (1974) 90 *L.Q.R.* 486, and Freeman, 'References to the Court of Justice under Article 177', (1975) 28 *C.L.P.* 176.

35. Notably *Schorsch Meier* v. *Hennin*, [1975] Q.B. 416, *R.* v. *Secchi*, [1975] 1 C.M.L.R. 383, *Re a Holiday in Italy*, (1975) C.M.L.R. 184, and *Kenny* v. *Insurance Officer*, [1978] C.M.L.R. 233.

36. As in *Lowenbrau* v. *Grunhalle Lager*, [1974] 1 C.M.L.R. 1, and *Van Duyn* v. *Home Office*, [1974] 1 W.L.R. 1107.

37. Loi no. 72–546 of 1 July 1972, found in the *Code Penal*, Arts 187–1 and 416. Its quiescence is reported by Aaron, in F. Schmidt (ed.) *Discrimination in Employment* (Stockholm, 1978) p. 59.

38. Regs 1408/71 and 574/72, made pursuant to Art. 51.

39. This is being accomplished by Directives pursuant to Art. 57. See further Wagenbaur, 'The Mutual Recognition of Qualifications in the EEC', chap. 6 of *Jacobs*.

*40 Cmnd 4862–I (1972) p. 118. Two groups for whom special provision was made were Gibraltarians, who are nationals for this purpose though they are not patrials, and Manxmen and Channel Islanders, who at their governments' request were excluded, despite being patrial.

41. Imm. Act 1971, s. 2 (1)(d).

42. Imm. Act 1971, ss. 1 (1), 2 (6).

43. Imm. Act 1971, s. 2 (1)(c).

44. On naturalisation of British protected persons see n. 48 below. Commonwealth citizens acquire U.K. citizenship by registration. In the case of non-patrial applicants the decision is entirely discretionary, and the conditions (and consequent EEC status) closely resemble those discussed in n. 48.

45. *de Smith* p. 425.

46. See, further, *de Smith*, pp. 419–26, and J. Evans, *Immigration Law* (Sweet & Maxwell, 1976) pp. 20–4 (hereafter *Evans*).

47. White Paper, *Racial Discrimination*, Cmnd 6234 (1975) para. 4.

*48. Under s. 2 (1) of the Uganda Independence Act 1962 the Uganda Asians were British protected persons, unlike the Kenya Asians, who were citizens of the United Kingdom and Colonies. They accordingly acquire citizenship by naturalisation, which requires residence in the United Kingdom and Colonies for four of the seven years preceding application. The new citizen gains the right of abode by being settled and ordinarily resident in this country for five years. No Uganda Asian refugee could therefore have become an EEC national until mid-1977. The rate at which they achieve this status will of course depend entirely upon the willingness of the Home Office to grant them citizenship. The varying conditions for nationalisation and registration are carefully set out in *de Smith*, pp. 421–2, esp. nn. 12 and 13.

49. See further, *Evans*, p. 48, discussing Imm. Act 1971, s. 3 (4) and (8).

50. The consequences of this change are discussed in ibid. p. 24.

51. Brought about by the House of Lords' decision in *Azam* v. *Sec. of State for Home Department*, [1974] A.C. 18.

*52. Non-patrial Commonwealth citizens can acquire U.K. citizenship only by discretionary registration. (See British Nationality Act 1948, s. 5 (A), incorporating Imm. Act 1971, sched. I, app. A.) S. 5 (A) (3) requires that the applicant have been 'ordinarily resident' for five years before he can be considered.

53. *Re Abdul Manan*, [1971] 2 All E.R. 1016.

*54. According to a letter from the DHSS to the author, this exclusion follows from the fact that the EEC Regulations governing social security entitlement for persons moving within the Nine are made under Art. 51 and are limited to workers who are nationals of a member state and their dependants. (This limitation was upheld in an analogous context by the Court of Justice in *Kermaschek*, [1976] E.C.R. 1969.) Since children are not workers then citizenship is irrelevant, and their exclusion follows from the status of their parents.

55. Thus his employment is not 'wholly or mainly outside Great Britain', which would put it outside the Act (s. 8 (1): see below, pp. 141–2).

56. I pass over the claim of indirect discrimination, in which the employer would have the opportunity to show that his requirement was 'justifiable', a term examined in detail in Chapter 2.

57. Limitation Act 1938, s. 21, and its predecessor, Public Authorities Protection Act 1893, s. 1.

58. *Bradford Corpn* v. *Myers*, [1916] A.C. 242, and *Turburville* v. *West Ham Corpn*, [1950] 2 All E.R. 54 (C.A.).

59. European Communities Act 1972, s. 2 (1)

60. Ibid. 1972, s. 1 (2)(a) and 1 (4).

61. Cmnd 4862–I (1972) p. 114.

62. *Evans*, p. 82.

63. See Bohning, 'The Scope of the EEC System of Free Movement of Workers: A Rejoinder', (1973) 10 *C.M.L. Rev.* 81

64. By Hartley, 'Provisions Concerning Free Movement of Workers', in *Jacobs*, pp. 26, 32.

65. [1976] E.C.R. 1669.

66. K. R. Simmonds, 'Immigration Control and the Free Movement of Labour: A Problem of Harmonisation', (1972) 21 *I.C.L.Q.* 307, 316.

67. Hartley, above n. 64, pp. 21–2. See further W. Bohning, *The Migration of Workers in the United Kingdom and the European Community* (O.U.P., 1972), pp. 130–136.

68. H. C. Deb. 16 June 1971, vol. 819 cols 576–86.

69. Hartley, above n. 64 *passim*.

70. See the discussion by Mbadinuju in [1977] *Pub. Law* 1, 8.

71. S. 34 (1).

72. S. 26.

73. In the *Ealing* case, above n. 11, [1972] 1 All E.R. at 112.

74. *Lester and Bindman*, pp. 154–5.

75. Cmnd 6234, para. 55.

76. *Singh* v. *Rowntree MacKintosh Ltd*, [1979] I.C.R. 554. A London Industrial Tribunal in an unreported decision cited in this judgment similarly accepted jurisdiction in a case raising the identical issue.

77. As in *Mills* v. *Cooper*, [1967] 2 Q.B. 459, construing the word as it appeared in the Highways Act 1959.

78. See the discussion in the paper issued by the Ministry of Housing and Local Government, *Gipsies and Other Travellers*, (H.M.S.O., 1967).

79. *Lester and Bindman*, p. 115 n. 4.

80. Fair Employment (Northern Ireland) Act 1976.

81. Official Report, Standing Comm. A, 29 April 1976, cols 84–92, and 4 May, cols 93–118.

82. Interview of 14 December 1977, London.

83. Both these statements are quoted in *Lester and Bindman*, p. 156.

*84. In a number of cases conciliation officers of the Board acted upon complaints of discrimination by Jews, and secured some form of redress for the victim. As it happens none of these cases was publicly reported, or reached the courts.

85. This was a successful prosecution of Colin Jordan, the Fascist leader, which included charges of distributing anti-black literature. It is described in *Lester and Bindman*, p. 368.

*86. In two cases described in the *Annual Report of the Race Relations Board* for 1970–1 (para. 19) Jewish parents complained that their children had been refused admission to fee-paying schools because of their ethnic origins. However, both schools did not reject all Jews, but maintained a quota system in order to preserve their 'Christian character'. One school was established by its charter as an Anglican foundation; in their application to the other the parents had described their religious denomination as 'Jewish'. The Board concluded that the exclusions were on religious rather than ethnic grounds, and outside the scope of the statute; nothing in the present Act would overturn this conclusion.

87. [1977] 3 W.L.R. 396

88. *Ostreicher* v. *Sec. of State for the Environment*, [1978] 3 All E.R. 82 (C.A.). See also the similar decision of the European Court in *Prais* v. *European Commission*, [1976] E.C.R. 1589.

89. EPCA, s. 58 (3).

90. Particularly in the litigation between Mr Saggers, a Jehovah's Witness (a sect which does not forbid trade union membership), and British Rail: *Saggers* v. *Brit. Railways Board (No. 1)*, [1977] I.R.L.R. 266, and *No. 2*, [1978] I.R.L.R. 435.

91. See the cases cited in Robillard, 'Should Parliament Enact a Religious Discrimination Act?, [1978] *Pub. L.* 379, 386–7. This article is valuable for its general review of the questions canvassed in this section of the present chapter.

92. [1977] 3 W.L.R. at 400.

93. 432 U.S. 63 (1977).

94. 432 U.S. at 85–97.

95. *Commis* v. *Heron Corpn*, decision of London Central Tribunal, COIT 912/249, 20 July 1979.

*96. In an unreported decision, *Bowen* v. *Motorcycle City (Sales) Ltd*, discussed in IDS Brief 159, p. 9 (June 1979), the complainant alleged he was denied employment because of his Australian accent! A Southampton tribunal found against him on the facts but went on to opine that even if true, discrimination on this basis would not come within the Act. For reasons stated in the text, it is submitted that these dicta were incorrect.

97. Decision of a Birmingham Tribunal, 18 January 1978, COIT 706/44.

98. *Race Relations Board* v. *Applin*, [1975] A.C. 259, [1974] 2 All E.R. 73, 92.

99. *Zarczynska* v. *Levy*, [1979] I.C.R. 184.

100. Idem at 189.

4
Victimisation

Two serious impediments to the enforcement of anti-discrimination laws have been the reluctance of victims to complain and the difficulties of producing evidence to substantiate claims of discrimination. Some of the sources of these obstacles cannot be affected by changes in the law: if victims are embarrassed, unwilling to relive the humiliation of an unpleasant experience in a judicial setting, or distrustful of receiving redress from 'white' institutions, there seems little that can be done. But one less emotional obstacle can be attacked: the fear, often well-founded, that complaining, or assisting someone else who complains, will bring retribution from one's employer or prospective employer.[1] In the history of trade union organisation the blacklisting of activists or sacking of those who sought to join a union were commonplace, and legislation now gives partial protection to trade unionists encountering this form of hostility.[2] No similar provision was present in the 1968 Act, and thus the Race Relations Board found itself helpless to assist an employment agency interviewer who was dismissed for providing the information enabling it to obtain a settlement on behalf of a victim of discrimination.[3] Partly in response to its representations, this lacuna is now filled by s. 2, which proscribes less favourable treatment 'by reasons that the person victimised' has brought proceedings, given evidence, made allegations of discrimination, or, in the sweeping language of s. 2 (1)(c), has 'otherwise done anything under or by reference to this Act'. The section applies even though the allegation, etc., was directed at a third person, i.e. not against the employer imposing the less favourable treatment. This is important, for it is tailored to the reality that a person who has complained of discrimination, or has assisted a complainant, is likely to be thought of as a 'troublemaker' by other employers: anyone who converts this thought into action now acts illegally. S. 2 also covers what might be called the pre-emptive strike: less favourable treatment 'by reason that the discriminator knows that the person victimised *intends* to do' (any of the acts enumerated above) or 'suspects' that he has done or will do them, is also unlawful.[4]

The prohibition of victimisation was deliberately drafted very broadly, and the Government vigorously resisted attempts to weaken it.[5] Its view was that the vexatious litigant, despite his popularity in legal folklore, is of far less social importance than the reluctance of people to put their jobs in jeopardy. Only one defence is explicitly permitted: if the less favourable treatment follows upon a false allegation not made in good faith, the section does not apply.[6] Indeed the breadth of the sections seems not to have been fully appreciated. In *Zarcyznska* v. *Levy*[7] the EAT held that a barmaid dismissed for refusing to follow her employer's instructions not to serve blacks had been dicriminated against 'on racial grounds'. Although the Appeal Tribunal's concern not to deny redress for the complaint is admirable, the same result could have been reached with far less analytical difficulty by reliance upon s. 2 (1)(c); indeed the word 'victimisation' was used in the judgment but only as a term of common speech, without appreciation that it carried legal implications.

However, because the section is awkwardly drafted, a second defence may be available. Contrary to what one might have expected, victimisation is not defined as *unfavourable* treatment in consequence of protected activities, only as *less* favourable treatment than would be meted out to others in similar circumstances. On a literal reading, an employee who complained to the CRE instead of first going through the company's complaints machinery could be disciplined or denied benefits or opportunities without violation of s. 2 – so long as the employer insists without exception upon the paramountcy of the internal procedures. Thus if similar sanctions were, or would be, imposed on others who complained to outside bodies, for example the Health and Safety Commission, the element of comparison that now seems to be required could not be made out. This result seems contrary to what was intended, but legislative amendment will be required to express that intention more faithfully.

One commentator has doubted whether even the present provision will be of much value in protecting complainants and those who assist them, because of the difficulties of proof.[8] One step not taken was that of reversing the burden of proof, a question to be discussed in greater detail in Chapter 11. Although normally in civil litigation the complainant must prove on balance pf probabilities the facts he alleges, where a person claims that he has been victimised by reason of membership in or activities on behalf of a trade union, the employer must prove that this is not so by demonstrating the true reason for the adverse treatment.[9] Since the evil is identical in both situations, and the normal burden of proof was reversed for the trade unionist precisely because of the difficulties of proof,[10] it is difficult to see why the same rule should not apply in the context of discrimination. If the complainant's case proves utterly without merit – vexatious or frivolous – the tribunal can deviate from normal practice and award costs against him – a sanction which, though rare, has been imposed in a number of instances.[11]

It is possible, however, that the difficulties of proof have been overstated.

There is a close parallel to the victimisation provision in the American statute,[12] and in a fair number of reported cases complainants have been able to vindicate their rights. For example,[13] a complainant contended she was sacked for refusing to falsify the test score of a black applicant, whilst the employer claimed that her inability to get on with her supervisors and subordinates was the true reason. The court, basing its conclusion on 'reasonable inferences drawn from the totality of facts ... and the entire web of circumstances presented ... in the record',[14] accepted her account. Not only did the defendant's affidavits contain serious inconsistencies, but the plaintiff's promotion and receipt of a bonus some months earlier, a good supervisor's report, and the fact that there was an unusual degree of consultation among her superiors before her dismissal suggested that something more sensitive than the discharge of an unsatisfactory employee had occurred. In another case[15] an account executive with an advertising agency who had filed a sex discrimination complaint was dismissed some time after obtaining a job description from a client for use in advancing her suit. Her employer claimed that she had 'acted disruptively' at an important meeting with the client. The court did not credit this explanation, since it was not mentioned at the time or in the letter of termination received by the plaintiff, who indeed had been asked to participate in a subsequent meeting with the same client before the employer learned of her approach to him for assistance with her sex discrimination claim. The court concluded that the employer did not attribute to the alleged incident the importance he subsequently claimed for it, and the chronology of events further supported the inference that he was casting round for an excuse. The absence of testimony from a supervisor who had been directly involved in the events reinforced this conclusion; the court reasoned that failure of the respondent to produce this witness suggested that he would not have supported the story presented.

These cases, which are not unique, suggest that contemporaneous or subsequent inconsistencies in the employer's account of what occurred, indications of previously favourable evaluations of the employee or applicant[16] before knowledge of his exercise of statutory rights had come to light, and the absence of corroborating testimony from persons who could be expected to support the employer's case, may all give rise to the inference that the complainant has been victimised. Moreover, unlike the United States, an employee in Britain with more than twenty-six weeks' service is entitled to a written statement for reasons of his dismissal; if the employer 'unreasonably' refuses to provide it, or if an industrial tribunal finds the reasons presented 'inadequate or untrue', it may award the employee two weeks' pay and make a declaration stating the true reasons.[17] Substantial discrepancies between the employer's written statement of reasons and the account offered at the hearing, or indeed inadequacies or falsity of the reasons themselves, provide the basis for an inference of victimisation even more readily than the 'totality of circumstances' approach the American

courts have perforce had to follow. However, the availability of this statement of reasons is subject to two important qualifications. It is not automatic
but requires the employee's request, placing an unduly high premium on his
legal knowledge, and it extends only to employees, not to applicants.

As a practical matter it may be expected that most acts of victimisation will
involve employees. Where victimisation takes the form of dismissal, actual
or constructive, complainants should be able to claim unfair dismissal as
well: it is argued below (p.126) that any dismissal for a reason unlawful
under the Act is *ipso facto* unfair.

This raises some complex legal questions. In general a dismissal will be
regarded as unfair unless the employer proves that it fell within one of
several enumerated acceptable reasons, and that in all the circumstances
dismissal on that ground was reasonable (see further below, p.125). One
of the potentially fair reasons is the conduct of the employee, and there is a
residual category of 'other substantial reason'. The common law imposes
upon employees a duty of confidence, which forbids them from revealing
information received in confidence in the course of their employment about
their employer's operations.[18] Moreover, although no case has squarely
raised the issue,[19*] it is unlikely that dismissal of an employee who passed on
confidential information to a third party such as a trade union organiser
would be upheld as fair. Thus the dismissal of an employee for reporting the
contents of confidential documents to a discrimination complainant, or for
providing him with copies, would seem prima facie lawful. However, he has
'otherwise done anything under or by reference to this Act', and it emerges
quite clearly from the Standing Committe Debates, in which this example
was given, that the Government intended that s. 2 (1)(c) protect the
employee in such circumstances, notwithstanding that his action might
technically be a breach of the law of theft.[20*]

This conflict of statutory application ought not to be a difficult one to
resolve. It is submitted that an activity made lawful by another statute
cannot as a matter of law be regarded as conduct justifying dismissal. This
broad principle is supported in the particular instance by the fact that the
unfair dismissal legislation itself regards dismissals constituting discrimination under the Act as particularly obnoxious: additional compensation is to
be awarded in such cases (see further, p.126). Victimisation is explicitly
encompassed within this category.[21] Moreover, in what admittedly were
dicta, Lord Denning M.R. has suggested that the employee's duty of
confidence must yield to the paramount consideration that information
concerning misconduct injurious to the public interest be disclosed to
appropriate bodies.[22] His remarks were uttered in a case involving the
exposure of a combination in restraint of trade, but it is submitted that the
important statutory policy of eliminating discrimination requires no less.
There is also the technical point that where statutes are inconsistent, the
latter is to prevail.[23] A corollary of the contention that a dismissal which
would amount to victimisation under the Act is automatically unfair is that

the normal rule that the employee's award should be reduced by the tribunal to reflect his contribution to his dismissal[24] may not be applied in these circumstances.

In certain circumstances victimisation may amount to criminal contempt of court. A century ago it was held emphatically that subjecting a person to any detriment because he gave evidence or otherwise participated in court proceedings constituted contempt;[25] *a fortiori* in the case of threats to do so to prevent his testimony. An industrial tribunal lacks power to punish contempts; they would be subject to the Supreme Court Rule requiring that any such actions committed in connection with proceedings in an 'inferior court' be dealt with by the Divisional Court.[26] The reasoning of Lord Widgery L.C.J. in *Atty-Gen.* v. *BBC*[27] suggests that industrial tribunals would be so classified. That case concerned the status of a local valuation court, which hears rating appeals. His Lordship applied four criteria: whether the tribunal (1) produces final and binding decisions, subject to appeal; (2) hears parties and has witnesses called before it; (3) has power to take evidence on oath; (4) has a formal procedure.[28] Industrial tribunals satisfy all of them. Hence a person threatened with or suffering any sanction or loss in retaliation for testimony or assistance in gathering evidence in a discrimination case[29]* may, entirely independently of a complaint under s. 2, inform the Clerk of the Industrial Tribunal, or indeed the Attorney-General's Office, and ask that contempt proceedings be brought.

CONCLUSION

S. 2 is important for two types of persons: those who have suffered discrimination and those who have assisted in the enforcement of the law. Its broad sweep offers them adequate safeguards, whilst the exclusion of those making malicious allegations accords due recognition to the valid interests of employers. The prohibition of victimisation is made especially necessary by the prevalent attitude in many firms, particularly smaller ones, that internal harmony and the reputation of the company must always be maintained above any other considerations. In this cosy atmosphere conspiracies of silence readily flourish when the law is broken, and it is a practical necessity that a law which often will require for its enforcement the assistance of persons within the firm be able to ensure that they are not punished for their 'whistleblowing'. However, the effectiveness of s. 2, like that of the basic prohibition of racial discrimination, will depend critically on matters of proof, particularly the willingness of tribunals to make reasonable inferences from the facts presented or omitted.

NOTES

1. S. 2 also applies to non-employment situations covered by the Act, but its most frequent use will obviously concern employment.

*2. These provisions, now found in EPCA, ss. 23–5, are described concisely by O. Kahn-Freund, *Labour and the Law* (Stevens, 2nd edn 1977) pp. 172–80. Their coverage is restricted to employees, those barred from employment for their activities having no redress. See *Birmingham City District Council* v. *Beyer*, [1977] I.R.L.R. 211 (EAT).

3. Report for 1973, H.C. 144 (1974) para. 58, and app. VI, case 1.

4. S. 2 (1) (italic supplied).

5. See Official Report, Standing Comm. A, 29 April 1976, cols 61–84.

6. S. 2(2).

7. [1979] I.C.R. 184.

8. *Macdonald*, para. 74.

9. EPCA, s. 25.

10. See the discussion in Standing Comm. F on the Employment Protection Bill: Official Report, 26 June 1975, cols 894–5.

11. See below, p.197. The leading case on when costs should be awarded is *Marler (E.T.) Ltd.* v. *Robertson*, [1974] I.C.R. 72 (N.I.R.C.).

12. Civil Rights Act of 1964, s. 704 (a).

13. *Tidwell* v. *American Oil Co.*, 332 F. Supp. 424 (D. Utah 1970).

14. 332 F. Supp. at 430.

15. *E.E.O.C.* v. *Kallir, Philips, Ross Inc.*, 401 F. Supp. 66 (S.D.N.Y. 1975).

16. As in *Barela* v. *United Nuclear Corp.*, 462 F. 2nd 149 (10th Cir. 1972).

17. EPCA, s. 53 (1) and (4).

18. In *Initial Services Ltd* v. *Putterill*, [1967] 3 All E.R. 145, 148, Lord Denning M.R. recognised the existence of this duty without need for discussion.

*19. There is a further complication in the few reported cases, in that employees engaged in such conduct allege victimisation by reason of trade union activities (prohibited by EPCA, s. 23), and the precise legal question is whether the employer can prove the dismissal was not on this ground. However, in *Archer* v. *Cheshire and Northwich Building Society*, [1976] I.R.L.R. 424, the EAT strongly hinted that had the industrial tribunal clearly stated that the complainant, a branch manager who disclosed the names of his employees to a trade union organiser, was dismissed for violating the duty of confidentiality expressly included in his contract of employment, the dismissal would have been upheld under the 'conduct' head.

*20. The point was explicitly covered in the Debates, in response to a proposed amendment that would have made s. 2 inapplicable where the complainant had 'acted in any way which is civilly or criminally unlawful'. See n. 5 above, cols 71–7, especially the Minister of State's remarks at cols 73–4.

21. S. 3 (3)(a) defines 'discrimination' as used throughout the Act to include victimisation. EPCA, s. 71 (3)(c) incorporates this definition by reference.

22. *Initial Services Ltd* v. *Putterill*, [1967] 3 All E.R. 145, 148.

23. *Craies on Statute Law* (7th edn, 1971) p. 371. The unfair dismissal provisions were first enacted as part of the Industrial Relations Act 1971, and in this respect have remained unaltered.

24. EPCA, s. 73 (7).

25. *Littler* v. *Thompson*, (1839) 2 Beav. 129.

26. S.C.R., Ord. 52, r. l.

27. [1978] 1 W.L.R. 477, *affd*, [1979] 3 All E.R. 45.

28. [1978] 1 W.L.R. at 482–3.

*29. That the contempt power applies where someone is victimised for activities short of actual participation before a court, such as giving information to a litigant's solicitor, was held in *Roebuck* v. *N.U.M. (Yorkshire Area)*, [1977] I.C.R. 573 (Ch. D).

Part II
Discrimination in Employment

5
Black Workers –
Discrimination and
Disadvantage

INTRODUCTION

The 1968 Act made racial discrimination in employment unlawful for the first time in English history. Although, or perhaps because, this is the area of paramount importance in ensuring a decent life for minorities, it has also been the one least amenable to improvement. PEP estimated that in the early 1970s, discrimination was occurring on a massive scale, including 'tens of thousands' of acts of direct discrimination in recruitment alone each year.[1] It further estimated that a black white-collar worker had a one in three chance of suffering discrimination when applying for a job, and that for an unskilled worker the odds rose to evens.[2] These figures omit discrimination in relation to promotion, progression and dismissal; they do not begin to take account of the incidence of indirect discrimination, which was not unlawful at the time the PEP survey was undertaken. Yet the same research showed substantially greater improvement in the area of housing, and in the view of the Race Relations Board, the 1968 Act led to the virtual disappearance of discriminatory advertisements, as well as to the removal of discriminatory conditions in insurance and other financial arrangements.[3] Although PEP did conclude that employment discrimination had lessened as well, its greater persistence makes it the testing case for the effectiveness of legislation.

However, neither employment discrimination nor legal attempts to suppress it can be sensibly understood except in the context of industrial relations, an important part of which is itself the contentious evolution of what now seems a solid consensus about the proper role for legal regulation.[4]* Between 1968 and 1976 there was an unprecedented outpouring of legislation protecting individuals in employment. Rights in relation to unfair dismissal, the contract of employment, the health and safety of working conditions and multiplicity of matters known generally as employment protection, as well as equal pay and sex discrimination, were all created or strengthened by Parliament in this period. Just as – after the fiasco of the Industrial Relations Act – the law was being withdrawn from the regulation of collective bargaining and its breakdown, so was reliance upon it for the advancement of individual rights given increasing importance. Workers now enjoy minimum standards in relation to numerous matters in which trade unions had lacked either interest or power to affect management decisions, and these safeguards apply to all workers, whether or not they enjoy union representation. Race discrimination law must thus be seen as one plank in this statutory 'floor of rights',[5] and comparison with other pieces of individual employment legislation provides one basis for critical evolution. In the pages following there will in particular be repeated reference to the rules governing unfair dismissal, now found in the Employment Protection (Consolidation) Act 1978 (EPCA).

However, legal similarities should not obscure sociological differences. The factor of race is an independent cause of individuals receiving inferior treatment, and members of minority groups may in addition lack certain economic or social skills whose absence blocks their employment opportunities even when decisions are made in the most fair-minded way. It is therefore essential, before examining the legislation, to consider what is known about the employment characteristics of blacks in Britain. There is a gargantuan body of literature of very uneven quality on this general subject,[6] and it is within neither the author's purpose nor competence to add to it. Moreover, most of the work has been done in the form of case studies, whereas for present purposes what is needed is an overall view of the situation of minority workers. Therefore great reliance has been placed upon the only systematic study conducted in the 1970s, the PEP survey of 1973–4, published in popular form under the title *Racial Disadvantage in Britain.*[7] This chapter will draw primarily upon chapter 3 and 4 of that work – though later albeit more localised studies will also be mentioned – to analyse the economic status of black workers in light of three paramount considerations. (To avoid a hailstorm of citations, statements of fact drawn from these two chapters have not been specifically noted.) First, to what extent do the disadvantages of blacks stem from discrimination – direct or indirect – or alternatively from other factors, such as lack of economic skills (including education), required for what would generally be regarded as satisfactory employment in the British economy of the early 1980s? Second, in view of the relative importance of discrimination and what might be termed insufficiencies in the human capital of non-whites, has the present law been adequately designed to dismantle the main obstacles to the advancement of blacks in employment? Third, in what arenas may discrimination as defined in the Act be expected to present the most serious and recurrent problems?

One limitation must be noted. All the analysis will focus on men. Attempting to disentangle the independent influences of racial and sex discrimination is simply too great a task, particularly when one must add to the mix important cultural influences, notably those keeping most Muslim married women out of employment, and conversely resulting in an extremely high proportion of West Indian women, many with young children, remaining in work.[8] Consequently some of the most serious disabilities associated with black female employment, notably homeworking,[9] are not discussed.

THE EMPLOYMENT PATTERN OF MINORITIES

The pre-eminent question is how immigrants – which remains the accurate description of the overwhelming number of black adults – found a place in the British labour market. The answer, concurred in by every writer, whether on the basis of a narrow case study or a broad overview, is that they took jobs native whites did not want, or perhaps more to the point, which employers could not fill from home-grown sources. It is difficult to remember that in the 1950s and early 1960s, the years of the greatest immigration of black workers, unemployment was consistently well below 3 per cent – less than half that of the late 1970s – with a chronic shortage of unskilled and semi-skilled labour. Thus, apart from East African Asians, who arrived in the late 1960s and 1972 as political refugees, black Commonwealth immigrants came as workers. This immigration closely paralleled the influx of millions of southern European and North African workers in the same capacity throughout the prosperous countries of northern and western Europe. Many did not expect to stay, and came without family; their outlook has been described as that of a 'target worker', a temporary immigrant who seeks to make as much money as possible in a short time, with the intention of returning to his homeland enriched.[10] The transformation of target workers into settlers cannot be explored in depth here, but it seems likely that one important influence was the increasingly restrictive immigration controls, which forced Commonwealth workers to choose between settlement and return; short-term working tours became virtually impossible after 1965.[11]

The role of immigrants as replacement labour conditioned their places of settlement and the work they did, although other factors, notably contacts with kin, were also important. Thus there are very few blacks in Scotland or the Northeast, both traditional areas of high unemployment; the ample supply of local labour precluded opportunities. Similarly, a surprisingly large proportion of the Asian immigrants had been farmers or agricultural labourers at home, but virtually none work in agriculture here; this is an industry in which employment has steadily declined for decades.

The replacement labour theory enables one to weave a coherent tapestry from otherwise apparently unrelated strands of data about black employment. Minority workers are about $1\frac{1}{2}$ times as likely as whites to work in manufacturing and transport and communications; they are also far more likely to be doing unskilled or semi-skilled manual work, and far less likely to hold professional, managerial or white-collar jobs. Only in skilled manual work are they found to the same extent as whites. These findings are of course tightly connected: low-skilled manual jobs predominate in the industries in which high proportions of minority workers are found. However, there are significant variations among the minority groups. West Indians and Sikhs are doing skilled manual work in substantially greater proportions than whites; Pakistanis/Bangladeshis are by far the worst placed of any group, with nearly 60 per cent doing unskilled or semi-skilled manual work; African Asians alone have penetrated white-collar (but not professional/managerial) jobs, indeed to a slightly greater extent than whites, but Pakistanis and West Indians are close to non-existent at these levels. There are also sharp regional differences among the groups, with Pakistanis heavily concentrated in textile work in the North, and Asians in the Midlands' foundries and car factories, although no similar grouping seems to have occurred among West Indians.

Blacks were recruited for the least desirable jobs, which seem to have been concentrated in older industries whose plants are located in the industrial areas of the nineteenth century: the decrepit areas of cities that are generally in economic decline. This conjunction of black immigrant settlement with inner-city decay and conflict has been emphasised by Professors Rex and Moore in relation to housing.[12] In employment terms it also meant that immigrants, who like most manual workers lived near where they worked, were geographically isolated from technologically advanced and innovative industries, for example electronics and computers, which have been the growth sector of the British economy, and which tend to be located in New Towns or on the fringes of established cities. The immigrants' place of settlement was not of course the whole story, for these industries demanded skills which most of them lacked; the concentration of minority workers was the result of independent but mutually reinforcing factors. However, certain government policy decisions, notably the encouragement of industry and branches of the civil service to move out of London, aggravated the problem, particularly for West Indians, two-thirds of whom live in London and the South-East. This policy was not reversed until the late 1970s.[13] Consequently the second generation of blacks will need to be geographically mobile if they are to find employment with reasonable prospects; those who, like thousands of Geordies and Scots, prefer to stay in the communities of their birth are likely to remain under-employed or unemployed. Meanwhile their fathers remain in industries in which there is risk of repeated lay-off, and ultimately redundancy.

One subject on which information is seriously incomplete is the extent to which opportunities for blacks remain restricted to large employers. The PEP survey excluded plants with less than 50 employees. Denis Brooks's study of Walsall found that the small employer sector (defined as 100 employees or less) employed about $3\frac{1}{2}$ per cent of the whites, but less than 1 in 200 blacks.[14] He explained this disparity as a result of the greater importance attached to 'personal acceptability' in small firms, coupled with racialist assumptions about behaviour of blacks which led to the conclusion that they would not 'fit in'.[15] On the other hand, the cultural strangeness of Asian immigrants may lend some credence to that perception, and it is possible too that vacancies are filled by friends and relations of those already employed in firms with a 'family' atmosphere, thus precluding the need for black labour. In any case it is simply unknown whether this absence of blacks from small firms was influenced by local peculiarities, or would be found nationwide. If it were, the implications would be serious: the Bolton Committee, defining small firms as those with under 200 employees, found that in 1968 they accounted for 29 per cent of all employment; five years earlier no less than 94 per cent of all manufacturing firms came within this definition.[16]

Their cumulative impact is thus significant, particularly because, as will be seen, a substantial number of large companies have remained virtually all-white. Moreover, each small employer is a separate legal entity. Hence any ruling in a discrimination case against one employer has no immediate legal effect upon any other even if their practices are in essence indistinguishable, as may well be the case in a particular trade or locality. In addition, the 'strategic' investigative role of the CRE examined in Chapter 13 is inevitably constrained by limited finances. It can hardly be expected to devote its resources to a series of investigations of firms which individually could not be expected to provide many openings, even if firmly commited to equal opportunity, If ten or fifteen of such firms were amalgamated the position might be very different, but so long as they remain legally distinct they will in reality enjoy considerable immunity from investigation.

A final general point concerns self-employment. The popular conception of Asians is of small shopkeepers; like most such images, this is a blend of accuracy and falsehood. Roughly 12 per cent of white men are self-employed, but this is true of only 8 per cent of Asians; of all minorities only African Asians are found in the distributive trades in (slightly) greater proportion than whites. However, among those Asians who *are* self-employed, nearly two-thirds are shopkeepers, compared with about one-quarter of whites. Thus at present, Asian enterprise is not a significant source of good employment for other Asians whose opportunities are blocked elsewhere, since shopkeepers usually have few employees, generally members of their immediate families. Whether such businesses will provide capital for a British-born generation of entrepreneurs remains to be seen. West Indians are only half as likely as whites to be self-employed, and of those who are, nearly half are in the building industry, probably as 'lump' workers.

THE CONDITION OF MINORITY EMPLOYEES

A.   Concentration

One of the striking findings of the PEP study was a sharp polarisation between plants employing black workers and those which do not; of their sample, which excluded areas with less than 1 per cent minority population, more than half the black workers were found in 14 per cent of the plants, while an estimated one-third of the plants were all-white. Their explanation stressed three contributing factors. First, workforces tend to reproduce themselves. Existing employees are often a source of new applicants. An employer who was able to fill vacancies by relying on this source would not have to recruit immigrants even if substantial numbers lived in the neighbourhood. One piece of indirect supporting evidence for this theory is that plants without minority workers used markedly fewer methods of search for staff, particularly for non-manual jobs; the suggestion is that these plants could as it were internally regenerate their workforce. Second, black applicants shied away from plants with a discriminatory reputation, even if located in areas with a large minority population. However, although this reputation may accurately reflect history, it does not of course prove that a black applicant would encounter discrimination at present, for changes in the demand for labour, in the personnel concerned with hiring, or even in awareness of the law, may have altered the firm's policies. Thus neither of these factors involved any breach of the law as it then stood. Only in relation to the third – refusal to hire on racial grounds – can changes in employment practices be required. Perhaps because unlawful discrimination was only one, and not always the most important, influence in channelling black workers into a relative narrow stream of potential employers, firms which have had little contact with them commonly take the view that racial discrimination is no concern of theirs.[17] Yet particularly in the present and prospective circumstances of continually high unemployment, it is precisely those firms whose employment practices require the most stringent scrutiny. Here the new concept of indirect discrimination may be of central importance: as we have seen (above, pp. 46 and 57), recruitment by reliance on personal referrals from the existing workforce may now be unlawful.

Research subsequent to the PEP survey has emphasised the prevalence and importance of 'crowding' of minorities into a narrow range of occupations, although not necessarily into low-paid employment.[18] Indeed two quite independent studies concluded that the primary effect of discrimination was to prevent the diffusion of blacks throughout the labour market.[19] Neither investigation sought to distinguish between the legal categories of discrimination nor to illuminate the specific forms it took, but it seems clear the occupational crowding – in effect a form of segregation – rather than total denial of employment, is the primary result of discrimination.

B. Unemployment

At the outset it must be emphasised how obsolete and unhelpful are the official statistics on minority unemployment. Whilst unemployment totals of persons born, or whose parents were born, in New Commonwealth countries are published quarterly by the Department of Employment, these are related only to the total of all unemployed persons; the same limitation applies to figures broken down by region or age. Consequently one can determine what percentage of all those unemployed are from various minorities, but on the vital question – the ratios of those unemployed to those working *within* each group, or in plain language ethnic unemployment rates – there are no figures available. Most writers use data from the 1971 Census, which are now virtually useless because of the very high proportion of non-whites who have only entered the labour force since then.[20] In May 1978, in response to a Parliamentary Question attempting to unearth this data,[21] the Secretary of State replied that although no figures were then available, he was 'considering' obtaining them from the next EEC Labour Force Survey, scheduled to be conducted a year later, and unavailable at the time of writing. Thus, although present statistics are useful for measuring trends, these are trends in indicators which are far from giving a precise measure of the differences that are a matter of concern.

Immigrants were most likely to be unemployed in the period immediately after their arrival; the constriction of the immigration of workers beginning in 1962 meant that by the late 1960s, when those permitted to settle had begun to carve a place for themselves, minorities were unemployed in roughly the same proportions as whites. However, in the generally prosperous period of the first Wilson Government, unskilled workers were badly burned by the white heat of technology: unemployment among them rose more rapidly than among the better qualified.[22] This underscored the vulnerable position of blacks whose lack of skill and seniority made them the most readily expendable when bad times arrived. Between November 1973 and May 1975, when unemployment throughout the country rose rapidly, the increase among black men was more than double that among all men.[23] Rex and Tomlinson's study of Handsworth presents figures for all of Birmingham which reveal that between February 1974 and February 1977 not only did unemployment among blacks rise faster than among whites, but that after the peak the rate of decline was slower; hence minorities comprised a steadily growing proportion of the city's unemployed.[24] These data would support the view that, despite the increasing number of years of work in Britain, blacks had remained at the tail of the employment queue – a supply of marginal labour which would enjoy neither opportunity nor security. The gloomy employment prospects nationwide in the next few years promise scant hope of improved opportunities; and new phenomenon of youth unemployment, in which Britain topped the EEC league table by a shockingly large margin,[25] gives a further turn to the screw. Unemployment among young West Indians has increasingly become a matter of public concern, as awareness of its magnitude – at least double the rate for young whites – and its connection with crime and conflict with the police can no longer be ignored.

However, no verdict can yet be brought in. Some encouraging signs appeared in 1977, when minorities dropped from 4.0 per cent to 3.7 per cent of the total unemployed between August and November, with a particularly large decrease among young people. Moreover, in the year ending in February 1978, white unemployment had increased at a higher rate. This trend continued through February 1979: in the preceding year, while the number of unemployed fell by 4.0 per cent, the corresponding figure for all minorities was 9.2 per cent, and 12.5 per cent for those aged 16–24. Unfortunately, young West Indians were an exception to this encouraging trend – among them the numbers unemployed rose by 8.5 per cent.[26] This reversal of trends is not readily explicable, especially as the various government-sponsored job-creation schemes, especially the Youth Opportunities Programme, have attracted disappointingly little minority participation.[27] It does, however, seem much too early to conclude that blacks are an underclass of superfluous low-skilled labourers, as has been forcefully argued is the case in the United States.[28]

C.   Wages and Hours of Work

Comparisons between white and minority earnings proved particularly difficult for the PEP investigators, since the age structure of the minority population is substantially different; blacks on average are considerably younger, and consequently a greater proportion are in work. Moreover, earnings vary with age – unskilled workers usually reach a peak in their thirties and suffer a marked drop in their fifties, whilst white-collar workers' earnings tend to reach a height in their forties, and then level out. When the researchers made statistical adjustments to remove the independent influence of age differences, they found that whilst unskilled and semi-skilled manual workers had identical earnings, white skilled workers earned about 10 per cent more than their black counterparts, and that the gap among non-manual workers was just under 30 per cent.

Moreover, the parity among low-skilled workers seems largely attributable to the fact that twice as many blacks did shiftwork,[29] which attracts premium payments. The greater amount of shiftwork among minorities cannot be explained simply by the fact that more of them work in low-skilled jobs involving such arrangements, although this contributes about one-third of the difference. The replacement-labour theory, sketched earlier, provides a fuller explanation: blacks were taken on for the unsocial hours which whites refused to work. In some cases, however, there seems to be complicating factors, best exemplified by Pakistanis in the Lancashire textile industry, almost half of whom work shifts. Asians with poor English are far more likely than any other group to do night-shift work, and PEP suggested that the convenience of working with others who speak the same language, coupled with limited opportunities elsewhere, has led low-skilled non-

English-speaking Asians to form ethnic work units. This isolation seriously hampers their acculturation to British industrial and social life, and keeps them physically apart from whites in the same plant, who work at different times and in more skilled jobs. The formation of ethnic work units has also been documented among Indians in Midlands foundries.[30] Here the methods of recruitment adopted by employers becomes critical: Brooks points out that one important advantage accruing to firms in the Walsall metal trades which have employed large numbers of Asians is that they can satisfy their need for labour without effort; existing workers are only too pleased to recommend friends or relations, and the job networks among kin 'do not of course stop at Walsall or the West Midlands [but] extend back to Kashmir or the Punjab'.[31] The new recruit is quite happy to have a job; that it involves working shifts, often in unpleasant physical conditions, and may provide no opportunities for advancement and little contact with anyone but his fellow countrymen seems of minor importance at the time. Ten years on, however, his perspective may be very different, and then the law relating to discrimination assumes greater relevance.

One critical difference between whites and blacks was in the effect of education on earnings. At the time of the survey, whites who had left school by 15 had median earnings of about 20 per cent less than those who remained longer. The corresponding difference among non-whites was under 5 per cent.

It is possible that the disparate age profiles may have partly affected these figures: if non-whites tend to be younger, they may be expected to narrow the gap as they rise with age to better-paid positions. But the survey also revealed that blacks with the same academic qualifications as whites were on average in much lower level jobs, which may also be inferred from the massive racial gap in earnings among those in non-manual employment. Moreover, African Asians, the only group to have penetrated non-manual employment to any significant extent, are the *worst* paid on average of all minorities, suggesting that they have gained access only to the lowest-level and least sought jobs of that description. It is here that the question of direct discrimination comes increasingly to prominence, for African Asians show the lowest incidence of poor English among Asians immigrants, and many were in middle-class occupations before their expulsion. In an important sense they are the testing case for the morality of British society: they present few of the problems of linguistic infirmity, cultural strangeness or alienation, or lack of economic skills that have been said to characterise other minority groups in varying degrees. If they remain submerged it will be as a consequence of racialism, not of their own defiencies.

More generally, an important feature of present-day economic life is that education normally results in higher earnings; as the economists put it, investment in 'human capital' is expected to pay dividends.[32] That this appears not to hold for blacks is a disturbing portent. It is possible that, for

low-skilled immigrants, the rise in living standard achieved by settlement
here, and the problems of adjustment to a new society and other more
personal matters, bulked far larger than denial of (mostly theoretical) job
opportunities. A sort of backhand confirmation of this comes from the PEP
findings on job satisfaction, in which Pakistanis – who are mostly likely to be
in the least skilled jobs, to do shift work, and who have the second lowest
average earnings – come top. This is rationally inexplicable except on the
basis that their reference group, to use Runciman's term,[33] is extremely
narrow, indeed is largely limited to their fellow countrymen; hence they
remain largely unaware of the comparatively inferior status. The same
cannot be said of their British-born children, nor of immigrants with higher
skills and less sense of distance from the way of life in this country. The fact
that 21 per cent of minority men with university degree standard qualifications were doing manual jobs is not merely a shocking waste of manpower; it
is certain to be a source of growing bitterness and disaffection with life in
Britain, an 'alienation' as profound, though perhaps not yet as visible, as that
experienced by West Indian youth.

Some data generated by the research of Dr C. Greenhalgh into sex-based
wage differentials suggests that there may have been some improvement in
relative earnings of non-whites in the mid-1970s.[34] Using data from the
General Household Survey, she found that in 1975 there was no racial
difference in earnings among single householders under 30 – although the
sample size was too small to support a broad conclusion – and that the
overall gap between earnings of white and black married men had narrowed
from 9½ per cent in 1971 to 7 per cent. The latter figure, of course, does not
take account of the variable of age, although most very young workers would
probably not be married. No more recent data have come to the author's
attention. The Royal Commission on the Distribution of Income and
Wealth, which commissioned no research on this subject, rather agnostically
concluded that there was 'no conclusive evidence that ethnic minority
groups as a whole have a disproportionately high incidence of low income'[35]
– of which male earnings would, of course, be only one component.

D.   The Impact of Direct Discrimination

The foregoing details of the inferior condition of black workers give rise to a
strong inference that their race has proved a serious handicap. On this basis
alone, however, one must say 'inference' rather than 'conclusion'. Other
factors, such as lower levels of skill, or simple inability to find one's way to
better jobs, might also be given prominence – although the low levels of
employment achieved by blacks with high academic qualifications, and the
substantial wage disparities among workers at all levels of skill, makes this
line of explanation a very weak reed. None the less, it is important to

document the patterns of clear-cut discrimination, and this too was part of the PEP research. Some of its more spectacular conclusions have been quoted on p. 95, and it established beyond question that discrimination, though less prevalent than before the 1968 Act, remained serious. Its findings were repeatedly cited in Parliamentary discussion, and were influential in persuading the Government, and those who spoke for the Opposition, that the legislation required strengthening. Moreover, this conclusion was reinforced by the limitations of the survey, which could not penetrate decisions made wholly within companies and therefore studied initial recruitment only. It was also limited to direct discrimination, then alone illegal; there has yet been no attempt to gauge the incidence of indirect discrimination. Consequently the analysis of indirect discrimination presented in Chapter 2 is based on the author's perceptions of what seem likely to be its most important manifestations, and it is quite possible that the subsequent research may indicate that emphasis should be placed on other policies and practices.

Apart from its general conclusions the detailed findings of the PEP study highlight areas in which direct discrimination seems especially serious. They further suggest that certain legal difficulties are likely to arise, and also that some unforeseen practical constraints may cramp the effectiveness of the methods chosen to enforce the reformed legislation.

The PEP investigators conducted a series of experiments using ostensible applicants – in reality actors – drawn from the various minority groups, white immigrants and white Britons, for a broad range of jobs ranging from unskilled manual labourer to management trainee. The varying responses to their applications enabled the extent of discrimination to be quantified.[36] Some of the most interesting results were in what they did not find. First, there were no significant regional variations, although since the tests were only carried out in six large English cities, it is unknown whether behaviour might be different in smaller towns, rural areas, and Wales and Scotland. However, a subsequent study, admittedly of so small a sample that the authors acknowledged that no firm conclusions could be drawn from it, found that Asian boy school-leavers were unable to get the same sort of jobs or apprenticeships as white Glaswegian boys of roughly the same educational qualifications.[37] Moreover, apart from Cardiff the black population outside English conurbations is minuscule; thus it is behaviour in this setting which determines the economic prospects of minorities.

Second, those who discriminate racially do so in undiscriminating fashion. There was virtually no variation in the extent of discrimination against the diverse ethnic groups. This undercuts one theory sometimes put forward, that the alienness of immigrants is what occasions hostility from the native-born. If this were so, one would expect substantially less discrimination against West Indians, many of whom felt a strong attachment to Britain when they emigrated, and who are plainly culturally closer to white Britons than they are many of the Asians. That this does not happen suggests that all 'coloureds' are simply commingled in the minds of those who discriminate. Furthermore, if strangeness were the important factor, one would expect that Italians or Greeks – the white immigrant nationalities used in the tests – would encounter discrimination to the same extent. This was not so; for both the manual and white-collar jobs these applicants met discrimination in 10 per cent of the cases, roughly one-third the figure for non-whites. This underlines the racialist nature of the behaviour of many employers, although it is also a reminder that unfavourable treatment on grounds of national origins is not simply a matter of academic concern.

The experience of discrimination against the test applicants broadly conforms to the pattern of inequalities that emerges from the more general data review in the preceding pages. Discrimination was most frequent among applicants for unskilled work (46 per cent) and white-collar jobs (30 per cent). This latter figure is probably a significant underestimate, since it measures only refusal to be invited to interview: there is no way of knowing whether applicants would have stumbled into further racial pitfalls in subsequent stages of hiring. Rather surprisingly, discrimination was higher for junior clerical jobs (48 per cent) than for management trainees (42 per cent) and accountants (35 per cent), although the latter two would either pay better or be more attractive for the career opportunities offered. None the less it is clear that the path to lucrative and high-status jobs is often blocked for reasons of race. This is confirmed by what is apparently the only study of the experience of black British students at British universities and polytechnics, which found that their applications were rejected at a far higher rate, and that they were given fewer offers of employment after interview, than white students of equivalent academic achievement.[38] As all had British qualifications and most were long-settled residents, racial bias alone can explain the outcome.

Equal treatment was most common for skilled workers, although even here discrimination occurred in 20 per cent of the applications. This accords with the findings that all groups except Pakistanis have found skilled manual jobs to the same or even greater extent than whites. It also agrees with an analysis based upon market demand. Even as the unemployment rates of the 1970s reached ever higher post-war peaks, shortages of skilled workers were widely reported. That black skilled workers meet the least resistance suggests that economic need is the most powerful factor overriding bigotry. Conversely, where there is a surplus of applicants, employers are far freer to make decisions based upon race. It follows that the attainments and skills of blacks are of far less importance to the incidence of discrimination than the general demand for a particular kind of labour and the availability of whites with competing skills. To fashion a paradox, one could most dramatically improve the employment prospects for blacks not by assisting them to better their education or acquire occupational skills, but by preventing whites from doing so. This point requires particular emphasis, because it may become the crux of a future, bitter debate. Restricting whites in this way is obviously politically impossible, as well as objectionable in principle. Racial preferences in the form of quotas or ratios attempt to achieve the same end by in effect devaluing the qualifications achieved by the whites. One common justification for their use in the United States is that without them blacks would be absent from first-rank academic institutions or desirable employment because the burden of history makes it impossible for them, taken as a group, to compete equally. It was suggested in Chapter 1 that this argument cannot yet plausibly be made in Britain. A corollary of this position, however, is that if blacks *are* able to compete equally, but are none the less denied positions unfairly, then the case for preferences for minorities or restrictions on whites becomes even more compelling as a matter of justice than would be true in the American context. An effective anti-discrimination law should be seen as the alternative to achieving justice by unjust means. The success of the present Act – Parliament's third attempt at controlling discrimination – is therefore critical if Britain is to avoid having to choose between open acceptance of permanent subordination of minorities and the use of racial preferences as compensation.

The PEP tests established what may be called the 'objective' facts about discrimination. The study of which they were a part also surveyed experience and beliefs about the same phenomenon. The most striking finding is that whilst roughly the same proportion of whites and West Indians – approximately three-quarters – believed that discrimination takes place in recruitment, this perception was shared by only half the Indians and 40 per cent of Pakistanis. This shatters the notion that minorities are over-sensitive or over-eager to complain. The greater extent to which whites acknowledge the existence of discrimination suggests that Asians either have a remarkable, and unfortunately mistaken, belief in British fairmindedness, or that they are simply unaware of what happens around them. That the latter seems likely is suggested by the fact that what PEP call 'culturally enclosed' Asians – those with poor English who are most likely to live and work largely with their own kind – least commonly believe that they have experienced discrimination, or that it exists, whereas the opinions of Asians with fluent English are much closer to those of whites and West Indians. Moreover, only among Asian women, the most rigidly 'enclosed' of all, does one find a greater belief that employers do not discriminate than the reverse, and a mere 3 per cent report personal experience of discrimination. A corollary of these findings is that one may expect the British-born generation of blacks to be more alive to discrimination, and presumably more resentful of it.

However, the study of the 'subjective' side also revealed some contrary indications. First, the percentage of those claiming personally to have experienced discrimination dropped dramatically – by almost two-thirds – compared with the PEP study seven years earlier. The critical, and unanswerable, question is to what extent this represents lessened as distinct from hidden or unperceived discrimination. It seems that the 1968 Act had at least one significant effect: it is now rare for an employer to reject applicants openly on the basis of race. Moreover, the sheer magnitude of the fall gives rise to a strong inference that there has been a real diminution in actual discrimination. This view receives further indirect support from the fact that men who came to Britain after 1969 were far less likely than earlier arrivals to believe that employers discriminate. One could argue that the newcomers were simply more ignorant, but it is equally plausible, and more consistent with the other responses, that the longer-settled men based their judgements on experiences that occurred before the statute began to make any impact. There are, then, some grounds for cautious optimism, for the 1968 Act, as we shall see, was a very limited measure; if it has none the less achieved some advance, one may reasonably expect that sharper legal tools will be able to make deeper incisions.

THE QUALIFICATIONS OF MINORITY WORKERS

The final point that must be considered is the extent to which the inferior economic position of blacks results from their lesser occupational skills. Employers cannot be expected to hire people incapable of doing the job; but evidence of even substantial disparities in qualifications overall would not necessarily cast doubt on the view that discrimination is widespread. The fact that proportionately fewer blacks than whites could reasonably be regarded as able to do a particular kind of work says nothing about the treatment meted out to those in fact qualified. Both factors can readily coexist, indeed could feed upon one another: if blacks learn that opportunities in a particular trade are blocked they may avoid wasting time acquiring skills they cannot use. This 'human capital' line of analysis is also worth pursuing because it may reveal significant differences among the minority groups, as well as isolating particular types or levels of jobs in which discrimination is particularly prevalent.

One analytical difficulty must be noted. What constitutes a qualification is itself a contentious and important question. A company may require that its cleaners have three 'O'-levels; anyone without these credentials would then be rejected as 'unqualified'. This example seems whimsical only because the gap between the job done and the achievement demanded is so obvious. Where, however, certain widely accepted preconditions for employment have never been evaluated and cannot be shown to be related to the demands of the work, under the new concept of indirect discrimination they may be regarded in law as being no different than the case of the over-educated cleaner (see above Chapter 2). Moreover, there is a plasticity about the use of qualifications: they are often ignored when labour is scarce, then insisted upon with great solemnity when applicant supply exceeds demand.[39] The apparent permanence of high unemployment suggests that this practice will be of critical importance. In both these circumstances the use of such employment qualifications may be unlawful if blacks are disproportionately excluded.

The most striking of PEP's finding was the variance between West Indians and all other groups. No less than 88 per cent of the West Indians had no educational qualifications at all, compared with 71 per cent of whites (62 per cent of those aged 16–44) and 59 per cent of Asians.[40] Asians, on the other hand, were roughly as academically qualified as whites: 24 per cent had 'O'-levels or above, compared with 22 per cent of whites (31 per cent of those aged 16–44). These figures – which conceal vast differences between ill-educated Pakistanis and East African Asians – if anything understate the level of Asian academic achievement, since to avoid arguments about the equivalence of overseas qualifications, PEP more or less arbitrarily lowered them by one notch; thus a foreign first degree was treated as an English 'A'-level.

These data suggest that even the most rigorously enforced anti-discrimination law will have limited effect on the number of West Indians employed in jobs requiring advanced education, but that Asians will be in a position to call upon its protection if needed. Indeed, the weight of direct and indirect evidence of discrimination in higher-level jobs suggest that Asians may be the main beneficiaries of the invigorated legislation, since only arbitrary barriers block the advancement of many into white-collar and managerial positions. On the other hand, West Indians are as likely as whites to have had some form of manual job training; for them the issue of fair application of qualifications arises in relation to skilled manual jobs – where, as we have seen, they are already found in large numbers though not in supervisory positions. However, they are much less likely to have been apprenticed,[41] and this appears to be one area in which the law may be of particular importance to them.

The substantial minority of academically advanced Asians coexists with much larger groups of those who barely speak English, and an even greater number who lack basic English literacy. Only among East African Asians did the PEP interviewers find a majority whose English could be described as 'fluent'; among Pakistanis, over 40 per cent of the men spoke English slightly or not at all. These and other indicators led PEP to conclude that there is a sharp polarisation among two types of Asians: the Westernised, well-educated, middle-class who have small families and tend to be dispersed among English people economically like themselves, and the culturally enclosed, foreign-language-speaking, ill-educated factory workers who live with large families in poor areas with high concentrations of immigrants. These groups participate in drastically dissimilar labour markets; thus the context, though not the motivation, of direct discrimination which they encounter will be radically different.

SUMMARY AND CONCLUSION

This chapter has reviewed the results of studies, notably those of PEP, on the forms and extent of disadvantage, and the incidence of direct discrimination suffered by racial minorities in Britain. The evidence of black disadvantage in employment is overwhelming, and can be seen in a wide range of indicators, notably in type of work done, wage and unemployment levels, and incidence of shiftwork. Some of the differentials may be set down to the lower level of educational qualifications among West Indians, and the lack of linguistic and occupational skills among older Asians, particularly Pakistanis. Much of it, however, is the result of intentional inferior treatment of racial minorities. Its most important manifestations are employers' unwillingness to recruit or hire them at all if an adequate supply of white labour is available, and a refusal to promote or engage qualified blacks to supervisory and managerial positions.

Legal regulation will perhaps be of secondary importance – though vital in rectifying the treatment accorded specific individuals – where labour shortages either minimise the extent of discrimination or, as in undesirable employment, create openings for blacks. However, where is there significant competition, as for managerial posts, or where employers fear adverse reactions from the workforce or customers, legal intervention is perhaps the only means even potentially capable of curbing inferior treatment on grounds of race. The present political consensus that massive unemployment is to be tolerated in the name of controlling inflation will expand the number of competitive situations, and hence both racial bitterness and the likelihood of discrimination. Thus quite apart from tackling indirect discrimination, the law has a major and probably increasing relevance to employment discrimination; particularly it would appear in relation to qualified Asians. It is beyond the scope of this book to consider what role trade unions may play in eliminating discrimination, whether by collective agreements or industrial action. Many would argue that this would be a method preferable to legal control. One may subscribe to this view as an ideal, but regrettably trade unions have taken limited concrete action in this respect. Indeed in some well-known cases they have failed their black members badly, and some of their practices may now be unlawful. These matters are considered further in Chapter 9.

NOTES

1. D. Smith and N. McIntosh, *The Extent of Racial Discrimination* (PEP, 1974) p. 35.
2. Ibid. pp. 20–8.
3. RRB Report for 1973 (H.C. 114, 1974) para. 55.

*4. Even the contentious proposals introduced in 1979 in the Conservative Government's Employment Bill do not reject this consensus. They propose changes in the substantive rules governing areas already regulated, e.g. picketing or the closed shop, but not a return to legal regulation of collective bargaining in the manner of the Industrial Relations Act 1971.

5. A term first coined by Professor Lord Wedderburn, and used by *Hepple*, pp. 252–3.

6. Interested readers may consult the Bibliography prepared by and available from the Runnymede Trust, *Briefing Paper 6/77* (1977).

7. D. Smith, *Racial Disadvantage in Britain* (Penguin Books, 1977). The original studies from which the material presented there was taken are listed on p. 11. The only other subsequent general survey, published by the Department of Employment as *The Role of Immigrants in the Labour Market* (1977), repeatedly cites *Racial Disadvantage* and adds little new information relevant to this chapter.

8. Discussed briefly in Smith, op. cit pp. 64–6.

9. See, further, the studies listed in *Briefing Paper 6/77*, op. cit., p. 23.

10. W. Bohning, *The Migration of Workers in the United Kingdom and the European Community* (O.U.P., 1972) p. 62. D. Brooks, *Black Employment in the Black Country* (Runnymede Trust, 1975) pp. 22–3, develops the implication of the 'target worker' mentality for the employment of immigrant workers.

11. Cf. C. Peach, *West Indian Migration to Britain* (O.U.P., 1968) chap. 5.

12. J. Rex and R. Moore, *Race, Community and Conflict* (O.U.P., 1967) *passim*.

13. In the White Paper *Policy and the Inner Cities*, Cmnd 6845 (H.M.S.O., 1977).

14. Brooks, op. cit. (see n.10, above) pp. 5–6.

15. Ibid. p. 20.

16. *Committee of Inquiry into Small Firms*, Cmnd 4811 (1971) p. 36 (table 3.v), and as cited in M. Chesterman, *Small Businesses* (Sweet & Maxwell, 1977) p. 11.

17. See the discussion of the reasons for the initiation of anti-discrimination policies in *Racial Disadvantage*, pp. 153–6.

18. Mayhew and Rosewell, 'Immigrant and Occupations Crowding in Great Britain', 40 *Ox. Bull. Econ. & Stats.* 223 (1978); Dex, 'A Note on Discrimination in Employment and its Effects on Black Youths', 8 *J. Soc. Pol.* 357 (1979).

19. Mayhew and Rosewell, op. cit. p. 241; Dex, op. cit. pp. 368–9.

20. In 1971 more than half (51%) of West Indians in Britain were under 14, double the proportion among the general population. Among Asians there were roughly half again as many persons of this age as among the U.K. total. These figures are found in the Report of the Select Comm. on Race Relations and Immigration, *The West Indian Community* (H.C. 180–1, 1976–7) vol. 1, p. xi.

21. Reported in the *D. E. Gazette* for July 1978, p. 827.

22. Bosanquet and Standing, 'Government and Unemployment, 1966–70', 10 *B.J.I.R.* 180 (1972).

23. *D.E. Gazette*, vol. 83, September 1975, pp. 868–9.

24. J. Rex and S. Tomlinson, *Colonial Immigrants in an English City* (Routledge & Kegan Paul, 1979) p. 110, table 4.7.

25. According to a summary of a Report compiled by the European Commission printed in the *Daily Telegraph* of 1 November 1977, there were 708,715 unemployed persons in Britain under 25; in no other EEC country did the corresponding figure reach even half a million.

26. These figures are taken from various tables in the *D.E. Gazette*, vols 85–7.

27. The *D.E. Gazette*, vol. 87, March 1979, p. 230, reported the formation of a joint working group of the Manpower Services Commission and the CRE to counter the problem of the under-representation of black youths in YOPS.

28. S. Willhelm, *Who Needs the Negro?* (Anchor Books, 1971) *passim*. As noted in

Chapter 1, there is a young minority within the American black community emerging into the middle class, to whom this argument would not be applied.

29. PEP Report, p. 81, table A24. As indicated there, this figure conceals a substantial difference between Pakistanis, who are twice as likely to be working night shifts as the other ethnic minorities.

30. See especially M. Rimmer, *Race and Industrial Conflict* (Heinemann, 1972) *passim*, and also Brooks, op. cit. (see n. 10, above).

31. Brooks, op. cit. pp. 22–3.

32. I am drawing on the summary of these theories presented in A. Atkinson, *The Economics of Inequality* (Clarendon Press, 1975) chap. 5.

33. W. Runciman, *Relative Deprivation and Social Justice* (Penguin Books, 1972) ch. 2.

34. 'Male–Female Wage Differentials in Great Britain: Is Marriage an Equal Opportunity?', unpublished MS., October 1979. I am grateful to Dr Greenhalgh for making this material available and taking the trouble to explain several technical points to me, which I hope I have managed to understand.

35. RCDIW, Report No. 6, *Low Incomes*, Cmnd 7175 (1978) para. 5.118.

36. The methodology of the actor tests is described briefly in *Racial Disadvantage*, pp. 105–8, and in more detail, with consideration of some possible criticisms, in Smith and McIntosh, op. cit. *passim* (see n. 1, above).

37. Fowler, Littlewood and Madigan, 'Immigrant School Leavers and the Search for Work', 11 *Sociology* 65 (1977).

38. Ballard and Holden, 'The Employment of Coloured Graduates in Britain', 4 *New Comm.* 325 (1975).

39. A point made in conversation by Dr. Michael Pearn of the Runnymede Trust. Cf. also White and Francis, 'Title VII and the Masters of Reality', 64 *Geo. L.J.* 1213 (1976).

40. PEP Report, pp. 57–9 and table B3 (pp. 338–9).

41. Ibid. p. 58.

6
Employment Discrimination Law – The Main Provisions

Employment discrimination is governed mainly by s. 4, reproduced in the Appendix. It will be seen that s. 4 (1) concerns applicants or inquirers, whilst s. 4 (2) relates to employees. The discussion of employment discrimination in this chapter will follow this sequence. However, three technical points, applicable equally to both subsections, may be examined first.

A. The 1976 Act, unlike its predecessor, gives 'employment' a definition of extremely broad compass. In several areas of law important consequences flow from whether a person is regarded as an employee or as self-employed; disputes over the categorisation have spawned a large body of case law, particularly concerning liability for national insurance contributions.[1] The dividing-line is roughly between someone under a contract of service, and someone who enters into a contract to provide services; only the former is engaged in what the law knows as 'employment'. Consequently, those falling into the latter category were not covered by the 1968 Act, as indeed they remain outside the unfair dismissal legislation.[2] Under the present Act, however, 'a contract personally to execute any work or labour' is also regarded as constituting 'employment'.[3]

This extension of the law to protect the self-employed has several important consequences. It may prove particularly valuable in the building industry, in which nearly half of all self-employed West Indians are found.[4] If they obtain work by direct arrangement with a builder they will now come under s. 4; if, as frequently occurs, they are sent to sites by an agency with whom they contract, they will benefit from the protection now extended to contract workers (s. 7, pp. 138–9). If the broad interpretation given the statutory phrase 'employment agency' by a Cambridge industrial tribunal[5] is followed generally, agents for self-employed persons like taxi drivers, actors and building workers will themselves be forbidden to discriminate.

Moreover, the wide definition would appear to encompass self-employed businessmen, not workers alone. Thus it would be illegal if for racial reasons a builder refused to engage a personal subcontractor, or a company refused to engage a firm of solicitors which employs Asian articled clerks. Both instances involve contracts to execute work; in the latter, the firm as complainant would draw upon the broad meaning of 'racial grounds' discussed on pp. 81–2. However, it is doubtful whether s. 4 would extend to discrimination against an incorporated enterprise, even if a one-man company, notwithstanding the fact that incorporated entities are legal persons.

None the less some ambiguities surround the meaning of employment. These arise in situations in which the job does not involve working entirely for the person who provides the opportunity. It is unlikely, for example, that the licensee of a pub would be regarded as 'employed' by a brewery, though the precise contractural and financial relationship in each case may be determinative. Even less open to doubt is that pupillages and tenancies in barristers' chambers are outside s. 4 (and indeed probably outside the Act entirely).

Yet more complex is the area of public appointments. Employment by the Civil Service or other public body is treated identically to other employment, since the Act applies to the Crown.[6] However, where the work in question involves the holding of a statutory office this is distinguished from 'employment', and the Act drifts into a sort of limbo. Such at any rate was the holding of the EAT in *Knight* v. *Attorney-General*,[7] decided under identical provisions of the SDA. The complainant alleged sex discrimination in relation to consideration for an appointment as a JP. This position was held to be outside the employment sections of the Act, and hence beyond the jurisdiction of an industrial tribunal to hear the complaint. The reasoning of the EAT is difficult to penetrate, but so are the provisions it purported to elucidate.[8] The judgment produced the striking conclusion that if any provision governed the selection of JPs it was the equivalent of s. 76, which covers government appointments outside s. 4 – a category presumably including everything from membership of quangos to the creation of Peers. If this view is correct, s. 76, which states that Ministers and government departments 'shall not do an act which would be unlawful under s. 4 if the Crown were the employer for the purposes of this Act', is unenforceable within the statutory structure described in Chapter 10. Although this does not preclude seeking prerogative writs from the High Court,[9] in view of the established principles governing the granting of these remedies, even in their present simplified form,[10] it is difficult to see how they could properly be claimed in relation to discrimination in public appointments. Although in *Knight* the EAT was at pains to limit its decision to the particular office of JP it subsequently relied on that judgment to reverse a tribunal which had taken jurisdiction over a claim of sex discrimination in the appointment of a rent officer.[11] It thus appears that a considerable number of positions may be effectively outside the Act.

B.   Whilst discrimination in respect of 'terms' offered or afforded is now forbidden, previously the prohibition extended to 'conditions of work' as well.[12] The effect of the omission of the latter phrase is obscure. 'Terms' has an extremely broad import: it would include not only the provisions specifically agreed between worker and employer – known as express terms – but also implied terms. These may be drawn from statute, collective agreement or unwritten but established patterns of behaviour in relation to a particular matter, e.g. whether the employee may be required to work far away from his initial job and place of engagement. The precise circumstances in which binding provisions may emerge from these sources is a matter of great legal complexity and practical importance. For present purposes it is enough to note that the current trend is for the individual's contract of employment to incorporate a growing number of implied terms drawn from collective agreements and statutes, particularly those which add to employees' rights.[13] Thus s. 4 would cover matters such as pay, pensions, hours, shifts, overtime, holidays and sick pay, as well as the employer's exercise of his disciplinary powers. Some of the crudest forms of discrimination, such as lower pay for the same work or requiring blacks to work longer hours for the same pay, fall under this head.[14]

It seems clear however that, expansive though it is, 'terms' would not include conditions of work in a physical sense. This view depends upon analogy to a series of statutory definitions of a 'trade dispute'. In an early formulation this meant anything 'connected with . . . terms of employment or conditions of labour'; the present one speaks of 'terms and conditions of employment or the physical conditions in which any workers are required to work'.[15] The repeated differentiation of contractual terms from physical conditions suggests that the former does not comprehend the latter; although the context is not precisely identical there is no apparent reason to interpret the present Act differently. Thus a bigoted foreman or interviewer who attempts to discourage a black applicant by telling him that he will be assigned to a dirty or noisy part of a factory does not break the law. The omission of 'conditions of work' occasioned no Parliamentary discussion and it is doubtful whether it was intended to restrict the scope of the new Act. It may be that the inclusion of 'other detriment' in s. 4 (2)(c) was thought to cover situations like the hypothetical example, but that subsection extends only to persons already in employment. At least as far as applicants are concerned, what may well have been a draftsman's error seems to have left a minor loop-hole.

C.   The precise language of s. 4 is addressed to 'a person, in relation to employment by him'.[16] Thus anyone whose job included responsibility for decisions relating to any of the matters coming within this section, whether generally or only in a specific case – for example, a foreman told by a personnel manager to choose a shop-floor worker from among applicants the latter has interviewed – would be liable for acts of discrimination. This language is in substance identical to 'any person concerned with the employment of others', the previous formulation.[17] However, it would be unduly harsh to require a victim of discrimination to unravel the threads of authority in a company at any given time in order to discover the proper defendant in his particular case. Moreover, for the statute to be an effective goad in eliminating discriminatory practices, companies and firms – rather than individuals who may in any event be effectively 'judgment proof' – must be faced with the ultimate liability if there is to be any financial incentive for them to make the necessary changes. The statute ensures this by following its predecessor in making employers vicariously liable for discrimination perpetrated by an employee 'in the course of his employment', even if the act was done without the employer's knowledge or approval.[18] The presence of this phrase – perhaps the most litigated in modern times – in the old Workmen's Compensation Acts provided a lucrative source of income for the legal profession, but over the years acquired an extremely broad meaning, and would include the acts of an employee who used a means expressly prohibited by the employer, provided the task itself was one he had been appointed to do.[19] *A fortiori* it would impose liability where the employer has said nothing at all about how a task is to be executed. However, because its breadth comes near to imposing strict, as well as vicarious, liability on the employer, he is provided with a defence: liability may be avoided if he proves that 'he took such steps as were reasonably praticable' to prevent the employee from doing the discriminatory act, or 'acts of that description'.[20]

The scope of this defence awaits authoritative interpretation. The danger is that the mere posting of notices or formalistic pronouncements by management that the law is to be obeyed would be regarded as sufficient. It is 'reasonably practicable' for management to undertake periodic reviews of its hiring policies to ensure non-discrimination, and of whether those who operate these policies have abided by them, and it is submitted that the defence should be accepted only if the employer has attempted this sort of monitoring and supervision. In the only case under the 1976 Act to have presented the issue, a Central London industrial tribunal took a similar view.[21] Although the respondent employment agency told employees that any form of discrimination would be regarded as a breach of their contract of employment amounting to gross misconduct warranting summary dismissal, and set out procedures to be followed for reporting instances where the agency's clients appeared to violate any anti-discrimination law, in practice these rules had been ignored several times. Consequently when an employee was found to have discriminated, the agency was held vicariously liable and the defence rejected.

However, the primary liability of the employer does not excuse illegal acts of employees. Knowingly aiding another person to violate the statute is itself unlawful[22] and where an employer is vicariously liable for his employee's act, the latter is deemed to have aided his employer.[23] Thus both could be made respondents before tribunals and the employee independently could be ordered to pay compensation, either for his own act of discrimination, or for 'aiding and abetting'.[24] In practice this last head of liability is likely to be of greater consequence in relation to trade union officials or shop stewards who influence or acquiesce in discrimination by management, a matter considered in greater detail in Chapter 9.

Having considered these preliminary points we may now turn to the general employment provisions.

DISCRIMINATION IN RECRUITMENT

The 1968 Act prohibited discrimination against a person seeking work 'which is available and for which he is qualified'.[25] The purpose of this clause was never clear, but its effect was to place two large stumbling blocks in the path of black job-seekers. It meant that a company which in pursuing a racialist hiring policy blatantly discriminated against a black inquirer, did not act unlawfully if in fact it had no vacancies at that particular moment. The same was true if a particular applicant was later proven to lack the necessary qualifications – itself often a very ambiguous standard. This language has been omitted from the present law; thus it is now illegal to treat a black applicant in any less favourable manner, for example by refusing to take his application while accepting that of a white, even if no openings exist or if he would not have been engaged for legitimate reasons.[26]*

In conjunction with this change, the Act now regulates 'arrangements made' in relation to recruitment or offers of employment (s. 4 (1)(a)). The great importance of this addition in relation to indirect discrimination has already been discussed (above, p. 46). Additionally, numerous 'arrangements' – practices and policies such as requiring higher levels of qualifications for blacks, or refusing to employ minorities for particular types of jobs (notably those involving contact with the public or visits to people's homes) – would constitute direct discrimination. If the policy ensured that an applicant was never fully considered – for example, by excluding him from a short list – his complaint would be based upon this subsection; if it was applied when the final hiring decision was taken he would complain of unlawful refusal to offer employment (s. 4 (1)(c)). However, where the arrangements have successfully kept minorities at arm's length from a particular company, so that none have actually applied and been personally affected by a discriminatory policy, the CRE is empowered to conduct a formal investigation and issue a non-discrimination notice if it finds the practice to be unlawful. (See further Chapter 13.)

DISCRIMINATORY ADVERTISEMENTS

One of the most important 'arrangements' concerning recruitment is of course advertisements of vacancies. These are subject to special regulation, as was true under the previous legislation. Because of the element of public insult and offensiveness involved in exclusionary advertisements they are illegal under s. 29 even if the particular form of discrimination is lawful, either because it is not made illegal by the Act, or is permitted by a specific exception therein. This is particularly important in relation to housing, and the widespread 'Flat to let – no coloureds please' notices disappeared after the passage of the 1968 Act, even though several explicit exemptions permitted discrimination. The same principle applies to employment; for example, those recruiting persons to work 'wholly or mainly outside Great Britain', or in a private household, are permitted to discriminate (see below, pp. 140–2) but not to indicate that intention in any advert. This broad sweep beyond the bounds of the statute is itself qualified by several specific exceptions, mainly concerning the special assistance provisions and cases where the genuine occupational qualification clause is invoked.[27] Moreover, as we have seen (p. 69), the proscription of discriminatory adverts does not reach exclusions based on nationality/citizenship if the employment is outside Great Britain. It would therefore be lawful to advertise for 'citizens of the United Kingdom' but not 'white Commonwealth citizens'. This is a tightening of the law, since the 1968 Act permitted the latter advertisement as well.[28] Indicating a preference for 'native-born U.K. citizens' would almost certainly be illegal, despite the fact that some blacks would fall within the category, since advertisements are unlawful not merely if they indicate, but if they 'might reasonably be understood as indicating' an intention to discriminate.[29] This language, carried over from the previous statute, appears to have been chosen to curb the use of ambiguous language and block searches for loop-holes, and also to direct the courts that in doubtful cases the advertisement should be suppressed. However, the Court of Appeal has analogised it to certain types of libel cases, and held that the test is whether the ordinary reasonable person, not one with specialist interest or knowledge, would understand the advert to suggest an intention to discriminate. 'Applying such a test, it is very much a matter of impression for the tribunal of fact'.[30] Thus where an advertisement in the *Daily Telegraph* for nursing jobs in South Africa included the phrase 'all white patients', Lord Denning M.R., although he found the question 'nicely balanced', refused to disturb the judgment of the County Court – which sat with assessors supposed to possess special expertise in matters of race relations (see below, p. 194) – that this did not restrict applications to white nurses, but merely informed potential applicants of all races that the institutions were segregated. The extent to which the advertising provisions have been undermined by the Court of Appeal's interpretation is difficult to predict: in the hypothetical advert for 'native-born U.K. citizens', one would assume that the reasonable reader would know that most adult blacks are immigrants and that many are not U.K. citizens, and would readily conclude that the advertiser intended to discriminate. In more ambiguous cases, however, the judicial test appears to weaken the law.

The public nature of advertisements makes them far easier to regulate and to prevent repetition, than is true of any other kind of discrimination. Moreover, those who publish, as well as those who 'cause to be published', unlawful advertisements are liable under the Act; hence it behoves anyone from a newsagent with a small notice-board to the editor of a mass-circulation magazine to vet the adverts received. Newsagents, merchants whose windows carry displays, and similarly situated persons are also covered because 'advertisement' is defined very broadly to include notices, even if not addressed to the public, and regardless of means of dissemination.[31] However, the publisher may escape liability if he reasonably relied upon the advertiser's statement that the advert fell within one of the exceptions permitted by the Act.[32]

The enforcement of s. 29 is reserved exclusively to the CRE.[33]* In employment cases the Commission may complain directly to an industrial tribunal that the respondent has commissioned or published an unlawful advert.[34] If the tribunal so finds, and if the Commission believe he is likely to continue violating the same sections, it may seek in a designated County Court to enjoin the anticipated illegality. The Court may grant an injunction or more limited order, and the prohibition need not be limited to a precise repetition of the previous violation, but may extend to all 'further acts which by virtue of [s. 29] are unlawful'.[35] In practice only the crudest and most clearly illegal advertisements are likely to be the subject of injunction proceedings. Thus far the Commission has preferred to proceed informally, attempting to secure voluntary withdrawal of unlawful publications, and in 1978 did so successfully in more than half the cases about which it had received complaints. Settlement effects continued in the others, and as of the end of that year no legal proceedings had been taken.[36]

There is of course a potential overlap between advertisements and the discriminatory 'arrangements' which may be the subject of an individual's complaint under s. 4 (1)(a), since the former may be part of the latter. In such circumstances a Scottish industrial tribunal held that it had jurisdiction to consider an individual complaint that an advert was discriminatory.[37] However, this overlap is more likely to arise, as in that case, in the context of sex rather than race discrimination, for numerous institutions cater for men and women exclusively and sometimes attempt to restrict their hiring to persons of that sex.

DISCRIMINATION AGAINST EMPLOYEES

Apart from the question of inferior terms the position of an applicant is likely to be straightforward: either he is offered employment or he is not.

The employee, on the other hand, is subject to a complex system of rules and opportunities, and among its different components the forms and frequency of discrimination will vary significantly. We shall therefore look in turn at each aspect of employment covered by s. 4 (2).

PROMOTION, TRAINING AND TRANSFER

A. Promotion

PEP did not attempt to measure the incidence of discrimination in promotion, since within a company the obstacles to any sort of controlled experiments such as the actor tests proved insuperable. It did find however that, at all job levels, whites were more than twice as likely as blacks to have supervisory responsibilities; and of the plants surveyed only 22 per cent had minority supervisors with white manual-worker subordinates.[38] Moreover, although only a relatively small fraction of men wished to be promoted at all, the proportion was slightly higher among minorities, as was the percentage of those dissatisfied with their promotion prospects.[39]

Three kinds of advancement within a firm may be distinguished. The first involves rising to supervisory positions within the same job level, as when a skilled worker becomes a foreman or chargehand overseeing the same type of work, or a clerk becomes head of the section in which he has been a junior. The second, sometimes called progression, means an ascent in the level of skill, usually involving a period of training, as when the most senior unskilled or semi-skilled assistant to a skilled worker is given a chance to learn the job. This often involves younger workers outside formal apprenticeship schemes. The third involves crossing the great divide in British industrial life, from manual to non-manual work – migration from the shop floor to junior managerial or white-collar work. Discrimination is equally unlawful in all these situations, but its contribution to the absence of black advance may vary enormously. For example, it has been reported that West Indians have been content to remain in the highest-paid skilled jobs not involving supervisory work, because they stand to gain little financially by becoming chargehands, and wish to avoid the personal abuse involved.[40] Not all the unpleasantness would be racial, and in any case this choice by an individual, no matter how much racial factors hovered in the background, does not involve discrimination as known to the law. The same Report stated that most complaints concerning promotion involved Asians, which coincides with the PEP finding that Indians and East African Asians were most keen on advancement.[41] For them the biggest stumbling-block is likely to be employers' insistence that only white necks wear white collars. Indeed, given the high degree of discrimination in white-collar jobs revealed by the PEP tests, one may predict that this will be one of the central areas of activity for anti-discrimination law in the coming decade, mostly concerning well-qualified Asians, especially Indians.

The key problem surrounding promotion is that most employers use criteria which allow extensive scope for subjective and arbitrary judgments, indeed which inevitably invite them. A characteristic example is those used by British Leyland when assessing potential Methods Analysts: 'Personal Health, Qualifications, Training, Experience, Intelligence, Social Abilities, Leadership, Self-Reliance, Stability, Motivation, Interests.'[42] This rag-bag of objective indicators of performance, assessment of aptitude, judgments about personality so subjective as to make criticism impossible, and matters entirely irrelevant to fitness for the job, is all too typical; indeed for higher-level positions there may be no formally proclaimed standards at all, with even greater weight attached to whether, in addition to relative competence, the candidate will 'fit in'.

No statute or rule of common law requires employers to base their decisions on standards of bureaucratic rationality. However, when the application of more vague and subjective standards leads to differentially high failure rates for minorities, the concept of indirect discrimination immediately becomes relevant. Although the legal issue arises in a whole range of employment contexts, it is of particular importance to promotion, where intangibles have traditionally been accorded such great emphasis – leaving vast scope for racial stereotypes to masquerade as legitimate judgment of personal characteristics. Indeed the shadowy quality of all such evaluations leaves the candidate with no real ground on which to contest a judgment based upon prejudice, conscious or unconscious. In these circumstances problems of direct and indirect discrimination converge: subjective assessments may mask deliberate racist decisions by individuals, or simply facilitate unintended but consistent disfavouring of non-whites. Indeed both factors may be at work concurrent where, as in a large company, many such decisions are taken over an extended period by several people.

These circumstances may call forth several positive responses: development, and consistent use, of evaluation criteria that as specifically as possible measure the candidate's past performance and other job-related characteristics; multiple evaluations, which reduce the power of any one person and dilute the effect of stereotypes that may influence an individual's views; and systematic review of promotions throughout the firm, to determine whether minorities are failing in disproportionate numbers. All these steps can, of course, be taken by employers of their own accord, and indeed would constitute essential parts of any realistic equal opportunity policy. But it is submitted that the use of subjective criteria where rates of promotion – or indeed of hiring – of blacks are 'considerably' below those for whites, is itself an indirectly discriminatory practice for which – given that these measures may readily be implemented – justification would be very difficult to establish. This is one area where the approach of the American courts should command respect, for they have had experience of a voluminous number of cases raising this issue, and the racially (and also sexually) discriminatory effect of standardless employment decisions has become so clearly manifest that numerous courts have declared them unlawful where they have not been shown to be related with some precision to job performance.[43] Moreover, as will be argued below (pp. 208–11), even in complaints by individuals of direct discrimination under the Act, statistical evidence of lower success rates of non-whites provides strong inferential support for the complainant's case where he purportedly was rejected for failure to satisfy subjective standards.

Thus far tribunals have been singularly resistant to claims of discrimination in promotion. Of the 33 successful cases decided up to the end of March 1979, precisely one concerned promotion, and there the failure of the respondent to call the key witness left the tribunal with no other plausible conclusion.[44] This is apparently due to their unwillingness to question the general use and specific application of subjective criteria, even in the relatively straightforward context of direct discrimination. Whatever may have been the truth about any specific case, as a general stance this is simply not good enough. The Act was not meant simply to prise open access for black people to low-level jobs; the same approach to facts, and the drawing of reasonable inferences from them, is to be taken in relation to all aspects of employment covered by the Act. Certainly for the present generation of British-born and educated black people, promotion will be as much a part of their career expectations as for their white contemporaries. In the long run ensuring fair promotion practices will be the touchstone of the effectiveness of the Act.

A further issue which companies must squarely face is that some employees will resent taking orders or being supervised by a black superior; hence promotion of a minority person may lead to greater disharmony than promotion of a white of lesser ability. Even assuming this attitude were widespread, it is legally irrelevant: discrimination to soothe racialist feelings of employees, or the preferences of customers, remains discrimination. Indeed any deliberate effort to induce or persuade a person responsible for promotions to take racialist feeling into account would be a form of pressure to discriminate and hence itself unlawful.[45]

There is also good evidence that this sort of white resistance is both relatively rare and easily overcome. Of those employers in the PEP survey who had appointed minority supervisors, only 5 per cent said that problems had ensued.[46] Moreover the study's conclusions on the nature of white resistance, drawn from experiences of both initial recruitment and promotion, are clear and quite persuasive.[47] They are that there is a sharp line between attitudes and behaviour, and that the former can be effectively neutralised if it is made plain that their expression will not be countenanced. This is not to say that racialist attitudes change when blacks are introduced to the workforce; they may even harden. But if it is made clear by management that the newcomers are there to stay, most of the recalcitrant whites – themselves usually a small minority – quickly come to accept them. The hard core of irreconcilables simply gnash their teeth, or even if individuals continue to abuse black workers verbally, their intensity simply mirrors their impotence. There were also numerous examples of what the Report called 'dissonance between attitudes of behaviour' – of strongly prejudiced people treating blacks politely and fairly because the situation required it. The corollary of these findings is not yet sufficiently appreciated: where ambiguity is allowed to prevail – as when key management or union personnel express their ambivalence, or hostility, to the presence of blacks – people who would have muted their objections in the presence of forceful leadership become less inhibited when they have only weak or contradictory cues to follow. Thus if senior management and unions decide to introduce an equal opportunity policy – in which widened promotion opportunities would be a vital element – and make it plain that obstruction will not be tolerated, they will face weaker opposition than if employees are asked hypothetical questions about their attitudes to black colleagues, or the effectuation of the policy is delayed or accompanied by obvious disagreement at lower levels of management.

Furthermore, although the conclusion must be hedged with qualifications owing to the complexities of unfair dismissal law, it would appear that employees who actively and deliberately obstruct the implementation of an equal opportunity policy may lawfully be sacked. One of the relatively few categories of action which in principle justifies summary dismissal for a single act is that of gross misconduct, which includes wilful disobedience to a legitimate order.[48] Thus so long as the employer makes it very clear that discriminatory decisions by personnel officials, racial abuse on the shop floor, or refusal to co-operate with or train newly-hired black employees, will be regarded as gross misconduct, and consistently treats such behaviour as a serious offence,[49] dismissal would probably be regarded as fair. This view assumes that the industrial tribunal, in applying the overarching statutory 'reasonableness' rule,[50] concludes that it was reasonable to classify racialist behaviour as gross misconduct. Given that, as we have seen, inducing or inciting others to discriminate is an unlawful act – as is assisting others to do so[51] – this conclusion would seem amply justified, if not indeed required as a matter of law. Moreover, the Court of Appeal decision in *Retarded Children's Aid Society Ltd* v. *Day*[52] suggests that where it is clear that an employee is opposed to the rules or policies operated by his employer and will carry on disobeying them, the usual concern with the need for warnings may be dispensed with, and he may be sacked forthwith.

In many instances the circumstances surrounding an employee's behaviour will be ambiguous, making it inappropriate to regard it as gross misconduct. There are however numerous cases in which dismissal for refusal to co-operate with management or for unpleasant and unjustified behaviour to other employees have been upheld as fair, particularly where warnings have been given in response to previous misconduct.[53] The important point is that employers will not find themselves caught in a vice of conflicting statutory commands, and may unequivocally insist upon compliance with the Act and with company policies designed to enhance opportunities. They cannot plausibly contend that opposition of white employees to the recruitment or promotion of blacks ties their hands.

B.   Training

Denial of opportunities for progression would probably technically not be regarded as discrimination in promotion, but in training, also specified in s. 4 (2)(b). The special assistance provisions discussed in Chapter 1 are strictly speaking derogations from this provision. An analogous exemption is for training of persons resident overseas who come to Britain to acquire skills which they intend to exercise wholly outside this country.[54] The employer may discriminate, but only to the benefit of such persons. The idea was to shield companies which set aside a fixed number of jobs for such overseas trainees from complaints of discrimination (presumably on grounds of nationality) by British residents. The exemption was also necessary for the various government-sponsored programmes which, it is hoped, will produce people who will favour British-made goods when exercising their skills in their home countries.

C.   Transfer

The question of transfer is encrusted with far greater legal complexity. The issues have been thoroughly canvassed by Macdonald, to whose account the reader is referred.[55] The one clear change brought about by the present Act is that the repeal of the racial balance clause (below, pp. 137–8) means that transfers of employees to achieve or maintain racial quotas no longer have statutory sanction. However, they probably do not violate s. 4 (2)(b), which speaks of 'access to opportunities for ... transfer'; they would either (depending on the factors Macdonald analyses) amount to dismissal, or to detriment (s. 4 (2)(c)). Complaints relating to transfers would be limited to the situation where the employee sought one and was denied it on racial grounds.

BENEFITS, FACILITIES OR SERVICES

The precise application of these terms is obscure. Its most likely use is as a plug for potential loop-holes: most things desirable to the employee and not regarded as a 'term' in the contract of employment should fall into this residual category. Examples would include Christmas bonuses and other employer largesse, permission to take time off for a wide variety of personal reasons on the same basis as other employees, or loans at below the market rate of interest to acquire shares in the company. If these desiderata are available only to employees, complaints involving discrimination in their provision are treated as matters of employment and heard by industrial tribunals. If, however, the employer is providing the same things to the public or a section of it – as when the complaint concerns accommodation provided by a hotel to its employees – the complaint is treated as one involving goods, facilities and services, and, like all such cases, must be taken to a County Court. This ordained by s. 4 (4), an indigestible jurisdictional provision whose impenetrability occasioned a good deal of jocularity in the Standing Committee. It also provides that in three instances – where the matter provided relates to training, or is regulated by the contract of employment, or is significantly different from what is offered the public (for example, banks offer loans to the public only at a market rate and commonly do not offer mortgages at all, but their higher-level employees are generally granted the important fringe benefit of low interest mortgages) – the complaint is to go to a tribunal.

DISMISSAL

One of the most valuable statutory rights in employment is that of redress for unfair dismissal. Introduced originally as part of the package of the Industrial Relations Act, and significantly expanded and strengthened in 1974 and 1975, the legislation (now found in EPCA) in effect deems dismissals unlawful unless they are based upon the employee's capability, qualifications or conduct, or are due to redundancy, statutory bar to continued employment or other substantial reason.[56] Moreover, a dismissal on one of the approved grounds may none the less be unfair if management failed to accord the employee appropriate procedural safeguards, particularly those recommended in the Code of Practice drafted by the Advisory, Conciliation and Arbitration Service (ACAS). The law concerning unfair dismissal is voluminous, complex and has been substantially altered in recent years by interpretations of the EAT; the reader may wish to consult detailed accounts.[57] The foregoing rough sketch is sufficient for background purposes; our present concern is the overlap between the Act and the law governing unfair dismissals. The consequence of this overlap is that while in some cases a complaint may have rights under both statutes, in others he may be barred by the qualifying rules of one but eligible under the other. Additional differences, notably in relation to remedies, create a legal labyrinth which requires exploration with some care.

A preliminary point is that 'dismissal' is defined in EPCA,[58] but not in the Act. This does not necessarily produce greater clarity in the former area of law, for an initially complex statutory definition has been further knotted by judicial interpretation. Speaking very broadly, a dismissal occurs not only where the employer overtly sacks the employee, but also where the latter resigns rather than accepts the employer's breach of contract, a situation known as constructive dismissal.[59] There are also a few less common situations, as when a fixed-term contract is not renewed, which are specifically enumerated as types of dismissal.[60] Since this has not been done for purposes of the Act, a victim of discrimination in these circumstances could only claim unfair dismissal, unless it could be argued that the refusal to renew was a 'detriment' (see below, pp. 130–1).

Although EPCA does not explicitly state that a discriminatory dismissal is automatically unfair, it is submitted that this is so for two reasons. First, it is difficult to see how a dismissal on racial grounds could ever fall within the set of potentially fair reasons just enumerated. Second, one of the major innovations in compensation for unfair dismissal introduced in 1975 is otherwise incomprehensible. As part of the attempt to strengthen the re-employment remedies of reinstatement and re-engagement tribunals were given more explicit guidance in the assessment of compensation where the employer failed to comply with such orders. They were also directed to give higher additional awards, calculated at double the normal range,[61] for two types of dismissal alone: those involving retaliation for trade union membership and activities, and discrimination unlawful under the Act or the Sex Discrimination Act.[62] In effect this adopts the concept of discrimination in the Act as a standard of unfairness in dismissal; it follows that a complaint of a discriminatory dismissal may be subsumed under a claim of unfair dismissal under EPCA. This is important, for, as will be seen, the remedies for unfair dismissal are generally more favourable to the complainant. Moreover, the racial element may make unfair a dismissal which would otherwise be lawful. Thus where an employee's conduct would have justified his dismissal, but other employees of different race received more lenient treatment for the same conduct, the dismissal would be racially discriminatory, and hence unfair. 'Different race' rather than white or black is the precisely accurate language, for harsher treatment of a white would be equally illegal under the Act.[63]

The same analysis has important application to cases where racialist reaction to black workers leads to their dismissal to 'restore shop-floor harmony'.[64] As with recruitment, compliance with the bigotry of others can never be a substantial reason justifying dismissal, which in these circumstances would be both unlawful discrimination and unfair. This conclusion is supported by the provision in the EPCA which bars a tribunal from taking account of pressure exerted on the employers by means of actual or threatened industrial action to bring about the employee's dismissal in deciding whether it was unfair.[65] Indeed as we have seen (p. 123 above) those agitating against minority workers would be acting illegally, and if their conduct disrupted production or normal working they could themselves be fairly dismissed. Any alternative interpretation of unfair dismissal law, or of the Act, would effectively grant racialists a veto over the employment of non-whites.

Although a complainant may submit claims under both statutes for the same wrong, in certain cases he may be ineligible under one of them. Unfair dismissal law is hedged about with qualifying conditions not found in the Act. The most important is that, as from 1 October 1979, the employee must have served for 52 continuous weeks.[66] Part-time workers – usually those whose contract states that their employment is for less than 16 hours per week – are excluded.[67] So are those who are over the 'normal retiring age' for someone in their position with that employer, or men over 65 and women over 60.[68] However, this last limitation has been curtailed by the curious decision of the Court of Appeal in *Nothman* v. *Barnet London Borough Council*[69] – affirmed by a sharply divided House of Lords[70] – which held that the age limits apply only where there is no normal retiring age in the complainant's occupation. This of course mainly benefits women like Miss Nothman, who would otherwise be barred at an earlier age than men in the same work. All persons in these categories can, however, complain of discriminatory dismissals under s. 4 (2)(c). Conversely, the only situation where the eligibility conditions of the Act are more restrictive is where the employee works in a private household. He has no rights under the Act (below, p. 140) but may claim unfair dismissal. Presumably as a result of the qualifying conditions, complaints about dismissals were by far the most common – 43.1 per cent, as compared with 28.1 per cent concerning refusal to hire – arising under the Act in its first year of operation.[71]

A dismissed employee who satisfies the qualifying conditions will virtually always be better advised to emphasise his claim of unfair dismissal, rather than of discriminatory dismissal under s. 4 (2)(c), because the remedies for the former are both broader and more generous. Under EPCA the primary remedy is supposed to be the return of the wrongly dismissed worker to his job under terms of an *order* either of reinstatement or re-engagement, although the remarkably low number of such orders suggests that tribunals have failed to appreciate the importance of the change of emphasis embodied in the legislation of 1975.[72] Compensation is supposed to be awarded only when the employee rejects a return, unless the employer can convincingly demonstrate that this is not 'practicable' for a precisely defined set of reasons, or where the employee has contributed to the dismissal.[73] In view of the prevailing high levels of unemployment, low-skilled workers particularly may be expected to prefer re-employment to a lump sum accompanied by long-term dole. Under the Act the tribunal can only issue a 'recommendation' – the term found so unsatisfactory in producing re-employment during the initial period of unfair dismissal law that it was replaced by 'order' in 1975 – that the respondent take action to reduce the discriminatory effect of his actions.[74] It is also given more discretion in ordering compensation if the respondent fails to comply; where this occurs after an order of reinstatement or re-engagement, the tribunal 'shall' make an award in accordance with a detailed statutory formula, but in discrimination cases a tribunal 'may' do so 'if it thinks it just and equitable'.[75] Thus the victim of a discriminatory dismissal is at any rate in theory more likely to obtain re-employment under EPCA. However, nothing in the Act *forbids* tribunals making a recommendation of reinstatement and backing it up with a heavy monetary award in the event of non-compliance. That this is unlikely to occur is as much the result of tribunal predilection as of statutory weakness.

The rules governing compensation come together in an extraordinary tangle. Duplicative payments are prohibited: tribunals are not to give damages for racial and/or sex discrimination which has been taken into account in computing an unfair dismissal award, and vice versa.[76] The extent of overlap is quite difficult to judge, although it is clear that complainants may simultaneously receive compensation under each statute for separate wrongs. The assessment of unfair dismissal compensation was recast in 1975, so that it now includes a 'basic award', calculated according to the same formula created for statutory redundancy payments, under which payment increases with the employee's age and length of service[77] and a 'compensatory award', which is supposed to replace actual financial losses occasioned by the dismissal.[78] Compensation under the Act, however, is governed by principles of tort law,[79] which would confine it to recognised categories of special and general damage and rule out anything like the abstract formula of the basic award. In practical terms this means that under the act the dismissed employee would receive only the equivalent of a compensatory award: his lost wages and ancillary benefits would be the complete measure of his pecuniary damages. In partial recompense the Act explicitly authorises damages to feelings,[80] which are not permitted in cases of unfair dismissal.[81] This is the only basis of compensation available under the Act but not permitted under EPCA. (Compensation for discrimination is considered in detail in Chapter 12.) In both cases, however, the complainant would be under a duty to mitigate his damages,[82] as for example by not refusing a reasonable offer of employment with another employer. Moreover, the principle of contributory negligence is probably equally applicable. Though mentioned explicitly only in relation to unfair dismissal,[83] it would be implicit in the use of tort principles to determine damages.

Compensation may differ substantially in two respects, however. The Act sets a flat maximum of compensation, now £5200.[84] For unfair dismissal the maximum basic award is now £3300, to which may be added a top compensatory figure of £5750.[85] These two awards are made either when reinstatement or re-engagement was not ordered, or when an employee is re-employed but the employer fails fully to comply with the conditions specified by the tribunal.[86] When the employer cannot satisfy the tribunal that it was not 'practicable' for him to comply with the order for reinstatement or re-engagement, compensation consists of these two awards plus an additional award; where the dismissal constituted unlawful discrimination under the Act this can be as high as another 52 weeks' pay, subject to the statutory limit of £110 per week – a total of £5720.[87] Thus, although it is highly unlikely,[88] the victim of a discriminatory dismissal could under the most aggravated circumstances receive £14,770 or nearly treble the compensation permitted under the Act. Moreover, since victimisation is explicitly treated under the Act as one specialised form of discrimination, [89] the higher additional award must be made in such cases, giving added protection to those whose willingness to assist victims of discrimination will often be essential to establishing the truth about disputed events (above, Chapter 4).

The second divergence may not have been intended. In the early years of unfair dismissal law tribunals deducted any employment or supplementary benefit received by complainants from their assessment of loss. The idea was to prevent double compensation, but it also shifted a substantial part of the cost of the employer's violation of the law to the social security system. This was altered in 1977; the deduction from the employee's award continues, but the DHSS now recoups the total state benefits from the employer.[90] The gist of a remarkably complex procedure is that if a tribunal decides that an unfairly dismissed man merited a total award of £1000, and he had already received £400 in state benefits for himself and all dependants, it would order the employer to pay him £600 and to pay £400 to the DHSS. On the other hand, assessment of compensation under tort law precludes consideration of any Supplementary Benefit (SB) received. This was settled by the House of Lords a decade ago in *Parry* v. *Cleaver*,[91] when it approved an earlier decision[92] to this effect. However, the treatment of Unemployment Benefit (UB) in tort cases remains a grey area awaiting judicial illumination: the Pearson Commission reported that present practice is a patchwork of inconsistency.[93] Hence if the dismissed employee in the above example brings a claim under the Act alone (thus forgoing any compensation equivalent to the basic award under EPCA) and is awarded damages of £1000 he could end up with anything between £1000 and £1400, depending upon whether he had received UB, SB or both, and upon whether the tribunal made any deduction for his UB. In this situation the dismissed employee is likely to have been eligible for SB only if his contributions were insufficient to entitle him to UB. There is no apparent reason why a person in this position should be favoured in the amount he may receive in compensation, especially since the extra money comes not from the discriminator, but from the Exchequer. This anomaly proceeds not from the Act, but from the logic of *Parry* v. *Cleaver*, in which the House of Lords was concerned that the creation of the Welfare State not provide a windfall for tortfeasors. It may most fairly be rectified by applying this policy with rigorous consistency and extending the provisions for recoupment to all tort cases in which the victim has received state income support, not by permitting reductions in the employer's liability for unfair dismissal or for discrimination.

The one remaining group of dismissals to be considered involves redundancy. In a number of circumstances the manner of selection of a particular employee may make his dismissal unfair, as where the employer breached a customary or agreed selection procedure[94] or did not make reasonable efforts to find him alternative employment within the undertaking or one of its associated companies.[95] Almost certainly selection of someone for redundancy on racial grounds would be regarded as unfair, as well as discriminatory; at least one tribunal so held where sex was the basis of selection, several years before sex-discrimination legislation was enacted.[96] The profound problem of indirect discrimination raised by the 'last-in – first-out' (LIFO) rule for redundancy selection has been considered in Chapter 2.

DETRIMENT

This last, 'sweeper-up', category seeks to catch any other form of ill treatment involving race which is not specifically mentioned elsewhere in s. 4 (2). The EAT has interpreted this word in the context of sex discrimination as connoting something 'serious or important'.[97] In doing so it purported to follow the decision of the Court of Appeal in *Peake* v. *Automotive Products Ltd*,[98] which rejected a complaint by a man who contended that he suffered a detriment under the Sex Discrimination Act because women in his factory were permitted to leave five minutes earlier than men. The basis of this decision, as subsequently recognised,[99]* was that the discrimination must be more than *de minimis* to constitute detriment, and the EAT's exposition should be understood to express no more rigorous test.[100] Moreover, unlike relations between men and women, any form of differentiation on grounds of race is inherently offensive, as the explicit prohibition of 'separate but equal' makes plain.[101] The judgments in *Peake* do suggest, however, that the test of whether any form of treatment of a complaint constitutes a detriment is objective rather than subjective – i.e. the complainant's statement that his treatment was demeaning in some way is not sufficient: the tribunal must be convinced that his perception was reasonable.[102]

One example of a detriment would be the opposite side of the coin of denying access to benefits: where the employee already had something desirable, e.g. regular opportunity to work overtime, and this was taken away on racial grounds, he will have suffered a detriment. More straightforward instances have emerged in early litigation: detriment has been found where the employer refused to operate a grievance procedure[103] or where a black employee received disciplinary warnings after provocation by racist co-workers.[104] Another example would be matters not covered by 'terms', as where a black employee (or group of employees) is given work in the dirtiest or noisiest part of a plant. Assuming this did not amount to segregation, if the physical placing of workers, or the actual allocation of work, were done on a racial basis, less favourable treatment of blacks would constitute detriment. A final instance would be discriminatory selection for layoff, which at least initially would not be classified as a dismissal.[105]*

NOTES

1. See the analysis in A. Ogus and E. Barendt, *The Law of Social Security* (Butterworth, 1978) pp. 48–52.
2. *Massey* v. *Crown Life Insurance Co.*, [1978] 1 W.L.R. 676.
3. S. 78 (1).
4. PEP Report, p. 93; above, p. 99.
5. *Bramble* v. *Clibbens Car Hire*, unreported, COIT 809/192 (1978), construing s. 14 (1) of the Act, which applies to an 'employment agency'.
6. See Chap. 8 for a discussion of discrimination in public sector employment. S. 75 brings the Crown at least partially within the Act.
7. [1979] I.C.R. 194.
8. S. 75 (1) and (2), the equivalent of SDA, s. 85 (1) and (2).
9. S. 53 (2) expressly reserves these remedies.
10. See S. de Smith, *Judicial Review of Administrative Action* (Sweet & Maxwell, 3rd edn, 1973) part III, especially chaps. 8 and 11, for the history and rules governing these remedies. On the present simplified form of the 'application for review' (Order 53) see Beatson and Matthews, (1978) 41 *M.L.R.* 437.
11. *Department of the Environment* v. *Fox*, [1980] 1 All E.R. 58.
12. RRA 1968, s. 3 (1)(b).
13. See the analysis by M. Freedland, *The Contract of Employment* (Clarendon Press, 1976) chap. 1, and especially the Postscript, pp. 372–6.
14. See, e.g., the examples cited in *Macdonald*, para. 160, and in the *Observer* account of 'Race on the Shop Floor', 23 July 1978.
15. For citations and discussion, see Simpson, 'Trade dispute and Industrial Dispute in English Law', (1977) 40 *M.L.R.* 16, 17–18.
16. This is a precise language of s. 4 (1); that of s. 4 (2) is slightly different, but in substance identical.
17. RRA 1968, s. 3.
18. S. 32 (1).
19. See, further, P. Atiyah, *Vacarious Liability in the Law of Torts* (Butterworth, 1967) chap. 19.
20. S. 32 (3).
21. *Mills* v. *Brook Street Bureau of Mayfair Ltd*, (1979) COIT 864/233.
22. S. 33 (1).
23. S. 33 (2).
24. Such was the holding of an Exeter Industrial Tribunal in a sex discrimination case, *Read* v. *Tiverton D.C.*, [1977] I.R.L.R. 202.
25. RRA 1968, s. 3 (1)(a).

*26. Cf. *Kirszak* v. *Swinnerton & Son Ltd*, COIT 851/201 (1979), a decision of a Birmingham Industrial Tribunal finding unlawful discrimination where the employer refused to interview Mr K. for a driver's job because of his foreign-sounding name. The fact that his bad driving record would probably have barred him was irrelevant.

27. S. 29 (2).

28. This was the Home Office interpretation of the 1968 Act, which it sought to alter in the present law. See White Paper, para. 76.

29. S. 29 (1).

30. *CRE* v. *Associated Newspapers Group Ltd*, [1978] 1 W.L.R. 905, 908, per Lord Denning M.R. Although this case was decided under the 1968 Act, the present s. 29 is in this respect identical.

31. S. 78 (1).

32. S. 29 (4). It is a summary offence knowingly or recklessly to make a false statement to this effect: s. 29 (5).

*33. S. 63 (1). The same enforcement procedure and jurisdictional monopoly applies to s. 30 (instructions to discriminate) and s. 31 (inducements). These are not separately discussed anywhere in this book.

34. S. 63 (2)(a).

35. S. 63 (4).

36. CRE, *Annual Report 1978*, H.C. 128 (H.M.S.O., 1979) p. 20.

37. *Brindley* v. *Tayside Health Bd*, [1976] I.R.L.R. 364.

38. *Racial Disadvantage*, pp. 186–7.

39. Ibid. p. 185.

40. 'Race on the Shop Floor', *The Observer*, 23 July 1978.

41. *Racial Disadvantage*, p. 186.

42. Quoted in the judgment of the Court of Appeal in *SRC* v. *Nassé, Vyas* v *Leyland Cars*, [1978] 3 All E.R. 1196, 1203. See Chap. 11 for discussion of this case.

43. The most-cited case seems to be *Rowe* v. *General Motors Corp.* 457 F. 2d 348 (5th Circ. 1972). For discussion of the broad issue and citation of numerous American cases on subjective criteria see B. Schlei and P. Grossman, *Employment Discrimination Law* (Bureau of National Affairs, Washington, 1976) pp. 72–6. A brief summary of several other promotion cases – none of which has been reported – may be found in I.D.S., Brief, Supp. 23, pp. 29–30.

44. *Davies* v. *British Railways Board*, unreported decision of a London Industrial Tribunal, 12 June 1978.

45. S. 31. Actions against violators of this section can only be brought by the CRE: s. 63 (1).

46. *Racial Disadvantage*, p. 187.

47. Ibid. pp. 170–81.

48. On gross misconduct and unfair dismissal see S. D. Anderman, *The Law of Unfair Dismissal* (Butterworth, 1978) pp. 104–10.

49. Where an employer has previously condoned breaches of his rules, or applied disciplinary rules inconsistently, dismissal in a particular case may be held unfair. See the discussion in ibid. pp. 120–3.

50. This is found in EPCA, s. 57 (3), and discussed at length in ibid. chap. 5. See especially pp. 108–9 on the reasonableness of classifying particular acts as gross misconduct.

51. S. 33, discussed in detail on p. 167.

52. [1978] I.R.L.R. 128.

53. Cases upholding the dismissal of persons whose behaviour caused disharmony within an enterprise are discussed by Anderman, op. cit., at p. 165 (see n. 48). Examples of fair dismissal for refusal to co-operate with management are two EAT decisions, *Boychuk* v. *J. Symons Holdings Ltd*, [1977] I.R.L.R. 395, and *Lawrence* v. *Newham Borough Council*, [1977] I.R.L.R. 396.

54. S. 6. Cf. s. 36, which is even broader.

55. *Macdonald*, paras 162–71.

56. EPCA s. 57 (1)(b) and (2), sets out the approved grounds.

57. The leading work is that of Anderman, op. cit. (see n. 48, above). See also D. Jackson, *Unfair Dismissal* (C.U.P., 1975).

58. EPCA, s. 55.

59. On which see Elias, 'Unraveling the Concept of Dismissal', (1978) 7 *I.L.J.* 16, 101.

60. EPCA, s. 55 (2)(b).

61. That is, based on 26 to 52 week's pay, rather than 13 to 26: EPCA, s. 71 (2)(b).

62. EPCA, s. 71 (3).

63. Cf. the similar reaction to harsher treatment of white employees under American anti-discrimination law in *McDonald* v. *Santa Fe Trail Trans. Co.* 427 U.S. 273 (1976).

64. Examples of such cases, decided (wrongly it is submitted) under the previous Act, are found in *Macdonald*, paras 195–7.

65. EPCA, s. 63.

66. EPCA, s. 64 (1)(a), as amended by S.I. 1979/959.

67. This follows, rather tortuously, from the exclusion of those not in 'continuous employment'. See EPCA, s. 151 and sched. 13.

68. EPCA, s. 64 (1)(b).

69. [1978] I.C.R. 336.

70. [1979] I.C.R. 111.

71. *D.E. Gazette*, October 1978, p. 1186, Table 5.

72. Figures on the number of such orders made in 1975–7 are given by B. Bercusson, *The Employment Protection (Consolidation) Act 1978* (Stevens, 1979) annotation to s. 68. For a discussion of how failure to perceive that reinstatement/ re-engagement are the primary remedies has affected judicial interpretation see the Note by M. Freedland, (1978) 7 *I.L.J.* 50.

73. The key provisions here are EPCA, ss. 68–70, esp. ss. 69 (5) and 70 (1).

74. S. 56 (1)(b).

75. S. 56 (4), which may be compared with EPCA, s. 71.

76. EPCA, s. 76.

77. EPCA, s. 73.

78. EPCA, s. 74. These losses would include lost earnings from the date of dismissal to the date of decision, and estimated future losses, both including ancillary benefits such as pension rights.

79. S. 57 (1).

80. S. 57 (4).

81. *Norton Tool Co. Ltd* v. *Tewson*, [1973] 1 All E. R. 183.

82. This is a basic principle applicable in all tort actions; EPCA, s. 74 (4) applies it to unfair dismissal claims.

83. EPCA, ss. 73 (7) and 74 (6).

84. S. 56 (2) and (3).

85. The method of calculation is explained by Bercusson, op. cit. (see n. 71, above), annotation to s. 72. The present maxima are laid down in The Employment Protection (Variation of Limits) Order 1978 (S.I. 1978/1777) and The Unfair Dismissal (Increase of Compensation Limit) Order 1978 (S.I. 1978/1778).

86. EPCA, s. 72.

87. EPCA, s. 71 (2) and (3); the maxima are found in the Statutory Instruments cited in n. 85 above.

88. Since the basic award is calculated according to age and period of employment with the respondent, the employee would have to have been with the employer

for at least twenty years, and be either near retirement age or very highly paid to secure the maximum sum. To achieve the highest possible compensatory award, which relates largely to lost wages, he would have to have very poor re-employment prospects indeed – which would probably be true only of someone near retirement age, or with a highly specialised skill made redundant by technological change.

89. S. 3 (3)(a).

90. EPCA, s. 132. The relevant delegated legislation putting the scheme into effect is the turgid Employment Protection (Recoupment of Unemployment Benefit and Supplementary Benefit) Regulations 1977 (S.I. 1977/674), explained in (1977) 6 *I.L.J.* 192.

91. [1970] A.C. 1.

92. *Foxley* v. *Olton*, [1965] 2 Q.B. 306. This decision has been criticised by commentators, notably P. Atiyah, *Accidents, Compensation and the Law* (2nd edn, Weidenfeld & Nicolson, 1975) p. 407, and A. Ogus, *The Law of Damages* (Butterworth, 1973) p. 224, but remains the governing law.

93. Royal Commission on Civil Liability, Cmnd 7054 (1978) para. 467.

94. EPCA, s. 59.

95. The leading case is *Vokes Ltd* v. *Bear*, [1974] I.C.R. 1.

96. *Lee* v. *British Domestic Appliances Ltd*, [1972] I.R.L.R. 8.

97. *Schmidt* v. *Austick's Bookshops Ltd*, [1978] I.C.R. 85.

98. [1977] I.C.R. 968.

*99. Lord Denning M.R. also rested his judgment in the *Peake* case on the grounds that the SDA was not intended to outlaw arrangements that reflected a chivalrous attitude toward women. In *Ministry of Defence* v. *Jeremiah*, [1979] 3 All E.R. 833, 836, he repudiated that position, and stated that the result should rest on the *de minimis* ground alone.

100. In *Jeremiah* Brandon L.J. equated detriment simply with 'putting at a disadvantage', [1979] 3 All E.R. at 837.

101. S. 1 (2).

102. Cf. the view of Brightman L.J. in *Jeremiah*, [1979] 3 All E.R. at 871, that the test of detriment is whether a 'reasonable' worker would so view the particular circumstances.

103. *Sheikh* v. *Focus Cinemas Ltd*, COIT 839/36 (1978).

104. *Ramsey* v. *John James Hawley (Speciality Works) Ltd*, COIT 804/139 (1978).

*105. At some point – exactly when is unclear – the layoff would constitute a constructive dismissal, which would bring the employee, if otherwise eligible, under EPCA.

7

Exclusions and Exceptions

Few enactments cover a particular field comprehensively. In response to the pressure of interest groups, belief that legal intervention is impractical or inappropriate in certain circumstances, a decision that certain manifestations of the problem addressed are of little importance, or sometimes simply due to draftsman's error, certain categories of people or activity are generally exempted. Yet however reasonable the case for a particular exception may seem, the cumulative effect of reasonable arguments may be that the net becomes a sieve. One respect in which the present Act is a marked improvement on its predecessor is that its employment provisions are subject to many fewer restrictions of scope and application. None the less some exceptions, considered in this chapter, remain.

The 1968 Act gave several hostages to fortune. Parliament was venturing into a field in which it had never trod. The key organisations on both sides of industry were united in their distrust of any legislation that intruded on the tradition of voluntarism in industrial relations – the settling of disputes arising at the workplace through collective bargaining and negotiation, without the intervention of outsiders. The TUC was at that time opposed to any form of legal regulation of industrial relations; it had not made the distinction – critical to its change of attitude towards legislation in the mid-1970s – between legislative protection of the rights of individuals at work and interference with collective bargaining. Neither the TUC nor the CBI regarded racial discrimination as different from any other problem of industrial relations. To obtain their support, and that of their numerous Parliamentary adherents, for the extension of anti-discrimination legislation to the sphere of employment, substantial concessions were made to the voluntarist tradition. Though none survived the legislative overhaul of 1976, they require some consideration here: they may be seen as milestones in the evolution both of anti-discrimination law and of the views of key elements in industry about the nature of discrimination and the means appropriate to its suppression.

The most important concession related to the method of enforcement

135

Normally the Race Relations Board or one of its conciliation committees would, on receiving a complaint, begin an investigation with a view to forming an opinion whether discrimination had occurred (see further below, p. 189). However, where the complaint concerned employment the statute required that it be referred to the Department of Employment, which had then to decide whether suitable 'voluntary industrial machinery', as it became known, existed to consider it.[1] Such a body, which could be established within a single company or cover an entire industry, would then be charged with establishing whether discrimination had occurred and with attempting to achieve a settlement. The detailed examination of the working of these bodies undertaken by Professor Hepple makes further description otiose.[2]

It soon became clear that his high hopes for the effectiveness of this machinery were not to be realised. One important limitation was that in 1968 less than half the workforce in Britain was unionised. The establishment and operation of voluntary machinery in practice required the agreement of organised workers and employers, and was thus only possible where recognised trade unions existed. Moreover, whether through indifference, inability to reach agreement within the industry, or to satisfy the Department of Employment guidelines[3] or for other reasons, establishment of such machinery was the exception rather than the rule. The Board reported in 1972 that only about one complaint of employment discrimination in five was referred to industry machinery,[4] and between November 1968 and June 1976 the Board disposed of just over five times as many cases as the voluntary bodies.[5] Even if allowance is made for the size of the non-unionised sector, it appears that the Board had become the primary body for dealing with employment discrimination.

More basic were the defects in the working of the industry machinery. In nearly eight years of its existence only twenty opinions of unlawful discrimination were formed; these comprised less than 3 per cent of the cases disposed of.[6] By contrast the Board formed opinions of discrimination in 16.2 per cent of such cases in 1975 and 11.6 per cent in the first half of 1976.[7] It is of course possible that the industries which established voluntary machinery also had less discrimination and/or effective informal methods for remedying it, but this argument has never been put forward. The Board, in its Final Report, recommended abolition of reliance on these bodies. Its tone was gentlemanly but unmistakably sharp: many of the hearings held before them were described as 'cursory' and often lacking the rudiments of natural justice.[8] Furthermore, in cases involving nationalised industries or public authorities, the specific employer who was the subject of the complaint was also represented on the hearing panel, which could hardly augment complainants' confidence in the impartiality of the process.[9]

No provision was made in the Sex Discrimination Act for special treatment of employment cases, which presaged the abandonment of the required use of voluntary bodies in the 1976 Act. That this change was accepted without controversy, indeed without interest, is quietly remarkable in the light of the importance attached to the industrial machinery less than a decade earlier. The absence of opposition may in part reflect increasing acceptance of the industrial tribunal as the proper forum for settling disputes arising under statutes establishing employment rights. More fundamentally it may be seen as a reflection of a growing understanding of discrimination and of the purposes and operation of legal means of combating it. In the 1960s some thought discrimination unexceptionable; many more held it to be infrequent and a matter for adjustment by negotiation. Leaders of both sides of industry now regard it as an infringement of the rights of black workers, which may appropriately be vindicated in law, not compromised by negotiation. This change of perspective is a firm indication that the enact-ment of legislation in this area has itself deepened the understanding of the evil at which it is directed; that quite apart from any impact it may have had on discriminatory practices, the 1968 Act was effective in changing the climate of opinion among persons whose influence and leadership are essential if employment practices are to be changed.

The other major concession to industry opinion was the inclusion of the so-called 'racial balance' provision. The idea here was that an employer might wish to counter the growth of ethnic work groups, or the concentration of minorities in particular sections or shifts. To do so he might either transfer some employees to other jobs, or refuse to hire any more members of a particular group. This obviously would entail discrimination against indi-vidual applicants or employees, so an exemption was provided for an act 'done in good faith for the purpose of securing or preserving a reasonable balance of different racial groups employed in the undertaking' or any specific part thereof.[10] The Government, heeding the recommendations of the Race Relations Board, and the TUC, proposed to abolish this exemp-tion, taking the view that opening up real equality of opportunity was the better way of breaking down isolation and concentration of black workers. The Board had earlier reported that the exemption was rarely used; it dealt with only one case in which an employer – rightly as it happened – had relied upon it.[11] However, the CBI felt strongly that the provision should be retained, and provided the Government and members of the Standing Committee considering the Bill with several examples in which it was purportedly used to good effect. Discussion of this matter took up by far the greatest amount of Committee time devoted to the main clause concerning employment, and it emerged that the Board – which lacked statutory authority to undertake general investigations – had not attempted to survey the extent to which the exemption was used.[12] The Government neverthe-less held fast, primarily on the basis of principle. It took the view that the special assistance provisions (above, pp. 00) afforded ample support to any employer who wished to assist non-whites to break out of undesirable jobs in which they were concentrated, and that there was no justification for any other form of different treatment of individuals on the basis of race or ethnic origin.

One point passed over in the Committee deliberations was the precise rationale of the racial balance exemption. The ambiguity is pinpointed by the remarkable refashioning of the English language perpetrated in the 1968 Act. Solely for purposes of determining racial balance, persons wholly or mainly educated in Great Britain were treated as members of the same 'racial group'.[13] Thus regardless of appearance or animosity between them, native whites and persons of Indian origin educated here were regarded as members of the same (undescribed and probably undescribable) racial group, whilst all foreigners were indiscriminately lumped together. The point of course was to prevent concentration of *immigrants*, who might be unable to communicate with supervisors, unfamiliar with British industrial practices, and easily open to exploitation. Yet workers' ability to speak English and acquisition of some experience on the shop floor would be far more important than time spent in a British school for avoiding such conditions. These criteria would however be impossible to apply in practice: the racial balance standards stood as an inadequate substitute. And in so far as concern was directed at the possibility of exploitation, effective trade union representation is a much more useful protection than quotas on hiring or compulsory transfers. It may be doubted whether the Government's stand on principle has led to any practical loss.

Moreover, the emphasis on immigrants meant the racial balance clause was inapplicable in one situation where workers' ethnic origins are plausibly relevant: the separation of Indians and Pakistanis, whose political and religious enmity has often spilled over on to the shop floor. An employer who merely wished to keep the peace, and thus maintained separate ethnic work units, or tried to hold a numerical balance in the total number of employees from each group, apparently could not lawfully differentiate between them under this provision if the people involved were educated abroad.[14*] Although this form of separation is qualitatively different from segregation of black and white because it is not imposed by the dominant group, it may still be regarded as objectionable in principle. None the less it is no more obnoxious than the sort of classifications permitted by the now-repealed clause, and it is ironic that this form of 'racial' balance was never permitted.

The final major exemption, for the shipping industry, has been temporarily and partially retained, and is discussed on pp. 143–5.

Over and above these three concessions the 1968 Act was further pockmarked by exclusions, all of which have been removed in the present legislation. The Act now applies to contract workers – persons technically employed by a third party but who actually work for another employer, known in the Acts as 'the principal'.[15] The latter is now subject to the same rules as any other employer. Thus secretaries, cleaners, building workers and others often under contract with recruiting agents cannot be denied work, receive inferior terms or suffer any other 'detriment' on racial grounds.

A second area now brought under control is discrimination in granting partnership status. Partnerships as employers have never enjoyed any special treatment in relation to discrimination, but the selection of partners is not classified in law as an employment relationship, and thus special regulation was required. S. 10 now outlaws discrimination by any firm of six or more partners, or any group of that size organising themselves into a partnership, in respect of selection and related arrangements, terms and expulsion or other detriment. The minimum of six seems to have been plucked from the sky. The Government, simultaneously pressed strongly in Committee to increase it to ten and to delete it entirely, essentially admitted as much, although its spokesman pointed to the principle stated in the White Paper of excluding 'personal and intimate relationships'.[16] However, this justification sits uncomfortably alongside the inclusion of all employers, no matter how small, particularly since the Sex Discrimination Act exempts employers of five or fewer persons;[17] it was never suggested that the exemption of small employers, included for administrative reasons in the 1968 Act and terminated in stages over four years,[18] should be revived.

The importance of even a minimum as small as six can be seen from a letter received by William Whitelaw, MP, and quoted in Committee, which stated that of some 20,000 unrestricted doctors engaged in general practice in England and Wales in 1974, just under 15,000 are in partnerships of less than six.[19] Thus the overseas doctors without whose work the National Health Service would be quite unable to provide care for millions of people – and of whom slightly over half have come from the Indian subcontinent[20] – may still be excluded from partnerships or offered inferior terms; and as the writer of the above letter stated, 'there is little doubt in anyone's mind' that discrimination of this kind frequently occurs. There seem to be no estimates of the proportion of partnerships among architects, solicitors, estate agents, dentists and the like, who similarly remain outside the Act. The Government have however reserved the power to 'alter' – which presumably means eliminate as well as increase or decrease – the minimum figure by order subject to Parliamentary approval;[21] the CRE must be consulted before the draft order is submitted.[22]

A third alteration is jurisdictional rather than substantive. The employment section of the 1968 Act extended only to 'persons concerned' with employment; training bodies, employment agencies and career advice services were therefore not covered under it, but were just as effectively regulated since they were offering facilities or services to the public within the meaning of s. 2 of that statute. The difference was of no practical significance, since complaints of discrimination by such bodies would all be handled by the Race Relations Board, regardless of the legal rubric under which they came. In at least one case an employment agency which gave effect to employers' racial preferences was found to have violated the law.[23] However, under the present Act employment complaints are heard in industrial tribunals, whilst all others go before County Courts, and there are important differences in procedure and expense between these two bodies (see further, Chapter 10). All matters relating to the sphere of employment are therefore now grouped together and made subject to the identical jurisdictional rules. Thus a person who suffers discrimination at the hands of either a statutory or private training body[24] or employment agency,[25] or the vocational guidance or employment service of a local education authority,[26] or in the other facilities or services provided by the Manpower Services Commission and its agencies[27] must bring his complaint to a tribunal. Where an employment agency has been told by an employer that he is entitled to discriminate by virtue of an exemption in the Act, and it was reasonable for the agency to rely on that statement, no liability attaches.[28] One of the few offences created by the statute is that of knowingly or recklessly making such a statement which in a material respect is false or misleading; the person making it may be fined up to £400.[29]

EMPLOYMENT IN A PRIVATE HOUSEHOLD

Tracking the footsteps of its predecessor, the present Act does not apply to employment in a private household.[30] This accords with the White Paper's stated intention of excluding 'personal and intimate relationships'[31] from the ambit of the legislation and is the sole such exemption in the area of employment. However, it applies only to discrimination on racial grounds and not to victimisation; the Government thought it more important to protect persons who assist in the enforcement of the legislation from retribution.[32] Its practical effect is slightly further narrowed in that an employee who has worked for one year can claim unfair dismissal, to which no such exception applies. Even though it remains lawful to refuse to hire a person of a particular race to work in a private household or to do so as agent for such an employer[33] – it is none the less unlawful to publish an advertisement indicating an intention thus to discriminate.[34] This was also the position under the 1968 Act, and led to the 'Scotch Porridge' case which received national attention in 1969. A doctor in Eastbourne advertised for 'Scottish daily for Scottish family able to do some plain cooking'; the Race Relations Board, having received a complaint, held that the advertisement infringed the statute. However, as we have seen, the CRE alone may bring an action against discriminatory advertisements; and since, unlike the Board, it has a discretion whether to take up any particular matter,[35] in cases where adverse public reaction is likely to outweigh the benefits of enforcement, it may refuse to take any action.

TERRITORIAL LIMITS

In constitutional principle there is no territorial restriction on the legislative competence of Parliament. To enlarge slightly Sir Ivor Jennings's famous example,[36] if Parliament wished to make it a crime for a Frenchman to smoke a cigarette in the streets of Paris, it is perfectly capable of making that act punishable in an English court. Though the present Act is understandably somewhat less ambitious, it appears to have been given an extensive reach. Delineating its precise limits is important, as increasing numbers of people work for British firms in Common Market countries or are employed by multinational companies and sent on tours of duty to various distant places.

The proscription of discrimination applies only to employment 'at an establishment in Great Britain',[37] defined in s. 8 (1) as applying to employment 'unless the employee does his work wholly or mainly outside Great Britain'.[38]* This establishes a straightforward quantitative test, under which the employee would receive protection unless the great preponderance of his work is done outside the country. By contrast the more convoluted territorial exclusions governing other employment legislation treat prospective complainants less generously.[39]* In particular, the rule pertaining to unfair dismissal, which requires consideration of where the employee 'ordinarily works',[40] should not be construed identically to s. 8 (1), especially as, in yet another provision, Parliament has plainly differentiated the two phrases.[41]*

The computational method, however, cannot be readily applied in cases of engagement for employment – whether initial hiring or promotion – which will produce the greatest number of discrimination actions. No applicant 'does his work' anywhere, nor is he an 'employee'. Since varying or abandoning the territorial limitations for applicants alone makes no sense whatever, the statute must be read in the conditional tense: 'would do his work'. To do so, one can only look to the terms of the proposed contract of employment. Theoretically regard might be had to where the successful applicant was deployed, but the three-month limit on complaints (below, p. 199) bars this approach, since such as short initial period cannot be taken as representative of the true nature of the work. However if, as is likely, the contract is silent on the matter, and by implied term the employer may determine where the employee will work, one is driven willy-nilly to adopt the mode of analysis the Court of Appeal applied to the determination of where the employee 'ordinarily works'. In *Wilson* v. *Maynard Shipbuilding Consultants A.B.*[42] Megaw L.J. instructed tribunals 'to ascertain where, *looking at the whole period contemplated by the contract*, the employee's base is to be'.[43] (italic supplied). This in turn depends upon a number of factors then set out in the judgment, including the location of the employee's headquarters and of his private residence, where and in what currency he is to be paid, and whether he pays British National Insurance contributions.[44] Since this test was devised to interpret a more restrictive statute it is submitted that in borderline cases it should be given an especially liberal application when interpreting s. 8.

The vital point is that a job which may entail substantial periods overseas may none the less be subject to the requirement of non-discrimination. Thus a British company looking for a young manager whom it intends to send to its South African subsidiary in the first two years of anticipated long-term employment cannot reject a black applicant simply on the ground that assignment to that country puts his work as wholly or mainly outside Britain. Just as Megaw L.J. adverted to the importance of unfair dismissal rights in according the territorial limitation there a narrow construction,[45] so licence to discriminate ought to be restricted to employment with only a remote connection with this country.

Even under the suggested interpretation the exemption seems unnecessarily wide. The American statute excludes only 'the employment of aliens outside any State'.[46] The difference may be seen by considering the case of a South African or Saudi employer who wishes to recruit in Britain or the United States. So long as the contract makes it sufficiently clear that the employment is for work in that country, Britain gives him full latitude to discriminate, on grounds of race, ethnic origin or indeed of sex,[47]* while in the United States he could only do so if he were seeking foreign nationals. It seems unexceptionable to permit a foreign employer to recruit only nationals of his country who happen to be resident here, but no reasons have ever been offered for any further derogation from the principle of non-discrimination. The fact that an employer who is able to take advantage of this exemption is none the less not permitted to advertise that he will discriminate on any grounds except nationality[48] may reduce the public insult, but not the violation of the principle.

At some point s. 8 may have to be interpreted in light of EEC law. The EEC Commission have issued a Draft Regulation on the Conflict of Laws and Labour Law which, if adopted, will be directly applicable in British courts. However, it appears that, in its present form, this instrument will not affect the territorial provisions of either the Act or EPCA.[49]

OFFSHORE OIL OPERATIONS

Britain's North Sea oil deposits are entirely located outside Great Britain, including its internationally recognised territorial waters. However, international agreements have resulted in the division of the North Sea into several areas, giving the nation adjacent to each area rights to the resources of the sea-bed within it.[50] The municipal law of the United Kingdom is extended to each area by means of Orders in Council pursuant to the Continental Shelf

Act 1964; in the absence of a specific Order a particular piece of legislation is assumed not to operate in offshore areas, since the courts have created a presumption that Parliament does not legislate extra-territorially.[51] Consequently legislation concerning individual employment rights contain an enabling provision permitting its application to offshore areas by delegated legislation.[52] Such orders have in fact been made in relation to all the rights now consolidated in EPCA.[53] The Act contains an analogous enabling power in s. 8 (5), but no order has as yet been forthcoming.

This cannot be due to the absence of need. On some rigs and supply vessels workers from Spain and other non-North European nations have been put in segregated living quarters,[54] a practice that seems prima facie unlawful.[55]* Nor is there reason to assume that the employment practices of oil companies are notably less discriminatory than those in other industries, although the American firms have over the past fifteen years been subject to the federal anti-discrimination in relation to all hiring done within the United States. The failure to extend discrimination legislation is only partly mitigated by the fact that persons working on a ship registered in Britain, are protected unless they work 'wholly' outside the country.[56] This does not mean, however, that all workers on British-registered drill ships are covered, since many are flown from elsewhere directly to the ship to work and never alight upon (or submerge themselves in) British territory.[57] In view of the extension of other major employment rights to offshore workers, and the partial coverage already established for some within the industry, the refusal to ensure that all workers within the industry do not suffer discrimination is without apparent justification. Furthermore, the anomaly will be compounded if, under the authority of recent statute,[58] the other employment rights are extended to workers in cross-boundary fields – areas which straddle the national boundaries of the divided continental shelf. This law specifically provides that discrimination legislation may be extended to those areas[59] – apparently at the behest of the Norwegian Government (with which Britain shares in the exploitation of a number of gas and oil fields), which argued that its legislation already guarantees similar rights.[60] It would be strange indeed if the only time British workers in the North Sea could secure redress against discrimination would be when within the jurisdiction of Norwegian law.

THE SHIPPING INDUSTRY

One of the less admirable features of Britain's great maritime empire was the employment of non-white colonial seamen in the worst jobs and conditions of work at vastly inferior rates of pay; aboard ship they were placed in segregated quarters and received inferior provisions. This was particularly true of Lascars, natives of India who were subject to additional discrimination imposed by various statutes designed to ensure that they would not remain in Britain.[61]

In 1968 this historic ill treatment was left untouched, although some of the most objectionable statutory provisions were repealed by the Merchant Shipping Act 1970. If anything the field for potential lawful discrimination was expanded, since the 1968 Act also contained various exemptions for discrimination on British or foreign aircraft operation outside Great Britain, even though recruitment took place in this country.[62] Employment in the shipping industry has severely contracted since then;[63] whether for this or other reasons, the National Union of Seamen became actively opposed to the continuance of the exemption, which permitted Indian nationals to be paid 75 per cent less than British ratings, while Hong Kong Chinese received approximately 25 per cent less.[64] The number of sailors and ships involved is remarkably large: Sidney Bidwell, MP, who had been briefed by the NUS, stated that just under 40 per cent of British flag ships employed low-wage crews, and that 19,000, or 44 per cent, of all jobs for seamen on British ships were filled by persons in this category.[65]

In the White Paper the Government acknowledged that the shipping industry exemptions in the 1968 Act 'could be inconsistent with the general principle of non-discrimination',[66] and began consultations with the Union and management with a view to their elimination. In the event only one exemption remains: s. 9 permits discrimination by an employer 'in or in connection with employment by him on any ship in the case of a person who applied or was engaged for that employment outside Great Britain'. It is clear from the lengthy Standing Committee discussions[67] that the Government and all Members understood this section only to permit payment of lower wages to foreign seamen. In particular no one supposed that the odious s. 8 (10) of the 1968 statute, which permitted discrimination in order to avoid persons of different racial origins 'being compelled' to share living quarters or mess or sanitary accommodation on a ship, was carried over into the present Act. One hopes this is so although the phrase 'in connection with employment' makes it at least doubtful, since living and eating arrangements are inevitably part of employment at sea. Should segregation persist, it may be expected that the Government would use the power it has specifically reserved to amend s. 9 by Order without the necessity of going through the normal lengthy legislative procedure.[68]

Ironically, the main reason for the decision not to abolish all exemptions relating to foreign seamen was the attitude of their home governments, particularly that of India, of which nearly 60 per cent are citizens. Even with the wage discrimination, they are very well paid in comparison with most of their fellow countrymen and Indian officials appear to have been worried about the 'distorting' effects of equal pay, not least on its own rising maritime industry.[69] None the less the Government viewed the continued discrimination with manifest distaste, and encouraged the formation of an industry-wide working group to decide how to phase out the differential. The Minister rejected a proposed amendment that would have removed the exemption after ten years in part because he regarded that period as excessive, and the power to remove it by draft order was inserted partly as a reserve measure to eliminate it if collective agreement failed.[70] The consultations began to bear fruit when a working party recommended in February 1978 that equal pay be implemented by staged rises for foreign seamen over a five-year period.[71] The redundancy of s. 9 cannot be far off.

GENUINE OCCUPATIONAL QUALIFICATION

The root assumption of anti-discrimination legislation is that, in the areas of behaviour it regulates, differences of race, ethnicity and the like are irrelevant. In rare circumstances this arguably is not true, and the American statute permits discrimination on grounds of religion, sex or national origin where one of those characteristics is 'a bona fide occupational qualification reasonably necessary to the normal operation of [a] particular business'.[72] It will be noted that under this provision race or colour can never be legitimate grounds for discrimination. The 1968 Act permitted 'selection of a person of particular nationality or particular descent for employment requiring attributes especially possessed by [such] persons'.[73] Fortunately this language never required judicial interpretation, for it was unusually ill chosen. Particularly confusing was the use of 'nationality', a political-legal category in no way related to what this exemption was attempting to permit. The idea was that certain situations require persons of particular appearance or skills which supposedly are possessed only by those from a specific minority group. The stock example is that of a restaurant with a Chinese decor which wishes to employ only waiters of Chinese physiognomy (whatever their citizenship). It may be wondered whether prospective patrons would really be put off by the prospect of receiving their chow mein at the hands of a red-haired Geordie, but the idea has never encountered Parliamentary opposition.

The present rules are intended to be 'narrower' than the section they replace.[74] They permit discrimination in all aspects of employment except 'terms', where being of a particular racial group is a 'genuine occupational qualification' for the job.[75] This 'GOQ' exemption – an anglicisation of the American 'bona fide occupational qualification or 'BFOQ', which first made its appearance in the analogous but broader provisions of the SDA[76] – applies in essentially two contexts.

The first is where, in a variety of specified situations, a person of a particular racial group is required 'for reasons of authenticity'. These include dramatic performances or other entertainment, work as a 'model' in painting, sculpture or films, or in a place where victuals are to be consumed in a 'particular setting'.[77]

Anyone who remembers the close-ups of Sir Laurence Olivier's pale eyes in the film version of *Othello* will appreciate the purpose of the first exemption, but it is none the less potentially a double-edge award. Can a theatre company planning to present Ibsen and Brecht refuse to audition black actors on the grounds that a play set in northern or central Europe requires whites 'for reasons of authenticity'? For that matter the same question applies to virtually all roles in Shakespeare's histories and tragedies except Othello himself. Yet the New York Shakespeare Company's unrestricted use of black actors, long before concern over discrimination became fashionable, did not detract from the quality of its performance and played an important role in opening up new opportunities for minorities in the theatre. This casts at least some doubt on what might seem to be a sensible standard: that being white may be a GOQ in an historical dramatisation or in depicting a famous individual, but not for any role concerning contemporary life in Britain's multi-racial community, apart from ensuring that members of the same family are of the same race. These 'authenticity' exemptions would perhaps be of more theoretical than practical concern, since decisions about casting are inherently so subjective that in the absence of unguarded remarks discrimination would be unprovable, but for the fact that the Act permits discriminatory advertisements where a GOQ is involved.[78] The proliferation of 'Persons of Appropriate Appearance Required' notices can hardly be welcome. Moreover, as one MP pointed out,[79] if the logic of these exemptions is accepted that pertaining to restaurants is too narrow, since many shops, e.g. one selling Yoruba crafts, try equally to establish a distinctive atmosphere or 'setting'.

Far more troublesome as a matter of principle than the question of 'authenticity' of appearance is the exemption in s. 5 (2)(d), which makes membership in a particular racial group a GOQ where 'the holder of the job provides persons of that racial group with personal services promoting their welfare, and those services can most effectively be provided by a person of that racial group'. This has been carried over from the SDA, in which its inclusion received little discussion, since criticism was concentrated upon other, more controversial GOQs relevant to sex. The government spokesman doubted it would be much use in the context of race, and instanced the hiring of a West Indian social worker or probation officer to work with 'disturbed or alienated West Indian adolescents'.[80]

In fact its potential use is far greater. This was seen in the furore occasioned by the employment policy announced by Camden Borough Council in January of 1978 (above, p. 26). The statement by the Council's spokesman that the under-representation of blacks among its employees would lead it to give preference to a black applicant over a white of equal ability attracted substantial attention and criticism, and if applied as a general hiring criterion would seem plainly to violate s. 1 (1)(a). However, it became clear from more detailed examination that the Council were particularly concerned to recruit black social workers, environmental and housing liaison officers, estate managers, interviewers and inquiry staff, and librarians to deal more effectively with the needs of their constituents, 20–25 per cent of whom are black. Most of these jobs can reasonably be described as providing welfare services, and it is irrelevant that a person hired in such capacity would also be providing services to whites living in the Borough, since the GOQ may be invoked where 'some only of the duties of the job' may best be carried out by a person of a particular racial group.[81]

Analysis of the legality of this policy cannot be separated from what elsewhere in the statute would be called its justification (Chapter 2). This follows from the fact that, to sustain a GOQ, the employer must demonstrate that a person of a given racial group can 'most effectively' provide the services.[82]* To support this contention he would have to rely on the argument that only members of the particular group possess the requisite skills, or that the state of race relations in the country is such that the intended recipients of the services would make substantially less use of them if they were provided by a person of a different racial group. This argument is probably only plausible in one direction, i.e. to support the hiring of minorities; the utter dependence of the National Health Service upon black nurses and doctors suggests that whites have little hesitation in accepting assistance from whomever is able to provide it.

In so far as a job involves working with immigrants – as distinct from non-whites – knowledge of their language and culture may well be an essential requirement of that employment. It may be assumed that most persons possessing that knowledge will in reality be of a minority group, but, unlike a racial classification, this is not an immutable fact; one may hope, for example, that increasing numbers of whites will take an interest in learning various Asian languages. The argument that race *per se* is a GOQ boils down to saying that people of West Indian or Asian origin are either so deeply distrustful of whites or are so culturally distant despite birth and education in this country, that any person of a particular minority group would understand and be accepted by members of that group far more fully than any white. Even taking the standard example, that of 'alienated' West Indian youth, convincing evidence has never been produced that most white social workers, health officers or neighbourhood lawyers have proven ineffective in working with them. Nor should it be assumed that educated and professionally qualified middle-aged West Indians would be more compatible; indeed the pronounced generational conflict among West Indians makes this at least doubtful. These considerations suggest that it is not necessary to depart from the principle of non-discrimination, which requires making judgments about the capabilities of particular individuals in particular situations, in order to select persons who are best suited to provide personal services to minority persons. It is apparent that what may loosely be called sensitivity to the attitudes and problems of particular groups, as well as more mundane skills such as ability to understand their dialect, is essential if the job is to be done well. Those selecting applicants for such a post are entitled to give great weight to these abilities in making their choice. It seems likely that, on average, members of the same group will more often possess them than outsiders, but this generalisation says nothing about the qualities of the individuals who actually must be evaluated. The statute in effect lays down an irrebuttable presumption that this is always so. As with all such presumptions, its arbitrariness will often be factually incorrect, as well as contrary to an important principle.

In one narrow situation the foregoing analysis applies, if at all, with greatly diminished force, and the case for race or ethnic origin as a GOQ becomes much more persuasive. This is where an association comprises members of a particular group, and it wishes to employ only persons of the same affiliation. There seems no reason why the Anglo-Polish Conservative Association or the Indian Workers' Association should not be permitted to employ persons of the same ethnic or national group to provide services to their members, just as such groups are specifically exempted from the prohibition against discrimination in membership of clubs (s. 26 (1)).

An amendment in these terms was proposed in place of the present s. 5 (2)(d),[83] and it is submitted that this tightly drawn exemption would suffice to mark out the narrow bounds within which the concept of GOQ may validly be applied to selection based upon race or ethnicity.

CONCLUSION

Unlike those of its predecessor the employment provisions of the 1976 Act are quite comprehensive. Virtually everyone, regardless of the technical nature of his contract of employment or the type of work in which he is engaged, now enjoys statutory protection. The shipping industry apart, the only persons excluded are those who may fall on the wrong side of blurred lines drawn by complex technical provisions, such as that defining territorial scope. The only seriously controversial exemption is that concerning the 'genuine occupational qualification' which, it is suggested, is substantially broader than is desirable.

NOTES

1. RRA 1968, s. 16 and sched. 2.
2. *Hepple*, pp. 184–201.
3. These are set out in *Lester and Bindman*, p. 318.
4. Report for 1971–2, para. 50.
5. This is calculated from the Final Report, para. 50 and app. IV, table 9.
6. Ibid. para. 60.
7. Calculated from ibid. para. 45.

8. Ibid. para. 60.

9. Report for 1973, para. 41.

10. RRA 1968, s. 8 (2).

11. Report for 1971–2, paras 55–6.

12. The discussion is found in Official Report, Standing Comm. A, 4 and 6 May 1976, cols 139–66.

13. RRA 1968, s. 8 (4).

*14. This is by no means clear. S. 8 (2) permitted discrimination if done 'in good faith for the purpose of securing or preserving a reasonable balance of persons of different "racial groups"'. Under s. 8 (4) 'racial group' meant 'persons defined by reference to colour, race or ethnic or national origins', which would appear to permit differentiation and 'balance' of Indians and Pakistanis. The question is whether the subsequent ascription in s. 8 (4) of all British-educated persons to the same racial group implies that all persons educated abroad would also be consigned to the same category. Despite what seems to be a rather widespread practice of employing members of one minority group exclusively – see e.g. Brooks, *Black Employment in the Black Country: A Study of Walsall* (Runnymede Trust, 1975) pp. 24–5 – this question never required interpretation by the Race Relations Board or produced litigation.

15. S. 7 (1).

16. The debate appears in Official Report, Standing Comm. A, 11 and 13 May 1976, pp. 237–58; the reference is to para. 59 of the White Paper.

17. Sex Discrimination Act 1975, s. 6 (3)(b).

18. RRA 1968, s. 8 (1).

19. Official Report, Standing Comm. A, 13 May 1976, cols 251–2.

20. See the figures in the study by the Community Relations Commission, *Doctors from Overseas: A Case for Consultation* (1976) pp. 10–13.

21. S. 72 (1)(c).

22. S. 73 (2).

23. See Final Report, para. 58 and app. VI.

24. S. 13 (2)(a)–(d).

25. S. 14 (1).

26. S. 14 (2).

27. S. 15 (1).

28. S. 14 (5).

29. S. 14 (6).

30. S. 4 (3).

31. Cmnd 6234, para. 59.

32. See the remarks of the Minister of State, John Grant, in response to an amendment which sought to extend the exemption to victimisation: Official Report, Standing Comm. A, 6 May 1976, col. 169.

33. S. 14 (4).

34. S. 29 (1). Employment in a private household is not one of the exceptions specified in s. 29 (2).

35. S. 15 (2)(b) of the 1968 Act, commanded that the Board or one of its conciliation committees 'shall respectively investigate any complaint received by them' . . . Though the investigation need not have resulted in a judicial proceeding, it did entail making formal enquiries to the alleged discriminator. No such mandatory language is contained in the present Act.

36. W. I. Jennings, *The Law and the Constitution* (Cambridge U.P., 5th edn, 1959), pp. 170–1.

37. S. 4.

*38. In addition, the rather impenetrable s. 8 (4) makes provision for commercial travellers and other itinerants to have a deemed 'establishment' at the place to which their work is most closely connected. Persons employed on a British-registered ship are covered unless their work is *wholly* outside Great Britain, and in their case the ship is treated as the establishment: s. 8 (2) and (3).

*39. EPCA, s. 141 contains five subsections with varying territorial exclusions for different employment rights. The conclusion that these are more stringent than s. 8 is shared by Forde, 'Transnational Employment and Employment Protection', (1978) 7 *I.L.J.* 228.

40. EPCA, s. 141 (2) has produced no less than seven reported decisions, which are analysed by Forde, op. cit. above, n. 4.

*41. ECPA, s. 141 (1), governing entitlement to written particulars of employment terms and minimum period of notice before termination, excludes 'any period when the employee is engaged in work wholly or mainly outside Great Britain unless the employee ordinarily works in Great Britain'.

42. [1977] I.R.L.R. 491, [1978] I.C.R. 376.

43. [1977] I.R.L.R., at 494.

44. Ibid.

45. Ibid. at 492, para. 8.

46. Civil Rights Act 1964, s. 702.

*47. SDA, s. 10 is identical to s. 8 of the RRA. In addition, under s. 7 (2)(g) of the SDA being a man is a genuine occupational qualification for employment if the job involves work in a foreign country whose laws or customs bar the employment of women in that position. This may be called the Arabian connection.

48. S. 29 (1) and (3), discussed above, pp. 118–19.

49. The Draft Regulation and the issues it raises are discussed by Forde, 'The Conflict of Individual Labour Laws and the E.E.C.'s Rules', (1978) *Leg. Issues of Eur. Integ.* 85.

50. A concise introduction to the international law context of British offshore oil operation is given by J. Kitchen, *Labour Law and Off-Shore Oil* (Croom Helm, 1977) pp. 31–4 and 54–5.

51. The presumption is discussed by Forde, op. cit. n. 49, at p. 88. The leading case is *Tomalin* v. *Pearson,* [1909] 2 K.B. 61.

52. EPCA, s. 137.

53. Employment Protection (Offshore Employment) Order 1976 (S.I. 1976/766, as amended by S.I. 1977/588).

54. Kitchen, op. cit., above n. 50, p. 82.

*55. In the special conditions of offshore work, the employer must provide accommodation. Thus, even if not expressly mentioned, accommodation would probably be regarded as an implied term of the contract of employment, and thus subject to s. 4 (2)(a). Even if this view is incorrect, segregation–deemed to be discriminatory by s. 1 (2) – of workers of a particular nationality or ethnic origin would be a 'detriment' within s. 4 (2)(c): above, pp. 130–1.

56. S. 8 (2) and (3); see above n. 38.

57. Kitchen, op. cit., above n. 50, p. 83.

58. Employment (Continental Shelf) Act 1978.

59. Ibid. s. 1 (2).

60. See the comment by I. Gault, (1978) 7 *I.L.J.* 239.

61. *Hepple*, pp. 62–7.

62. RRA 1968, s. 8 (7)–(9).

63. Membership of the NUS, which operates a strong closed shop in the industry, dropped from 70,000 in the early 1960s to 43,000 a decade later. B. Weekes *et al.*, *Industrial Relations and the Limits of Law* (Blackwell, 1975) p. 39.

64. These figures were given by the Minister during the debate on s. 9: Official Report, Comm. A, 11 May 1976, col. 230.

65. Ibid. col. 216.

66. Cmnd 6234, para. 64.

67. Official Report, op. cit., above, n. 64, cols 211–38.

68. S. 73 (1)(a). Prior consultation with the CRE is required: s. 73 (2).

69. Official Report, op. cit., above, n. 64, cols 227–8.

70. Ibid. col. 234.

71. Department of Trade, *Report of the Working Group on the Employment of Non-domiciled Seafarers* (H.M.S.O., 1978).

72. Civil Rights Act of 1964, s. 703 (e)(1).

73. RRA 1968, s. 8 (11).

74. This was the White Paper's description of the proposed changes, Cmnd 6234, para. 63.

75. S. 5 (1)(a).

76. SDA, s. 7 (2) permits eight separate GOQs.

77. S. 5 (2)(a), (b), (c), respectively.

78. S. 29 (2).

79. Mr Walter Clegg, Official Report, Standing Comm. A, 6 May 1976, col. 181.

80. Ibid. col. 189.

81. S. 5 (3).

*82. The statute is silent on the question of burden of proof, but as the claim of GOQ is an affirmative defence to a complaint of discrimination, the burden must, on established principles, rest with he who offers the defence, i.e. the employer.

83. Official Report, op. cit., above, n. 79, cols 186–8.

8

The Public Sector

Thus far we have looked at the problems of employment discrimination either in terms of national patterns or in relation to the practices of private employers. The public sector, in which hiring policies are much more standardised and centralised, and which may be more directly guided by government policy, requires separate treatment. In this chapter we first look at employment in the Civil Service and the nationalised industries. Next considered is the potential use of the power of central government in the market-place – as a consumer of goods produced in the private sector – as a means of securing that its contractors do not discriminate, or indeed make active efforts to ensure equal opportunity. The last area examined is employment by the police, in which decisions are largely made independently by each Force, though in some respects uniform national standards must be applied.

CROWN EMPLOYMENT

At common law the King can do no wrong, nor can he be sued in his own courts. It therefore required the reform introduced in the Crown Proceedings Act 1947 to permit government bodies to be sued for wrongs such as torts or breaches of contract,[1] and the same waiver of immunity is incorporated in the Act.[2] At common law a Crown servant probably held office at Her Majesty's pleasure,[3] but for purposes of the Act any possible doubts are quieted by the equation of his terms of service with a contract of employment.[4] For the first time the employment provisions have been explicitly extended to the armed forces, although complainants must follow internal procedures rather than going before an industrial tribunal.[5] As we have seen (above, p. 114), certain public appointments may also effectively be outside the Act.

The largest category of Crown employees are of course civil servants, defined in the Fulton Report as 'servants of the Crown, other than holders of political or judicial offices, who are employed in a civil capacity and whose remuneration is paid wholly and directly out of moneys voted by Parliament'.[6] This is a relatively narrow definition, excluding among others employees of the National Health Service, the nationalised industries, local government, universities and the police. The practical importance of the categorisation is that the Civil Service Commission has no power to affect the employment policies of the other public sector bodies; thus even a Government committed to an energetic equal employment programme would not have as great a direct formal influence as would be true in countries such as West Germany in which the category of civil servant is far more extensive. None the less, the Civil Service is the nation's largest single employer; in 1974 it employed approximately half a million persons, plus nearly 200,000 industrial staff.[7]

In one respect discrimination in the Civil Service is open and deliberate. This is in the exclusion of aliens, which also extends to the armed forces. As both Hepple and Lester and Bindman have surveyed the applicable rules thoroughly, the reader is referred to their accounts.[8] The present statute carries over the exemption of its predecessor for rules restricting employment by the Crown or any public body to 'persons of particular birth, nationality, descent or residence'.[9] Discrimination based on race or colour is not thereby permitted, although there remains the blanket national security exemption[10] whose origins are obscure and which apparently has never been invoked. Regulations made under the 1968 Act detail the public bodies entitled to discriminate on these grounds; strangely, the great majority are museums of various kinds.[11] By special provision these Regulations were carried over as if made under the new Act.[12] It should be borne in mind, however, that the Civil Service Commission have interpreted the so-called Nationality Rule to permit Commonwealth citizens to be regarded as 'British', so most non-white immigrants are eligible for Civil Service employment.[13] In its discussion paper proposing a new and more exclusionary concept of British nationality[14] the Government did not discuss whether enactment of its proposals would affect this interpretation. Entrance into the EEC has not affected the Rule, since the Treaty specifically exempts public service employment from its prohibition of nationality discrimination.[15]

The element of public accountability, the ability of ministers and officials to have a direct impact on employment practices, and the educative and exemplary effect of government action all make it vital that the Civil Service function as a model employer in relation to discrimination. The Civil Service Department took its responsibilities seriously enough to invite the Tavistock Institute of Human Relations to study its employment practices, with emphasis upon whether any of them worked to the disadvantage of minorities, and how the avowed policy of equal opportunity could be monitored. The Report, published in November 1978,[16] documented strikingly lower acceptance rates for black applicants – disparities that would easily satisfy the 'considerably smaller' requirement of s. 1 (1)(b)(i) – for Executive Officer, Clerical Officer and Clerical Assistant grades, and consistently lower job ratings and rates of promotion among blacks in situations as diverse as the Portsmouth Docks and a DHSS Regional Office. The researchers made no allegations of direct or indirect discrimination, which would have taken them beyond their remit. However, they did emphasise that the lack of explicit criteria both at the 'sifting' and interview stages, and the consequent prominence of subjective judgments, must be thoroughly scrutinised since they presented major potential 'hazards to fairness'. In blunter language, the Report documents a prima facie case of, at the least, large-scale indirect discrimination.

The then Government responded by establishing a Working Party to consider, in light of the Report, how the Civil Service equal opportunity policy might best be implemented. One obvious, and urgent, question raised by the Report is whether the tests and selection criteria, formal or informal, used by selectors, are job-related and can be justified under the *Steel* guidelines (above, pp. 57–8). The fact is that, at the time of writing (1979), the Government has only barely begun to put its own house in order, and is hardly in a position to fault other employers, at least in respect of indirect discrimination. Indeed, despite Ministerial exhortation to employers to keep records of their employees' racial and ethnic origins as part of an equal opportunity policy, the Civil Service does not do so, and has no accurate figures of the number of its own black employees, still less of applicants.[17] Inadequacies in the Civil Service's record as an employer do not, of course, excuse deficiencies elsewhere, but the moral authority of government policy statements and the work of individual Ministers must be badly weakened when the performance of those most closely under their control cannot be held out as a model. Even if Civil Service recruitment remains severely curtailed over the next few years, matters such as evaluation and promotion will be a test of the genuineness of public pronouncements.

Of even greater importance, in terms of the number of persons employed, are the nationalised industries, which, with other public corporations, accounted in 1975 for approximately 8 per cent of the entire U.K. labour force, or just under 2 million persons.[18] They occupy a peculiar constitutional position, being neither departments of government nor wholly independent of ministerial control. Legally, they do not share the status of the Crown.[19] In the words of the late Professor de Smith, 'Broad policy control rests in the hands of the Minister; day-to-day administrative control lies in the hands of the governing bodies; an indeterminate zone where policy and administration lies between.'[20] Most statutes creating the board governing a particular industry empower a designated Minister to give the board directions of a general nature about the exercise of its functions on matters he considers are related to the national interest.[21] Quite apart from such formal authority, a House of Commons Committee concluded in 1968 that informal intervention by Ministers had increased since the establishment of the nationalised industries two decades earlier.[22] Thus there is legal authority and, even more, practical precedent, for the Government to ensure that the nationalised industries adopt policies that are particularly sensitive to the elimination of discrimination and the creation of increased opportunities for minorities.

This they have signally failed to do. The consensus among those knowledgeable about employment discrimination is that their record is in general no better than that of the private sector, and that in particular industries it may be substantially worse.[23] In one respect the hiring practices of the nationalised industries are distinctive: their use of tests is far greater than among private companies. However, few efforts appear to have been made to assess their validity,[24] and many may therefore be impossible to justify if shown to have a discriminatory effect. Successive Governments had fought shy of attempts to influence the practices of public industries until in 1978 the race relations advisory group of the Department of Employment asked thirty of them to issue a clear written statement of a policy of non-discrimination. In late March 1979 the Minister in charge of the effort, John Grant, stated more than half had done so, and that his Department would then attempt to ensure that these policies would be implemented by effective procedures.[25] It is not known whether the present Government will continue in this direction.

GOVERNMENT CONTRACTS

Another manner in which a Government determined to eliminate discrimination can exert particular influence is by use of its economic power in the marketplace. Central government is a massive consumer of the products of many and diverse industries throughout the economy. Although no overall figures of the total value of government purchases are released – or indeed, apparently, compiled – it is possible by piecing together scattered bits of information to arrive at a crude estimate. In 1975–6 the minimum value of government contracts was about £3,000,000,000, and almost certainly substantially higher. Roughly half this figure consisted of non-competitive contracts, mostly involving the Department of Defence.[26]

That governments use their expenditure on procurement as one means of achieving various policy objectives is now well-established.[27] The best-known recent example was the insertion in 1978 of a wage control compliance clause in all government contracts.[28] However, the most important precedent for the use of governmental purchasing power to ensure that those with whom it does business observe socially desirable practices is the Fair Wages Resolution of 1946. This 'set of directives', whose pedigree extends back to 1891, has never taken statutory form, but Parliament has required its insertion in all government contracts, loans, grants of licences or subsidies.[29] As its title suggests, it requires contractors to pay wage rates, and establish hours and conditions of work, that meet certain minimum standards. In addition they must agree not to interfere with the freedom of employees to become members of a trade union. The contractor is also responsible for ensuring that any subcontractor he engages adheres to these conditions, and he is required to post copies of the Resolution at his establishment.

The Resolution is part of the contract between the Government and the contractor; under settled contract law principles, it cannot be enforced by an employee or any other third party.[30] The primary sanction envisaged is denial of future contracts for failure to observe the conditions. Apparently no firm has been struck off the list of approved contractors for more than forty years,[31] but no information is available on how frequently compliance is secured by threats from the Department concerned or by the Department of Employment, which has overall responsibility for enforcement. It appears that the ultimate weapon, cancellation of an existing contract for failure to comply with this clause, has never been used.

The Street Report recommended that a non-discrimination clause be inserted into all government contracts, but with greater responsibilities imposed on contractors and more powerful enforcement machinery established. Its proposals were heavily influenced by American practice, to be examined below. The Government did not adopt them. Instead it followed the Fair Wages Resolution approach, and in October 1969 the Chancellor of the Exchequer announced that a clause would be included in all government contracts requiring that the provisions of the Race Relations Act then in force be observed, and that the 'Government Departments will be prepared to withhold contracts from firms practising racial discrimination in employment'.[32]

The Race Relations Board criticised this approach, as have numerous commentators.[33] Four main objections have been offered. First, the contractor is not required to take any positive steps, e.g. special recruitment efforts or training programmes, to promote equal opportunity, but must simply obey the negative condition of non-discrimination. Second, no specific government Department has been given responsibility for enforcing this clause. Each Department is responsible for its own contracts, and inevitably will be more concerned about getting its work completed than about considerations it regards as peripheral. Third, neither the Race Relations Board nor the CRE, for which such matters are central, were given special responsibility for monitoring compliance by contractors, as recommended in the Street Report. Fourth, no provision was made for cancelling existing contracts, as distinct from withholding future ones.

It may be said too that this clause is only inserted in contracts, and is not imposed as a condition of the massive subsidies or loans which have so frequently been granted in recent years. Moreover, unlike the Fair Wages Resolution, the contractor is under no duty to ensure that a subcontractor he engages is obeying the law. No contract has in fact ever been withheld, despite the 1969 announcement.

In the White Paper the Government stated that in future a new condition would be added, requiring a contractor to 'provide on request to the Department of Employment such information about its employment policies and practices as the Department may reasonably require'.[34] In its Final Report the Race Relations Board sharply criticised what it regarded as the timidity of this proposal, particularly faulting the absence of sanctions and the refusal to give the new Commission any monitoring responsibility. Rather belatedly its views seem to have been accepted. In November of 1978 the Government announced proposals that would have given the Department of Employment powers to request a range of information from its contractors, including details of employment policies and steps taken to avoid all forms of discrimination; of the use made of English-language testing and reasons for it; and of the overall ethnic composition of the workforce.[35] If the Department found the replies unsatisfactory, it would refer them to the CRE for consideration of possible illegality. If a firm refused to co-operate with the Commission, or the latter found prima facie evidence of discrimination, the Government would be prepared to withhold contracts, although not, apparently, to cancel existing ones. These proposals, which were to be the subject of consultation, met immediate strong opposition from the CBI[36] and the present Government has not yet indicated its position.

Advocates of vigorous use of the contract compliance power regard it as a major enforcement device; the Board described it potentially the Government's strongest weapon in the attack on discrimination.[37] This view purports to draw on the experience of the American programme, but there is reason to believe that its effectiveness, which on paper looks formidable, has been exaggerated. No published work has systematically evaluated its impact, but a series of papers given at a seminar devoted to this purpose[38] while emphasising the difficulties of coming to firm conclusions, support a rather pessimistic view.

Federal contract compliance, though its antecedents go back to the Second War, really began in a serious way only in 1965.[39] The programme not only forbids discrimination, but requires any firm whose contract totals more than $50,000 – which means virtually every supplier – to undertake 'affirmative action' to correct deficiencies in its employment of minorities and women. Any contractor who fails to make a 'good-faith effort' to fulfil this obligation is subject to the cancellation or suspension of its existing contracts, as well as future debarment.

Form does not necessarily equal substance. As of 1969, the cancellation and debarment sanctions had never been invoked,[40] and a study of compliance efforts in 1970–2 found that, although thousands of companies were cited for non-compliance, the sanctions were imposed at the rate of two times every three years, and that more than four contractors in five were subject to no compliance review at all in this period.[41] One commentator, who spoke of the 'ineptness' of the performance of the office of Federal Contract Compliance, also pointed out that its relative low status within the hierarchy of government prevents it from ensuring that powerful departments, such as Defense, cancel contracts with violators.[42] Subsequent review of the programme by the Department of Labor concluded that compliance efforts had been devoted excessively to paper requirements, rather than to truly improving opportunities.[43]

If the contract compliance approach has had but limited value in the United States, the significant differences in the economic structure of the two countries suggest that substantially less may be expected of it in Britain. In many areas it is simply unnecessary, for in the public sector – virtually non-existent in the United States – we have seen that there is ample scope for more direct Ministerial intervention. Indeed, directly or indirectly the nationalised industries could themselves be made active agents of equal opportunity policies, by requiring those doing business with them to comply with specified conditions. This possibility seems never to have been seriously considered, and would doubtless be resisted strongly by those bodies. Yet the degree of public ownership gives a British Government determined to eliminate employment discrimination a degree of influence far greater than would be possible in the United States. Thus a NEDO study of the nationalised industries found that in 1971 the purchases of plant and machinery by the largest six accounted for approximately one-third of *all* expenditure on plant and equipment by U.K. industry.[44] Excluding purchases from other nationalised industries, the total 'purchased inputs' of these six alone totalled almost two thousand million pounds – a figure that by now inflation will surely have doubled.[45] Moreover, in several instances they are virtually their suppliers' sole customers.

Paradoxically, however, the degree of direct and indirect government involvement in the economy may severely limit its ability to enforce an equal opportunity policy. In recent years nationalisation has been particularly directed at ailing industries which required substantial financial support. In other instances, large dollops of public money have been given to private companies whose troubles threatened to cause large-scale unemployment. It is very difficult in these circumstances to imagine that a threat to refuse future contracts, let alone cancel those in existence, could be uttered, or taken, seriously. The difficulty is compounded by the fact that in so many industries real domestic competition does not exist; the alternative to doing business with a discriminatory British employer would be placing orders overseas. The uproar inevitably accompanying foreign purchases, from the farcical affair of House of Commons tableware to the prolonged struggle over new planes for British Airways, further inhibits the use of the most powerful and direct sanctions.

However, if as with nuclear arms the ultimate weapon is too awful to use, there remain less devastating devices. Perhaps most valuable is the co-ordination between the Department of Employment and the Commission envisaged in the November 1978 proposals, whereby information received by the latter could be turned over to the CRE to provide the basis for a formal investigation (see further, Chapter 13). Although a company might argue that this transfer of information constituted a breach of confidence, it is thought unlikely that this view would prevail. The information would not, in Viscount Dilhorne's words, be 'of a personal character obtained in the exercise of a statutory power', nor would 'the giver of it . . . not expect it to be used for any purpose other than that for which it is given, or disclosed to any other person not concerned with that purpose'.[46] Indeed it would be obvious that the purpose of requiring the information related to a matter of funda-mental concern to the CRE. For avoidance of doubt, a standard clause could be inserted in future government contracts stating that all such information may be referred to the EOC and CRE.

POLICE EMPLOYMENT

The police occupy a unique constitutional position, both in terms of their governance and of the legal status of a police officer.[47] Since a constable is neither a servant of the Crown nor, at common law, of the police authority which in fact pays him, legislation was required to make Chief Constables vicariously liable for the tortious acts of constables under their control.[48] The Act follows this pattern. It deems the holding of the office of constable to be an employment by the chief officer of police where his action has affected a constable, or by the police authority where their action is in issue.[49] Police cadets are also included.[50] As the Chief Constable has sole authority to appoint police officers below the rank of Assistant Chief Constable, in most complaints of employment discrimination he will be the nominal respon-dent; as under the Police Act 1964 he has the right to indemnification if he is ordered to pay compensation or settles a claim with the approval of the police authority.[51] Like all employment-related complaints, claims of dis-crimination in the appointment or promotion of police officers or cadets go to industrial tribunals. Specialised police forces such as those under the control of London Transport or the Atomic Energy Authority are also subject to the Act.[52]

Overt discrimination in the hiring of black policemen was at one time openly acknowledged; in 1963 a spokesman for the Metropolitan Police said that the people of London were not yet prepared for blacks in uniform.[53] The colour bar was first breached in 1966, when black constables were appointed in Coventry and Leamington Spa. The Metropolitan Police – the only force over which the Home Office has any direct responsibility – subsequently changed their stance. Late in 1975 they began a £25,000 advertising campaign to recruit black police, which included use of the ethnic minority press; by April 1977 the number of minority policemen had doubled – to 78 – and by the close of the year stood at 82.[54] This total comprises just under three-eighths of the 1 per cent (0.0375 per cent) of the Metropolitan Police, who serve an area with a non-white population of around 8 per cent. However, only the West Midlands Police, with 36 black officers out of 6114 (just under 0.06 per cent), have a better record in this respect.[55]

In view of the extensive recruitment campaigns, both by particular Forces and, in 1976, nationally, it seems unlikely that direct discrimination is now of major importance in keeping the numbers so small. Moreover, as Commonwealth citizens, few blacks would be barred by the prohibition in the Act of Settlement 1700 against aliens holding an office of trust, a category including the office of constable.[56] The author has had the benefit of an interview with the Assistant Chief Constable and Chief Inspector concerned with recruitment to the West Midlands Police,[57] who take the view that the main problems are of two quite different sorts. The first is the reluctance of blacks to apply, which their active recruitment efforts have yet to overcome. This in turn derives from a widespread antipathy to the police as well as hostility individuals have encountered from their friends and families when they appeared in police or cadet uniforms.

The second obstacle is the selection criteria. The most important hurdle is a nationwide examination, devised by the Home Office, which is supposed to demonstrate 'O'-level or Grade 1 CSE competence in language ability and numeracy. Although no figures are kept, the responsible officials estimate that whilst roughly one-half of all applicants to the West Midlands Police fail this exam, the proportion among non-whites is more like 80 per cent. Prima facie this raises the question of indirect discrimination, but since the test is confidential it is impossible to assess whether it is truly job-related, although many of the skills it seeks to test do seem likely to arise in police work. Moreover – a point likely to weigh heavily in any contested case – they are necessary for the academic aspects of the training programme attended by all probationary constables. On the other hand, use of the test began in 1974, before the concept of indirect discrimination appeared, and it is doubtful whether the impact on minorities was considered when the test was devised, or indeed whether it has since been reviewed with this point in mind. However, interest has been shown in the use of a 'culture fair' test, whose object would be to achieve a truer estimate of minority applicants' abilities by taking account of their relative unfamiliarity with the language.

The other important selection stages are an interview, a home inquiry visit, and height, weight and eyesight requirements. Although the White

Paper instanced height requirements as an example of what would come under legal scrutiny under the new concept of discrimination,[58] the officials stated that police standards (172 cm. for men, 162 cm. for women) did not in their experience disproportionately exclude Asians, and were firm that the requirement was necessary to ensure respect from the public and the self-confidence of the constable in dealing with them. In their estimation, those blacks who passed the examination were at least as likely as whites to get through the remaining stages.

The prospects for brightening this picture in the short term are minimal. The massive pay rises received after the Edmund-Davies Report have made police work far more attractive than previously, and Forces like the West Midlands which were several hundred below their establishment have begun to fill vacancies and apply their selection standards more rigorously. As the ACC pointed out, one consequence of this otherwise welcome development is that the more intense competition may well increase the difficulties of black applicants, whose high rates of rejection occurred during a period when Forces were desperate for manpower. This can only be a bad omen for the success of the energetic efforts of some Forces to reduce the animosity existing between many blacks, particularly the young, and the police.

NOTES

1. See further, *de Smith*, chap. 28; *W & P/B*, chap. 36.
2. S. 75 (6) and (7).
3. Some cases suggested the existence of a contractual relationship between the Crown and its employees. See the discussion in *de Smith*, pp. 194–5, and the cases cited therein.
4. S. 75 (2).
5. S. 75 (8) and (9).
6. Cmnd 3638 (1968) app. A.
7. 'Civil Servants and Change' (C.S. Dept 1975), quoted in *W & P/B*, p. 259.
8. *Lester and Bindman*, pp. 218–21; *Hepple*, pp. 270–2.
9. S. 75 (5), which repeats s. 27 (9) of the previous Act.
10. S. 42, carrying over s. 10 (1) of the previous Act.
11. These are now to be found in the Race Relations (Prescribed Public Bodies) Regulations 1977, S.I. 1977/1774. The Bank of England and the Science Research Council are also among those listed.
12. Sched. 2, para. 9.
13. *Hepple*, p. 271.
14. *British Nationality Law*, Cmnd 6795 (1977).
15. Art. 48 (4).
16. *Application of Race Relations Policy in the Civil Service* (C.S. Dept H.M.S.O., 1978).
17. According to the Tavistock Report (ibid. para. 2.2) the C.S.C. does not record race or ethnic origin on any of its application documents.

18. These estimates appear in NEDO, *A Study of United Kingdom Nationalised Industries* (HMSO, 1976) p. 13 (main volume).

19. *Tamlin* v. *Hannaford*, [1950] 1 K.B. 18. See, further, *de Smith*, pp. 216–25; *W & P/B*, pp. 280–92.

20. *de Smith*, p. 218.

21. See some of the examples given ibid., and in *W & P/B*, pp. 284–5. This power is of course constrained by the notion of *vires*.

22. First Report of the Select Comm. on Nationalised Industries, H.C. 371–I (1967–8).

23. This view was expressed by participants in a conference the author attended on the workings of the 1976 Act, held in March 1979 under the sponsorship of the Runnymede Trust.

24. Information about the use of these tests and the absence of validation efforts, by the nationalised industries, was received in a private communication from Dr M. A. Pearn, author of several pamphlets and articles on employment testing and discrimination, and Assistant Director of the Runnymede Trust.

25. H.C. Hansard, 27 March 1979, cols 109–10 (W.A.).

26. These estimates are derived from figures taken from the following sources: Non-competitive contracts – *Report of the Second General Review of the Profit Formula for Non-Competitive Government Contracts* (Chairman: Sir W. K. M. Slimmings) (H.M.S.O., 1977). Competitive contracts – various Votes listed in *Appropriation Accounts*, 1975–6 (H.C. 93) (H.M.S.O., 1977) vols 2 and 3.

27. See generally, C. Turpin, *Government Contracts* (Penguin Books, 1969) chap. 9, entitled 'Procurement as an Instrument of Public Policy'.

28. See further, Elliott, (1978) 7 *I.L.J.* 120, and Ganz, [1978] *Pub. L.* 333.

29. See further, B. Bercusson, *Fair Wages Resolutions* (Mansell, 1978); O. Kahn-Freund, *Labour and the Law* (Stevens, 2nd edn, 1977) pp. 158–60.

30. An employee's attempt to do so failed in *Simpson* v. *Kodak Ltd* [1948] 2 K.B. 184.

31. The last such instance recorded in Bercusson's study, op. cit. p. 215, occurred in 1934.

32. Quoted in *Macdonald*, para. 357.

33. See the remarks in the Board's Annual Report for 1971–2, paras 94–5; *Lester and Bindman*, pp. 205–7; *Hepple*, pp. 280–1.

34. Cmnd 6234, para. 20.

35. The proposals are summarised in *Ind. Rel. Legal Information Bull.*, no. 133, 21 March 1979, p. 11. Initially only the 300 largest contractors were to be approached.

36. See the report of the letter sent by the Director-General of the CBI to the Department of Employment, in *The Guardian*, 28 February 1979.

37. RRB, *Final Report*, H.C. 3 (1976) app. VIII, paras 6–13.

38. 'Evaluating the Impact of Affirmative Action: A Look at the Federal Contract Compliance Program', *Ind. & Lab. Rel. Rev.* vol. 29, no. 4, July 1976. The published symposium consisted of five papers and several comments.

39. That year saw the promulgation of Executive Order No. 11246 which, though often amended, remains the paramount legal instrument. See further, B. Schlei and P. Grossman, *Employment Discrimination Law* (Washington, BNA, 1976) chap. 25; Note, 44 *N.Y.U.L. Rev.* 590 (1969).

40. Note, 44 *N.Y.U.L. Rev.* 590, 592.

41. Goldstein and Smith, 'The Estimated Impact of the Anti-discrimination Program Aimed at Federal Contractors', 29 *Ind. & Lab. Rel. Rev.* 523, 524 (1976).

42. Jones, 'Comment' on p. 581 of the Symposium cited in n. 38.

43. See the testimony of the Assistant Secretary of Labor in charge of the review to

a House of Representatives Committee, published as Read, 'Equal Opportunity Under Federal Contracts', 28 *Lab. L.J.* 3 (1977).

44. NEDO Study, above, n. 18, p. 14 (main volume).

45. This is an estimate calculated from figures presented in ibid, appx volume, pp. 32–3, especially table B.24, and Background Paper No. 6, p. 2.

46. *Norwich Pharmacal Co.* v. *Commissioners of Customs and Excise*, [1974] A.C. 133, 189; [1973] 2 All E.R. 943, 961.

47. See further, G. Marshall, *Police and Government* (1965) *passim*, and *W & P/B*, chap. 20.

48. Police Act 1964, s. 48. An attempt to hold local police authorities liable for the wrongdoing of constables failed in *Fisher* v. *Oldham Corpn*, [1930] 2 K.B. 364.

49. S. 16 (1)(a) and (b), respectively.

50. S. 16 (4).

51. S. 16 (2).

52. This was the intention of the definitions in s. 16 (5), as explained by the Minister to the Standing Committee: *Official Report*, 18 May 1976, cols 316–17.

53. Quoted in *Hepple*, p. 273.

54. H.C. Hansard, 11 May 1977, vol. 931, col. 498 (W.A.) and 14 February 1978, vol. 944, col. 104, (W.A.).

55. The latter figures were received from the police officials mentioned in the text in the interview cited in n. 57 below.

56. This was decided more than two centuries ago, in *R.* v. *De Mierre*, (1771) 5 Burr. 2788.

57. Interview of 20 September 1979 with Asst Chief Constable J. Glynn and Chief Inspector R. Cross, from which the factual statements made in the ensuing paragraphs derive. I should like to thank Mr Glynn and Mr Cross for their whole-hearted co-operation and provision of information.

58. Cmnd 6234, para. 55.

9
Trade Unions and
Shop Stewards

Confining discussion of discrimination in the area of employment to actions by managers and their subordinates would present a seriously incomplete picture. With a growing majority of the workforce composed of trade union members, the performance of unions is critical. Perhaps the most unique feature of British trade unionism is the role of shop stewards, with their double-sided relationship to the autonomous work group which elects them and the organisation of which they are the purported delegates. Their equally unique and highly controversial position under the Act must also be examined in detail.

The relevant provision is s. 11.[1] Protection is extended to members of trade unions, and to those seeking membership. It is unlawful to discriminate against the former in relation to access to benefits, facilities or services, expulsions or varying terms of membership, or by subjecting [them] to any other 'detriment'.[2] The latter are covered with regard to refusal and terms of membership.[3]

These provisions are in essence identical to those contained in the 1968 Act. From a reading of the Race Relations Board's Annual Reports it appears that they were little used: in the 1970s only one opinion of discrimination was formed, and that in the notorious situation at Mansfield Hosiery Mills Ltd, described below. However, one should not conclude from the quiescence of the law that discrimination is absent from trade unions. In 1978 alone the CRE received 57 requests for assistance concerning discrimination in admission to membership.[4] Both the PEP research and the outbreak of several prolonged strikes by Asian workers in the early 1970s further attest to its importance.

The PEP study revealed that, contrary to earlier suggestions,[5] trade-union membership is substantially higher among all minorities groups than among whites, especially those doing unskilled and semi-skilled manual work.[6] Later in the 1970s, several bitter recognition strikes – of which Grunwick was only the most notorious – attested to the importance black workers attach to trade unionism. The question is whether their loyalty has been adequately recognised and repaid. As early as 1955 the TUC passed a resolution condemning racial discrimination in employment, but virtually nothing concrete was done at any level to combat its manifestations either by employers or among member unions. This too changed in the last decade, more specifically from 1973 onwards, when a number of local and national conferences adopted resolutions against racialism.[7] In March 1975 the TUC produced a model equal opportunity clause for inclusion in collective agreements, which in some instances has occurred.[8] Later in the same year it established an Equal Rights and a Race Relations Advisory Committee. And in contrast to its official position in the 1960s it supported the passage of the Sex Discrimination Act and the strengthening of racial discrimination legislation.[9]

At ground level the picture is less sanguine. In their survey PEP found several instances of unions acting in concert with management to exclude non-whites or limit their numbers, or where poor representation or absence of efforts to remedy situations which white workers would not have tolerated had facilitated discrimination or exploitation by management. It was also clear that unions at national level had done little to remedy such situations, or even to learn of their existence.[10] Other studies have documented a substantial under-representation of blacks as shop stewards,[11] which cannot be entirely explained by linguistic incapacity or lack of familiarity with industrial custom and practice.

One of the significant triggers awakening the interest of higher-level trade-union officials in the problems of racialism was the outbreak of strikes by Asian workers in opposition to their own unions.[12]* Perhaps the most spectacular occurred at Mansfield Hosiery Mills Ltd in 1972. The company operated a promotion structure with the assistance of white skilled workers which excluded Asians from promotion to skilled jobs. The Asians took strike action alone; white workers not only refused support, but negotiated a productivity deal that had previously been resisted. Some aided the intrusion of the National Front, as the long strike produced increasing racial enmity throughout the area. The dispute received national attention, and was the subject of separate inquiries by the Department of Employment and the Commission on Industrial Relations.[13] The strike was eventually successful, not only in demonstrating the ability of Asian workers to draw upon their community for support, but in ending the discrimination and securing the immediate promotion of twenty-eight Asians to skilled positions.

Another challenge to a union was presented by the fourteen-week strike at Imperial Typewriters at Leicester, which began on May Day of 1974.[14] Roughly two-thirds of the workers were Asians, mostly refugees from Uganda, who were engaged in tedious assembly-line work. Initially a small group struck about the bonus system, but when the Branch Committee of their union, the Transport and General Workers' Union (TGWU), refused to take part in talks with the Strike Committee, positions stiffened. The number of strikers increased tenfold and their demands mushroomed to include an end to racial discrimination in promotion, increased shop-steward representation, and no victimisation of strike leaders. Increasingly their antagonism was directed at the union, and after a month the Regional Secretary held an Inquiry. Eventually, Regional officials overruled actions by local union bodies, and the strike was settled on the basis that the results of the Inquiry would determine the action to be taken on the strikers' grievances. Attempts by the National Front to destroy the settlement failed, but succeeded in worsening the racial divisions among the workforce.

Public self-criticism is hardly a distinguishing feature of large organisations of any kind, and the remarkable feature of the Report of Inquiry[15] was the extent to which the TGWU accepted that it was in error in failing to back some of the strikers' key demands, and in acknowledging its deficiencies in representing Asian workers effectively. The Report recommended elimination of the two-year membership rule for shop stewards, which had made most of the Asians ineligible, and also suggested better communication and explanation of the negotiated grievance procedure, including distributing printed summaries in the immigrants' languages.

In these and other cases there can be no doubt that several local officials and shop stewards either committed acts of direct discrimination or assisted or tolerated their commission by management. Yet the law does not treat them alike; the critical precondition for its application to trade unionists is the status of the person committing or aiding the discrimination. If he is a full-time official, or otherwise employed by a trade union, the position is clear. Under the provision concerning vicarious liability (see above, pp. 115–16) the union – like any employer – is legally responsible for the acts of its employees. However, under the 1968 legislation, liability extended not only to the organisation, but also to 'any person concerned with the affairs of such an organisation'.[16] This phrase encompassed shop stewards, who at plant level are the key trade-union figures in British industry.[17] They are elected, unpaid part-time representatives of their workmates, who are responsible for the day-to-day workings of industrial relations. In particular it is they who at the first instance take up the grievances of a worker or group of workers in matters such as work allocation, discipline and plant rules; who participate in joint management–union selection of apprentices or other agreed hiring and promotion procedures; who often are responsible for recruitment to the union; who represent their members in the plant bargaining which has become an increasingly important supplement to national wage agreements; and who negotiate with management over redundancies. Their importance is the precise measure of the impact their acts of discrimination may have on black workers, and makes their exclusion from the 1976 Act all the more controversial. For s. 11 is limited to organisations, and does not extend to 'persons concerned' with their activities.

This exclusion was the subject of long and at times acrimonious debate in both Houses of Parliament.[18] The Lords inserted the 'persons concerned' language into the section, but the Commons insisted upon its deletion. Although some Labour MPs had questioned the provision in the Standing Committee, voting in the Commons broke along party lines, with Labour alone in favour.

It must be emphasised that in practical terms the extent of the immunity is quite narrow. Nothing in s. 11 affects the liability of a shop steward who, like everyone else, violates s. 33 of the statute if he knowingly aids another person to commit a discriminatory act. Thus where management and shop stewards connive to limit the hiring or block promotion of black workers,[19] the primary liability rests with the employer under s. 4, for he has final responsibility for the decision (below, p. 177). The shop steward who knowingly assists in this discrimination is, however, independently liable as an aider and abettor, and may be ordered to pay compensation for injury to feelings, a head of damages independent of any economic loss suffered by the complainant (s. 57 (4); see below, pp. 228–9). It is only in relation to purely internal trade union functions and activities, of which the prime example is refusal to take up a member's grievance against management,[20] that the immunity has been conferred.

Thus what might otherwise have been the strongest argument favouring the present provision has been undercut. The voluntarist tradition of strict exclusion of the law from industrial relations (see above, p. 135) has in relation to stewards already been so severely breached by s. 33 that the existing immunity no longer expresses a norm but an isolated exception, an obeisance to an historical totem. It should be emphasised too that the voluntarist regime long upheld sweeping discrimination against certain groups such as aliens and, above all, women. The proponents of voluntarism, when emphasising its value in regulating conflicts between unions and management, or indeed rival unions, have blandly overlooked its toleration of these injustices. Minorities within the workforce, until recently silent and ignored, have been badly served by voluntarism, and it is no longer enough simply to invoke the authority of tradition in the absence of credible evidence that their interests, and those of blacks, will be adequately protected.

None the less the competing considerations are many and finely balanced. On the one side, shop stewards, unlike managers, do not carry out their tasks as employees. They are the elected representatives of a work group which may be largely autonomous from official union control. Local councillors or MPs, in carrying out their ancillary functions of making representations to administrators on behalf of their constituents, are arguably outside the Act if they treat requests for assistance from blacks less favourably than those received from whites;[21]* it may be thought that a shop steward exercising an analogous function should enjoy a similar immunity. Moreover, it is often difficult to find people willing to take on the time-consuming and unpaid position;[22] the prospect of having to justify one's behaviour to an industrial tribunal may deepen the general reluctance to serve.

Second, recent research has shown that the relationship between shop stewards and their members is highly complex.[23] Many are 'populists' rather than leaders; that is, they see themselves, and behave, as delegates of those who elected them. In the plant studied, this tendency was particularly marked among staff, as distinct from shop-floor, stewards. Thus in so far as the steward's discrimination reflects the wishes of his members, imposition of personal liability may be seen as unfair scapegoating. Moreover, stewards do their jobs and exercise their powers by means of complex 'networks of influence' which depend on personal relationships, rather than formal invocation of institutional controls. In such intimate situations the intervention of formal legal rules and institutions is regarded as undesirable, bad for industrial relations, and in reality likely to produce unenforceable dictates. A final and related contention is that trade union principles, as embodied in the day-to-day behaviour and expression of stewards themselves, place primary emphasis on unity and collective advance.[24] Permitting members to hale stewards before tribunals would create personal bitterness and cleavages within the work-group that would destroy stewards' ability to mobilise workers for effective action against management, which requires a united workforce.

The opposing view does not ignore the realities of trade-union organisation, nor the intricate dynamics of shop steward behaviour. However, different inferences and conclusions of policy may be drawn from the same factual perceptions.

First, a steward who discriminates in response to his members' promptings acts no differently from an employer who refuses to hire or promote a black person for fear of his employees' or customers' reaction. Yet, as we have seen (above, pp. 4 and 122), the law has never accepted this justification for discrimination. Indeed the prospect of liability may *strengthen* the ability of a shop steward to resist his members' pressures, since an appeal to avoiding unpleasant personal consequences would carry more weight in such a situation than invocation of abstract principles of equality. Moreover, a sizeable number of shop-floor stewards function as leaders, rather than mere delegates,[25] and in so far as their own inclinations lead them to discriminate, they deserve no more lenient treatment than any other person with power to cause difficulty for minority persons.

Second, powerful as the argument based upon the need for union solidarity must be, it is simply unacceptable that the cry for unity should be used as a shibboleth for shabby treatment of a weak minority. Forbidding gains by individual workers via 'private deals' with management is justified by the greater reward for all that collective action may achieve; but where the collectivity imposes or tolerates inferior treatment, black workers required to make such sacrifices are denied the reciprocal advantages. Moreover, stewards also describe 'fairness and justice' as important trade-union principles;[26] if this is to be taken as more than rhetoric, public policy in the form of legislation is justified in upholding it when racial bigotry exposes an internal conflict of principles.

Another objection stresses the inherent limitations of the effectiveness of legal intervention in the personal relationships involved. This really involves two distinct points. The first arises from the particular context of industrial relations. It emphasises that the great practical failure of the Industrial Relations Act 1971 occurred with its attempt to impose liability upon shop stewards, an effort abandoned after the *Heatons* case (below, p. 170) made it possible to shift primary liability to the unions.[27]* The present position under the Act simply carries over this eventual outcome, and the Government's contention was essentially that it represents a hard lesson learned.

This view, however, runs together two radically different situations. Legally, unlike their responsibility for industrial action, it is very unlikely that unions can be held liable for shop stewards' discriminatory acts (see below, p. 171). Morally, direct discrimination by a shop steward, even if acting as representative of an autonomous work-group, hardly deserves the same protection that is rightly required where the steward is engaged in advancing the interests of his members against their at least equally powerful employer in the competitive arena of collective bargaining.

Nor is there much realistic possibility that stewards would be liable for indirect discrimination. It seems unlikely that a work-group would unwittingly evolve anything as subtle as an apparently even-handed rule or practice which in reality disproportionately disqualified or excluded minorities; its exclusions are likely to be overt and intentional. Even in the rare instance, no financial liability would be incurred since compensation for indirect discrimination is not available under the Act (above, p. 13 and below, p. 233–4). Indeed if a tribunal recommended abolition of an indirectly discriminatory practice and the work-group refused to comply, the steward would still incur no liability. By a strange weakness in the Act failure to comply with a so-called 'action recommendation' can result in an order of greater compensation, but only in cases in which compensation could initially have been ordered.[28] Whatever one may think of this enforcement mechanism in principle, its limitations undercut the important argument against shop-steward liability.

The second limb of objection emphasises the inappropriateness of legal intervention in relationships of a highly personal quality, such as exists between shop stewards and the work-group. Though carrying some force, it perhaps proves too much. It was repeatedly urged by the Conservative Opposition in their unsuccessful efforts to stop the extension of the Act to clubs of more than twenty-five members and partnerships of six or more persons.[29] Small family businesses often maintain a highly personal atmosphere as well, yet no one has suggested that this entitles them to remain free to discriminate. Had the Government chosen in all these instances to permit exceptions the limited immunity of shop stewards would have rested upon an explicable, if arguable, decision of principle. It did no such thing. Rather it steadfastly insisted upon the paramount need for comprehensive proscription of discrimination, even as Ministers acknowledged the practical limits of law in these areas.[30] In this light singling out shop stewards for exemption seems a combination of conclusions mistakenly transposed from a greatly dissimilar context and some politically inspired special pleading.

It might appear that in practical terms the omission of shop stewards is of minor importance, for tribunals are likely to award minimal damages against men of modest incomes. This overlooks one of the most important means of influence of law, particularly when applied to private individuals: the deterrent effect of the legal process itself, of being compelled to take the time and trouble, and undergo the embarrassment, of justifying one's behaviour to the scrutiny of outsiders. Moreover, where a shop steward does discriminate and deterrence by definition has failed, the question of redress for the victim becomes paramount. In most analogous situations under the Act this is covered by the agency liability principle embodied in s. 32 (2). This simply states a basic principle of the law of agency: where someone acts on behalf of another person, having received his authority to do so, the latter, known as the principle, is liable for the acts of his agent. This authority may, in the language of s. 32 (2), be expressed or implied, precedent or subsequent.

The application of agency principles to shop stewards, or more precisely the legal responsibility of trade unions for their activity, was at the centre of the storm surrounding the Industrial Relations Act.[31] The problem has twice come before the House of Lords. In the leading case, *Heatons Transport (St Helens) Ltd* v. *Transport and General Workers' Union*,[32] the question was whether the union was liable under the Industrial Relations Act 1971 for the decision of its shop stewards to 'black' container depots at particular docks. Lord Wilberforce, who spoke for the whole House in a rare joint opinion, stated – on the basis of evidence demonstrating the unusually decentralised character of the union – that the stewards had a general implied authority to act in the interest of those they represented, but that his authority did not extend to acts outside union rules or policy. Since union policy was to oppose loss of members' work caused by the introduction of containers, and the stewards had implied authority to take industrial action in furtherance of it, liability was found.[33]

Lord Wilberforce was at pains to stress that, in the absence of express authority, the result in each case would depend heavily upon the evidence about union policy and the action of its officials.[34] The importance of these questions of fact received even greater emphasis in *General Aviation Services (UK) Ltd,* v. *TGWU*,[35] in which meticulous examination of the evidence concerning conduct of union officials in relation to the action of shop stewards led both the Court of Appeal and House of Lords to reject the conclusion that an implied authority existed.

The practical import of these cases is that trade unions will seldom be responsible for discrimination by their shop stewards. We have seen that the official policy of the TUC, supported by virtually all unions, is one of non-discrimination.[36]* Consequently there would be no general express authority for any act of direct discrimination, and the more centralised the union structure, the less likely that an implied authority would be found. Only if it could be proven that an authority had been conferred on the steward in particular circumstances would liability fall upon the union. This restrictive approach seems appropriate in light of the tenuous connection which in reality exists between shop stewards and the union organisation outside the plant;[37] given the independence of stewards, imposition upon the union of liability for their actions would simply be arbitrary.

To the foregoing analysis must be added one footnote. S. 32 (2) refers to acts of agents 'for another person'. After the House of Lords had voted to amend s. 11, Lord Simon of Glaisdale, the only Law Lord to have spoken during the Debate, asked the government spokesman whether a trade union would be a 'person' within this subsection. Though he never received the promised written reply, subsequently he was informally given an affirmative answer by a Home Office legal official.[38]

This view, which seems correct, is based upon established rules of statutory interpretation, under which the expression 'person' extends to bodies both corporate and unincorporate.[39] Although present legislation specifically excludes trade unions from the former category,[40] in the context of discrimination they would unequivocally fall within the latter. Thus trade unions, like other principals, would be subject to the same rules of agency liability.

To summarise the position in relation to direct discrimination, trade unions are liable for the acts of full-time officials and other employees (s. 32 (1)), subject to the defence of taking reasonably practical steps to prevent such discriminatory acts (s. 32 (3)). Shop stewards – or indeed other worker representatives who are not union officials – are not liable as individuals, nor does liability extend to the union, unless it had conferred an authority upon the steward to discriminate. Where such authority exists, it would appear that the phrase 'person' in the context of s. 32 (2) includes a trade union.

It may be wondered whether the present provisions adequately protect the interests of black workers. In the early 1970s there were some disturbing cases of mass dismissals of Asians who had fallen out with their union, which had accepted, or then proceeded to negotiate, new work arrangements without consulting them or in opposition to their wishes. In instances where complaints of unfair dismissal were made they were rejected by industrial tribunals, which seem to have regarded the Asians' attitude as obstructive.[41]

Both the TGWU's unusually honest assessment of its own shortcomings in the Imperial Typewriters dispute and the linguistic and other problems of communication that often arise with Asian immigrant workers suggest an equally plausible but sharply opposed conclusion: that the unions may not have taken adequate account of these workers' interests and desires, or simply failed to ensure that they understood the new arrangements and the reasons for them. Nor can outright disregard of their wishes by individual shop stewards or union officials for racialist reasons be entirely ruled out. In situations where the workforce is divided on racial lines, minority workers are without legal protection. American law has attempted to counterbalance this weakness by imposing a 'duty of fair representation' on trade unions and their representatives, requiring them to process grievances and negotiate with management on behalf of all groups within the workforce.[42] However, this has arisen in the radically different context of American labour law, which creates a 'bargaining unit' within which a single union is granted monopoly representation. This structure is entirely alien to British industrial relations, and is supported by legal paraphernalia which have never, even under the regime of the Industrial Relations Act 1971, had any counterpart here. One cannot see how such a duty, even if created by statute, could be enforced. It should be noted too that one expert on trade-union discrimination in the United States has expressed serious doubt whether the rule has in reality achieved equal treatment for black union members.[43]

An alternate possibility is for minority workers to join a union responsive to their interests. In some situations, particularly where a union representing white skilled workers chooses to ignore non-whites doing unskilled jobs, this has occurred.[44] But where they are already members of a union with which they are dissatisfied, the 'Bridlington Agreement' – rules initially established at the TUC Congress of 1939 to govern relations among affiliated unions in matters including rivalry in recruitment and transfers of members – will often stand in the way.[45] Their general tenor is best exemplified by the vocabulary of the Regulations concerning the settlement of inter-union disputes, which makes specific provision for cases of 'alleged poaching'. In harmony with this approach is Principle 5, which specifically forbids a union to organise workers represented by another without the latter's consent; the fact the new union may have been invited to do so by disaffected workers is not taken into account. The Bridlington Principles play an important role in preventing divisions within the trade-union movement and avoiding unnecessary industrial disputes, but not surprisingly they were designed without contemplation of the possibility that racial minorities might be locked in a subordinate position within their union. Consequently in such cases effectively unrepresented workers may be left out in the cold.

Moreover, there appears to be little room within the existing procedural structure to remedy this situation. Principles 2 and 4 prohibit a union from immediately admitting an applicant who has been a member of another

TUC affiliate within the previous year, and lay down a time-consuming procedure which permits the applicant's former union to object. If the two organisations cannot reach a satisfactory settlement the matter must be taken to the Disputes Committee of the TUC, which is empowered to make an award if it cannot achieve an agreement 'acceptable to all the parties involved' – which does not however primarily mean the dissatisfied members. The recent detailed study of the adjucations of this Committee[46] reveals that it consistently subordinates the wishes of individual or small groups of unionists to institutional considerations. The paramount criteria are organisational dominance, existing negotiating rights, and compliance with procedural rules laid down in the Bridlington Agreement.[47] All of them, but particularly the first – which has assumed increasing importance over the years[48] – virtually guarantee that black workers whose union serves them badly will be rebuffed; a conclusion following *a fortiori* from the fact that the existing union's organisational dominance rests securely on the white majority. An illustration of the Committee's approach is provided by one case with no racial element, in which dissatisfied workers sought new union affiliation. The receiving organisation was held to have violated the Bridlington Agreement in accepting them.[49] Only where disaffected unionists are in a majority – as might occur where ethnic concentrations among different grades of workers have developed and blacks in a particular grade sought to transfer membership – would the principles evolved by the Disputes Committee over the years permit the transfer. As the author of the study commented elsewhere: 'individual rights are left by the Committee to be vindicated within TUC member unions and not by means of transferring unions'.[50] Nor is there any reason to think that this attitude will change, for the Committee is not concerned with imposing fundamental reforms on trade unions, but with providing an adjudicative forum for settling inter-union squabbling in a manner that staves off pressures for outside intervention, and is acceptable to established trade union leaders.[51] An active concern for just treatment of racial minorities is simply outside the universe it inhabits.

Although ill treatment of black workers within a union may only occur infrequently, it is none the less imperative that some avenue of redress be created within the TUC procedural framework. Failure to do so could produce several unfortunate consequences: increasing pressure for greater legal intervention in the conduct of internal trade union affairs; investigations by the CRE, which need not attend upon an individual complaint; and ultimately the formation of separate unions on ethnic lines. The growth of such organisations is undesirable from everyone's viewpoint: it would reinforce the social isolation of Asians from the wider community, and result in a divided and embittered workforce, incapable of effective negotiation and industrial action. Ensuring fair treatment of black unionists is a matter of self-interest for organised trade unionism.

It is doubtful whether anti-discrimination law can assist black workers in this situation. Although trade union officials in their negotiations and presentation of individual grievances would doubtless be providing 'benefits, facilities or services' to their members, it is unlikely that they would be held to have violated the Act if the outcome of their negotiations was a wage structure or shift arrangement that most whites in a plant favoured but blacks opposed. Industrial tribunals, rightly, would be loath to set themselves up as review bodies to evaluate the wisdom of a collective agreement negotiated by constitutionally chosen shop stewards and union officials. The problem of 'fair representation' can only be effectively resolved within the union, by a combination of unflinching refusal by union leaders to tolerate racialism and energetic participation by black members.

TRADE UNIONS AND
INDIRECT DISCRIMINATION

In their work of negotiation and representation it is doubtful whether trade-union officials or shop stewards will be in a position to commit acts of indirect discrimination. When one looks at what has been called the 'job control functions' of trade unions[52] the picture is very different. In particular, some of the practices associated with the pre-entry closed shops – in which the worker must be accepted into the union before he can obtain work – would now seem to be unlawful. As this possibility was never discussed when the Act went through Parliament, and seems to have gone at least publicly unrecognised in trade-union circles, it will be examined in some detail.

Lord McCarthy in his classic study distinguishes four types of pre-entry closed shop.[53] There is the *labour supply shop*, in which membership in the union is an essential prerequisite of obtaining employment, and the union also acts as a labour exchange; employers in the industry will inform its representatives of vacancies and through them receive new employees. A variant is the *labour pool* closed shop, of which the best-known example is the National Dock Labour Board (NDLB) scheme. Here the employers and the union agree to form a recognised labour force, consisting entirely of union members. Once accepted into the pool a member may take up or change employment without reference to the union, and the employer is not obligated to 'clear' its employees with union representatives, so long as they are part of the pool.

Where skilled workers are involved, and apprenticeship is a necessary qualification for the job, the union simply limits its intake to properly qualified apprentices. It then usually seeks to limit the numbers trained each year, by insisting upon a fixed ratio of apprentices to workers. This forms the *craft qualification* shop. A variant involves recruitment of skilled workers from among the unskilled who have generally worked alongside present union members; this progression cannot occur unless the union admits the new man as a member, hence the name *promotion veto* shop.

The importance of the closed shop can hardly be exaggerated. McCarthy found that approximately one-half of manual-worker trade unionists worked in a closed shop, and that in several skilled trades the entire craft was closed to the non-unionists. He also estimated that about 1 in 5 closed shops are of the pre-entry type.[54] Later research has demonstrated that the closed shop has become increasingly prevalent, having taken hold in industries in which it had earlier been uncommon, and has acquired a remarkable degree of management support.[55]

Nothing in the pre-entry closed shop inherently involves or requires racial discrimination. Overt racial exclusion, though more devastating in its impact on the rejected applicant for membership, is no more likely to occur in this context than in any other aspect of employment. A unique problem does arise because unions have used their restrictions on entry to give preference on a personal basis, particularly by favouring the admission of sons and relations of existing members. Thus the NDLB labour-pool shop operates several pools, the most desirable being known as the Main Register. 'The Board recognises the priority claim of dockers' sons to be taken on the Main Register'; when Lord McCarthy wrote, they comprised 18 per cent of the annual intake.[56] Subsequent developments do not suggest that nepotism on the docks has lost its importance.[57] Similarly, the labour supply shop which exists for unskilled workers in the printing industry means that the unions are besieged with applications for membership. In large towns a list of would-be members is maintained; this is known colloquially as the 'Sons and Brothers list'.[58]

In the craft qualification shop, which operates in its most developed form among skilled printing workers, the limitation on apprentices, together with union participation in their selection, has also enabled nepotism to flourish.[59]

Applying s. 1 (1)(b), it is obvious that the requirement or condition of being related to a union member, when the existing membership is over-whelmingly white, is one that a considerably smaller proportion of blacks than whites will be able to fulfil. As noted in the context of word-of-mouth hiring, the same would be true if the preference were given to friends of existing members. If in either instance a black applicant is denied union membership, s. 11 (2)(b) would be violated. Moreover, where knowledge of such practices has discouraged blacks from even attempting to join, the Commission for Racial Equality could seek to ban their use: s. 28 of the Act outlaws 'discriminatory practices' – the operation of indirectly discriminatory criteria which need not actually have been applied to a particular person. However, the Commission alone may attack such practices and must proceed by means of a formal investigation and issuance of a non-discrimination notice (see below, Chapter 13). This process is elaborate and time-consuming and, as with individual complaints, would have to be repeated with each organisation separately if proceedings against one union did not spur voluntary changes by others with similar practices.

In the pre-entry closed shop the union stands on the same footing as an employer in terms of its impact on those seeking work, and there is no basis for treating it differently under the Act. To uphold nepotistic preferences the union would have to prove that this hiring policy was 'justifiable'. Under either the test of job-relatedness suggested earlier, or the guidelines outlined in *Steel*, this would not be possible. Certainly under the American statute, nepotistic trade-union practices in various crafts have been struck down by the courts consistently and with little hesitation.[60]

When the relevant standard is confined to whether a challenged practice contributes to business efficiency it is difficult to see how it could be otherwise. The closed shop is the pre-eminent example of the point made on p. 60, that trade-union practices are not designed to maximise profitability or market efficiency, but to protect members. It was also suggested there that the interests of workers may not be adequately taken into account under the justification provision in its present form. Nepotism in hiring can hardly claim the same respect as the last-in-first-out principle, the closed shop, or other practices which safeguard union bargaining power or prevent management exploitation. But despite its emotive connotation it is merely one manifestation of inheritance, an institution generally regarded with favour. For skilled workers, whose wages are insufficient to enable them to accumulate any sizeable amount of wealth, access to membership of a union which operates a pre-entry closed shop may be the most valuable asset they can confer upon their children. It is difficult to distinguish their actions and motives from those of a businessman or solicitor who brings his child into the family firm,[61] or to deny the importance that family connections retain in education, merchant banking, the legal profession and other key centres of power and influence. This is not to suggest that nepotism among trade unionists is acceptable, but to throw into sharp relief the narrow scope of anti-discrimination law generally. No statute in any country has yet been able to penetrate elite institutions; even American employment case law – by far the most highly developed and voluminous – has concerned mainly manual and lower-level service jobs.[62] This class bias, whether or not intentional, is one of the striking features of the practical working of anti-discrimination legislation in its early stages. Its elimination will be one of the primary tasks in the next generation of legal control.

The peculiar position of shop stewards raises the question of where liability would rest in the case of indirect discrimination. Assuming that stewards or other persons who were not trade-union officials were responsible for the selection of members, the union's liability would depend upon the existence of an authority for the nepotism preference. Although open recognition of the practice seems to be greatest on the docks, its existence in other industries could hardly be maintained without the knowledge and approval of union officials – who would themselves have seen it in operation when they sought entrance to the union. In these circumstances, and particularly because prior to the enactment of the indirect discrimination provision preference for sons and relations was not unlawful,[63]* it should not be difficult to establish that those operating such a membership policy had union authorisation to do so. Evidence of persons with knowledge of the particular industry and union concerned may be required, since admissions by those immediately involved may not be readily forthcoming.

Where as with the craft qualification shop the actual selection of apprentices is done by management, it is they who will be liable under the Act, even though their choice may be heavily influenced by the union.[64]* This emerges clearly from the *Steel* case (see above, pp. 13) in which the complaint against the union which negotiated a discriminatory provision was dismissed by the Employment Appeal Tribunal. Since 'at the end of the day it was the Post Office who had to make the decisions and made the decision', and an effective order would run against them, Phillips J. saw no reason for the union to remain a party to subsequent proceedings.[65] Although trade-union representatives who assisted in selection could be individually liable under s. 33, they could not, as we have seen, be ordered to pay compensation to a victim of indirect discrimination.

TRADE UNION DISCIPLINE

The final area in which the Act may require modification of trade-union practices is that of discipline. Many trade-union rules contain vague 'catch-all' or 'omnibus' clauses authorising expulsion or lesser sanctions for conduct 'detrimental to the union' or which 'renders the member unfit for membership', among other formulations.[66] Like all union rules these are regarded in law as part of a contract of membership between the individual and the union, and discipline imposed for reasons other than, or contrary to, those authorised in the rules constitutes a breach of contract for which redress at common law may be sought in the courts.

Expulsion on overtly racial grounds presents an easy case, since no trade-union rule would authorise such action, and the breach of contract would be patent. However, it is certainly possible that a member who alleged discrimination by his union, either by means of a formal complaint to a tribunal or informally to the CRE, or who assisted the Commission in an investigation into discrimination by the union, would be expelled under an omnibus clause, or for failing to follow the established internal union complaints procedure.

All of these activities would readily come within s. 2 of the Act and the member could complain of victimisation (above, Chapter 4) regardless of the precise sanction imposed.[67] However, if expelled the most he could expect under the Act would be a recommendation of readmission by the tribunal, backed by an award of compensation if it went unheeded: the union could not be required to accept him (see further below, pp. 233–5). If he worked in a closed shop his ostensible legal victory might well leave him unemployed, although he could appeal to the Independent Review Committee of the TUC – a body with no formal power but considerable persuasive authority established in 1976 under the chairmanship of Professor Lord Wedderburn to hear appeals in cases of expulsion from membership where a closed shop exists.[68] The courts however possess the injunctive power which industrial tribunals have never been granted, and could compel readmission or even, in a case of clear illegality, forbid the impending expulsion.[69]

What remains problematical is whether the victimised member has any rights at common law that would gain him access to its superior remedies. The procedural rules of natural justice have long been held applicable to disciplinary proceedings.[70] However, although Lord Denning M.R. had suggested that the courts could vet trade-union rules for substantive unreasonableness,[71] his dicta had generally been rejected,[72] and he has recently resiled from that position.[73] Judicial intervention in these circumstances would require enunciation of a principle that activities falling within s. 2 could never be regarded as 'conduct detrimental'. As in *Esterman* v. *NALGO*[74] it would be expressed in the terms that no reasonable disciplinary tribunal could *bona fide* reach that conclusion. Such a rule of law could draw support from cases invalidating expulsion of members who have brought suits against their union to restrain illegal activities.[75]

That this analysis is inconclusive is hardly surprising. No case raising the issue has yet arisen, and the courts would have to strike a delicate balance between avoiding undue interference in trade-union self-government and protecting the livelihood of members whose defiance of the majority may vindicate important policies expressed in Acts of Parliament. What does emerge clearly is the relative feebleness of the remedies available under the Act, a point to which we shall return in Chapter 12.

CONCLUSIONS

As yet the Act has had little direct application to trade unions. However, serious problems of discrimination in relation to admission and equal treatment of existing members unquestionably exist, and may be expected to provide the raw material for litigation of individual complaints and investigations by the CRE. Although at official levels encouraging steps have been taken by the TUC and some unions, a great deal remains to be done, particularly at the workplace itself. The refusal to impose liability for discrimination upon shop stewards who act on behalf of work-groups, contrary to union authorisation, is a dubious anomaly in a statute otherwise noteworthy for its comprehensive scope. At present the rigidities of TUC rules concerning transfer of union membership may lock black workers into unions which ignore their interests in favour of the white majority. The statute provides no remedy and it is difficult to imagine how legal intervention could work effectively in these circumstances. Precisely because of the statutory exemption and practical limitations, shop stewards and trade-union officers have a particularly great responsibility to exercise moral leadership in confronting problems of discrimination.

NOTES

1. This section also applies to employers' and professional associations, not discussed in this book.
2. S. 11 (3)(a), (b) and (c), respectively.
3. S. 11 (2)(b) and (a), respectively.
4. *CRE Annual Report 1978*, H.C. 128 (H.M.S.O., 1979) p. 8.
5. Runnymede Trust, *Trade Unions and Immigrant Workers* (Workers' Educational Association, Dec 1974) p. 9 (hereafter Runnymede Survey).
6. *Racial Disadvantage*, pp. 191–2. These findings refer to men only.
7. These are discussed and several reprinted in the Runnymede Survey, pp. 12–14 and 20–2.
8. The text may be found in *Macdonald*, para. 222. The Race Relations Board reported its inclusion in several collective agreements in its Final Report: H.C. 3 (1976) para. 56.
9. Compare its attitude in 1968 as chronicled by *Lester and Bindman*, pp. 126–7, with its evidence of the House of Commons Select Committee on Race Relations and Immigration, 10 July 1974.
10. *Racial Disadvantage*, pp. 196–207.
11. Notably D. Brooks, *Black Employment in the Black Country* (Runnymede Trust, 1975) p. 30, who found that there were black shop stewards in only 15% of the firms in his survey with black employees, despite roughly equivalent trade-union membership among all races.
*12. Miles and Phizacklea, 'The TUC and Black Workers, 1974–1976' (1978) 16 *B.J.I.R.* 195, suggest that top-level TUC officials were moved even more forcefully in the direction of active efforts towards advancing equal opportunities by their alarm at the growth of National Front support among trade unionists in this period.
13. Report of a Committee of Inquiry into a Dispute between Employees of the Mansfield Hosiery Mills Ltd, Loughborough, and their Employer (Dec 1972) (Chairman: Kenneth Robinson); CIR Report No. 76, *Mansfield Hosiery Mills Ltd.*
14. The strike and its aftermath are well described in the Runnymede Survey, pp. 21–2.
15. The Report is summarised in the Runnymede Survey, pp. 17–18, and IDS Brief no. 48 (Nov 1974) p. 8.
16. RRA, 1968, s. 4 (1).
17. On the role of shop stewards see, further, J. Goodman and T. Whittingham, *Shop Stewards* (McGraw-Hill, rev. edn, 1973) esp. chaps 7 and 8; and W. E. J. McCarthy, *The Role of Shop Stewards in British Industrial Relations*, Donovan Commission Research Paper No. 1 (H.M.S.O., 1967).

18. Official Report, Standing Comm. A, 13 May 1976, cols 259–70; H.L. Deb. vol 374, cols 482–502 (29 Sep 1976); H.C. Deb. vol 918, cols 539–50 (27 Oct 1976).

19. As in some of the instances detailed in the PEP Report, pp. 196–200.

20. This would constitute discrimination in relation to access to benefits, facilities or services of membership, contrary to s. 11 (3)(a).

*21. This is to take the view most favourable to those opposed to shop steward liability, but it is very much open to doubt. S. 20 forbids discrimination in the provision of 'facilities' and 'service' provided by any person to the public or a section thereof, 'for payment or not'. Whilst in voting or otherwise taking political decisions, a councillor would be regarded as acting on behalf of the public generally, in taking up complaints from that section of the public comprising his constituents, he would seem to be providing an unpaid service, or possibly a facility for redress of grievances. A reading of the legislative history is of no assistance, as the problem seems not to have been envisaged. But the literal wording of s. 20 would indeed encompass these 'representational' activities of elected officials.

22. E. Batstone *et al.*, *Shop Stewards in Action* (Blackwell, 1978) p. 25.

23. This paragraph is based upon ibid. chaps 2 and 5.

24. Ibid. pp. 27–8.

25. Ibid. pp. 29–31.

26. Ibid. pp. 27–8.

*27. A. Thomson and S. Engleman, *The Industrial Relations Act* (Martin Robertson, 1975) pp. 106–9 show how, after the *Heatons* case, the National Industrial Relations Court actively discouraged employers from joining shop stewards as defendants along with unions, and attempted to use the latter as policemen of their stewards' activities.

28. The action recommendation is authorised by s. 56 (4)(c), and the restriction on compensation for non-compliance is found in s. 56 (4)(b). See Appendix for full text.

29. S. 25 and s. 10, respectively.

30. E.g. the remarks of the Home Secretary, Merlyn Rees, on the regulation of racial exclusions from clubs: H.C. Deb. vol. 918, col. 570.

31. The extra-judicial background of the *Heatons* case, including the serious possibility of a general strike, is fully described in Thompson and Engleman, op. cit. pp. 99–104.

32. [1973] A.C. 15; [1972] 3 All E.R. 101.

33. [1972] 3 All E.R., at 112–13.

34. Idem at 109.

35. [1976] I.R.L.R. 225 (H.L.).

*36. The one exception to this is the various agreements limiting the employment, or otherwise requiring inferior treatment, of alien workers. These are discussed by *Hepple*, pp. 49–54, who notes that many disappeared in the late 1960s. Those that remain are now almost certainly unlawful in light of the extension of the Act in 1976 to encompass nationality discrimination (above, Chapter 3).

37. See the discussion of this point by Batstone *et al.,* op. cit. pp. 179–87.

38. I am grateful to Lord Simon of Glaisdale for providing me with this information and, in correspondence, explaining this point to me.

39. Now found in Interpretation Act 1978, sched. 1. The only exception is for penal enactments, within which 'person' refers only to a body corporate. This, however, has no application in relation to discrimination under the Act.

40. Trade Union and Labour Relations Act 1974, s. 2 (1)

41. See especially *Singh* v. *British Steel Corpn*, [1974] I.R.L.R. 131, and the comment by Hepple, [1974] 3 *I.L.J.* 166, and *Ram* v. *Midland Motor Cylinder Co. Ltd*, reported in IDS Brief 16 (IT decision) and 19 (NIRC decision) June and August 1973.

42. See H. Wellington, *Labor and the Legal Process* (Yale U.P. 1968) pp. 145–75. This duty is not limited to racial minorities and women, but extends generally to sub-groups within the bargaining unit.

43. W. Gould, *Black Workers in White Unions* (Cornell U.P. 1977) pp. 35–8.

44. See, e.g., M. Rimmer's study of a group of Midlands foundries, documenting the different attitudes of the AEF, the established union which catered for white skilled workers, and the TGWU, which the immigrants joined: *Race and Industrial Conflict* (Heinemann, 1972).

45. This is in fact what occurred in the *Singh* case, above, n. 41, in which the Asian workers left BISAKTA and wished to join the TGWU. The Bridlington Rules, which have been amended several times, may be found in their present form in a booklet, *TUC Disputes Principles and Procedures*, issued by the TUC in 1978.

46. Kalis, 'The Adjudication of Inter-Union Membership Disputes: The TUC Disputes Committee Revisited', (1977) 6 *I.L.J.* 19.

47. Ibid. pp. 20–5.

48. Ibid. p. 34.

49. Ibid. p. 23, n. 27.

50. Kalis, 'The Effectiveness and Utility of the Disputes Committee of the TUC', (1978) 16 *B.J.I.R.* 41, 49. For a similar view see C. Grunfeld, *Modern Trade Union Law* (Sweet & Maxwell, 1966) p. 227.

51. Kalis, op. cit., above, n. 50, *passim*.

52. W. McCarthy, *The Closed Shop in Britain* (Blackwell, 1964) pp. 16–17.

53. Ibid. pp. 17–27.

54. Ibid. pp. 78–9.

55. Weekes, 'Law and Practice of the Closed Shop', (1976) 5 *I.L.J.* 211, and Brown, 'Trade Union Organisation at the Workplace', unpublished MS. I am grateful to William Brown, of the Industrial Relations Research Unit at Warwick University, for providing me with a copy of this paper which reviews developments in the manufacturing sector up to the end of 1977.

56. McCarthy, op. cit. p. 43.

57. E.g. the dispute that came before the National Industrial Relations Court as *O'Farrell* v. *N.D.L.B.*, [1974] I.C.R. 266.

58. McCarthy, op. cit. p. 39.

59. Ibid. p. 45.

60. The leading case is *Local 53, Heat and Frost Insulators* v. *Vogler*, 407, F. 2d 1047 (5th Cir. 1969). For others see W. Gould, op. cit. n. 43, pp. 288–9, and cases cited therein.

61. And who, as has been seen above (p. 139), may discriminate in the selection of partners in a partnership of less than six.

62. Cf. Note, 'Title VII and Employment Discrimination in "Upper Level" Jobs', 73 Col. L. Rev. 1614 (1973). This orientation may have become a bit less marked by the late 1970s.

*63. This passes over the obvious problems arising under the Sex Discrimination Act.

*64. An apprenticeship is a form of 'employment' covered by s. 4: see s. 78 (1).

65. [1977] I.R.L.R. 288, 291.

66. See generally, Rideout, 'The Content of Trade Union Disciplinary Rules', (1965) 3 *B.J. Ind. Rel.* 153.

67. Expulsion would come under s. 11 (3)(b); lesser sanctions, which would constitute 'detriment', under s. 11 (3)(c).

68. A brief description of this body, and the circumstances of its establishment, appears in O. Kahn-Freund, *Labour and the Law* (Stevens, 2nd ed, 1977), pp. 190–2.

69. As happened in *Esterman* v. *NALGO,* [1974] I.C.R. 625.

70. See further, R. Rideout, *Principles of Labour Law* (Sweet & Maxwell, 3rd edn, 1979) pp. 274–80.

71. Notably in *Edwards* v. *SOGAT*, [1970] 3 All E.R. 681, 695–6, in which he was joined by Sachs L.J., and *Bonsor* v. *Musicians Union*, [1954] Ch. 479, 488.

72. The clearest rejection of the Denning view is the speech of Diplock L.J. (as he then was) in *Faramus* v. *Film Artistes' Association*, [1963] 2 Q.B. 527, 554–6, approved in the House of Lords, [1964] A.C. 925, 940, 943, 947–8. See generally, Grunfeld, op. cit. n. 50, pp. 59–61.

73. In *British Actors Equity Assn* v. *Goring*, [1977] I.C.R. 393, 395–6.

74. [1974] I.C.R. 625, 632.

75. See the cases cited in Grunfeld, op. cit. p. 182, notably *Osborne* v. *A.S.R.S.*, [1911] 1 Ch. 540.

Part III
Enforcement

Part III
Enforcement

Introduction

In this portion of the study attention turns to the precise mechanisms by which the prohibitions proclaimed on the paper of the statute are given effective force. It is here that the distinctively *legal* controls on discrimination operate in their unique environment. There are of course other means by which discrimination might conceivably be reduced. Market forces might make it uneconomic for employers to cut themselves off from the supply of black labour, or for vendors of houses to restrict their pool of potential purchasers. Given the high level of unemployment, and brisk demand for good housing, reliance on the market would only exceptionally be an effective strategy; indeed even with nearly full employment in the 1960s, blacks were largely restricted to the least desirable jobs and encountered massive discrimination in other aspects of life.[1] Other factors, notably the attenuated influence of market considerations in vital matters such as the provision of council housing and public sector employment, and the influence of collective bargaining, make the strategy even less plausible in present-day Britain. Alternatively, it might be argued that education and exhortation are the appropriate means of altering discriminatory behaviour, a tactic that would require no legal mechanisms at all.

The legal approach involves the use of specialised institutions – an adjudicative body with its own characteristic procedures and, usually, authorised actors (lawyers) – providing remedies backed by unique powers of compulsion to alter the relations between the parties before it. Use of law may also involve creation of governmental bodies with power to regulate behaviour; unlike adjudicative institutions, they are not concerned primarily with applying law to individuals. They may exercise their powers on their own initiative and in pursuance of statutory policies, and the weapons at their disposal may be quite different from those in the judicial armoury available to successful litigants. Their manner of exercise of these powers is subject to overall supervision of the courts; defining the occasions and the grounds of judicial intervention is the gravamen of the complex and controversial area known as administrative law.

The nature and availability of remedies, and the exercise of statutory powers, are grist to the lawyer's mill, a central element in what is sometimes called 'lawyer's law'. But they are also the testing ground for evaluating the effectiveness of legal intervention in any area of human behaviour. Their substance reflects philosophical assumptions and policy judgments which tend to remain submerged until dissatisfaction outside the legal system requires a reconsideration during which these fundamentals are forced to the surface. Perhaps the clearest contemporary example is the mammoth body of literature on the nature, purpose and function of tort law, spawned by the widespread realisation of its inadequacy as a system of compensation for accident victims.[2] Within a much narrower compass a similar debate, startlingly acrimonious, between the Court of Appeal and the House of Lords, occurred in recent years over the availability and justifications of exemplary damages.[3]*

These philosophical issues merge inevitably with practical considerations. Assuming that newly enacted legislation is actually intended to alter behaviour,[4]* it may none the less be ineffective because the means chosen are inadequate. This may occur for a variety of reasons: perhaps the most important are that the enforcement measures either permit widespread evasion or are too weak to overcome countervailing social or economic pressures. Alternatively either the statute as a whole, or particular coercive powers exercised under it, may generate such widespread resistance that it becomes a dead letter. The Industrial Relations Act 1971, and most spectacularly the contempt powers used against the docker stewards in 1972, provide the classic recent instances.[5] However, neither in Britain nor elsewhere – except perhaps in relation to bussing of schoolchildren in northern American cities – has such intense opposition to anti-discrimination laws developed. Indeed the problem has been quite the reverse. The characteristic failing of many of these statutes has been the flaccidity or unworkability of their powers of enforcement and remedy. The earliest American and Canadian statutes, enacted between the end of the Second World War and the early 1960s, either provided only criminal penalties for their enforcement, or established administrative bodies lacking power to compel termination of discriminatory practices.[6] Although the lessons of this experience were available to those drafting British legislation, they were heeded only in part, leaving severe weaknesses in the structure devised in 1968 to regulate employment and housing discrimination. Dis-satisfaction with the working of those provisions was reflected in the making of the present Act. For this reason analysis of the present provisions is prefaced by a brief account of the previous method of enforcement and its inadequacies. Tracking the path of the present law the discussion will then separate individual complaints, or private enforcement, from action by the Commission for Racial Equality. What will emerge is a vivid contrast between the wide-ranging scope of the law and its sophisticated definition of discrimination, and the relatively primitive and toothless devices created for the realisation of rights under it. So severe are these deficiencies that a grave question-mark hangs over the entire effort to control discrimination in Britain by legal means.

But – and this is vital – the procedural and remedial weaknesses are not simply the result of errors of judgment in the Home Office. Any social policy innovation must inevitably be fitted into the existing legal structure, however ill contrived that may be for effectuating it. It is hardly realistic to expect proponents of policies controversial in themselves to attempt to restructure the legal system simultaneously. Yet the burden of the argument offered below is that certain doctrines of substantive law, and still more the prevailing ethos among judges and other legal actors, are virtually guaranteed to undermine the remedial measures required to eradicate discrimination. To put it bluntly, there is a real possibility that anti-discrimination efforts will fall a casualty to English legal conservatism. This gloomy prospect also raises a theoretical question concerning what comparative lawyers now call 'legal transplants'.[7]* One of the primary purposes for which one legal system may borrow the substantive law of another is to effectuate 'at home a social change which foreign law is designed either to express or to produce'.[8] Can this be accomplished if the substantive law is wrenched from the procedural and remedial structure within which it was formulated and evolved? Further, and more immediately pertinent to the present study, if Professor Kahn-Freund is correct in suggesting that procedural law is essentially untransplantable,[9] can existing institutions and habits of thought be adapted to enable the substantive transplant to flourish in the stonier soil of its new legal environment?

NOTES

1. Documented fully in the 1967 PEP Report, published in popular form as W. Daniel, *Racial Discrimination in England* (Penguin Books, 1968).
2. For a convenient summary and review of this literature see Miers and Veitch, 'Assault on the Law of Tort', (1975) 38 *M.L.R.* 139. See also P. Atiyah, *Accidents, Compensation and the Law* (Weidenfeld & Nicolson, 2nd edn, 1975) parts 1–3.
*3. In *Cassell & Co. Ltd* v. *Broome*, [1971] 2 Q.B. 354, the Court of Appeal simply refused to follow *Rookes* v. *Barnard*, [1964] A.C. 1129, on the grounds that the House of Lords decided that case *per incuriam*, i.e. in their view erroneously. Their knuckles were firmly rapped when *Broome* reached the Lords, [1972] A.C. 1027, although the latter judgment in fact affirmed the award of exemplary damages in the particular case.
*4. As indicated in the Preface, I reject the 'pacification' theory of racial discrimination legislation in Britain. Nor do theories of 'symbolic' legislation, such as the interpretation of Prohibition laws in the United States in J. Gusfield, *Symbolic Crusade* (University of Illinois Press, 1963), pertain here.

5. On which see B. Weekes *et al.*, *Industrial Relations and the Limits of Law* (Blackwell, 1975) chap. 7.

6. See, e.g., M. Sovern, *Legal Restraints on Racial Discrimination in Employment* (Twentieth Century Fund, 1966) chap. 3; Tarnopolsky, 'The Iron Hand in the Velvet Glove', 46 *Can. B. Rev.* 565, 568–72 (1968).

*7. The analysis of this question offered in chap. 12 is deeply influenced by the late Sir Otto Kahn-Freund's lecture, 'On Uses and Misuses of Comparative Law', (1974) 37 *M.L.R.* 1, reprinted as chap. 12 in his *Selected Writings* (Stevens, 1978). See also A. Watson, *Legal Transplants* (Scottish Academic Press, 1974), which is concerned only with rules of private law.

8. Kahn-Freund, op. cit. p. 2.

9. Ibid. pp. 19–20.

10
Individual Enforcement of the Act

One of the significant innovations of the 1976 Act is that an individual who feels he has suffered discrimination may bring an action on his own behalf. On the face of it this hardly seems remarkable; where a statute creates new rights for the benefit of a category of individuals it usually enables the protected group to enforce those rights in some judicial forum. Yet this was not the position under the previous legislation, and in order to understand the present provisions fully a brief review of the structure of enforcement under the 1968 Act is necessary.

Under that statute all complaints of discrimination had to be made to the Race Relations Board, which was then required to investigate the complaint, and to 'form an opinion' whether the law had been broken. If it so concluded, it was empowered to initiate a process known as conciliation, the object of which was to achieve a settlement, which might – or might not – include a payment of compensation from the discriminator to the victim, and a 'satisfactory written assurance' against repetition of the discriminatory action. If conciliation failed, the Board, and it alone, had power to initiate legal proceedings in a County Court. In so doing it was acting on behalf of the victim, who would receive any damages awarded; but the decision whether to take legal action rested entirely within the discretion of the Board: no appeal from that decision was provided.[1]

This process of enforcement engendered great dissatisfaction. One cannot improve on the criticisms expressed in the White Paper of 'procedures which may seem cumbersome, ineffective or unduly paternalistic':[2]

> The complainant may feel aggrieved at being denied the right to seek legal redress while his complaint is being processed. If his complaint is not upheld, he is likely to resent the fact that he is denied direct access to legal remedies. Even if it is upheld, he may feel aggrieved because, in his view, the Board or conciliation committee has accepted a settlement or assurance which he regards as inadequate; or, worse still, because after conciliation has failed, the Board has decided not to bring legal proceedings, whether because it considered it had insufficient prospects of proving the case in court or for some other reason.[3]

There were additional difficulties. If a complaint concerned employment, it had first to be referred by the Board to the Secretary of State for Employment. If he decided that suitable voluntary machinery existed the complaint would be routed there for consideration. As we have seen (above, pp. 136–7), the voluntary machinery was often deficient in its procedures and notably reluctant to come to the conclusion that discrimination had occurred. This is not to suggest that the Board's own procedures were faultless. It consisted of a full-time Chairman and nine part-time Members, nearly all of whom were members of numerous voluntary bodies, pressure groups and quangos.[4] It was inherently implausible that they could personally investigate one thousand complaints each year, notwithstanding the appointment of nine regional conciliation committees to assist them in this work. In fact the actual investigation was carried out by conciliation officers. These civil servants, employed by the Board, did the fieldwork and presented written documents detailing their findings to a Committee of the Board, or the appropriate conciliation committee, which then gave both complainant and respondent the opportunity to make oral or written representations. However, when the relevant committee met to formulate its opinion, not all members would have seen the documentary evidence thus assembled, and had to base their judgment on a brief summary of the material prepared by the conciliation officer. When in one case, *Selvarajan* v. *Race Relations Board*,[5] a majority of committee members had before them only a skeletal factual summary headed 'clearly predictable case', the proceedings were assailed as a denial of natural justice, but the Court of Appeal gave the argument short shrift. All three judges evinced great solicitude for the practical administrative difficulties faced by the Board, but little regard for the plight of the complainant, who could neither challenge the committee's decision nor take further legal action against the alleged discriminator. Moreover, what Hepple called the 'very strong professional middle-class bias' of the membership of conciliation committees[6] (shared by the Board itself) – which seems to have remained unaltered since his study[7] – could hardly enhance the conviction of complainants that the reality of what had happened to them was adequately understood.

None the less the procedure had one major advantage. It enabled the victim of discrimination to acquire, without cost, the services of the Board's staff, who over the years developed a substantial expertise in tunnelling beneath the surface of denials and pleas of ignorance. They were able to interview witnesses, question alleged discriminators and – within the limits of their circumscribed statutory powers (see below, p. 240) – otherwise obtain information throwing clearer light on the disputed events. Moreover, once the committee formed the opinion that discrimination had occurred, the conciliation officer would attempt to negotiate a settlement. Often his knowledge of the law and experience in negotiation exceeded that of the respondent, and it was not unknown for complainants to receive reasonable settlements in cases that the courts might have rejected.

Few complainants can realistically be expected to come near doing any of these things as well. Limitations of time, money, self-confidence and, often enough, education ensure this. Even fewer will have legal competence – the knowledge, not merely of substantive law, but of what materials and information are relevant to their claim, and of how they may be obtained. In the most closely analogous situation, that of unfair dismissal, the complainant at least knows he has been sacked, there is no difficulty determining who made the decision, and, if the dismissal arose out of an incident at work, witnesses are known and available. In discrimination cases, particularly those involving hiring, a substantial amount of time and effort is often needed simply to establish analogous elementary facts. Victims of discrimination face the most formidable practical difficulties of evidence and proof of all those who seek to realise the rights laid down in social legislation. These will be examined in depth in the following chapter; what must be emphasised at this point is that assistance, if not indeed representation, by specialists is indispensable if these rights are to be more than paper proclamations.

Thus any change that freed the complainant from total dependence on an administrative body but left him without support would have been a serious retrograde step. In light of the emphasis in the White Paper on the 'strategic role' envisaged for the new Commission for Racial Equality (CRE) (below, Chapter 13) there were considerable grounds for apprehension about how individual complainants would fare.

The disquiet has been allayed both by the provisions of the legislation and the use thus far made of them by the Commission. Any 'actual or prospective complainant or claimant' may apply for assistance to the CRE which may grant it on one of several broad grounds: that the case raises a question of principle; that it is unreasonable in light of its complexity or the applicant's position to expect him to deal with it unaided; or by reason of any other special consideration.[8] Assistance covers a wide range: advice; help with obtaining evidence – particularly aiding the complainant to fill out the official forms for questioning respondents (below, p. 205); attempting to reach a settlement; arranging – and financing – representation in legal proceedings; and – most important – providing representation by the specialists of its own staff. Essentially the Commission has been given a free hand to represent complainants itself where it thinks it appropriate, and to offer a range of less comprehensive services to others. Virtually the only statutory constraints upon it is that it must make its decision and inform the applicant within two months of receiving the request.[9] It has sought to preserve this wide discretion, and has not established formal criteria to govern requests for assistance. This view is understandable, particularly in light of its limited resources, but – rather like subjective employment decisions – it may readily give rise to dissatisfaction and complaints of arbitrariness. In the *Bohon–Mitchell* case (above, pp. 45–6) the complainant encountered a series of delays, had to undertake most of the preliminary discovery inquiries virtually unaided, and was only informed ten days before the hearing that the Commission would not represent her. No reason for this decision was ever given. Only her good fortune in securing the services without fee of an expert barrister ensured that her case was effectively presented.

The Commission's ability to represent and support applicants is quite unusual. Despite a recommendation by the Lord Chancellor's Advisory Committee some years ago, legal aid is not available for representation before any tribunal,[10] although some preparatory assistance at public expense may be obtained under the so-called 'green form' scheme. Only in cases falling under the Race Relations and Sex Discrimination Acts do aggrieved persons bringing cases to industrial tribunals have the possibility of public support. In view of the singular set of difficulties they face, this can hardly be regarded as favouritism; rather it may go some way toward redressing the great imbalance. Of course it is a compensation available only to those whom the CRE decides to assist.

The Commission has made active use of its powers to aid individual complainants. In early 1979 thirteen of its officers were working on assistance to individuals, compared with thirty-six concerned with 'strategic' formal investigations.[11] Of the 644 applications for assistance received in the first nine months of 1979 which had received full consideration, only about one-eighth resulted in complete denial of assistance or withdrawal of the complaint. The Commission's most common response (to just over 40 per cent of applications) was to provide help with filling out the official Question Form (below, p. 205), subsequently discussing the respondent's reply with the complainant, and aiding him to prepare the originating application for an industrial tribunal hearing. People in this category would also be referred to local law centres or other sources of representation. A further 30 per cent of applicants, whose cases raised more complex issues or who had received no response to their Questionnaire, received more intensive counselling. Those remaining – slightly more than one-sixth – were granted legal representation, either by a Complaints Officer from the Commission's staff or, much more commonly, by solicitor or counsel whose fees were paid by the Commission. These decisions are taken by the Complaints Committee, which consists of five of the statutory Commissioners (below, p. 244). For no very evident reason there is a decided regional variation in the incidence of legal representation; applicants from the areas served by the Commission's office in Leeds much more frequently received representation than those from anywhere else, whilst Midlands complainants fell substantially below the national average, particularly in 1979.

When 1979 is compared with the initial two years of the Act's operation a distinct downward trend can be seen in the proportion of cases in which legal representation has been granted. This appears to be less a response to financial austerity than the result of a policy decision by the Commission that its credibility with industrial tribunals would be strengthened if it were seen to support only cases with more than fair probability of success. Whilst the consequence may be to help those applicants it does represent, meritorious cases it misjudges, or difficult cases which require particularly skilful handling not readily available outside Commission, may now be lost. One striking fact has already emerged: virtually no one who has brought a complaint without some form of assistance from the CRE has prevailed before an industrial tribunal.

Thus the early experience under the new Act has been that individual complainants have not suffered from the creation of a wider investigatory role for the Commission, and that there has been little injurious competition between the twin functions of aiding individuals and seeking more general changes in discriminatory practices. The picture could readily change however, either if the CRE altered its policies or a government decision to pare its resources intensified the competition between the two strands of enforcement effort.

THE STRUCTURE OF PRIVATE ENFORCEMENT

All proceedings arising under the Act are funnelled through the jurisdictional structure therein established.[12] Consequently a complainant may not seek redress in the High Court, under the well-established principle that where a statute creates new rights, it may set out the exclusive procedure for their vindication.[13] However, in the rare case where the common law imposes a duty of non-discrimination,[14]* or in other instances, notably unfair dismissal, where there are alternative statutory remedies for victims of discrimination (above, pp. 127–8) these rights remain undisturbed. This leaves the person affected a choice of remedies, for the restriction on proceedings applies only where the complaint alleges that the discrimination was 'unlawful by virtue of a provision of this Act'.[15] Where discrimination is unlawful 'by virtue of' some other law, the procedural avenues of the Act need not be travelled.

Conversely, claims brought under directly applicable European Community law involving nationality discrimination (above, Chapter 3) probably cannot be brought before industrial tribunals. This was squarely held by the EAT in *Amies* v. *ILEA*,[16] in which the plaintiff attempted to invoke the Treaty provision concerning sex discrimination in employment. Bristow J. rejected her substantive complaint, and also stated that the industrial tribunals lacked jurisdiction to entertain it: themselves creatures of statute, they can exercise no powers other than those conferred on them by statute.[17] As no statute confers jurisdiction upon them to hear cases arising under the Treaty, it would follow that the High Court is the sole forum for any claim of this form of discrimination. Nevertheless, Lord Denning M.R. subsequently attacked this view.[18] However his Lordship's comments were *obiter*, his fellow judges did not address the question, and the present position remains uncertain.

The *Amies* rule is a significant deterrent to vindication of one's rights. Actions in the courts are expensive, time-consuming and governed by highly formal rules of evidence. These characteristics are of course prominent among the reasons for the proliferation of tribunals, but it can be little consolation to someone seeking to enforce his rights under the Treaty that he is a textbook illustration of the advantages of the legal structure of the Welfare State. Fortunately most people in this situation will also have a cause of action under the Act.

The statute creates in outline a bifurcated structure of enforcement. Employment matters are heard before industrial tribunals, with appeal first to the Employment Appeal Tribunal (EAT) then to the Court of Appeal. All other cases are heard in specially designated County Courts,[19] with appeal then to the Court of Appeal. Despite the general limitation of the present study it is necessary in this chapter to consider enforcement in the County Court as well, since the need to overcome its defects is an important element in the suggestion below that the entire enforcement apparatus be scrapped and replaced by discrimination tribunals. There are in addition minor special cases. Where the complaint concerns the action of a professional qualifying body whose decision is already subject to a statutory appeals procedure, that path must be taken.[20] This provision would encompass, for example, actions taken by the Medical Council in striking off doctors, from which an appeal to the Privy Council is provided.[21] Where it concerns employment discrimination within the armed forces, the complaints procedures set down in the various Services Acts must be followed.[22]

The question of where discrimination cases should be heard is more contentious and important than may first appear. The Street Report recommended that special tribunals be constituted to deal with racial discrimination cases. The Government rejected this in 1968, and all cases in which settlement efforts failed and the Board initiated proceedings were heard in the County Courts. A concession was made to those who believed that it was desirable to enlist the services of persons specially knowledgeable in matters of race relations by the requirement that the County Court judge be assisted by two assessors, selected from a list of persons thought by the Lord Chancellor to possess this expertise. Their function was limited to advising the judge, who retained sole power to decide the case. Use of assessors in County Courts is not peculiar to discrimination cases,[23] but no serious effort was made to select people with real knowledge of race relations issues, and as of 1972, not a single black assessor had been appointed.[24] Moreover, since cases often raised a purely legal point on which lay assessors could make no particular contribution, to require their participation seemed unnecessary. The present Act retains the possibility of their appointment, but also provides that their services may be dispensed with if both parties consent.[25]

The one possibility no one considered in 1968 was use of industrial tribunals. These bodies had only been established four years earlier to hear a small number of cases relating to industrial training levies. Their jurisdiction was rapidly expanded by a number of statutes and, with the enactment of unfair dismissal legislation in 1971, they became one of the most important and active adjudicatory bodies in Britain.[26] Approximately 47,000 applications were referred to them in 1976 and in 1977; of these, roughly 80 per cent concerned unfair dismissal.[27]

Like tribunals generally, these bodies are supposed to be cheap, informal and not unduly legalistic. Unlike the County Courts, one need not be legally qualified to have the right of audience, and applicants are most commonly represented by trade-union officials. Hence also CRE complaints officers, who may have good knowledge of discrimination law but lack a legal qualification, are fully able to provide representation. Similarly, lay advocates may appear before the EAT.[28] Tribunals are composed of a lawyer chairman and two 'wingmen', each of whom is drawn from a panel appointed by the Department of Employment, which, by law, must consult representatives of employers and organised employees.[29] The wingmen on the EAT must be similarly recruited.[30] In reality this means they are nominated by the CBI and TUC. This contribution of laymen to tribunal adjudication can in theory by justified as a counterweight to the chairman's legalism – although 96 per cent of decisions are unanimous[31] – and by their experience of industrial relations. However, others besides those affiliated with the TUC and CBI are equally qualified, and the composition of industrial tribunals is best understood as the entrenchment of participation by the key interest groups in industrial relations.

Thus by 1975, when the Sex Discrimination Act was passed, industrial tribunals were naturally seen as the appropriate forum for employment discrimination cases, and the draftsmen of the Race Relations Act could hardly have avoided following the same pattern. Yet precisely because of their membership, use of industrial tribunals may well have been a mistake. Nothing in the background or experience of most wingmen can be expected to equip them with an understanding of discrimination or empathy with its victims. Indeed in so far as discrimination has come about through understandings between unions and management, or merely as the inadvertent result of long-standing practice, they can be expected to be instinctively unsympathetic to complainants. Moreover, their experience as tribunal members cannot be expected to educate them rapidly since, taking figures from the first quarter of 1978, only 1 per cent of the applications received by tribunals concerned racial discrimination.[32]

The Government was aware of the problem, but its response was strange. In the sex discrimination White Paper it stated: 'The number of women appointed to the tribunals is being increased. The aim is to have sufficient women so that at least one person of each sex will normally be on a tribunal which is hearing a sex discrimination or equal pay case.'[33] This aim has apparently been realised, and the same approach is taken when EAT panels are selected. The race discrimination White Paper simply said that '[t]he Government will draw attention of the nominating organisations to the desirability of including members of racial minorities among the nominees'.[34] This far less positive tone, coupled with the unfortunate substitution of 'members of racial minorities' for persons with some knowledge of discrimination in industry, led black organisations and the Race Relations Board itself to make anxious representations to MPs, who debated the matter at some length in Standing Committee.[35] In the event the Government rejected a clause that would have required the appointment of a lay member with race relations experience to hear discrimination cases, but did urge the nominating bodies to put forward individuals who had served as members of conciliation committees under the 1968 Act, or who had otherwise acquired knowledge of race relations in employment. By May 1979, sixty-nine such persons had been appointed. Presidents of tribunals have also been asked to assign someone from this 'pool' of wingmen to each tribunal hearing a discrimination complaint.[36] Whether this relatively small group (less than 3 per cent of all wingmen) can be effectively deployed in this way remains to be seen.

The purpose of selecting people with this background for tribunal work is not to guarantee one vote for the complainant. Because legal proof of discrimination is largely a matter of inference from ambiguous facts (see further, Chapter 11) those hearing the complaint need to be familiar with the pattern and practices of discrimination, as well as of industrial relations generally, to have a 'feel' for which of the conflicting narrations and explanations of the parties seems more credible. The presence of such people may also be a necessary counterweight to the instinctive scepticism, if not outright hostility, to discrimination complaints manifested by other tribunal members. This is borne out by the experience of adjudication in the first eighteen months of the Act: in *every* case in which there was a split tribunal decision against the complainant, the non-specialist wingmen joined the chairman to make the majority.[37]*

Moreover, the unusual prominence of questions of fact in discrimination cases makes the role of the industrial tribunal more than usually definitive. It is settled law that the findings of fact of industrial tribunals are to be accorded extreme deference by appellate bodies; as Phillips J. expressed the principle, they must stand unless the evidence was 'wholly contradictory to [the tribunal's] conclusion'.[38] Thus it is not rhetoric to state that the Act could effectively be paralysed by tribunal members who unconsciously regard discrimination complaints as troublemakers, or instinctively give greater credence to the evidence of more 'respectable' management witnesses, or who simply fail to understand the different patterns of behaviour among immigrants.

It would also, given the matter in which certain interests are institutionalised in tribunal membership, be a quite unjustifiable anomaly to exclude other tribunal users from representation. All the more so since the principle of representative membership has long been accepted for a variety of tribunals. Thus National Insurance Local Tribunals, which hear appeals concerning entitlement to contributory social security benefits, include wingmen drawn from panels representing employers and the self-employed, and 'employed earners';[39] where the claimant is a woman, at least one of the tribunal members should be female as well.[40] Similarly, Supplementary Benefit Appeal Tribunals (SBATs) must contain at least one member 'appointed from among persons . . . [who] represent work-people'[41] a provision carried over from the 1930s when their predecessor body was concerned with unemployment benefit appeals. With the enactment of the Social Security Act 1979 the principle of consumer representation has been greatly extended: the other SBAT wingman is now to be drawn from panel of persons reputed to have knowledge or experience of conditions in the local area and of the problems of people living on low incomes.[42] Also it is now specified that at least one of the tribunal members should if practicable be of the same sex as the appellant.[43]

The question remains whether even an adequately constituted industrial tribunal is the best forum for discrimination cases. Its importance is reinforced by doubts about whether County Courts are particularly suited to hear the non-employment cases: all the reasons that have traditionally been invoked to support the creation of specialist tribunals, of which there are now over fifty, as alternatives to the courts apply equally here.[44] Apart from the establishment of racial discrimination tribunals, all cases arising under race and sex discrimination legislation, including equal pay, could be heard by discrimination tribunals, whose lay membership would be composed of persons with experience of the reality of discrimination, and less institutionally connected with the entrenched forces of industrial life. This latter proposal would not require amalgamation of the administrative bodies created to enforce the legislation, since their functions go well beyond dealing with legal violations and the very different problems of blacks and women demand separate attention. It would, however, permit the tribunals to develop an expertise and experience that the present adjudicative bodies, whose main concerns are far removed from discrimination issues, can never be expected to acquire.

A final consequence of the split enforcement structure is that very different rules apply in relation to costs. In industrial tribunals, each party bears his own costs, regardless of the outcome; only where the tribunal concludes that a party has acted 'frivolously or vexatiously' may it require the complainant to make some payment to the respondent.[45] This happens but rarely,[46] and in only two racial discrimination cases were costs awarded (once in the extraordinary total of £1000) during the first year of the working of the new system.[47] Similar although slightly more rigorous rules apply in the EAT.[48]

In the County Court the normal 'fruits of victory' rule applies. Because of its more time-consuming procedures and the necessity of what in the seventeenth century was called 'feeing a lawyer', costs can be substantial, and many times higher than actual damage awards in cases where pubs, restaurants and the like refuse to provide services or goods. Indeed, under the 1968 Act the real financial sting felt by discriminators in this field was in the award of costs, since damages seldom exceeded £20. However, since cases could then only be brought by the Board, no individual complainant had to face the impossible dilemma of risking several hundred pounds to redress an insult for which damages of £5 might be awarded. This is precisely the situation in which complainants now find themselves, unless the CRE supports them. As this type of case is generally confined in its implications to the individual and is least likely to raise legal issues of public importance, it would be rational for a body with limited funds to treat it as having the lowest priority. Thus, apparently unintentionally, the new enforcement provisions will severely cripple the effectiveness of s. 20. The same may be true of the strengthened prohibition of discrimination by clubs (s. 25), which the then Government thought important enough to override unusually intense and acrimonious opposition.

A further snare awaits the unwary litigant. Costs in the County Court, which in any event seldom equal the full charges incurred by the winner,[49] are taxed on the basis of scales which increase according to the amount awarded. However, in an action limited to damages, solicitors' charges – by far the dominant element in the total of the costs – are not allowed when the award is less than £100. This is subject to exceptions, of which the most relevant is that if the judge certifies that 'the case involves a question of fact or law or exceptional complexity' he may award costs on whatever scale he chooses.[50] It is impossible to estimate how commonly the exception will be invoked, but it is safe to assume that most cases concerning goods, facilities and services, and probably many concerning the rental or sale of housing, will not satisfy the criterion. However, the limitation of the award of costs applies only where damages alone are sought, and it appears that no restriction pertains where other remedies are sought simultaneously.

Complainants in the County Court are entitled to all remedies available in the High Court,[51] notably a declaration and an injunction. Hence on a literal reading the costs rule would not apply to most discrimination cases. However, an injunction is unlikely to be granted unless it appears that in future the defendant may again discriminate against the particular plaintiff, and the granting of a declaration is wholly a matter for judicial discretion.[52] It remains quite unclear how plausible the prayer for these remedies must be to oust the costs rule. However, the declaration was one of the primary remedies available under the 1968 Act,[53] and there is no indication that Parliament intended any change. This problem remains fraught with uncertainties, and the risk may deter perfectly good claims. In this, as in other respects, the inadequacies of the County Court as a forum for discrimination cases is manifest. This conclusion, of course, applies equally to complaints under the Sex Discrimination Act, and the case for the creation of a single tribunal with jurisdiction over all discrimination matters, including those arising under the EEC Treaty, seems firmly established.

TIME LIMITS

The standard period within which complaints within the jurisdiction of industrial tribunals may be brought is three months from the day the act complained of was done. The Act follows this pattern.[54] Since whether discrimination has occurred, particularly in hiring, is a far less clearcut matter then whether one has been dismissed or made redundant, the wisdom of imitation is open to doubt. The same time-limit formerly applied in the United States, but was doubled in 1972. The Government resisted a suggestion in Committee that the period be six months on the ground that this would unduly complicate the position of people who might have claims under different statutes, as with a discriminatory dismissal.[55] Since such persons could only gain by the extended time-limits, and since in any case the majority of cases do not concern dismissal, this reasoning seems thin. However, the present limit is more liberal than that of the 1968 Act, which was two months. Furthermore, the tribunal is given an overriding discretion to hear late applications if it considers it 'just and equitable' to do so.[56] It remains to be seen how this will be interpreted, and in particular whether the courts will take the same miserly attitude manifested in decisions concerning the discretionary extension for hearing unfair dismissal claims where it was not 'reasonably practical' for the complaint to be presented within the alloted time.[57] The EAT has ruled in a sex discrimination case that tribunals should consider all relevant factors in exercising their discretion, one of which is whether prime facie the complainant's case is strong.[58] Other relevant factors may be diligence in pursuing alternate remedies, and poor English.[59]

In non-employment cases the statute is more generous. The period is normally six months, with an automatic two-month extension where the applicant has requested assistance from the CRE.[60] There is a strong case for treating employment cases identically, since the present rules either encourage unnecessary applications to avoid prejudicing the complainant's rights, or may leave him out of time if the three-month period expires while the Commission is making up its mind. It would be particularly appropriate for tribunals to involve their 'just and equitable' discretion in such cases.

CONCILIATION

An underlying premise of all employment legislation is that litigation is to be minimised. Consequently a statutory body, the Advisory, Conciliation and

Arbitration Service (ACAS), has been established to promote good industrial relations and to help to achieve settlement of industrial disputes.[61]
Under the Act ACAS has a similar role; it is required to promote a
settlement of any complaint received by an industrial tribunal if requested
by either party or if a conciliation officer believes he has a reasonable chance
of achieving it.[62] He must make similar efforts if requested to do so before a
complaint is presented.[63] The conciliation officer interviews the applicant
and respondent to ascertain the relative strength of their cases, advises each
side of the other's position, and recommends what appears to him a
reasonable settlement. His ability to work effectively would be badly
handicapped if the parties could not speak in complete freedom, including
making admissions damaging to their position if given as evidence before a
tribunal. Hence nothing communicated to a conciliation officer in the course
of his settlement attempts is admissible in tribunal proceedings without the
consent of the person from whom he received it.[64] The same rule applied to
communications received by the Race Relations Board and its officials
under the old procedure.[65] However, because ACAS is concerned only with
industrial matters, there is now no statutory body which could perform
analogous functions in non-employment cases, and thus no requirement that
conciliation be attempted in them.

The role of ACAS in discrimination cases is the subject of intense
controversy. After the first year of the Equal Pay Act a National Council of
Civil Liberties study accused ACAS conciliators of exerting undue pressure
on complainants to withdraw their applications.[66] Many people concerned
with the working of the 1976 Act have also sharply criticised their work,
claiming that their sympathies lean toward employers and that they wrongly
discourage complainants from pursuing their claims.[67] On the other hand,
the average settlement achieved by ACAS is higher than that achieved by
CRE officials negotiating on behalf of persons who have come to the
Commission for assistance.[68]

A major source of the controversy is the difference in perspective between
those committed to a vigorous policy of use of the new law to compel
changes in employment practices and that of ACAS officials, whose working
ethos leads them to view each dispute as an individual problem which should
be resolved quietly and without recourse to tribunals. If one may judge from
reading the Service's Annual Reports, it defines its function and judges its
success in what it calls 'individual conciliation' matters in large part by the
number of cases it can 'clear' without reference to a tribunal. Thus an ACAS
conciliation officer would regard achievement of a not unreasonable settlement as a success, whereas a CRE complainant aid official would regard it,
particularly in a strong case presenting an important legal question, with
very mixed feelings. Given this difference of organisational orientation,
some degree of suspicion and hostility seems inevitable.

The real issue is whether the diverse aims of complainants, who range from those who see their cases as part of a political struggle to those who want public acknowledgement of ill treatment to those who simply want their financial loss made good, are adequately understood and respected by the conciliators. The Service's *Annual Report 1978* suggests that the unique character of discrimination cases has begun to be appreciated. Figures therein indicate that in percentage terms, four times as many unfair dismissal complaints as racial discrimination complaints are conciliated; all of matters within ACAS jurisdiction, racial discrimination complaints are almost twice as likely to come before a tribunal.[69] The Report suggests that one reason for the disparity is that 'the parties may be more interested in the principles involved than in reaching a compromise settlement'.[70] One hopes that this awareness is transmitted from those at the higher levels of the Service to the officers on the line.

When conciliation fails, and the case goes forward to a tribunal, the complainant's legal problems have only just begun. He faces the unusual difficulties in gathering and presenting the evidence required to establish his case. These are considered in the following chapter.

NOTES

1. The key sections of the 1968 Act were ss. 14–15, 19 and 21. *Lester and Bindman*, chaps 8 and 9, give a full account of the Board's work in conciliation and legal proceedings, respectively.

2. Cmnd 6234, para. 41.

3. Ibid. para. 40.

4. This may be seen from the biographies of the Members appearing in the CRE's *First Annual Report – 1977* (H.M.S.O., 1978) appx 12.

5. [1975] 1 W.L.R. 1686.

6. *Hepple*, p. 264.

7. See *First Annual Report*, op. cit. n. 4, appx 13 for biographies of conciliation committee members.

8. S. 66 (1)(a), (b) and (c), respectively.

9. S. 66 (3). Note also s. 66 (4), permitting the Commission an additional month if they so inform the applicant.

10. This is not true of the EAT, a superior court of record, for proceedings before which legal aid is available.

11. I should like to thank Mr Goolam Meeran, Complaints Principal of the CRE, for providing me with the figures, unpublished at time of writing, used in the ensuing paragraphs.

12. S. 53 (1).

13. *Barraclough* v. *Brown*, [1897] A.C. 615.

*14. The primary instance is the duty of innkeepers and common carriers to provide their facilities without discrimination. This is outside the scope of the present work. The common law imposes no limits on racial discrimination in employment, save whatever may grow out of the Court of Appeal decision in *Nagle* v. *Feilden*, [1966] 2 Q.B. 633; see *Lester and Bindman*, pp. 51–3.

15. S. 53 (1).

16. [1977] I.C.R. 308, followed in *Charles Early Ltd* v. *Smith* [1978] Q.B. 11, 26 (EAT). These decisions have been heavily criticised, e.g. by Freestone, (1978) 41 *M.L.R.* 346.

17. [1977] I.C.R., at p. 313.

18. *Shields* v. *E. Coombes (Holdings) Ltd*, [1979] 1 All E.R. 456, 461–2.

19. There are sixteen of these, specified by Statutory Instrument (S.I. 1968/1978, as amended). They are basically the County Courts in the larger towns. The others lack jurisdiction to hear cases under the Act.

20. S. 54 (2).

21. Medical Act 1956, s. 36 (3).

22. S. 54 (2); see s. 75 (9) for the relevant statutes concerning the Forces.

23. Their use is authorised by s. 91 of the County Courts Act 1959, and s. 98 of the Judicature Act 1925.

24. *Lester and Bindman*, p. 330. These authors also criticise the quality of appointments.

25. S. 67 (4).

26. On the inception of industrial tribunals see K. Whitesides and G. Hawker, *Industrial Tribunals* (Sweet & Maxwell, 1975) chap. 1.

27. The figures, taken from Department of Employment statistics, appear in B. Bercusson's annotation of *The Employment Protection (Consolidation) Act 1978* (Sweet & Maxwell, 1979) s. 128.

28. EPCA, sched. 11, para. 20.

29. Industrial Tribunal (England and Wales) Regulations 1965, S.I. 1965/1101, as amended by S.I. 1977/1473.

30. EPCA, s. 135 (3).

31. Bercusson, op. cit. n. 26, annotation to s. 128.

32. Ibid.

33. Cmnd 5724 (1974), para. 83.

34. Cmnd 6234, para. 83.

35. Official Report, Standing Comm. A, 15 June 1976, cols 623–39.

36. Letter from the Department of Employment to the author, 11 May 1979.

*37. Interview with Mr Goolam Meeran, 20 April 1979, who also informed me that in one unreported tribunal decision, the lay wingmen joined to outvote the chairman and find for the complainant.

38. *Watling* v. *William Bird*, (1976) 11 *I.T.R.* 70. Several cases establishing this point are discussed by S. Anderman, *The Law of Unfair Dismissal* (Butterworth, 1978) pp. 67–8.

39. Social Security Act 1975, s. 97 (2).

40. SSA 1975, sched. 10, para. 1 (4), proviso (c).

41. Supplementary Benefit Act 1976, sched. 4, para. 3 (1).

42. Social Security Act 1979, sched. 2 (inserted into SBA 1976 as sched. 4) para. 1 (a).

43. SSA 1979, sched. 2, para. 5 (a).

44. For an overview of the origins, purposes and working of tribunals see H. Street, *Justice in the Welfare State* (Sweet & Maxwell), 2nd edn, 1975, chap. 1.

45. Industrial Tribunals (Labour Relations) Regulations S.I. 1974/1386, rule 10.

46. See *Macdonald*, para. 370, and the cases discussed in n. 6 therein.

47. See cases discussed in Incomes Data Service Brief No. 150, February 1979, p. 16.

48. Employment Appeal Tribunal Rules, S.I. 1976/322, rule 21.

49. A concise explanation of why this is so may be found in D. Barnard, *The Civil Court in Action* (Butterworth, 1977) p. 168.

50. The cost rules are found in County Court Rules, ord. 47, rule 5. The exception quoted in the text is found in rule 13.

51. S. 57 (2).

52. See, generally, I. Zamir, *The Declaratory Judgment* (Stevens, 1962).

53. *Lester and Bindman*, pp. 337–8, point out that they were the sole class of cases in which a declaration alone, without a prayer for damages could be sought in the County Court.

54. S. 68 (1).

55. Official Report, Standing Comm. A, 22 June 1976, cols 692–7.

56. S. 68 (6).

57. EPCA, s. 67 (2). See Bercusson's annotation of this subsection (op. cit. n. 27), which has generated an extraordinary number of cases.

58. *Hutchinson* v. *Westward Television*, [1977] I.C.R. 279.

59. See tribunal decisions cited in IDS Brief, Supp. 23, May 1979, p. 24.

60. S. 68 (2) and (3).

61. Employment Protection Act 1975, ss. 1–6.

62. S. 55 (1).

63. S. 55 (2).

64. S. 55 (4).

65. RRA 1968, s. 24.

66. J. Coussins, *Equality Report* (NCCL, 1976) p. 18.

67. This view emerged clearly in the day-long seminar organised by the Runnymede Trust and held on 30 March 1979, on the working of the Act, which the author attended. Proceedings have been published by the Trust under the title *A Review of the Race Relations Act 1976* (June 1979).

68. Meeran interview, *above*, n. 37.

69. ACAS, *Annual Report 1978* (H.M.S.O. 1979) table 25. Sixty-one per cent of racial discrimination complaints dealt with by the Service reached a tribunal, compared with 37 per cent of all cases, and 43 per cent of sex discrimination complaints.

70. Ibid. p. 83. The Report also suggests that another reason may be 'that a settlement in such cases usually results in a continuing commitment sometimes affecting a group of employees', i.e. that the collective dimension of the problem may make *employers* reluctant to settle.

11
Problems of Proof

The broadened definition of the evil, and the enlarged scope and application of the present Act, do not of themselves ensure its increased effectiveness in combating discrimination. This will depend above all else on whether the legal principles and procedures developed to govern proof of discrimination are not unduly restrictive. This chapter will explore the practical difficulties, perhaps seemingly humdrum but ultimately crucial to the effective enforcement of the law, that seem likely to arise in litigation. It will first look at problems specific to direct discrimination, then at those of indirect discrimination, and finally at matters common to both. Whilst they will be discussed in the context of the adjudication of individual complaints, most are equally relevant to formal investigations undertaken by the CRE. A final section will analyse the remarkably contentious question whether an employer is entitled to withhold information in his possession from a complainant on grounds of confidentiality.

DIRECT DISCRIMINATION

Apart from the increasingly rare situation where the applicant is told flatly, 'No blacks wanted',[1] he will know two things only: that he did not get what he sought, and that he is black. The employer's monopoly of knowledge about the process of decision, and the power derived from the control of information, ultimately rests upon the common law. He is under no obligation to explain, still less to justify, his decision to reject an applicant: as Lord Davey made clear three-quarters of a century ago, the common law permits refusal to hire a workman for any reason whatever, or for no reason at all.[2] To be effective, anti-discrimination law cannot merely formally curtail the employer's prerogative; it must also enable a reviewing body to determine whether the forbidden factor influenced the decision.

This could be done in at least three ways. The employer could be required by statute to state reasons, buttressed by the sanction of compensation if the reasons given prove to be false. Such legislation now governs dismissals.[3] Its inclusion in the Act does not seem to have been seriously considered, perhaps because it would have been a radical departure in relation to hiring where, unlike dismissal, the common law never sought to protect the applicant's expectations. It is unfortunate that this step was not taken, for it would have ensured the ready availability of information about the decision, compiled close enough to the time of the event to be highly reliable.

Instead an inadequate substitute has been provided. The Home Office has been given power to prescribe forms, obtainable from the Department of Employment, which complainants may use to obtain information from the alleged discriminator.[4] The replies received are admissible as evidence before the industrial tribunal, and whilst the employer may lawfully refuse to respond, the tribunal is empowered to infer that he violated the law if he deliberately refuses to reply, or if his response is 'evasive or equivocal'.[5] Thus where an Asian rejected for a supervisory post was asked at interview whether he had ever supervised whites, and the respondent gave patently inadequate answers to his questions, an industrial tribunal readily drew the inference that discrimination had occurred.[6] None the less this so-called 'Questions Procedure' has two major defects. It puts the entire initiative for invoking the process on those suffering discrimination, who for a variety of reasons have already shown great reluctance to complain.[7] Second, it may not be utilised until several weeks or even months after the event, when memories have faded; if, as is common, no records are kept of rejected applications, what actually happened may be impossible to reconstruct. The questionnaire now used is also open to criticism, especially for not including any specific question about indirect discrimination. At best a prospective complainant merely obtains after a long delay the same information the employer could without undue burden have furnished him at the time. As with the controversy about reinstatement or re-engagement of those unfairly dismissed, the price for obeisance to the common law is high.

A second method would be to carry over one of the significant innovations of unfair dismissal law, which puts the burden of proof on the employer to show that the dismissal was fair.[8] This reverses the normal principle of civil litigation, under which the complainant or plaintiff must prove on balance of probabilities that the defendant has infringed the law in the way he alleges, and in ambiguous cases the courts always interpret statutes so as to follow this rule. The usual justification for this allocation of the burden of proof is that otherwise the defendant would be placed in the supposedly unreasonable position of having to prove a negative – for example, that he was not negligent, did not break the contract, and so forth. None the less in certain situations, notably where the fairness of a dismissal or the victimisation of trade unions[9] is in issue, Parliament has made clear that it is for the respondent to prove that he has acted lawfully. Similarly, in cases of indirect discrimination, damages are denied only if the employer can satisfy the tribunal that he did not use the discriminatory requirement with the intention of discriminating on racial grounds.[10]

The common thread in all these instances is that the relevant issue is the motivation behind the respondent's actions. Thus it remains for the employee to prove that he was dismissed – not always easy or obvious, particularly where constructive dismissal is claimed – but if the employer is to satisfy the tribunal that the dismissal fell within one of the approved statutory categories he must establish the real reason for his action. On this question of motivation he alone can provide information.

Precisely the same problems arise in claims of discrimination, and it is to be severely regretted that the Act did not adopt the same procedural response. Despite the recent precedents lawyers' hackles would doubtless have levitated at such a 'radical' measure, but the result is that the difficulties of proof confronting individual complainants are at present so great that the effectiveness of the statute is at risk. In effect the *complainant* in a discrimination case is compelled to prove a negative: that the employer did not have a legitimate reason for denying him what he sought. Short of overturning the common law rule and requiring that all applicants for hiring or promotion be furnished with a reasoned explanation for their rejection, reversal of the burden of proof is the most effective way to accomplish the same result in the relatively small number of instances where a legal controversy arises and a complaint actually reaches a tribunal. It is submitted that, in the light of the realities of discrimination cases, this step is both reasonable and necessary.

It is, however, quite possible that the foregoing argument implicitly exaggerates the real impact that shifting the onus of proof would have. It has been argued that in reality the dismissed employee must shoulder a substantial burden of proof if he is to prevail;[11] and in race cases, even those brought under EPCA, this seems inevitable. Thus if an employer claims that the worker was dismissed for misconduct, but fails to satisfy the tribunal on this score, that only entitles the applicant to the ordinary remedies for unfair dismissal. The factor of race, and hence the greater compensation available in cases of discriminatory dismissal (above, pp. 126), will only be introduced into the case if *he* proves that it was the real ground of the employer's action.

The third approach to determining whether the law was broken is that adopted by the EAT in its initial decisions on this question under the SDA. In the first, *Moberley* v. *Commonwealth Hall*, Kilner-Brown J. stated that 'where it has been established that one party to the act of discrimination [i.e. of differential treatment of any sort] is male and the other party is female, prima facie that raises a case which calls for an answer'.[12] In *Oxford* v. *Department of Health and Social Security*,[13] Phillips J. explored the issues somewhat more fully. He accepted that the Act, which is silent on the burden of proof, must under accepted principles place the formal burden on the complainant. But he also explicitly recognised that the complainant labours under a burden of lack of information, and therefore held that 'it would only be in exceptional or frivolous cases that it would be right for the industrial tribunal to find at the end of the applicant's case there was no case to answer and that it was not necessary to hear what the respondent had to say about it'.[14] Thus a woman who feels she has been discriminated against need only show that a man was accorded different treatment, and it will then fall to the employer to show either that her treatment was not less favourable, or that the less favourable treatment was not on the basis of sex, but on some legitimate ground. The identical wording of the two statutes in this respect prescribes the same approach in race cases, which indeed the EAT has taken without extended comment.[15]

The realism of the EAT's decisions is to be welcomed. However, it must be recognised that this is but the beginning of the process of proof. The employer's response to most claims of discrimination generally consists of denial of the complainant's statement of the facts, presentation of his own version, and/or assertion that a better qualified person was found for the job. The key question for the tribunal then becomes one of credibility. Usually the evidence is sharply conflicting, with neither side obviously engaged in fabrication. The witnesses normally are interested parties – the complainant and those who dealt with him: disinterested observers do not exist. In these circumstances relatively minor inconsistencies in the complainant's story have weighed heavily against a finding of discrimination, as credibility is translated into a fine balance of probabilities.[16]

It is essential that tribunals not take on unduly narrow approach to their task of adjudication. Although the question they ultimately must determine is whether a specific act of discrimination against the particular complainant occurred, it does not follow that they are limited to consideration only of the facts of the particular incident. For the purpose, not of proving discrimination, but of assessing credibility, evidence about the employer's hiring policies and practices is relevant, though not determinative. Thus a complainant who produces witnesses who state they have suffered discrimination by the respondent, or who can testify to his reputation as a discriminatory employer, enhances his case. Equally an employer who can summon black employees to testify to even-handed treatment thereby supports his denial of discrimination.[17]* Also pertinent would be testimony similar to the PEP actor tests (above p. 105), as where a white friend is offered or considered for a job after a black applicant has been told that the vacancy has been filled. That this kind of evidence has probative value follows from the precise wording of s. 1 (1)(a), which defines discrimination as, on racial grounds, treating someone 'less favourably than he treats or *would treat* other persons' (emphasis added). The employer's response to subsequent applicants whom he believes to be genuine is one of the very few ways in which this otherwise hypothetical comparison can be undertaken.[18]*

Moreover, refusal to draw inferences from such indirect evidence would simply encourage duplicity and subterfuge. Put another way, the statute would be enforceable only where the employer was foolish enough to admit what he was doing. Discrimination, not candour, was what Parliament sought to eliminate; this requires that deeds, not words, be evaluated.

Admission of this sort of evidence conforms to the normal principles guiding the use of 'similar fact' evidence in civil cases. In Eggleston's words:

> Where, however, the behaviour of a person on other occasions throws light on his behaviour on the occasion in question, otherwise than by showing that he is the sort of person who would be likely to behave in that way, for example, if evidence is available to show that the defendant is engaged in a systematic course of conduct, evidence of similar facts is admissible.[19]

An example is *Hales* v. *Kerr*[20] in which a plaintiff who alleged that he had contracted an infection from the defendant barber's unsterilised razors was permitted to call evidence of two customers who had been infected in the same manner. The point requires emphasis because in a recent EAT judgment, *Jalota* v. *Imperial Metal Industry (Kynoch) Ltd,*[21] Talbot J. opined that the number of black employees in the respondent's workforce was irrelevant to a claim of discrimination. With respect, it is submitted that this dictum is quite unsound even under established rules of evidence, and is further contradicted both by common practice in the County Courts under the 1968 Act,[22] and by the practical necessities of giving effect to Parliament's decision to outlaw race and sex discrimination in employment. It is also contrary to common sense; discrimination is the paradigm case of a 'continuing course of conduct' – a bar or a quota on minority hiring is by definition not an individualised decision – and evidence of the employer's hiring practices is in fact the most relevant information that may be sought on this point. It can of course refute as well as support an allegation of discrimination.

To say that such information is highly relevant is neither to argue that it is dispositive nor that the question in litigation is one of mathematical probability: the lawyer's concern is with specificity and individuality to a degree that a social scientist would find quixotic. None the less, where flatly contradictory accounts are given by the parties, more reliable evidence than inconsistencies extracted in cross-examination or the general impression made by a witness should be sought, particularly since most complainants are unrepresented and cannot be expected to possess an advocate's forensic skills.

Such testimony broadens the field of investigation, but is perforce limited to the experience of particular witnesses. The rationale of its use, however, points the way towards further widening the focus of inquiry. Here it seems appropriate to take a leaf from the lawbook of the American federal courts, which have had to confront identical evidentiary issues over the past dozen years. They have accepted as probative evidence statistical data demonstrating disparity between the percentage of blacks employed by the respondent and the percentage of blacks in the population from which he draws his workforce, or – of greater probative value – data showing that blacks have a lower rate of hiring or promotion by the employer than whites.[23] Indeed in the American courts such evidence *of itself* constitutes prima facie evidence of discrimination, and thus one finds cases in which the employer proves that the named plaintiff did not personally encounter discrimination, but in which remedial action is ordered against practices whose discriminatory effect is demonstrated.[24] This would not be possible in Britain, where the absence of anything like the American class action procedure limits the scope of inquiry and remedy to the individual complainant. Thus statistical evidence would play a far more modest role in direct discrimination litigation in Britain: it would not be used of itself to establish discrimination, only to attack the credibility of the employer's denial, and it would be used in a much narrower forensic context where the ultimate question concerned the treatment accorded a particular person. It should be noted that the Northern Ireland Commissioner of Complaints, in investigations of cases of religious discrimination, has used statistical data of the type described above to support a finding of discrimination in the absence of convincing contrary evidence.[25] It seems proper for the CRE in their investigations to use such statistical data along with other material to support a conclusion of discrimination and the issuance of a non-discrimination notice.

Other considerations support the proposed use of statistical evidence in direct discrimination cases. First, discrimination is fundamentally a group wrong: a person is badly treated because he is, involuntarily, a member of a group the discriminator dislikes or thinks should not occupy certain positions. The legal corollary is that treatment accorded the group, which can only be collected and presented in some numerical form, is probative of the treatment of an individual in a contested case.

Second, by definition discrimination is not a response to a given individual's character or behaviour, but rather a repeated and unthinking reaction to any person who possesses a particular trait. Thus if an employer does engage in direct discrimination, he is likely to do so against all non-whites, rather than just the particular complainant. Over time, one would expect the result to be clearly a demonstrable pattern of a low proportion of non-white employees and/or a high proportion of rejected applicants. Statistical data merely express this common-sense observation in a convenient manner.

Finally, jobs vary in the extent to which qualifications for them can be measured objectively. For white-collar and supervisory posts in particular, great weight is given intangible characteristics like 'leadership potential' or 'ability to get on with fellow workers'. Though necessary for effective performance, their evaluation is inevitably highly subjective. The employer's judgment is therefore very difficult to criticise, even when the successful applicant's subsequent work shows it to have been clearly erroneous. Thus it is equally difficult to show in a given case that racial animosity or preconceptions, rather than considered judgment about an individual, led to the rejection, or the failure to short list, a non-white applicant or inquirer. But a higher rate of rejection of blacks than of whites, or a notable disparity of black employees compared with blacks in the labour market, is strong evidence that the employer is not making good-faith individualised judgments, however inaccurate; rather, they suggest that either he has refused to hire blacks as a matter of policy, or that he includes race as an element in the candidate's qualifications which counts against him. This latter view is not wholly irrational – some employees *will* resent being supervised by a non-white, or having to work closely alongside him – but the statute provides no exemption for those who discriminate to propitiate others. For positions governed largely by subjective and intangible criteria, statistics indicating the hiring patterns of the respondent should weigh even more heavily than in situations where more obviously verifiable criteria are used.

The relevance and appropriateness of statistical evidence in direct discrimination cases have been discussed at such length because the point awaits authoritative resolution by the EAT and the Court of Appeal, and the practice of industrial tribunals has varied enormously.[26] It also seemed necessary to argue against the conclusion that the problem of proof has been adequately resolved by the EAT's creatively in helping complainants leap the hurdle of the formal burden of proof. The judgments in *Moberley* and *Oxford*, although they enable the complainant to pierce the veil of secrecy surrounding the employer's decision, do not speak to the more fundamental problem of how, other than by more or less intuitive evaluations of the truthfulness of witnesses whose evidence is contradictory, the existence of discrimination is to be established. It is submitted that the use of statistical data for the purposes and in the manner outlined above will bring the fact-finding process closer to the reality of employment discrimination without loading the dice against the employer, who can contest the accuracy and validity of the complainant's data, or produce his own.

Two distinct types of statistical analysis may be employed: demographic or comparative. The first contrasts the presence of non-whites in the workforce, or a particular level of it, with that of the population in the surrounding area. Quite apart from the difficulties attending definition of the relevant categories,[27] this method is relatively crude. A substantial disparity between blacks in the workforce and in the area may mask the fact that the proportion of successful black applicants is the same or even greater than that of whites: the demographic disparity may be due to the fact that relatively few blacks have the requisite skills. By contrast, the second type of data, also called applicant-flow statistics, measure the success or failure rates of various racial groups in their treatment by the employer.

The difference may be illustrated by the following example. Demographic statistics would show that an employer's workforce was 3 per cent black, whilst the area from which he normally recruited was 10 per cent black.

Applicant-flow statistics would compare the percentages of successful black and white applicants for employment, e.g. the respondent hired 5 of 50 (10 per cent) black applicants, but 80 of 200 (40 per cent) white applicants. The employer could show that the demographic statistics are an inaccurate portrait of his hiring practices by producing comparative statistics of his own: e.g. that of the 18 blacks who applied, he hired 6 (33⅓ per cent), whilst he only hired 50 of the 300 whites who applied (16⅔ per cent). By contrast he could only rebut the suggestion of discrimination appearing in the above example of applicant-flow statistics by showing that black applicants lacked necessary qualifications in proportions commensurate with their higher rate of rejection.

Clearly the comparison produced by applicant-flow data is far more precise, and where they are available, they are always to be preferred, indeed required. Where they cannot be obtained, demographic statistics should be accepted as the best available evidence; this would require the complainant to seek the most competent evidence, but not cause his claim to fail if the evidence does not exist because the opposing party has not compiled it. Indeed, particularly when the case concerns progression or promotion decisions which have been entirely a matter of the employer's decision about existing employees, his failure to present data demonstrating lack of disparity in white and non-white success rates should have particular force in denigrating the credibility of his denial of discrimination.

The conclusion that statistics may be used to buttress or undermine either side's contentions in employment discrimination cases indicates nothing about the *degree* of disparity needed to give rise to the suggested inference. The statute itself offers no guidance. It seems impossible to formulate general principles; to construct a legal standard on the basis of purely quantitative differences is to build upon quicksand. The most that can be suggested is that relatively small disparities should be sufficient to cast doubt on the employer's credibility. Such a rule, in addition to emphasising the law's firm stance against conscious bias, would conform to and reinforce the distinction between direct and indirect discrimination: only the latter requires a showing of 'considerable' disparity before discrimination may be found.

INDIRECT DISCRIMINATION

The gravamen of indirect discrimination is whether a policy or practice governing employment has a disproprtionately heavy adverse impact on non-whites or women. The practical problem of proof is how this disparate racial impact is to be demonstrated.

Since the question to be determined is the adverse racial effect of an employment criterion or policy which on its face is racially neutral, statistical data become the primary, if not indeed the sole kind of relevant evidence. In the measurement of comparative group performance it is difficult to see what other sort of evidence could be probative; put another way, in what form other than percentage data, ratios or similar expressions can the behaviour of large numbers of people be compared?

Thus statistical evidence will be part of both kinds of discrimination cases, but it is important to notice that its purpose and importance are decidedly different in each. Whereas the focus in direct discrimination cases is on the decisions and practices of the particular respondent, the concept of indirect discrimination requires a more global comparison – between the 'posture and condition' of the relevant minority and majority populations. In the former case statistical evidence is used to undermine, or to buttress, the credibility of witnesses; it cannot of itself furnish a legal conclusion of discrimination. In the latter, statistics demonstrating disparity are *themselves* the direct evidence of what the statute proscribes. Comparative statistics thus comport precisely with the concept of indirect discrimination; in contrast, demographic statistics, which are not designed to measure the effect of any particular employment criterion, are of no value in cases of this kind.

The most reliable type of evidence would be applicant-flow statistics demonstrating differential success or failure rates of whites and non-whites to whom the requirement was applied. These could only be compiled by the employer, who hardly has an interest in collecting evidence that might prove that he has acted illegally. Nor is he under any statutory obligation to keep such records. Moreover, records kept by firms with few employees or few black applicants may be statistically unreliable. Thus, in the great majority of cases, evidence of the effect of a given policy or employment qualification must inevitably be drawn from more general data. Census material, Department of Employment statistics, surveys undertaken by the CRE or government departments, and academic research may all form the basis of the complainant's case.

An example of the kind of evidence that tribunals will have to consider may be seen in the case of *Price* v. *The Civil Service Commission*.[28]* Mrs Price complained that the maximum age limit of 28 years for applicants for Executive Officers in the Civil Service indirectly discriminated against women, many of whom would be unable to work in their twenties because of responsibility for care of their children. She produced evidence comparing rates of labour force participation of women and men of various ages to support her claim. The EAT accepted the validity and utility of this evidence, and further accepted that interpretation and analysis of it by a statistician should guide the tribunal in reaching its decision. Thus a corollary of the use of statistics to establish indirect discrimination is that expert testimony will play a central role in such cases.

Not every relevant fact will require formal proof. In *Price*, for example, the EAT relied on 'knowledge and experience' to conclude that women in their mid-twenties to mid-thirties are active in birthing and minding children, and that many among them therefore cannot work. Doubtless the complainant could have produced some statistics on this point, though it would merely have been a time-consuming irritant to require her to do so. But many matters of common observation may be impossible to prove. For example, the practice of word-of-mouth hiring (above, p. 46) puts non-whites at a serious disadvantage in finding employment, since persons of the same race tend to associate more commonly and closely with one another. Data about marriage apart, the racial pattern of association is probably impossible to prove, but as a matter of 'knowledge and experience' it seems an uncontroversial conclusion, which indeed has been readily reached by American courts.[29] In technical terms it is to be accepted as a matter of judicial notice. No radical extension of the doctrine is required: the role of women in child-rearing or the racial pattern of friendship is as readily apparent as the fact that the streets of London are crowded and dangerous; that boys are naturally reckless and mischievous; or that people who go to hotels do not like their nights disturbed, all of which have been judicially noticed as 'notorious facts'.[30] Judicial notice is a matter of particular importance in discrimination cases, which are acted out against the back-cloth of established patterns of social behaviour. This is not to say that the complainant may rely on judicial notice alone to establish discrimination. The line is between what may be called general social facts, and facts specifically related to the acts or practices of the parties to the case, or which – as with differential rates of compliance – that statute itself specifically requires the complainant to prove.[31]*

Despite the fundamental differences in the importance and manner and purpose of use of statistical evidence in direct and indirect discrimination cases, several common problems surround its use in both types of case. These may be analysed under the heads of availability, competence and definition. It may be noted that whilst they are present in promotion cases as well as those concerning initial hiring, they are far less severe in the former, in which there will be fewer competitors – whose identity will be known or readily ascertainable by the employer – and who will all be drawn from the same source, i.e. the existing workforce.

AVAILABILTY

To say that a complainant may use statistics as evidence entails two presuppositions: that they exist, and can be obtained. Yet either or both are likely to be false. Most employers do not keep records of the race of their employees, still less of applicants, and the same is true of trade unions. The new law imposes no obligation to do so: a very mild proposal by Frederick

Willey MP, then Chairman of the Select Committee of Race Relations and Immigration, that would have authorised the Home Secretary at some future time to require employers of more than twenty-five persons to keep records of their employees' race was resisted by the Government and received little support in the Commons.[32] Much of the resistance seems to have been due to a generalised distaste for the intrusive and time-consuming record-keeping requirements now imposed on American federal contractors. Though Mr Willey shared this attitude, neither he nor any of his fellow committee members who visited the United States appears to have realised that one of the main objections to the American practice is that reports must be filed annually; a requirement that records be maintained, but produced only where legally relevant, is far less onerous. It is also plain that the failure even to attempt to devise some more acceptable alternative will have serious consequences. During the Commons Debate insufficient attention was given the critical question how, in the absence of some sort of record-keeping obligation, anyone – a complainant, the CRE, or the employer – is supposed to prove, or controvert, a charge of discrimination. Since indirect discrimination by definition requires comparisons between racial groups, this omission is puzzling.

The problem is by no means limited to record-keeping by employers. The global comparisons required for indirect discrimination require data from other sources. For example, a challenge to educational credentials or test results as an employment prerequisite – the precise issue presented in the *Griggs* case – obviously demands information about comparative performance on 'O'-levels, 'A'-levels or the particular test, and this simply does not exist. Indeed data on the number of non-white students do not exist, in part because for several years in the 1970s members of the National Union of Teachers refused to collect them. Apart from Department of Employment figures on unemployment, most information on non-whites comes from sources which distinguish only between those born abroad and native British; though useful in the 1960s, they are increasingly misleading as the proportion of non-whites born here approaches 50 per cent.

It is difficult in these circumstances to see how the necessary information can emerge. The source of the problem is that the concept of indirect discrimination originated with the legislation against sex discrimination. Educational and employment records of this kind are widely kept and readily available; the social attitudes that have led to resistance to racial record-keeping have no counterpart with respect to sex. One possible solution would be for the CRE to undertake studies of the effect of a particular requirement, which may then be used as evidence of discriminatory impact by the complainant. This is analogous to what happened in *Griggs*: as evidence of the discriminatory effect of the tests at issue, the judgment cited a case heard by the Equal Employment Opportunities Commisssion some years previously which revealed a gross racial disparity in performance on the same tests. Such efforts by the CRE often may not be possible, and in any case it would be some years before they were of any use to complainants. Moreover, such studies would be of no use in direct discrimination cases, where the inquiry is directed solely to the respondent's own operations.

Despite the lack of statutory compulsion it may be that practical realities will lead many employers of their own volition to keep records. In the *Oxford* case the EAT held that information as to the qualifications, though not the names, of successful applicants should be disclosed to the complainant.[33] This ruling points towards putting a responsibility on the employer to keep records of all applications, although the precise issue did not arise in *Oxford* because the respondent in fact had such records. Once it becomes regular practice to record details of applicants, it is but a short step, either by means of a specific question, or – as in now done by Department of Employment officials – visual identification, to note an applicant's race. Certainly employers may expect requests for such information, either via the Questions Procedure or from the CRE in the course of an investigation. Moreover, many employers will be concerned about adopting policies that further equal opportunity. A booklet prepared by the Industrial Society to explain the provisions of the Act to its members strongly recommends that, for this purpose alone, careful records be kept and periodically reviewed of the distribution of minority group workers at various job levels.[34] The idea, dominant in the 1960s, that racial equality requires racial blindness is increasingly seen to be unrealistic and unhelpful.

In three special situations the pressures for keeping records of this kind will be even stronger. Local authorities have been put under a general statutory duty to 'make appropriate arrangements' to eliminate unlawful racial discrimination.[35] Among their numerous other functions, local authorities are large-scale employers, and if they are to monitor their equal opportunity policies effectively, it is an appropriate, indeed necessary, arrangement that they compile data on the racial distribution of their workforce and applicants for employment.

Second, the CRE has been given substantial power to ensure compliance with its non-discrimination notices. Among other things it may require that the person on whom the notice is served furnish information demonstrating compliance, in a manner and form specified by the Commission.[36] This provides ample authority for a requirement of effective monitoring that would include racial record keeping.

Finally, if the Government ever follows up the White Paper's promise that all contractors will be required to provide information about their hiring practices on request to the Department of Employment (above, p. 157) a very large number of employers indeed will find it difficult to avoid compiling ethnic data if they are to be able to answer the questions the Department may reasonably be expected to put.

The arguments against recording racial data – whether by government bodies, schools or private employers and trade unions – cannot be peremptorily dismissed, and the controversy over whether, and in what form, a question on ethnic origin should be included in the 1981 Census attests to the difficulties involved. But there is no denying the imperative need for means of monitoring the extent of discrimination, the effectiveness of equal opportunity policies, or compliance with tribunal recommendations or non-discrimination notices. The Act's resolution of the conflicting considerations is unduly one-sided, and it is increasingly clear that further government initiatives in this matter will be required.

COMPETENCE

One important consequence of taking employment discrimination cases out of the ordinary courts is to limit the role played by the legal profession on behalf of complainants.[37] With compensation so severely restricted (below, pp. 228–33), substantial time required for adequate preparation, complaints often of limited means and legal aid unavailable for tribunal litigation, very few solicitors outside law centres can be expected to take discrimination cases. This would not necessarily be a tragic loss if there were an alternative source of able and committed persons who could represent complainants, as shop stewards and other trade-union officials now do in unfair dismissal and industrial injury benefit cases. However, in many cases the discriminatory practice will have been jointly agreed by management and the trade unions concerned, so that little help could realistically be expected. Moreover, the expertise of the lay advocate is the product of personal involvement in industrial life; a shop steward who has helped operate a code of practice has a far clearer idea than a solicitor about whether a dismissal was unfair. This does not apply to compiling, organising and presenting somewhat abstract data, as required in indirect discrimination cases, nor to questioning witnesses about distant events; here neither lay advocates nor indeed many solicitors have any particular skill or experience to offer. *A fortiori* many complainants, who may have a limited education or language difficulties, will be unable to represent themselves adequately.

The statute addresses these difficulties by empowering the CRE to represent complainants directly, or to provide various forms of advice and assistance (above, pp. 191–2). However, to strike a now-familiar sad chord, even a vigorous complainant aid programme will inevitably be limited by the resources available to the Commission as well as by the competing demands of its other functions. Nor can it conjure up skilled representatives outside its own staff where none exist. Perhaps the most satisfactory solution would be the development of an independent body, with private financial support, that would act as an institutional litigant, representing complainants in all types of discrimination cases with a skill born of the experience that comes of specialisation. Whether finance for such a project would be available is another matter.

DEFINITION

Since discrimination is inherently a matter of comparison, it is essential that the realms of comparison be properly defined. The EAT has given attention to this question only in passing, in relation to indirect discrimination. In the course of remitting the *Price* case to an industrial tribunal to determine whether the age maximum was unlawful, it observed that the 'pool' of women and men whose ability to comply with the requirement was to be determined was something less than the entire male and female population of the relevant age: there was much to be said for that view that the appropriate pool was that of qualified men and qualified women.[38]

This approach may open a Pandora's box. Where is information on the number of men and women meeting particular qualifications to be found? The more numerous and specific these are, the less likely the statistics corresponding to them will exist. If a complainant cannot produce these more detailed figures, does her claim necessarily fail? Moreover, this approach tends to confuse the SDA with the Equal Pay Act 1970. Thus if a woman were to complain of indirect discrimination in respect of a job done by women – for example, various kinds of office work – there might only be a relatively small pool of men with whom comparison could be made.[39]* This should not foreclose the complainant's case; there is no justification, in the absence of clear statutory command, for importing the conundra arising under the 'equality clause' when no men are employed on 'like work' with women into the differently worded provisions of the discrimination statutes.[40] The EAT'S suggestion is appropriate, but merely tautologous, in cases where the challenged qualification, unlike the age maximum in *Price*, is purportedly concerned with applicants' ability to do the job. Finally, whatever may be true with respect to sex discrimination cases, racial data are scarce and unreliable enough without the complainant being burdened with the additional task of producing more refined comparisons. Thus it is submitted that the complainant may rely on any figures, whether national, regional or the product of an adequate sample survey, which may be regarded as presenting a reasonably representative picture. It may then fall to the respondent to produce more refined data which, if they measure the effect of the challenged requirement more precisely, are to be preferred. But the complainant's case should not suffer if he is unable to produce the more sophisticated data.

A final point may be emphasised, which was also present in *Price*. Among the reasons the industrial tribunal had rejected the complainant's claim was that the record disclosed that of those who were accepted as executive officers, 53·7 per cent were women. Although this datum would be important if direct discrimination were in issue, it is irrelevant in a case of indirect discrimination, where the question is whether the particular policy had a disparate effect on non-whites or women. This can only be determined, as the EAT pointed out, by comparing its impact on men as against women, or whites as against non-whites, not by looking at overall hiring or promotion figures, in which this precise comparison would be hidden. Conversely, the fact that the absolute numbers of persons affected is small does not disprove discrimination, so long as the proportion of the minority group disadvantaged is 'considerably' greater than that of the majority.

In cases of direct discrimination, which concern only the respondent's operations, the bounds of comparison are different. Where demographic statistics are used in hiring cases, the primary definitional issue is what constitutes the relevant general population with which to compare the workforce. The ideal measure would be the labour market from which the workforce is drawn, but that may be too abstract a concept to satisfy tribunals, and in any case population figures are not kept on the basis of labour markets.[41]* Alternatively, one could arbitrarily select a unit of local government – city, county or borough (in London). The question is important because blacks are usually concentrated in central city areas and thus, speaking broadly, the wider the area considered the smaller will be the percentage of non-whites in the entire population, and consequently the less likely that a sizeable demographic disparity between workforce and population will be shown. (This assumes the plant is located in a traditional industrial area: if it were on the outskirts of a conurbation, the reverse would be true.) For example, if an employer in Wandsworth is alleged to have committed an act of direct discrimination, is the proper area for comparison the factory's immediate environs (such as the surrounding square mile); the Borough; Inner London; South London including suburban areas; or Greater London? One might combine both possibilities by defining the labour market as the governmental units where most of the present employees live. Thus if three-quarters of the workforce are clustered in five boroughs, that would comprise the relevant area. One suspects that this approach might prove useful only when manual jobs are in issue, for higher-level employees would tend to be dispersed over greater distances from their place of work. However the area is designated, a substantial amount of analysing the workforce by area of residence will be required, which can only be done by the employer. It is proper to require that he furnish such information, because how the relevant population is defined for purposes of the litigation will have significant bearing on the outcome.

A second definitional question concerns the relevant workforce. This could range from those employed at a particular job level, to all employees of the division, works or the entire company in its regional or even national operations. The most important factor would seem to be where employment decisions and policies are made within the company: if promotions are governed by the head office but unskilled labourers hired by one official at each plant, the relevant workforce should be determined by the scope of authority in each case.

In progression or promotion cases the appropriate 'pool' is more apparent: those below the level of the job in question. Demographic statistics may be used in direct discrimination cases of this kind: a showing that the workforce is 15 per cent non-white, but only 5 per cent of all non-whites occupy the high position, will call into question the credibility of the employer's denial of discrimination where the evidence is conflicting. But, as always, comparative statistics demonstrating the pattern of the employer's decisions – here, disparate promotion rates within the relevant workforce – would cast much graver doubt on the employer's case. Thus the following hypothetical figures would be more valuable for the complainant than the crude demographic comparison:

No. blacks in lowest-level jobs	*No. promoted over five-year period*	*Promotion percentages*
500	125	25

No. blacks in lowest-level jobs		
50	8	16

It would remain open to the employer, however, to show that these figures merely reflect the lack of interest or skills among non-whites, or represent the application of a requirement or condition that is not indirectly discriminatory.

A quite separate issue is that of obtaining information the employer does possess. Normally this is done in litigation by a pre-hearing process called discovery, which permits each party access to information in his opponent's possession that is necessary and relevant to his case. The Industrial Tribunal Rules incorporate the County Court's discovery Rules,[42] and give tribunals a general discretion to order discovery, subject to the qualification that they shall not do so if they believe it is 'not necessary either for disposing fairly of the proceedings or for saving costs'.[43]

Since discrimination by definition entails comparison of the treatment received by different persons, the critical factor in an individual case is evaluation of the qualifications of the complainant and the person hired or promoted; the more clearly those of the former appear superior the stronger the inference of discrimination. Particularly in promotion cases, where the candidates are relatively few and internal to the firm, the employer almost certainly has, or could readily piece together, information about the past performance and evaluations of all those considered. Even where initial selection is in issue, data about the successful candidate and those short-listed probably remain on file. Not surprisingly, complainants commonly seek discovery of such information. However, much of it has been given under the promise or expectation that it would remain confidential; not only the employer, but also the other candidates, may object to its disclosure to their unsuccessful rival, now a complainant.

It is a striking illustration of the divergence between what issues are regarded as important within the legal system, and what matters affect the working of society, that the single issue generating the largest amount of reported case law under both discrimination statutes, has been the claim of confidentiality to avoid disclosure of information to complainants. No less than seven appeals, some consolidated, have reached the EAT. The Court of Appeal gave great deference to the claim of testimonial privilege:[44] Lord Denning M.R. seemed extraordinarily hostile to the statutory powers of the CRE to obtain information (see further, below, p. 246), apparently under the misapprehension that these could be used on behalf of individual complainants.[45] When the issue reached the House of Lords in *Science Research Council* v. *Nassé*,[46] it formally affirmed the judgment of the Court of Appeal, but with such major differences in tone and emphasis as to substantially broaden complainants' access to information vital to documenting their allegations.

One point raised by each side was rejected. No 'public interest immunity' shields confidential information, even if, as one of the parties claimed with little supporting evidence,[47]* industrial unrest would result from its disclosure. On the other hand, the complainants, who were supported by both Commissions, failed to establish that any document satisfying the test of relevance must be disclosed, notwithstanding that it was given in confidence or contained intimate details about other persons. Rather, the Lords' judgments in essence emphasised the primacy of the language of the discovery Rule: disclosure is required where the evidence is 'necessary for disposing fairly of the proceedings'.[48] Greatest weight was given to the interests of justice, in the sense of full and effective presentation of a litigant's case. Once it becomes clear that a document is indeed 'necessary' the interest in confidentiality must be subordinated. It should not, however, be ignored: if – as seems unlikely – the relevant information can be obtained from other sources, disclosure should not be ordered, and all confidential material not essential to the proceedings should, if contained in a document handed over to a complainant, be covered up.[49] The view of the Master of the Rolls that disclosure of confidential documents should occur only rarely was decisively repudiated.[50]

Having established these general principles the House of Lords refrained from laying down any rules governing the vital practical question of how chairmen of tribunals should decide whether to examine the documents for which confidentiality is claimed, rather than accepting the respondent's assertion that disclosure would be undesirable. The four speeches which discussed the matter all approved the approach of Arnold J. in *British Railways Board* v. *Natarajan*,[51] which must now be regarded as the Baedeker for chairmen in this respect. Examination should be undertaken if 'there is any prima facie prospect of relevance of the confidential materials to an issue which arises in the litigation; put another way, whether it is reasonable to expect that there is any real likelihood of such relevance emerging from the examination'.[52] This test would appear to ensure that information generally requested in cases like *Nassé* – covering matters such as education, qualifications, length of service and supervisors' reports on the complainant and rival candidates – would at the least require examination by the chairman, since prima facie they would be the most relevant material the complainant could offer. Earlier decisions taking a more restrictive view, such as that in the *Jalota* case (above, p. 208), must now be regarded as discredited. The task that will now challenge the ingenuity of chairmen is that of devising ways to avoid unnecessary revelations about individuals; one possibility approved earlier by Phillips J., when President of the EAT, is to provide the factual information without identifying the individuals, who may be denominated by letter or number.[53]

NOTES

1. For a rare example see *Race Relations Board* v. *Mecca Ltd*, [1976] I.R.L.R. 15. Even this situation presents a question of credibility when, as in the *Mecca* case, the defendant denies in court that any such remarks were made.

2. *Allen* v. *Flood*, [1898] A.C. 1, 172–3.

3. EPCA, s. 53 (1) and (4). This written statement is not received automatically, only at the request of the dismissed employee – a serious weakness in the legislation.

4. S. 65 (1)(a). The form and its manner of use are specified in the Race Relations (Questions and Replies) Order, S.I. 1977/842.

5. S. 65 (2).

6. *Virdee* v. *E.C.C. Quarries Ltd*, [1978] I.R.L.R. 294.

7. For analyses of the reasons for this reluctance see *Lester and Bindman*, pp. 304–5, and the *Final Report* of the Race Relations Board (H.C. 3, 1976) para. 114.

8. EPCA, s. 57 (1).

9. EPCA, s. 25; see above, p. 88.

10. S. 57 (3); below, p. 233.

11. B. Bercusson, *The Employment Protection (Consolidation) Act* (Sweet & Maxwell, 1979), annotation to s. 57.

12. [1977] I.R.L.R. 176, 177.

13. [1977] I.R.L.R. 225.

14. Idem at 226.

15. Notably in *Bourne* v. *London Transport Executive*, (1978) EAT 123/78.

16. I am generalising here from the cases discussed in the Annual Reports of the Race Relations Board, especially the *Final Report*, op. cit., which details the greatest number.

*17. This kind of evidence has been admitted in numerous cases under the 1968 Act of alleged racial discrimination by publicans, in which the defendant has called black customers to testify that he has treated them without discrimination, the purpose of such testimony being to support his denial of the alleged discrimination in the particular instance in issue. I am grateful to Geoffrey Bindman for informing me of this practice.

*18. An example is *Mills* v. *Brook Street Bureau of Mayfair Ltd*, (1978) COIT 864/233, in which the complainant's white husband made a subsequent (spurious) application. Unlike the County Court judge in a case under the 1968 Act who dismissed such a technique as 'an exercise in lying' that would diminish the credibility of the witness (quoted in *Macdonald*, para. 152), the industrial tribunal fully accepted the husband's account. The judge's view seems distinctly wrong-headed, since misleading someone who one suspects of unlawful conduct hardly suggests that the person so doing would lie to a judicial body.

19. R. Eggleston, *Evidence, Proof and Probability* (Weidenfield & Nicolson, 1978) p. 45 and, more generally, chap. 7.

20. [1908] 2 K.B. 601, D.C.

21 [1979] I.R.L.R. 313, 314.

22. See note 17, above.

23. Here I am largely drawing on two student notes, appearing in 59 *Va. L. Rev.* 461 (1973) and 89 *Harv. L. Rev.* 387 (1975). The ambiguities in the precise bases of comparison, and the various possible kinds of comparisons, are explored further on pp. 210–12.

24. E.g. *Brown* v. *Gaston County Dyeing Machine Co.*, 457 F. 2d 1377 (4th Circ. 1972); *Barnett* v. *W. T. Grant Co.*, 518 F. 2d 543 (4th Circ. 1975).

25. See, especially, the Erne Hospital Case, CC Case No. 175/74 and the comments in the *Fourth Report of the Commissioner*, para. 40 (1972).

26. Several tribunal decisions are summarised in IDS Brief, Supp. 23, pp. 20–1 (May 1979). A bold use of statistical evidence, requiring certain assumptions to fill in unavailable data, was undertaken by a Gloucester tribunal in *Patel* v. *The Post Office*, (1978) COIT 9982/78.

27. These are discussed on pp. 217–19.

*28. [1977] I.R.L.R. 291. See also *Meeks* v. *National Union of Agricultural and Allied Workers*, [1976] I.R.L.R. 198, where the issue was whether a lower rate of pay for part-time workers constituted indirect sex discrimination, and the tribunal accepted the complainant's evidence that whilst 97% of employed men were engaged in full-time work, the figure for women was 68%.

29. See, e.g. *Parham* v. *Southwestern Bell Tel. Co.*, 433 F. 2d 421 (8th Circ. 1971); *Barnett* v. *W. T. Grant Co.*, 518 F. 2d 543, 549 (4th Circ. 1975) and cases cited therein.

30. *Phipson on Evidence* (11th edn. 1970) s. 59.

*31. Matters of judicial notice will arise primarily under the 'can comply' element of indirect discrimination. This is because in *Price* the EAT interpreted this phrase liberally to mean whether the applicant can comply 'in practice' which involved taking into account 'current usual behaviour' of men and women (above, p. 49). It is this test that opens the door to judicial notice.

32. 8 July 1976, Hansard (H.C.) vol. 914, cols 1627–56.

33. [1977] I.R.L.R. 225, 226.

34. M. A. Pearn, *A Guide to the Race Relations Act* 1976 (Ind. Soc., 1976). See especially appx I. The Guide also suggests inquiry into whether non-whites fail to apply for employment, or for training and promotion to higher-level jobs, and further suggests monitoring to ensure that 'suggested situations' within the workforce do not develop.

35. S. 71 (a).

36. S. 58 (3) and (4); below, p. 247.

37. A government survey in October 1977 showed that only 33% of complainants were legally represented when their case was heard by an industrial tribunal. Even for employers, the corresponding figure was only 49%. Bercusson, op. cit. n. 11, annotation to s. 128.

38. [1977] I.R.L.R. 291, 294. Presumably this meant those qualified but for the use of the requirement or condition.

*39. In the *Meeks* case, op. cit. n. 28, the complainant was a secretary and all those employed in that capacity by the respondent were women. Her claim of indirect discrimination succeeded, although her action failed on other grounds.

40. See especially, *Waddington* v. *Leicester Council for Voluntary Services*, [1977] I.R.L.R. 32, and *Macarthys Ltd* v. *Smith*, [1978] 2 All E.R. 746, which required the EAT to grapple with the difficulties inherent in s. 1 (4) of the Equal Pay Act. The latter case has now been referred to the European Court of Justice by the Court of Appeal: [1979] I.C.R. 785.

*41. This is subject to the important exception that high-level jobs, and those involving specialised training (e.g. university lectureships), draw upon a nation-wide labour market. Thus national data, generally readily available, would be appropriate in such cases.

42. Industrial Tribunal (Labour Relations) Regulations 1974, S.I. 1974/1386, reg. 3, rule 4 (1)(6).

43 CCR, ord. 14, rule 2.

44. *S.R.C.* v. *Nassé*, [1978] 3 All E.R. 1196.

45. See his comments at [1978] 3 All. E.R. 1207.

46. [1979] 3 All E.R. 673.

*47. The appeal of Mrs Nassé was heard together with a related case, *Vyas* v. *Leyland Cars*. Leyland alone claimed public interest immunity, which it supported with an affadavit submitted to the Court of Appeal and never subject to cross-examination, in which the industrial unrest card was played. While Lord Denning gave the point much play, [1978] 3 All E.R. at 1204 and 1207, it was firmly repudiated by Lord Salmon and Lord Fraser of Tullybelton (who was joined by Lord Scarman), at [1979] 3 All E.R. at 683–4 and 692, respectively.

48. See the speeches of Lord Wilberforce, [1979] 3 All E.R. at 680c, Lord Salmon at 684f, and Lord Fraser at 693–94.

49. Per Lord Wilberforce, [1979] 3 All E.R. at 680d, Lord Salmon at 685g, Lord Fraser at 695g–h.

50. Per Lord Salmon at 685g, Lord Edmund-Davies at 689c, Lord Fraser at 693g–h.

51 [1979] I.C.R. 326.

52. Ibid. at 333.

53. In *Oxford* v. *DHSS*, [1977] I.R.L.R. 225, 226.

12
Individual Remedies

To have any real effect a law that seeks to alter behaviour must be used by its addressees to guide their conduct on their own initiative. If no one were influenced by a law except after the fact – when required to pay compensation for its breach – it would prove effectively impotent, for litigation – a time-consuming, costly and idiosyncratic method of enforcement – is unsuitable to ensure systematic compliance, and the sheer volume of actions would choke the enforcement machinery. The reasons why people obey laws is a large question which has received a great deal of speculation and insufficient empirical research,[1] and about which it is not proposed to theorise here. Without denigrating the importance of any number of other factors, one clearly vital consideration is the threat of sanction, the *deterrent* effect that shapes behaviour by making compliance more attractive than the financial costs or physical and psychological punishment that follows upon non-compliance.[2] Although countervailing factors pointing in the direction of immobility or active resistance may carry the day in particular instances,[3]* in principle a reforming statute should contain credible sanctions, readily capable of being invoked and carrying sufficient sting to stimulate its addressees to obedience. These postulates about remedies – a small sub-set of the general problem of the dynamics of legal compliance – form the criteria by which the provisions of the Act discussed in this chapter will be evaluated.

However, depending upon the legislative goal, alternate or multiple remedies may be required. Where a law is either prohibitive, seeking to halt what is regarded as wrongdoing, or mandatory, attempting only to require minimum standards of conduct, it generally relies upon imposition of penalties. However, where it seeks to achieve more programmatic ends, requiring changing actions of people working in complex organisations, then it will contain or provide for positive directions. The difference may be epitomised by two statutes, one imposing upon each landlord responsible for premises let, the duty to take reasonable care to ensure that the premises are free from defects that might cause personal injury,[4] the other being the unfair dismissal provisions described on pp. 125–7. Compliance with the first necessitates only that each landlord individually survey his premises and carry out necessary repairs. The second requires those in charge of employment within firms to frame rules or guidelines, communicate them to others within the organisation, and perhaps discuss and negotiate about them with employees, whose representatives will also have to learn about the legislation and transmit that knowledge in some form to their members.[5]*

Negative sanctions are less costly and easier to administer, but their simplicity exacts a price: they cannot shape action in any specific direction. They are the form in which most remedies of private law have traditionally been cast; partly as a consequence, they have been the dominant form of judicial remedy.[6] Even the injunctive power of equity is usually used to forbid certain conduct; mandatory injunctions are relatively rare. Conversely, regulatory orders are a creature of public law, and usually carried out by specially constituted administrative bodies.

The distinction between the two kinds of remedies is an abstracted 'ideal type', and in American law in recent years the lines between them have been blurred.[7] Because of the influence this development has had on discrimination law, it merits discussion here. It is not due simply to the role of American courts as arbiters of a written constitution. Congressional legislation has required to courts to formulate wide-ranging, directive remedies simply as a matter of statutory interpretation. The courts have been made an instrument of legislatively designed public policy, and their role has been augmented both by the often open-ended way in which key statutory terms have been expressed, and by the breadth of the powers conferred upon them. This can be seen in a vast range of substantive areas,[8] but most pertinently in the Civil Rights Act itself. Once a court finds that discrimination (of any kind) has occurred, it is given power to issue an injunction forbidding illegal practices, and in addition

order such affirmative action as may be appropriate, which may include, but is not limited to, reinstatement or hiring of employees, with or without backpay ... or any other equitable relief as the court deems appropriate.[9]

These remedial devices have been used by the American courts in a way consciously calculated to further the *legislative* purpose of eradicating discrimination. In *Albermarle Paper Co.* v. *Moody*[10] the Supreme Court had to determine in what circumstances backpay – i.e. compensation for past lost earnings opportunities – should be awarded. It began by affirming that in addition to the statute's traditional tort-like purpose of compensating plaintiffs for economic injury, the primary objective was one of social policy: 'to achieve equality of economic opportunity and remove barriers'. It continued:

Backpay has an obvious connection with this purpose. If employers faced only the prospect of an injunctive order, they would have little incentive to shun practices of dubious legality. It is the reasonably certain prospect of a backpay award that 'provides the spur or catalyst which causes employers and unions to self-examine their employment practices'.[11]

Consequently it held that there is a strong presumption favouring awards of backpay, which can be overcome only in exceptional circumstances in which these dual objectives would not be frustrated.[12]

The striking thing about this judgment is that the Court saw no contradiction at all between the compensatory and regulatory purposes of the statute. By contrast English courts have regarded other purposes of awards of damages besides compensation with disfavour, and as *alternatives* to this accepted traditional aim. Thus the long judgments in the House of Lords in *Rookes* v. *Barnard*[13] and *Cassell & Co. Ltd* v. *Broome*[14] restricting the availability of exemplary damages were largely based on the view that anything other than *restitutio in integrum* as a guiding principle represented 'punishment', said to be properly a matter for criminal law.[15] There was no awareness that damages might have a broader regulatory function, effectuated through deterrence in the manner suggested in *Moody* and in the preceding argument here. The difference is a fundamental one of perspective. Those steeped in the common law see the choices as bounded by the poles of compensation and punishment because they restrict their focus to the plaintiff and the defendant in individual litigation.[16]* The deterrent-regulatory view becomes possible only when one's focus shifts to encompass the world beyond the specific case. The former is an intellectual framework deriving from and perhaps appropriate to private law, and has the virtues of encouraging meticulous attention to specific facts, individual differences and the achievement of justice between persons.[17] It is however badly suited to achieving social justice, or even to accommodating the reality of collective action and interests. The continued suzerainty of common-law thinking – even in cases requiring the interpretation of statutes which impose public ordering on hitherto private decisions – must subtly but inevitably confine their scope and impact.

Parliament's response to the twin problems of the appropriate role of courts and tribunals as policymakers, and the type of remedial powers they should be granted, has been ill considered and contradictory. It has not hesitated to involve tribunals in the framing of substantive policies: upon them has fallen the main burden of putting flesh on the very bare bones of the statutory standards of 'fairness' in dismissal; and, as has been seen (above, pp. 55–6) the decision to import the concept of indirect discrimination will also immerse them in adjudication based upon policy choices. Yet at the same time Parliament has kept the remedial powers in its legislation tightly corseted. It seems to have followed unreflectingly in the judges' conceptual track and has remained intellectually imprisoned within the framework of private law. Thus discrimination actions are explicitly analogised to claims in tort; tribunals have been denied injunctive power; and the so-called 'action recommendation' is a pale shadow of the 'affirmative action' powers contained in the American provision quoted earlier. All these matters receive detailed discussion below.

It is remarkable how the teachings of Maitland and Maine have been forgotten, how the interaction of process and substance, indeed the dependence of the latter on the former, has been ignored. Yet nothing illustrates this truth better than the concept of indirect discrimination itself. The unspoken precondition of the creative act of statutory interpretation by the Supreme Court in *Griggs* was the presence in the statute of the potent arsenal of remedies that would enable the courts to give the new concept practical effect: the Court was not required to reach the result it did by the presence of these remedies, but it *could not* have done so in their absence. The elimination of indirect discrimination requires the extensive use of public law remedies, for the tools of private law simply will not cut deep enough. Yet Parliament has transplanted the substance of American law whilst cutting away its remedial and procedural roots. In so doing it may well have provided a textbook example of ineffective legislation, as well as an object lesson in the impossibility of partial transplantation. The statute has not been in force long enough to state this conclusion with a confidence grounded in solid evidence. We can however examine the remedies available under the Act to individual litigants, exploring their potential uses and practical limitations.

Industrial tribunals are empowered to order any or all of the following remedies they consider 'just and equitable': a declaration of the rights of the parties in relation to the complaint; an order of compensation; and a 'recommendation' that the respondent take certain action (s. 56 (1); see Statutory Appendix). These remedies vary considerably in breadth, value to the complainant and impact on the respondent. Each will be examined in relation to both forms of discrimination.

DECLARATION

This is simply a statement that respondent has violated the complainant's statutory rights. It accompanies, and is a precondition of, more extensive remedies, but of itself is of no tangible benefit to the complainant, except perhaps as an authoritative vindication of his allegation of ill treatment. However, in certain circumstances it may have broader consequences. Where a respondent has been found to have committed a discriminatory act – as would be stated in the declaration issued by a tribunal – the CRE may, if it 'appears' that he will do another discriminatory act or is operating a discriminatory policy, apply to a County Court for an injunction.[18] This 'persistent discrimination' provision effectively allows the Commission to short-circuit the lengthy formal investigation process (below, pp. 243–6) once a prior act of discrimination has been committed, and to achieve a more specific and mandatory remedy, although the issuance of an injunction is of course at the Court's discretion. Moreover, the terms of the section do not limit the Commission's ability to seek the injunction to instances of similar conduct; thus where the tribunal's finding occurs in a case of directly discriminatory hiring, the injunction may be sought in relation to a dismissal or indeed to an act of indirect discrimination. It is obviously essential that the CRE maintain systematic oversight of tribunal decisions as part of the more general task of co-ordinating its enforcement efforts with those of private litigants. As yet it has not done so.

COMPENSATION

1. Injury to Feelings

A tribunal may order payment of compensation for damages suffered by the victim of discrimination, subject to a maximum and to rules preventing duplicative awards (above, pp. 128–9). By far the most commonly used head of damages, and one specifically mentioned in the statute,[19] is that of compensation for injury to feelings. Analytically this occupies a somewhat unusual position, for generally English law does not impose a duty to respect the feelings of others: as Lord Wensleydale said in 1861, 'Mental pain and anxiety the law cannot value, and does not pretend to redress, when the unlawful act complained of causes that alone.'[20] This may be contrasted with the position in civil law systems, in which personal dignity is protected by means of liability for 'moral damage', which includes all injuries to feelings and reputation.[21] However, injury to feelings may be compensated as a form of 'parasitic' damages, a term not intended as disparagement, but to denote its so to speak piggy-back status.[22] Thus, to take the most common instance, damages for injury to feelings are often awarded in defamation cases on top of recovery for injury to reputation or social position. Moreover, where the defendant has acted in a particularly deliberate, high-handed or insulting manner, an additional sum may be awarded under this head as a form of aggravated damages.[23]

Virtually all successful complainants in employment discrimination cases have received some award for injury to feelings. The sums involved have been small, rarely exceeding £100.[24] Neither the EAT nor the Court of Appeal has yet had occasion to set out any guidelines, and one has the sense when reading industrial tribunal decisions that the awards are made almost at random, in that two tribunals confronted with similar acts of discrimination may award substantially different amounts. To a significant extent this is inevitable, since any attempt to place an economic value on psychological injury involves subjective reactions which will vary with the membership of each tribunal, and promulgation of a tariff would remove that element of sensitivity to individual circumstances which awards under this head are particularly supposed to reflect. None the less, whilst it is inappropriate to suggest that awards under this head be used as a means of regulation, since their purpose is solely to compensate the individual, the normal level of award may be said to be too low. What is missing from most decisions is an active sense of the humiliation of suffering discrimination – of the denial of the dignity of the victim. The impossible task of deciding in the abstract what this is worth is avoided by the statutory command that one look to the law of tort.

Clearly the closest similarity is to libel cases, and it is significant that what appears to be the largest award for injury to feelings – £400 – occurred in a sex discrimination case in which the tribunal drew its inspiration from the awards made by judges in such actions, and explicitly stated that injury under this head should be regarded as substantial.[25] Whilst precision as to quantum seems impossible, it is submitted that the latter approach should be followed, and that current tribunal practice shows insufficient sensitivity to the nature of the injury involved.

2. Economic Loss

Compensation for injury to feelings is the most individual-orientated and purely tort-like of the damages available under the Act. That it is the most common basis of recovery emphasises the timidity with which tribunals have used their remedial powers in the initial years of the Act. Potentially more wide-ranging, and better adapted to performing the function of catalyst or goad, are awards for the economic injuries inflicted by discrimination: loss of wages and ancillary benefits (such as pension rights), promotion opportunities and benefits arising from seniority. This type of compensation is not concerned with the psychological damage suffered by the individual who has personally received discriminatory treatment. Its focus is no longer exclusively upon the victim, but equally upon the discriminator. Hence an unlawful practice – for example, a blanket refusal to promote blacks – properly calls forth the remedy of payment of lost wages and other benefits to all otherwise eligible black employees, regardless of whether they went through the pointless exercise of actually applying for promotion. The way is thus open to a more realistic assessment of the full impact of the unlawful conduct. However, as will be seen, English law is at the moment ill equipped to take account of this collective dimension.

The most substantial category of loss is that of potential earnings. Here, as in personal injury actions, in the model case a tribunal should be able to calculate how much the complainant would have earned, subject to his duty of mitigation, make whatever deduction for collateral benefits is required, and award the difference. However, this is almost never possible in discrimination cases except perhaps those involving dismissal – where ironically the statutory formula for unfair dismissal awards would displace it in most instances (see above, p. 128). The problem is that jobs are almost invariably the object of competition, which discrimination prevents minority applicants from entering. Yet even after fair consideration a given complainant might not have been employed. It is usually impossible to assess accurately how his credentials compared with others, particularly as the discriminatory exclusion is likely to have meant that subsequent evaluation procedures, such as taking up references, were never undertaken.

Thus the true extent of the complainant's loss cannot be known, and no matter how the question of compensation for loss of earnings is answered, a legal presumption must take the place of unascertainable facts. A tribunal can take one of two approaches, and either award such damages only upon a showing that the complainant was the best-qualified candidate, or require proof only that he fell within the range of qualified candidates.[26]* Neither approach infringes the principle that the complainant must establish legal injury; the difference lies only in which unavoidable assumption is used in the calculation of compensation.

The relatively small number of awards under this head, plus statements appearing in some tribunal judgments,[27] suggest strongly that the more restrictive former approach has been dominant. It is submitted that this is mistaken. Once the complainant has discharged his onus of proving injury he should not be further required to carry the burden in relation to matters which are incapable of firm demonstration and, more importantly, which concern decisions within the prerogative of the respondent, who has, or has had, all the relevant information in his possession. Moreover, *ex hypothesi* the employer has violated the law, and if use of a presumption is unavoidable, it seems fair to make the one favourable to the innocent party. Confronted with an analogous 'inherent evidential difficulty' in a case of breach of statutory duty, Lord Wilberforce offered similar reasons for adopting the same approach.[28] Thus a rebuttable presumption should be established entitling a victim of hiring discrimination to compensation for lost earnings, which the employer may overcome by a showing that the person appointed was clearly superior to the complainant. By contrast present tribunal practice in effect requires complainants who claim compensation for lost earnings to prove their superiority over all competitors, which imposes upon them an additional difficulty not required by the Act itself, and which indeed obstructs one of its primary objects. It does so by sharply reducing the quantum of awards, and hence lowering the cost of discrimination. It thus removes a strong incentive for change, and undermines the central policy of the Act of achieving equal opportunity by self-initiated abandonment of unlawful practices, a manner of reform greatly preferable to litigation. Moreover, were compensation for lost earnings the common practice, employers would find it to their greater self-interest to resist customer or workforce pressure to discriminate. At present it is economically rational simply to sit back and await the occasional complaint, indeed to offer a relatively large settlement, rather than face the complexities and opposition that changes in employment practices would call forth.

A further form of compensation that should be considered has become known in the United States as 'front pay'. This arises in promotion cases in which a black worker has been excluded from a higher-paid post which he cannot immediately occupy after winning his case because it would be unfair to oust the incumbent white to redress the employer's wrongdoing. The remedy is to require the employer to pay the employee the difference between his present salary and what he would have earned in the higher-level job, covering the period from the date of judgment to the date when it seems likely he will assume the new position.[29] This obviously involves estimation, but no more so than the usual practice of estimating a plaintiff's prospects of promotion in determining the quantum of damages in personal injury actions. Front pay would be of particular importance where employers have been willing to engage blacks for menial tasks but deny them promotion to skilled or supervisory work. One tribunal has adopted this remedy in a very recent sex discrimination case.[30]

One critical handicap to the potential 'catalytic' effect of remedies for economic loss in England is the absence of any form of collective redress. Virtually every suit under the American civil rights laws is brought as a class action. This is a device by no means peculiar to American law, and is found in legal systems which bear a much stronger English imprint, notably that of Canada, and is under active consideration in Australia.[31] Indeed the class action has recognisable antecedents in several centuries of English practice which were lost in the single-minded individualism of the mid-nineteenth century.[32] In America it was designed and first used in commercial and corporate litigation, but also proved ideal for plaintiffs in discrimination cases, all of whom were suffering identical treatment. It enables a litigant whose claims are typical of numerous other persons to represent their interests in court. If he prevails, remedial action – including substantial compensation – may be granted to all members of the class. This multiplies the bill manyfold: hence the deterrent effect. By emphasising the extent to which the challenged action has had widespread impact, it has the additional value of directing the Court's attention to the societal implications and questions of policy embedded in the particular case before it.

Nothing like a class action can now be brought in England. At best, and only with the agreement of the respondent, it may sometimes be possible to treat a particular decision as a test case which will affect other previously identified individuals. This makes it even more vital that tribunals when framing their awards of compensation attempt to further the overarching purposes of the statute. However it is plain that, in the absence of a general overhaul of civil procedure which seems less than imminent, the full potential of the catalytic effect of litigation brought by individuals will not be realised.

3. Exemplary Damages

The upshot of Lord Devlin's leading judgment in *Rookes* v. *Barnard*,[33] reaffirmed by the House of Lords in *Cassell & Co. Ltd* v. *Broome*,[34] is that in principle damage awards in tort actions should not be used to 'punish' the defendant. This would preclude exemplary damages, but Lord Devlin recognised three exceptions based upon precedent and statute. The most important, derived from some of the great cases of English constitutional history, was that of 'oppressive, arbitrary or unconstitutional action by servants of the government'.[35] This category has been interpreted broadly; in *Broome* Lord Diplock said, 'It would embrace all persons purporting to exercise powers of government, central or local, conferred upon them by statute or held at common law by virtue of the official status or employment which they held.'[36] Thus most public officers – but not employees of nationalised industries, which we have seen are in law independent of 'the Government' (p. 154 above) – would come within its ambit. Although the point would doubtless be urged, nothing in Lord Diplock's elucidation, still less in broader consideration of policy, limits 'power of government' to the exercise of its traditional functions: it should comprehend the full range of twentieth-century Welfare State activities and the employment of those required to carry them out.

Earlier in this century it is doubtful whether the courts would have treated racial discrimination as falling within this exception. In *Weinberger* v. *Inglis*[37] a naturalised British subject who had been a member of the Stock Exchange for over twenty years was not permitted to renew his membership – and hence deprived of his livelihood – because of his German origins. The House of Lords affirmed lower court rulings that this action was not arbitrary or capricious.[38] This decision, in which some of the judges expressed the identical anti-German hysteria that had led to Weinberger's exclusion, cannot simply be explained as the usual judicial abdication of responsibility during war-time,[39] for roughly contemporaneous peace-time decisions show a similar toleration of bigotry.[40] It has however been regarded with disdain by present-day judges, notably by Lord Justice (now Lord) Salmon in *Nagle* v. *Feilden*,[41] who described the decision as 'astonishing'. Indeed the latter case marked an important change of judicial attitude. Mrs Nagle had been denied a training licence by the Jockey Club solely on grounds of her sex, and sought a declaration that this was unlawful. A unanimous Court of Appeal decided in her favour, and Lord Denning M.R. joined Salmon L.J. in describing the defendant's action as 'arbitrary and capricious'.[42] In subsequent dicta the Master of the Rolls declared that allocation of pupils to schools by colour of skin would, like allocation by colour of hair, be so capricious and unreasonable that the courts would strike it down as ultra vires[43] and, also in dicta, Sachs L.J. applied the identical description to racially motivated expulsion from a trade union which maintained a closed shop.[44] Thus, taking 'capricious' to be synonymous with 'arbitrary' it appears strongly that racial discrimination by public officials would now come within the exception recognised by Lord Devlin, particularly as the disparity of power between perpetrator and victim fully merits the adjective 'oppressive' as well.

This conclusion will have important application in relation to discrimination in the provision of local authority services, notably housing, which are outside the scope of this work. However, the extent of employment by local authorities and central government will make it applicable in numerous tribunal cases. As yet the availability of exemplary damages appears not to have been appreciated by complainants, their representatives, or tribunals, and indeed it is doubtful whether those responsible for initiating the legislation contemplated the possibility. Nevertheless, by assimilating discrimination cases to tort actions without qualification, they unavoidably incorporated all the rules relating to damages into the Act. It would be wholly unjust to refuse to grant punitive damages against an appropriate respondent, since other general principles of compensation adverse to complainants, such as the duty to mitigate damages, are routinely applied. Purely as a doctrinal matter, exemplary damages must be allowed. And on the level of policy, in so far as the prospect of exemplary damages would act as an additional deterrent, the unfortunate remedial limitations of the Act would in this important class of cases be partly overcome.

The foregoing discussion of damages pertains only to direct discrimination, for the Acts forbids damage awards in cases of indirect discrimination, provided the employer proves that the requirement or condition was not applied with the intention of treating the complainant unfavourably on racial grounds.[45] Here the burden of proof is on the respondent, who presumably must show that some genuine non-racial purpose led him to adopt the unlawful practice. Unless the reason professed is patently specious this would not seem difficult to discharge, and indeed the author has been unable to find any such case under the SDA, which contains an identical rule, in which damages have been awarded. This limitation removes a potentially significant incentive to employers to alter indirectly discriminatory practices before they are challenged, and may further prove a substantial disincentive to a person contemplating bringing a case. Without the possibility of an award of costs or legal aid in the tribunals, unless the complainant can represent himself or get CRE support, even a successful action will leave him out-of-pocket. The rationale for the restriction on damages to cases involving intent is far from clear: in tort actions negligence is usually sufficient for liability. The rule might be defensible if the statute created superior remedies for economic loss but, as we have seen, it does not. Hence the successful complainant is left in a decidedly inferior situation, by the ordinary standards of private law. He receives no compensation, bears his own costs and may not even be able to bring about a change of policy by means of an action recommendation.

ACTION RECOMMENDATION

The final power granted to tribunals is to make a 'recommendation' that the employer take action the tribunal believes 'practicable' in order to obviate or reduce the discriminatory effect of his action on the complainant.[46] This suffers from two serious weaknesses.

The most important is that it is a *recommendation*, not a mandatory injunction. If the respondent 'without reasonable justification' refuses to comply, the tribunal may then order compensation or increase its previous award,[47] but an employer who is prepared to pay the price may simply carry on. However, the awards here are at large, and vigorous use of this sanction – limited only by the maximum set by EPCA for non-compliance with order of re-employment, at present £5750[48] – should ensure that all but the most obstinate employers follow the tribunal's lead. Cases of indirect discrimination are very different. Elimination of the unlawful practice is likely to be the primary aim of the complainant, who we have seen cannot receive financial compensation. Yet the statute provides no sanction whatever for failure to comply with a recommendation. Compensation for non-compliance may only be awarded where compensation could initially have been awarded.[49] By definition this excludes indirect discrimination; the only conceivable way in which this might be circumvented is if a tribunal were to exercise its power to review its decision if the interests of justice so require,[50] and conclude from the respondent's refusal to comply that his indirectly discriminatory practice was in fact intended to exclude minorities, and then order payment of initial compensation and a further award for non-compliance. It is not at all clear whether this course is permissible and in any case it would only be adopted at the tribunal's discretion. Otherwise the Act is shockingly feeble in giving force to its own commands.

The lack of power behind the action recommendation is not accidental. The Act carefully separates employment cases from all others, in which there is no restriction on the power of County Courts to issue injunctions or other mandatory remedies.[51] However, industrial tribunals are subject to the same limitation imposed upon them in unfair dismissal cases: they cannot compel reinstatement or re-engagement, but can only respond to recalcitrance with an award of additional compensation.[52] Thus the refusal to permit tribunals to command the hiring or promotion of victims of discrimination, which is common practice under the American statute quoted earlier, is not due to policy decisions concerning discrimination, but to a broader attitude toward the employment relationship. The most convincing explanation for the refusal to equip tribunals with the most obvious and potent remedial tool, was that offered by the late Professor Sir Otto Kahn-Freund, speaking of remedies for unfair dismissal:

> We see the power of a legal shibboleth – here it is the ancient doctrine that a contract of employment cannot be specifically enforced against either side because Equity does nothing in vain and also because an order for specific performance against the worker would savour of compulsory labour, and the rule of mutuality demands that if no such order can be made against the employee, it cannot be made against the employer either.[53]

This 'legal shibboleth' is of course a fundamental doctrine of the common law. Its emphasis upon dispute settlement among individuals – its orientation to private law – confined the thinking of judges within the narrow framework of contract law doctrine, and Parliament has not broken out of this restricted space. In jurisdictions where a broader public policy approach has been taken – notably in the labour legislation of several Canadian provinces and the American Congress – this shibboleth has long since lost its power and reinstatement is a primary legislative remedy.[54] Legislatures in those jurisdictions consciously followed the pattern of those statutes when they subsequently enacted anti-discrimination laws which included the power to order the employment of those whose statutory rights were violated.[55]* Conversely, common law concepts have become a straitjacket upon social legislation in Britain, constricting the imaginations of those who have devised remedies to give effect to new rights.

The second limitation is that the remedies are limited to removal of the discriminatory effect on the *complainant*. This is strikingly out of joint with the recognition – clearest in relation to the concept of indirect discrimination – of the collective character of the injuries inflicted and the interests protected. But this perception has not been carried through to its necessary consequence: remedies are not extended to the group. The omission is not simply a function of the absence of anything like the class action device, but seems also the result of an intellectual failing: to the writer's knowledge the possibility was never considered during the drafting or the Parliamentary consideration of the legislation. There are difficulties attending collective remedies – particularly in defining the class entitled to benefit and in avoiding outright racial preferences; and the manner in which the American courts have resolved them, notably the latter, may serve more as a warning than a model. But such pitfalls hardly justify the failure even to attempt to devise any alternative solutions.

Moreover, the restriction on the scope of remedies severely weakens the regulatory function of the Act by curtailing the ability of tribunals to curb discriminatory practices. Thus although a tribunal may declare a particular recruitment practice unlawful it apparently could not recommend adoption of other methods of recruitment less adverse to minorities generally if the complainant has found other employment or is otherwise uninterested in employment with the respondent.[56] Once again[57] excessive concentration on the situation of the individual litigant makes the effectiveness of the Act largely a matter of chance.

Similarly, this limitation of focus may also sharply circumscribe the ambit of any permissible recommendation. Whilst a tribunal could always suggest specific positive steps – such as training programmes to upgrade black unskilled employees, or recruitment through channels heavily used by blacks – it would seem beyond its powers to embody such ideas in a recommendation backed upon by the sanction of compensation: by definition, these practices would not affect the complainant, but would be intended to assist non-whites in future.

The recommendation is thus limited to steps like abandoning a discriminatory practice declared illegal, or to reinstating the complainant or offering him the next available job. Some tribunals, taking a conservative view of what is 'practicable', may decline to recommend employment of the complainant if the post has been filled, although the Act does not compel this result and there appears no reason why an employer who has broken the law should not incur the full cost of making the victim whole in this way, particularly as the cost may be otherwise borne by the taxpayer in the form of unemployment benefit. An additional problem is that tribunals, with a massive caseload and no administrative support, are unlikely to make action recommendations requiring any substantial effort of oversight or even review, which will seriously reduce the value of the action recommendation as an instrument of reform.

At the very least tribunals ought conscientiously to ensure that the effect of the unlawful act on the complainant is truly 'obviated'. This approach would not only entail recommending the employment of any complainant who so desired, but also attempts to offset the continuing effects of discrimination. One example is the award of front pay discussed on pp. 230–1. Another is that where the complainant is to be offered employment, he should be accorded seniority with effect from the state of the discrimination. Otherwise the illegality is given permanent effect: someone engaged after the complainant was turned away would receive preference in matters governed by seniority.[58] In the second round of the *Steel* case (above, pp. 13–14) the industrial tribunal went part way to taking this course when it awarded Mrs Steel a compromise retrospective seniority status.[59]

It could of course be argued that the foregoing criticism of the individual remedies is misplaced, in that elimination of practices and policies with wide-ranging adverse effects on blacks will be the essence of the CRE's 'strategic role'. Constraints on the Commission are considered in detail in Chapter 13, but it may be mentioned quickly that financial and manpower limitations make this view unrealistic. In 1978 the CRE initiated only fifteen investigations relating to employment; a number of these were in response to individual complaints and had few wider ramifications.[60] Other spheres of concern, and other functions of the Commission, must compete for its very scarce resources. It is obvious that this scale of investigative activity cannot be expected to shoulder the main burden of changing discriminatory policies, and the central role that could be taken by action recommendations in individual cases has been obstructed by the inadequacies we have reviewed.

The weaknesses of the remedies in individual cases make the role of the CRE all the more critical. Unfortunately, although it has been given a wide brief, its powers are hobbled by analogous restrictions, as well as others growing out of its peculiar administrative character. These are considered in the following pages.

NOTES

1. E.g. the materials collected in L. Friedman and S. Macaulay, *Law and the Behavioural Sciences* (Bobbs-Merrill, 2nd edn, 1977) chap. 3B; several of the essays in J. Pennock and J. Chapman (eds), *Nomos XV – The Limits of Law* (Lieber-Atherton, 1974); and many of the articles in Issue No. 2 of *J. Soc. Iss.* (1971).

2. On deterrence see F. Zimring and G. Hawkins, *Deterrence: The Legal Threat in Crime Control* (Chicago U.P., 1973), and their article in *J. Soc. Iss.*, op. cit.; and several articles by the Norwegian scholar J. Andeneas, particularly 'The General Preventive Effects of Punishment', 114 *U. Pa. L. Rev. 949* (1966) and 'The Morality of Deterrence', 37 *U. Chi. L. Rev.* 649 (1970).

3. Perhaps – systematic empirical data are lacking – the most important sources of successful resistance are *communal*, as where a cohesive group – trade unionists, white Southerners, or nationals of a country occupied by foreigners – see the law as an imposition of the fiat of outsiders; and *moral*, as where users of cannabis see prohibition of its use as part of a broader attack on their way of life, or objectionable in principle. Ignorance or lack of familiarity with the legal process on the part of the protected class may also make a law ineffective even without active opposition, e.g. Aubert, 'Some Social Functions of Legislation', in V. Aubert (ed.) *Sociology of Law* (Penguin Books, 1969) chap. 11.

4. Defective Premises Act 1972, s. 4.

*5. This is, of course, over-simplified, since it omits the choice of doing nothing and running the risk of the financial consequences.

6. F. Lawson, *Remedies of English Law* (Penguin Books, 1972) *passim.*

7. I draw here particularly on the excellent article by Chayes, 'The Role of the Judge in Public Law Litigation', 89 *Harv. L. Rev.* 1281 (1976). See also D. Horowitz, *The Courts and Social Policy* (Brookings Institution, 1977).

8. E.g. in anti-trust law, where the governing statutory standard is 'reasonableness', to which the courts have had to give concrete content for nearly seventy years, in important areas of labour law, and much of the environmental and consumer legislation of the 1970s.

9. S. 706 (g).

10. 422 U.S. 405 (1975).

11. 422 U.S. at 417–18.

12. Ibid. at 419–21.

13. [1964] A.C. 1129.

14. [1972] A.C. 1027.

15. Commentators adopt the same perspective and reach the same conclusion. See A. Ogus, *The Law of Damages* (Butterworth, 1973) pp. 32–4; H. Street, *Principles of the Law of Damages* (Sweet & Maxwell, 1962) pp. 34–6.

*16. Cf. O. Kahn-Freund, *Labour and the Law* (Stevens, 2nd edn, 1977) pp.1–2, who attributes the 'infinitestimal' contribution of the common law to good labour relations, and its recurrent harmful forays in that area, to its individualistic orientation.

17. The point is well made in an otherwise rather overwrought essay by Tay, 'Law, the Citizen and the State', in E. Kamenka *et al.* (eds) *Law and Society: The Crisis in Legal Ideals* (Edward Arnold, 1978).

18. S. 62 (1); see Statutory Appendix.

19. S. 57 (4); see Statutory Appendix.

20. *Lynch* v. *Knight*, (1861) 9 H.L.C. 577, 598.

21. See further, Handford, 'Moral Damage in Germany', (1978) 27 *I.C.L.Q.* 849.

22. Cf. H. Street, op. cit. pp. 26–8.

23. See especially *McCarey* v. *Associated Newspapers Ltd* (No. 2), [1965] 2 Q.B. 86, per Pearson L.J. at 104–5 and Diplock L.J. at 107; Ogus, op. cit. pp. 237–8.

24. See, e.g., the sample of cases reported in CRE, *Annual Report 1978* (H.C. 128, 1979), app 11, and the remarks of Ian Macdonald, a barrister active in this area, in *Runnymede Seminar*, p. 13.

25. *Gubala* v. *Crompton Parkinson Ltd*, [1977] I.R.L.R. 10.

*26. A compromise approach could be devised: a tribunal could make a percentage reduction of the full award, based on its assessment of the likelihood that the complainant would have been engaged. Though more favourable to complainants than present tribunal practice, for reasons stated in the text it is submitted that the second alternative there mentioned is preferable. Moreover, unlike the analogous practice in unfair dismissal cases, this 'compromise approach' would lack explicit statutory grounding.

27. E.g. in *Virdee* v. *E.C.C. Quarries Ltd*, [1978] I.R.L.R. 295, para. 17, and *Patel* v. *The Post Office*, COIT 9982/78 (1978) para. 15.

28. *McGhee* v. *N.C.B.*, [1972] 3 All E.R. 1008, 1012.

29. The leading case appears to be *Patterson* v. *Amer. Tobacco Co.*, 535 F. 2d 257 (4th Circ. 1976). See, further, W. Gould, *Black Workers in White Unions* (Cornell U.P. 1977) pp. 147–9.

30. *Irvine* v. *Prestcold Ltd*, COIT 907/186 (1979), decision of a London Central Tribunal.

31. Discussion Paper No. 11 of the Australian Law Reform Commission, of June 1979, advocated its adoption with some adaptations to Australian conditions.

32. See further, 'Developments in the Law – Class Actions', 89 *Harv. L. Rev.* 1318, 1332–5 (1976).

33. [1964] A.C. 1129.

34. [1972] A.C. 1027.

35. [1964] A.C. at 1226–7.

36. [1972] A.C. at 1130. Lord Hailsham, at 1078, and Lord Reid, at 1088, express similar views.

37. [1919] A.C. 606.

38. This judgment was presaged by the result in the similar case of *Cassel* v. *Inglis*, [1916] 2 Ch. 211.

39. Most notably in English law in *Liversidge* v. *Anderson*, [1942] A.C. 206; see also *Cooperative Committee on Japanese Canadians* v. *A.-G. for Canada*, [1947] A.C. 87 (Privy Council). The existence of an entrenched Bill of Rights is of little avail in these circumstances, as *Korematsu* v. *United States*, 323 U.S. 214 (1944), clearly illustrates.

40. Notably *Horne* v. *Poland*, [1922] 2 K.B. 364, discussed by *Lester and Bindman*, pp. 54–7.

41. [1966] 2 Q.B. 633, 653.

42. [1966] 2 Q.B. at 647.

43. *Cumings* v. *Birkenhead Corpn*, [1972] Ch. 12, 37.

44. *Edwards* v. *SOGAT*, [1971] Ch. 354, 388.

45. S. 57 (3); see Statutory Appendix.

46. S. 56 (1)(c); see Statutory Appendix.

47. S. 56 (4); see Statutory Appendix.

48. S. 56 (2), as amended by S.I. 1978, no. 1778.

49. S. 56 (4)(b).

50. Industrial Tribunal (Labour Relations) Regs, S.I. 1974, no. 1386, rule 9 (1)(e).

51. S. 57 (2).

52. EPCA, s. 71.

53. Op. cit. (1974) 37 *M.L.R.* at 24.

54. S. 10 (c) of the National Labour Relations Act of 1935, now 29 U.S.C., s. 160 (c), specifically authorised reinstatement of employees by order of the NLRB if the employer had acted illegally.

*55. Congress and the Supreme Court were fully aware of the labour law precedents; see the judgment in the *Moody* case, op. cit. at 419, n. 11.

56. Cf. *Turton* v. *MacGregor Wallcoverings Ltd*, [1977] I.R.L.R. 249 (IT), *revd on other grounds,* [1979] I.R.L.R. 244 (C.A.), in which no action recommendation was made because the complainant was no longer in the respondent's employment.

57. Cf. the difficulties surrounding the 'detriment' requirement of s. 1 (1)(b); above, pp. 50–2.

58. This problem has been recognised by the American Supreme Court, which approved granting retrospective seniority status as a normal remedial practice in *Franks* v. *Bowman Transport Co.*, 424 U.S. 747 (1976).

59. *Steel* v. *The Post Office*, [1978] I.R.L.R. 198.

60. For details see *Annual Report 1978*, op. cit. n. 24, p. 7.

13
Administrative Enforcement

I

One of the most substantial changes effected by the 1976 Act was the reorganisation of the administration of race relations legislation. Previously what may be called the enforcement arm – the Race Relations Board – and the hortatory voice – the Community Relations Commission – were separately constituted and funded. The new legislation amalgamated their functions into one body, the Commission for Racial Equality (CRE), with legal responsibility for both types of activities. Nothing further is said here about the Commission's role in giving financial assistance to community and self-help groups, including local Community Relations Councils (s. 44), or in supporting research and educational activities (s. 45). Substantial discussion and criticism surrounded the decision to fuse the two structures; Lord Hailsham described the new Commission as combining the functions of the Archbishop of Canterbury and the Director of Public Prosecutions. None the less, separate divisions within the Commission are responsible for the disparate tasks and there is no indication that its enforcement activities – the concern of this chapter – are in any way constrained by the existence under the same roof of activities from which legal regulation and conflict are far removed.

The enforcement powers granted the new body were a direct response to dissatisfaction with restrictions imposed on the Board, which was itself one of the most influential critics of those provisions.[1] Three key changes were enacted:

(1)   The CRE may now, entirely of its own initiative, and without need to wait upon receipt of a complaint by a putative victim,[2*] carry out 'formal investigations' into discrimination against individuals or the existence of discriminatory practices.

(2)   In the course of such investigations it may compel the production of relevant documents and the testimony of witnesses.

(3)   If it concludes that the target of the investigation has discriminated or continues to do so, it may issue a 'non-discrimination notice' requiring him to cease his illegal activity and provide subsequent information demonstrating compliance.

These and related powers will be considered in the following pages. It should be stressed, however, that at present only the barest outlines of the process of administrative enforcement are visible. At the time of writing, the Commission has announced commencement of well over thirty formal investigations, but has issued only four non-discrimination notices, none in the field of employment.[3]* Thus to a regrettable extent the focus here is on the formal statutory structure of enforcement, and in discussing the actual behaviour of the Commission I have relied heavily on information gathered in an interview with Dr Peter Sanders, Director of its Equal Opportunities Division (responsible for investigations), as well as a paper on the subject he has published.[4] Factual statements about the work, if not otherwise footnoted, derive from these sources.[5]

II

The RRB had a statutory obligation to receive and investigate every complaint received.[6] This derived from its monopoly of access to judicial remedies (above, p. 189); as a corollary to permitting complainants direct access to a tribunal or court, it has not been imposed upon the CRE. Indeed, as we have seen (above, pp. 191–2), the Commission now has a very wide discretion as to what forms of assistance, if any, it may choose to provide individual complainants. These changes are the product of an altered conception of what should be the main thrust of administrative action against discrimination. This is the much-proclaimed 'strategic role', a term which became an instant cliché but none the less expressed a heightened understanding of how a public body with unusual powers but limited resources may most usefully direct its energies. Individual enforcement can at best produce an erratic series of changes in the behaviour of individual employers. Moreover, as Mayhew's study of the Massachusetts Commission Against Discrimination revealed:

> The pattern of complaints did not correspond to the structure of discrimination. By and large, the complaints did not attack the major bastions of discrimination. Rather, the complaints reflected the current structure of Negro employment; they tended to be directed toward areas where racial barriers had already fallen.[7]

In other words, the pattern of complaints is moulded by the day-to-day experience of black workers: if a plant's low labour turnover, location, reputation as a discriminator or ability to play upon a rejected applicant's credulity ensure that no complaints are forthcoming, the enforcement process will remain in abeyance. Nor can individuals be expected to have the interest or capability required to survey the general field of employment, pinpoint areas likely to present the greatest stumbling-blocks to significant numbers of minority persons, and concentrate particular attention upon them. To these factors should be added the manifest reluctance of victims of discrimination, particularly in Britain, to complain at all,[8] which in the experience of the Board also exhibited a class dimension: manual workers – a disproportionate majority of blacks – showed the greatest disinclination.[9] The conclusion seems clear: an independent body capable of choosing when and how to intervene, acting on behalf of the public interest in reducing discrimination and hence able to concentrate upon targets that seem to its expert officials (who may be expected to be aware of the views of minority organisations) to be of long-term importance, is more likely to make a general impact on the incidence of discrimination than even a substantial number of successful individual complaints. To this must be linked the PEP estimate that one-third of all plants in areas with at least 1 per cent immigrant settlement employed no blacks at all, and their inference of a significant tendency for black applicants to avoid plants with a discriminatory reputation.[10] Thus without some so to speak external force legally competent to apply pressure, a large proportion of industry could be expected to remain almost untouched by enforcement activity.

To emphasise the 'strategic role' is not to belittle the importance of redressing wrongs suffered by individuals, nor of ensuring that they feel they have received substantial justice. Nor does it contradict the earlier statement (p. 52) that individual litigation is likely to be the central means of enforcing the Act. That prediction was based on what seem the practical realities, particularly the small number of major investigations the Commission will be able to undertake in light of its finances; it was anything but a suggestion of the most likely effective procedure. Second, it was also a peculiar lawyer's point: though a change in hiring policies in one industry or even a large firm may open more opportunities than numerous successful complaints, it may produce no litigation or issues of legal interpretation that find their way into the Law Reports. Conversely, individual complaints raising such questions, even if of limited behavioural significance, serve to define the precise jurisdictional scope of the law. They are therefore not to be denigrated, particularly because an unfavourable ruling may seriously constrain administrative efforts. One of the Commission's most delicate tasks is to allocate its manpower and funds in a manner that neither prevents it from undertaking a sufficient number of formal investigations with the requisite thoroughness, nor results in denying effective assistance to a substantial number of individuals with meritorious complaints. This is to say that the *sine qua non* of its effectiveness is quite simply money, efficiently used; however sophisticated the substance of the law, or useful its remedies may appear on paper, if lack of funds keeps the enforcement machinery in store much of the time, it cannot produce results. A Government which wished to undermine the Act need not amend it drastically, thereby issuing an open challenge and bringing political opposition upon itself; it need only turn off the financial tap. It is not yet discernible whether reductions imposed by the incoming Conservative Government – which effectively froze the Commission's budget at the level set by its predecessor, with no allowance for the inflation that rose so rapidly in 1979 – will significantly weaken its enforcement activities. In March 1979, thirty-six persons, including administrators and secretaries, were working in this area. Although a staff inspection had concluded that another twenty people should be added to the relevant Division, this decision was countermanded when the cuts were imposed. It is difficult to see how the Commission can carry out an adequate number of complex formal investigations with this level of resources.

The Commission is not limited in initiating investigations to organisations or persons alleged or thought to have discriminated against a specific individual. Where discrimination has been practised so effectively that no overt act need to have taken place, it may proceed against what the Act terms a 'discriminatory practice'. This concept appears to have been inspired, though not expressly borrowed, from the power granted the American Equal Employment Opportunities Commission to bring suit against a 'pattern or practice' of discrimination.[11] It is set out in s. 28 (see Appendix) and in essence means any manifestation or policy with an indirectly discriminatory effect; rather dubiously the CRE have taken the position that it also includes an overt colour bar.[12]* Examples would be successful use of indirectly discriminatory selection criteria, and cruder devices such as calculated rudeness to discourage applications. The Commission alone may proceed under s. 28. In view of the complete absence of blacks from a high proportion of large plants and a perhaps even greater percentage of small ones (above, pp. 98–100) this section is of potentially great importance.

The Commission's strategy in selecting areas and specific employers, as summarised by Dr Sanders, places particular emphasis on industries in which blacks are particularly numerous, such as passenger transport, textiles and engineering. It attempts to ensure some degree of geographical spread. It is alert as well to the practical problem that an area of employment composed of numerous small unconnected enterprises is less amenable to investigation than one dominated by a few centralised large ones. While most of the investigations came about as a result of an individual complaint, approximately one-third did not, and these seem to involve some of the larger and more complex efforts.

III

The Commission 'may if they think fit . . . conduct a formal investigation for any purposes connected with the carrying out' of any of its statutory duties

(s. 48 (1)). These duties include promotion of equality of opportunity and good race relations.[13] Thus an investigation need not be directed toward issuance of a non-discrimination notice; it may be concerned to identify and publicise the discriminatory impact of a particular practice, or may result only in a report to the Home Secretary urging legislative changes, or in a recommendation to a company or local authority to alter a certain policy.[14] Thus the CRE could examine a level of employment, such as apprenticeships or managerial positions, in a cross-section of industries; a particular practice, e.g. the use of general aptitude tests; or the activities of related institutions like industrial language training courses.

Despite this seemingly all-embracing sweep the Home Office has resisted the Commission's intention to investigate the administration of the immigration laws. Its position is that investigations may only be undertaken into activities unlawful under the Act; as we have seen (p. 65), s. 41 exempts statutes and delegated legislation. This contention not only is difficult to reconcile with the plain wording of s. 48 (1); it also overlooks the distinction between substantive provisions and their manner of enforcement. Both sides have agreed to seek adjudication of the dispute in the High Court; at the time of writing no decision has been rendered. Even if the Home Office were to prevail, the Commission's ability to investigate discrimination by the Civil Service Commission or a government Department would not be restricted; there is no question of a broad claim of Crown immunity.[15]*

Thus far all the Commission's formal investigations have been undertaken at the exercise of its own discretion, although it may also be required by the Home Secretary to conduct a specified investigation;[16] no such request has yet been made. Conduct of a formal investigation is under the nominal supervision of one or more Commissioners specifically assigned that task, although in addition to what may be termed the Standing Commissioners, individuals may be appointed as additional Commissioners for purposes of a particular investigation.[17] The actual field work is undertaken by staff with the Equal Opportunities Division.

The manner in which a formal investigation is conducted is laid down in the statute. The Commission must draw up terms of reference and give general notice of the holding of the investigation; if it chooses to revise the original terms it must again circulate notice.[18] If, however, the terms of reference confine the investigation to the activities of named persons – hereafter somewhat loosely called 'the respondent'[19]* – whom the Commission believe may have violated the Act, it must inform such persons[20] that their activities will be investigated in this light, and offer them the opportunity to make oral or written representations, and to be represented by counsel at any hearing. These rules are laid down in the controversial s. 49 (4), which originated as an Opposition amendment originally rejected in the House of Commons, but accepted after its insertion by the Lords. It was not included in the Sex Discrimination Act when enacted in 1975, but an identical provision was added to that statute.[21] The new subsection gives a respondent the right to be heard prior to the initiation of the investigation, notwithstanding that the right to make representations before a non-discrimination notice could be issued had always been provided (s. 58 (5)). The effect is that a sort of mini-hearing must be allowed before a 'targeted' investigation may be commenced, which at the very least introduces a delay of several weeks.[22] Since even small investigations have thus far taken approximately a year to complete, any unnecessary cause of delay is unfortunate. However, information obviously would have to be sought from the employer in the ordinary course of the investigation, and it is possible that his representations would either clarify the issues or direct the Commission's attention to a narrower range of matters. It seems unlikely, despite the hope of the proponents of the provision, that representations at this stage might dissuade the Commission from pursuing the investigation, since their accuracy could only be determined by further probing.

It is clear that s. 49 (4) goes well beyond the requirements that the common law would impose upon the Commission in the name of natural justice or, as it has increasingly come to be understood in relation to administrative gathering of evidence, the duty to act fairly.[23] In one recent case a claim by a company that natural justice required the Department of Trade to give it an opportunity to answer complaints before inspectors were appointed under the Companies Act – the stage of the inquiry precisely analogous to that in which s. 49 (4) operates – was struck out as frivolous and vexatious.[24] Indeed a general analogy to the investigative procedure under the Companies Acts seems appropriate, since the result may also be a public report or further legal proceedings against the respondent. Some years ago Lord Denning M.R. said that the inspectors 'must be masters of their own procedure' and, although they must act fairly, this required only that 'before they condemn or criticise a man, they must give him a fair opportunity for correcting or contradicting what is said against him'.[25] This principle is satisfied by s. 58(5) (above); thus the added procedural step seems otiose. What remains unclear is whether, and at what stage of the investigation, a respondent may resort to the courts. In the *Ealing* case (above, pp. 66–7) after the Board had completed its investigation but before it had initiated proceedings, the Council sought a declaration that it had acted lawfully in applying the 'nationality rule' to Mr Zesko. The Board argued that the High Court lacked jurisdiction, since the 1968 Act set out an elaborate procedure which required the Board to take any legal proceedings in specified and specially constituted County Courts. This view was sharply rebuffed, all judges[26] stating that, whatever restrictions the statute may have placed upon the Board, none whatever had been imposed on any respondent, and repeating the settled principle that ouster of Higher Court jurisdiction is not to be lightly implied. However, in that case the Board had obtained all the necessary information from the Council and no factual issues remained to be determined; whether a declaration could have been sought before the administrative fact-finding process had been completed did not arise and was not considered. The most closely analogous procedural stage under the present Act is the point at which the Commission give notice to the respondent that it is minded to issue a non-discrimination notice against him, but the Act provides an appeal from any such notice to an industrial tribunal or County Court (s. 59 (1)) – unlike the 1968 Act, which established no procedures for a respondent to contest the Board's opinion that he had discriminated. It is therefore possible that the provisions governing formal investigations would be regarded as a comprehensive procedural code, ousting the jurisdiction of the High Court,[27] but this can hardly be stated with confidence.

In carrying out formal investigations the Commission now has power, subject to the limits on production of evidence obtaining in High Court proceedings, to obtain oral and documentary evidence.[28] The evidence must be sought by a notice whose precise form is prescribed in a statutory instrument.[29] In a general investigation, however, the notice must be authorised by the Home Secretary.[30] Alteration, suppression or destruction of any document is a summary offence, as is knowingly or recklessly making any false statement in response to a notice.[31]

The Commission is seriously restricted in the use which it can make of the information thus acquired. In particular, as Lord Fraser of Tullybelton pointed out in *SRC* v. *Nassé*,[32] if the investigation uncovers evidence of discrimination against a particular individual it cannot provide him with that material to enable him to bring a complaint; such evidence can only be disclosed in a form that does not identify any person to whom it relates.[33] Similarly it would be unable to provide detailed information to the Equal Opportunities Commission if it discovered evidence of sex discrimination, although it could indicate in general terms that such evidence existed.[34] The prohibition is supported by a criminal sanction.[35]

The CRE's power to issue a non-discrimination notice – essentially an administrative prohibition whose form is prescribed by Regulation[36] – is quite unusual in British administrative law. The nearest parallel is to the power granted inspectors under the Health and Safety at Work Act 1974 to issue improvement and prohibition notices.[37] It is circumscribed by several procedural and substantive statutory requirements. As has been seen, no notice may be issued unless the respondent has been given at least twenty-eight days to make oral or written representations, of which the Commission much have 'taken account'.[38] Within six weeks of issuance the respondent may appeal against any requirement in the notice, which an industrial tribunal may quash if it considers the requirement 'unreasonable because it is based on an incorrect finding of fact or *for any other reason*'.[39] The italicised clause seems extraordinarily vague, and gives the tribunal wide-ranging and virtually unreviewable power to substitute its judgment for that of a purportedly expert administrative body. Indeed the full measure of its power in this respect is even greater, for it may substitute any alternative requirement of its design.[40] Whilst it seems unexceptionable for the tribunal to have power of review in relation to issues of fact, since it presumably will hear the relevant evidence and normally serves as a fact-finding body, to regard it as more competent than the Commission to determine what corrective steps would best achieve compliance with the law seems quite implausible. Indeed in view of the serious doubts that must surround the suitability of industrial tribunals and County Courts to consider discrimination cases (above, Chapter 10) this provision is particularly unfortunate. Respondents' rights would have been adequately protected had tribunal jurisdiction been limited to quashing recommendations based upon substantial mistake of fact or error of law.

Apart from proscription of discriminatory practices as defined by s. 28 or specified acts of discrimination, the notice may require the respondent, if compliance necessitates changes in his practices, to inform the CRE of the manner in which he has implemented those changes, and of 'such other information as may reasonably be required' to verify compliance.[41] This latter provision opens the door to compulsory recording of the ethnic origins of applicants for selection and promotion. Once the notice has become final the information may be required for a period not exceeding five years.[42] If the respondent fails to provide it the Commission may apply to a County Court for an order requiring him to do so; the ultimate sanction is the penalty for neglecting witness summons under s. 84 of the County Courts Act 1959, which is a maximum of £50.[43] Equally important, the respondent may be obliged to inform 'other persons concerned' of his changed employment practices.[44] In addition to mandating prominent notices at the workplace and specific instructions to personnel concerned with employment, this provision would appear to support an order that announcement of the changes be inserted in places likely to command the attention of black workers, such as the ethnic minority press, school careers offices and Jobcentres.

It should be emphasised that, information relating to compliance apart, the Commission have no power to compel the discriminator to take any positive steps.[45] Its powers are limited to ensuring the cessation of illegality; it cannot prescribe adoption of a particular policy, such as recruitment arrangements or promotion criteria, that would actively expand opportunities for minorities. It can, however, recommend initiation of such policies by the respondent during or at the conclusion of the investigation;[46] such recommendations apparently may be made privately.

IV

A non-discrimination notice is not a coercive instrument, in that violation does not automatically call forth monetary penalties, nor is it a contempt.

Indeed the process of ensuring compliance is extraordinarily cumbersome. If the notice has been in force[47] less than five years, and information received from the respondent, or indeed from any source, reveals evidence of non-compliance, the Commission may apply under s. 62 for an injunction. The forum must be a designated County Court, not an industrial tribunal, which lacks injunctive power. If the evidence concerns discrimination against an individual, a matter over which an industrial tribunal would ordinarily have jurisdiction, the so-called preliminary action procedure under s. 64 (1) permits the Commission to seek a ruling from a tribunal that discrimination occurred in the particular case; thus armed, and only when thus armed,[48] it may seek the injunction. This is the sole instance in which the CRE may itself bring a complaint alleging discrimination against an individual directly to a tribunal, rather than undertaking a full-scale formal investigation or assisting or representing someone in an action he has brought. Moreover, apparently the process may be reversed: if in the course of a formal investigation of a respondent who has been found by a tribunal to have discriminated within the previous five years, the Commission discovers evidence of subsequent illegality, the wording of s. 62 (1) (see Appendix) would permit it to take 'preliminary action' and then seek an injunction, thus short-circuiting the rest of the lengthy formal investigation. However, the Commission cannot seek an injunction where the previous violation concerned discriminatory advertisements, instructions or inducements, unless these have been included in a previous non-discrimination notice.[49]* It is not enough that it has previously obtained a declaration under s. 63 against someone who has violated these provisions (above, p. 119).

Alternatively, the Commission could mount a 'follow-up' investigation into the respondent's compliance, and presumably use the information thus obtained to activate the persistent discrimination procedure set out in s. 62. Special provisions permit it in these circumstances to issue notices to acquire information without securing Home Office approval where that would otherwise be required.[50]

V

The Commission's final role is preparation of a Code of Practice. By s. 47, added to the Bill late in the Standing Committee stage, it may issue codes containing such practical guidance as it believes useful to eliminate discrimination and promote equal opportunity – but only in the field of employment, a restriction that was never explained. Doubtless the reason is that this function is modelled directly upon the work of ACAS in industrial relations; indeed in many details the language of s. 47 is identical to that of s. 6 of the Employment Protection Act 1975. Yet whilst ACAS obviously is concerned only with employment, the CRE is not, and one would have thought that a

Code of Practice in matters like allocation of council housing would be very useful indeed.

In another important respect, the authoring bodies stand on a very different footing. One use of a Code is in cases before tribunals, which may take it into account where it appears relevant. In many cases the CRE will either be directly involved – as when a non-discrimination notice is challenged – or may be assisting the complainant. It may therefore be using provisions of its own Code to support its position in a specific case. This will doubtless somewhat diminish the importance of the Code in litigation; in any event, the statute states that failure to observe a provision of any code is not itself unlawful.[51]

The practical importance of a Code of Practice is unclear. Legal writers take the view that the ACAS Code on disciplinary procedure[52] was instrumental in developing procedural protections for employees;[53] industrial relations specialists are less persuaded.[54] It may well be that the Code had greater importance *post hoc* – in guiding tribunal decisions once a dismissal had occurred – that in structuring management policies and behaviour. In all events any Code issued under the Act must inevitably be more concerned than the dismissal Code with influencing management than with shaping the law. Dismissals are governed primarily by the standard or reasonableness, which the Code helps to define, whereas under the Act discrimination is much more tightly defined and specific acts must be proven.[55]

Before a Code of Practice may be issued the Commission must consult interested organisations and consider their representations.[56] The final product must be approved by the Employment Secretary and then laid before Parliament.[57] At the time of writing, the Commission has circulated a draft Code and is considering the responses of interested bodies. Compared with the various ACAS codes the draft seems considerably more detailed, and evinces a greater concern to educate managers and alert them to matters of which they are likely to be aware. Many of these go well beyond discrimination as known to the law, and are directed to problems that may arise with a multicultural and multilingual workforce.

VI

It would be premature to attempt to assess the Commission's effectiveness as an enforcement agent. At first blush it appears to have adequate powers, but the time required for formal investigations, and the lack of effective force in the non-discrimination notice, are potentially serious weaknesses. Above all, it remains open to doubt whether the Commission will receive sufficient funds to carry out its work effectively.

NOTES

1. Notably in its Report for 1971–2, paras 72–90. See also *Lester and Bindman*, chap. 11.

*2. Under s. 17 of the 1968 Act the Board could not begin an investigation unless it had either received a complaint from an individual, or had otherwise cause to suspect that an individual had suffered discrimination not more than two months after the matter had come to its notice (for example, as a result of allegations by a third party). Thus some victim had always to be identifiable.

*3. The published investigations have concerned a pub, a restaurant, a working-men's club and a children's home.

4. P. Sanders, 'The Strategic Use of the Law', in *Runnymede Seminar*.

5. See also Creighton, 'Enforcing the Sex Discrimination Act', (1976) 5 *I.L.J.* 42, for description of the identical procedure under that statute.

6. RRA 1968, s. 15 (2).

7. L. Mayhew, *Law and Equal Opportunity* (Harvard U.P. 1968) p. 159.

*8. For an analysis of the factors discouraging complaints under the previous system, see the Board's *Final Report*, para. 114 (H.C. 3, 1976). This reluctance is not unique to Britain – see Professor Jowell's findings among blacks in Boston, reported in chap. 3 of his *Law and Bureaucracy* (Dunellen, 1975) – but it does seem particularly marked here, probably reflecting the generally low level of litigation compared with the United States.

9. *Final Report*, op. cit. app. VIII, para. 17.

10. PEP Report, pp. 94–5, 102–3. Indeed PEP found (p. 182) that over half the men surveyed had never applied to a firm unless they knew it employed some blacks.

11. Civil Rights Act of 1964, s. 706. This jurisdiction was transferred from the Justice Department to the EEOC in 1972.

*12. Dubiously, because it seems a strained reading of the notion of indirect discrimination: being white is indeed a condition fewer blacks than whites can satisfy, but this is hardly the intended meaning. Since there seems no reason why the CRE should not be empowered to proceed against a fully effective colour bar, amendment of s. 28 to include directly discriminatory policies would be desirable.

13. S. 43 (1)(b).

14. The power to make such recommendations is conferred by s. 51 (1): the remainder of the section requires the CRE to make public reports of all its formal investigations.

*15. Nor could there be, as ss. 75 and 76 (above, p. 114) ensure. It is uncertain whether the Home Office will also argue that Immigration officials are Crown servants, who do not provide facilities or services to the public or a section of it, and hence are outside s. 20 and any other provision of the Act.

16. S. 48 (1).

17. S. 48 (2). The number of Standing Commissioners may vary between eight and fifteen: s. 43 (1).

18. S. 49 (2), (3) and (5), respectively.

*19. Somewhat loosely because no formal proceedings have been taken, and indeed the Commission may decide that none is warranted. But 'target' or 'subject' seemed even less appropriate descriptions.

20. 'Person', of course, includes a limited company or partnership and, in this context, a trade union.

21. Sched. 4, para. 2 of the RRA 1976.

22. No time-limits are specified in the statute or regulations. In practice the

Commission apparently allows at least twenty-eight days, the same period specified in s. 58 (5) after the respondent is told of an impending non-discrimination notice.

23. Cf. *Selvarajan* v. *RRB*, [1975] 1 W.L.R. 1686 (above, p. 190), in which the obligations of the Board in investigating complaints were thus described. Perhaps the best review of the case law in the complex and controversial area of natural justice is by a Canadian scholar; see Mullan, 'Fairness: the New Natural Justice', 25 *U. Tor. L.J.* 281 (1975).

24. *Norwest Holst Ltd* v. *Department of Trade*, [1978] 3 All E.R. 1280 (C.A.).

25. In *re Pergamon Press Ltd* [1971] Ch. 388, 400.

26. Swanwick J. at first instance, [1971] Q.B. 309, and all the Lords who discussed the point, [1972] A.C. 342.

27. Under the rule in *Barraclough* v. *Brown*, [1897] A.C. 615; above, p. 193 and n. 13.

28. S. 50 (1) and (3).

29. Race Relations (Formal Investigations) Regulations 1977, S.I. 1977, no. 841, reg. 5 and sched. 1.

30. S. 50 (2)(a).

31. S. 50 (6).

32. [1979] 3 All E.R. 673, 695; discussed in detail on pp. 220–1.

33. S. 52 (1)(c).

34. An amendment that would have permitted such pooling of information was resisted by the Government: Official Report, Standing Comm. A, 15 June 1976, cols 619–21.

35. S. 52 (2).

36. Formal Investigations Regulations, op. cit. reg. 6 and sched. 2.

37. Under ss. 21 and 22, respectively, of that statute. The use of the Health and Safety provisions as a model was acknowledged when the new machinery was discussed in the context of the SDA: Official Report, Standing Comm. B, 15 May 1975, col. 402 (John Fraser).

38. S. 58 (5)(c).

39. S. 59 (2) (emphasis supplied). Designated County Courts have identical powers in non-employment cases. The appeals procedure in employment cases is set out in the Industrial Tribunals (Non-Discrimination Notice Appeals) Regulation 1977, S.I. 1977, no. 1094.

40. S. 59 (3).

41. S. 58 (2) and (3).

42. S. 58 (4).

43. This emerges when s. 58 (7) and s. 50 (4) and (5) are read together.

44. S. 58 (2)(b)(ii).

45. This follows from the wording of s. 58 (2) (a) – see Appendix – which permits the CRE to require only that a respondent 'not . . . commit any such acts'.

46. S. 51 (1)(a).

47. Technically, has 'become final', defined in s. 78 (4) to mean essentially that all appeals have been taken or the relevant time-limits expired.

48. S. 62 (2) requires the Commission to wait until the tribunal's finding has become final.

*49. This follows from the language of s. 62 (1)(a) and (b) (see Appendix), which requires that the previous violation has either been the subject of a non-discrimination notice or has been adjudicated under s. 54 or s. 57; the matters mentioned in the text are governed jurisdictionally by s. 63.

50. S. 60.

51. S. 47 (10). Cf. *W. Devis & Sons* v. *Atkins*, [1977] A.C. 931, per Viscount Dilhorne, confirming that this principle applies under the analogous provision of the unfair dismissal legislation.

52. Now found in the Employment Protection Code of Practice (Disciplinary Practice and Procedures) Order 1977, S.I. 1977, no. 867.

53. E.g. B. Bercusson in his annotation of s. 6 (11) of *The Employment Protection Act 1975* (Sweet & Maxwell, 1976) and S. Anderman, *The Law of Unfair Dismissal* (Butterworth, 1978) pp. 81–2.

54. B. Weekes *et al.*, *Industrial Relations and the Limits of Law* (Blackwell, 1975) p. 179.

55. Cf. *Macdonald*, para. 369.

56. S. 47 (2) and (3).

57. S. 47 (4)–(7).

Coda

The spirit of this study has been one of qualified pessimism. This results partly from the particular failings of the Act which have been criticised in various chapters. Four especially stand out: the weakness of the remedial powers available, and their timid use by industrial tribunals; the refusal to establish separate tribunals to hear all cases under the Act (possibly combined with jurisdiction over sex discrimination cases as well); the absence of effective devices to overcome the severe difficulties of proof under which discrimination complainants inevitably labour; and the failure of central government and the public sector generally to take the lead in eradicating discrimination. However, the disquiet runs deeper than criticisms at this level of specificity.

Anti-discrimination legislation is no more than a means to an end – purging decisions of bias and broadening opportunities for members of minority groups. It is, however, only one means to that end, and to be effective other forces must pull in the same direction. The economic, political and moral environment must reinforce the legal commitment. This is very far from true in Britain at present.

One of the striking political changes of the 1970s was the bipartisan acceptance of high unemployment as a permanent condition of economic life. Whatever the broader justifications, the effect is to increase the likelihood and exacerbate the effects of discrimination, by intensifying the competition for employment and providing employers with a surplus of suitable candidates from whom to choose. The unskilled and ill educated are likely to be particularly hard hit, as the unemployment rate among young West Indians demonstrates. The invocation of legal rights will thus occur in a setting of scarcity, hence intensifying conflict, which can only weaken public support for effective legislation. Were the number of opportunities greater, doors would be more readily open to all comers, and those who lost out on merit would at least find some reasonable alternative.

Like all attempts at legal regulation the Act attempts to achieve its end by means of sanctions. Elementary psychology suggests that this approach is of limited value: rewards rather than punishments are generally more effective in altering behaviour. The use of positive inducements for non-discrimination – which could range from tax concessions or subsidies to firms which implement effective equal-opportunity policies to knighthoods for their managing directors – is beyond the scope of the legal system. Only government policy can promote efforts to reduce racial inequality in this way, and the political will has thus far largely been absent. What is required is an effort that is both highly visible and directed towards concrete results. The kinds of policies that are needed, and the tactics required to ensure their effectiveness, have not been explored in this book, which emphasises the role of the legal system. However, an excellent and practical discussion of these matters is contained in Section III of David Wainwright's recent work, *Discrimination in Employment.*[1] Measures like the programmes elaborated there need to be implemented over the whole range of industry and the process of implementation must be conducted in a manner that recognises the dislocations companies attempting to change their personnel policies will inevitably encounter, and assists them to weather any storms. Government alone can co-ordinate such an undertaking, and provide the necessary mixture of positive inducements and negative sanctions. Reliance on even strengthened legislation may help a limited number of individuals secure some *post hoc* redress; augmenting the powers of the administrative enforcement body may, after prolonged investigation and litigation, alter the practices of a limited number of employers, whose total workforce may not be large. At best private litigation and administrative investigations may have substantial spillover effects on those not directly involved, but these will be intermittent and random. The impact of these means of enforcement is not to be disparaged, but to use the legal approach as the primary weapon is to begin with second best.

Discussion of the moral environment must inevitably be less precise. However, it seems most unlikely that when prominent Ministers and politicians persist in equating racial minorities with immigrants, and label immigration as a problem to be countered by police measures, and when racist jokes are readily retailed in the media, which also give prominence to stories about crime or other undesirable behaviour among minorities, that the employers and workmates of black workers will regard them with the respect their individual talents happen to deserve. Racism is the abiding curse of this country, and it is fed by institutions and persons who should know better. One repeatedly encounters social attitudes and hears remarks unpleasantly echoing those commonplace in the United States twenty years ago, and which since have become publicly unacceptable.

The pessimism is, as noted, qualified. At the time of writing, the Act has been in force less than three years, and the CRE was badly disorganised during its first months. If the Commission were to issue several far-reaching non-discrimination notices requiring significant changes in the employment practices of a number of large companies, and these withstood legal challenge, the momentum of progress might accelerate, with employers beginning to take the Act seriously and initiating equal opportunity policies of their own design. Similarly, judicial backing for a trenchant interpretation of indirect discrimination, and a greater willingness to make imaginative use of the power of action recommendations, could yet achieve greater impact than at present seems likely. Predictions that are merely projections are certain to prove false.

NOTE

1. Published by Associated Business Press, 1979. I should like to thank Mr Wainwright and his publishers for providing me with a page-proof copy of this book before its formal publication. The work covers sex discrimination and equal pay as well as racial discrimination.

Statutory Appendix

PART I

DISCRIMINATION TO WHICH ACT APPLIES

Racial discrimination

1.—(1) A person discriminates against another in any circumstances relevant for the purposes of any provision of this Act if—

(a) on racial grounds he treats that other less favourably than he treats or would treat other persons; or

(b) he applies to that other a requirement or condition which he applies or would apply equally to persons not of the same racial group as that other but—

(i) which is such that the proportion of persons of the same racial group as that other who can comply with it is considerably smaller than the proportion of persons not of that racial group who can comply with it; and

(ii) which he cannot show to be justifiable irrespective of the colour, race, nationality or ethnic or national origins of the person to whom it is applied; and

(iii) which is to the detriment of that other because he cannot comply with it.

. . .

PART II

DISCRIMINATION IN THE EMPLOYMENT FIELD

Discrimination by employers

Discrimination against applicants and employees

4.—(1) It is unlawful for a person, in relation to employment by him at an establishment in Great Britain, to discriminate against another—

(a) in the arrangements he makes for the purpose of determining who should be offered that employment; or

(b) in the terms on which he offers him that employment; or

(c) by refusing or deliberately omitting to offer him that employment.

(2) It is unlawful for a person, in the case of a person employed by him at an establishment in Great Britain, to discriminate against that employee –

(a) in the terms of employment which he affords him; or

(b) in the way he affords him access to opportunities for promotion, transfer or training, or to any other benefits, facilities or services, or by refusing or deliberately omitting to afford him access to them; or

(c) by dismissing him, or subjecting him to any other detriment.

OTHER UNLAWFUL ACTS

Discriminatory practices

28. – (1) In this section 'discriminatory practice' means the application of a requirement or condition which results in an act of discrimination which is unlawful by virtue of any provision of Part II or III taken with section 1 (1)(b), or which would be likely to result in such an act of discrimination if the persons to whom it is applied included persons of any particular racial group as regards which there has been no occasion for applying it.

(2) A person acts in the contravention of this section if and so long as –

(a) he applies a discriminatory practice; or

(b) he operates practices or other arrangements which in any circumstances would call for the application by him of a discriminatory practice.

(3) Proceedings in respect of a contravention of this section shall be brought only by the Commission in accordance with sections 58 to 62.

. . .

Enforcement in employment field

Jurisdiction of industrial tribunals

54. – (1) A complaint by any person ('the complainant') that another person ('the respondent') –

(a) has committed an act of discrimination against the complainant which is unlawful by virtue of Part III; or

(b) is by virtue of section 32 or 33 to be treated as having committed such an act of discrimination against the complainant,

. . .

Remedies on complaint under s. 54

56. – (1) Where an industrial tribunal finds that a complaint presented to it

under section 54 is well-founded, the tribunal shall make such of the following as it considers just and equitable –

(a) an order declaring the rights of the complainant and the respondent in relation to the act to which the complaint relates;

(b) an order requiring the respondent to pay the complainant compensation of an amount corresponding to any damages he could have been ordered by a county court or by a sheriff court to pay to the complainant if the complaint had fallen to be dealt with under section 57;

(c) a recommendation that the respondent take within a specified period action appearing to the tribunal to be practicable for the purpose of obviating or reducing the adverse effect on the complainant of any act of discrimination to which the complaint relates.

. . .

(4) If without reasonable justification the respondent to a complaint fails to comply with a recommendation made by an industrial tribunal under subsection 1 (c), then, if it thinks it just and equitable to do so –

(a) the tribunal may (subject to the limit in subsection (2)) increase the amount of compensation required to be paid to the complainant in respect of the complaint by an order made under subsection (1) (b); or

(b) if an order under subsection (1) (b) could have been made but was not, the tribunal may make such an order.

. . .

Enforcement of Part III

Claims under Part III

57. –(1) A claim by any person ('the claimant') that another person ('the respondent') –

(a) has committed an act of discrimination against the claimant which is unlawful by virtue of Part III, or

(b) is by virtue of section 32 or 33 to be treated as having committed such an act of discrimination against the claimant,

may be made the subject of civil proceedings in like manner as any other claim in tort or (in Scotland) in reparation for breach of statutory duty.

(2) Proceedings under subsection (1) –

(a) shall be brought in England and Wales only in a county court, and

(b) shall be brought in Scotland only in a sheriff court,

but all such remedies shall be obtainable in such proceedings as, apart from this subsection, would be obtainable in the High Court or the Court of Session, as the case may be.

(3) As respects an unlawful act of discrimination falling within section 1 (1) (b), no award of damages shall be made if the respondent proves that the requirement or condition in question was not applied with the intention of treating the claimant unfavourably on racial grounds.

(4) For the avoidance of doubt it is hereby declared that damages in respect of an unlawful act of discrimination may include compensation for injury to feelings whether or not they include compensation under any other head.

. . .

Non-discrimination notices

Issue of non-discrimination notice

58.–(1) This section applies to–

(a) an unlawful discriminatory act; and
(b) an act contravening section 28; and
(b) an act contravening section 29, 30 or 31,

and so applies whether or not proceedings have been brought in respect of the act.

(2) If in the course of a formal investigation the Commission becomes satisfied that a person is committing, or has committed, any such acts, the Commission may in the prescribed manner serve on him a notice in the prescribed form ('a non-discrimination notice') requiring him–

(a) not to commit any such acts; and
(b) where compliance with paragraph (a) involves changes in any of his practices or other arrangements–

(i) to inform the Commission that he has effected those changes and what those changes are; and

(ii) to take such steps as may be reasonably required by the notice for the purpose of affording that information to other persons concerned.

(3) A non-discrimination notice may also require the person on whom it is served to furnish the Commission with such other information as may be reasonably required by the notice in order to verify that the notice has been complied with.

. . .

Other enforcement by Commission

Persistent discrimination

62.–(1) If, during the period of five years beginning on the date on which any of the following became final in the case of any person, namely–

(a) a non-discrimination notice served on him; or

(b) a finding by a tribunal or court under section 54 or 57 that he has done an unlawful discriminatory act; or

(c) a finding by a court in proceedings under section 19 or 20 of the Race Relations Act 1968 that he has done an act which was unlawful by virtue of any provision of Part I of that Act,

it appears to the Commission that unless restrained he is likely to do one or more acts falling within paragraph (b), or contravening section 28, the Commission may apply to a designated county court for an injunction, or to a sheriff court for an order, restraining him from doing so; and the court, if satisfied that the application is well-founded, may grant the injunction or order in the terms applied for or in more limited terms.

Index